the Market!

MW00987031

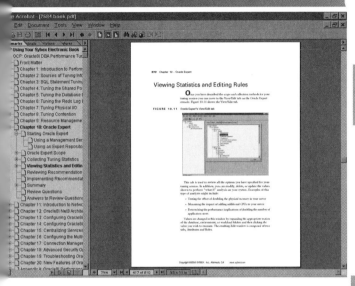

Search the DBA Study Guide ebook in PDF

- Access the entire *Oracle8i DBA Study Guide*, complete with figures and tables, in electronic format.

- Use the Adobe Acrobat Reader (included on the CD-ROM) to view the electronic book.

- Search chapters to find information on any topic in seconds.

Oracle8i Evaluation Version

- Preview Oracle8i in this downloadable evaluation version.

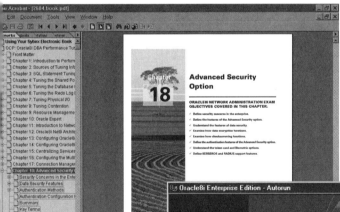

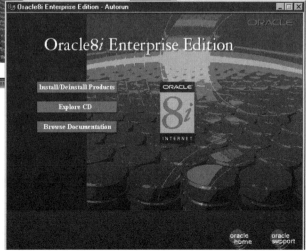

SYBEX

OCP: Oracle8i DBA SQL and PL/SQL Study Guide

OCP: Oracle8i™ DBA SQL and PL/SQL Study Guide

Chip Dawes

Biju Thomas

San Francisco • Paris • Düsseldorf • Soest • London

Associate Publisher: Richard Mills
Contracts and Licensing Manager: Kristine O'Callaghan
Acquisitions & Developmental Editor: Kim Goodfriend
Associate Developmental Editor: Ben Tompkins
Editor: Nancy Conner, Marilyn Smith
Production Editors: Lisa Duran, Leslie E. H. Light
Technical Editors: Betty MacEwen, Ashok Hanumanth
Book Designer: Bill Gibson
Graphic Illustrator: Tony Jonick
Electronic Publishing Specialist: Susie Hendrickson
Proofreader: Lindy Wolf
Indexer: Matthew Spence
CD Coordinator: Kara Eve Schwartz
CD Technician: Keith McNeil
Cover Design: Archer Design
Cover/Photograph: Photo Researchers

Library of Congress Card Number: 00-105388

ISBN: 0-7821-2682-0

SYBEX and the SYBEX logo are trademarks of SYBEX Inc. in the USA and other countries.

The CD interface was created using Macromedia Director, COPYRIGHT 1994, 1997-1999 Macromedia Inc. For more information on Macromedia and Macromedia Director, visit http://www.macromedia.com.

SYBEX is an independent entity from Oracle Corporation and is not affiliated with Oracle Corporation in any manner. This publication may be used in assisting students to prepare for an Oracle Certified Professional exam. Neither Oracle Corporation nor SYBEX warrants that use of this publication will ensure passing the relevant exam. Oracle is either a registered trademark or a trademark of Oracle Corporation in the United States and/or other countries.

TRADEMARKS: SYBEX has attempted throughout this book to distinguish proprietary trademarks from descriptive terms by following the capitalization style used by the manufacturer.

Manufactured in the United States of America

10 9 8 7 6 5 4 3 2 1

To my wife Mary and my children Zachary and Charlie.

-Chip Dawes

To my wife Shiji and my parents, who are there whenever I need support and guidance.

-Biju Thomas

Acknowledgments

I would like to thank the folks at Sybex who helped with this book. Ben, your prodding to stay on schedule kept us going; Lisa and Nancy; and Kim (good luck at Organic.com). Thank you, Betty—your technical reviews and insights raised the quality of this book. I'd like to thank Oracle for producing a great database and language. Thank you, Biju, for jumping into the book and helping to make it possible.

I owe a big thanks to my family: Mary, Zachary, and Charlie. They put up with a lot of lost time with me while I was working on this book.

-Chip Dawes

Anything is possible with hard work and dedication from a group of people. I would like to thank Sybex for giving me the opportunity to write this book. I thank the excellent team at Sybex for their support and patience, especially Kim, Ben, Nancy, Betty, Lisa, and Chip, who helped to bring the best out of me.

I thank my parents and sisters, who simply are the best. I thank all my friends—you helped all through my career knowingly or unknowingly. This book is for all of you who have been a source of inspiration in my life.

Thank you, Shiji, for being there when I was busy working and for all your support and love.

-Biju Thomas

Contents at a Glance

Contents

Introduction

There is high demand and competition for professionals in the Information Technology (IT) industry, and the Oracle Certified Professional (OCP) certification is the hottest credential in the database world. You have made the right decision to pursue certification: Being an OCP will give you a distinct advantage in this highly competitive market.

Many readers may already be familiar with Oracle and do not need an introduction to the Oracle database world. For those who aren't familiar with the company, Oracle (founded in 1977), is the world's leading database company and second-largest independent software company, with revenues of more than $9 billion, serving more than 145 countries. Oracle databases are the *de facto* standard for large Internet sites, and Oracle has positioned itself to continue this dominance of the Internet market.

This book is intended to help you on your exciting path toward obtaining the Oracle8i Certified Database Administrator and Oracle8i Certified Application Developer certifications. Basic knowledge of Oracle SQL and PL/SQL is an advantage when reading this book but is not mandatory. Using this book and a practice database, you can start learning Oracle and pass the IZ0-001 test: Introduction to Oracle: SQL and PL/SQL.

Why Become an Oracle Certified Professional?

The number one reason to become an Oracle Certified Professional is to gain more visibility and greater access to the industry's most challenging opportunities. The OCP program is the best way to demonstrate your knowledge and skills in Oracle database systems. The certification tests are scenario-based, which is the most effective way to assess your hands-on expertise and critical problem-solving skills.

Certification is proof of your knowledge and shows that you have the skills required to support Oracle core products. The OCP program can help a company to identify proven performers who have demonstrated their skills and who can support the company's investment in Oracle technology. It demonstrates that you have a solid understanding of your role and the Oracle products used in that role.

So, whether you are beginning a career, changing careers, securing your present position, or seeking to refine and promote your position, this book is for you!

Oracle Certifications

Oracle has several certification tracks designed to meet different skill levels. Each track consists of several tests, and these tests can be taken in any order. The following tracks are available:

- Oracle Database Administrator
- Oracle Application Developer
- Oracle Database Operator
- Oracle Java Developer
- Oracle Financial Applications Consultant

Database Administrator (DBA)

The role of the Database Administrator (DBA) has become a key to success in today's highly complex database systems. The best DBAs work behind the scenes but are in the spotlight when critical issues arise. They plan, create, maintain, and ensure that the database is available for the business. They are always watching the database for performance issues and to prevent unscheduled downtime. The DBA's job requires broad understanding of the architecture of Oracle databases and expertise in solving problems. The Oracle8i Certified Database Administrator track consists of the following five tests:

- 1Z0-001: Introduction to Oracle: SQL and PL/SQL
- 1Z0-023: Oracle8i: Architecture and Administration
- 1Z0-025: Oracle8i: Backup and Recovery
- 1Z1-024: Oracle8i: Performance and Tuning
- 1Z1-026: Oracle8i: Network Administration

Oracle Application Developer

This track tests your skills in client-server application development using Oracle application development tools, such as Developer/2000, SQL, PL/SQL, and SQL*Plus. The following five tests comprise this track:

- 1Z0-001: Introduction to Oracle: SQL and PL/SQL
- 1Z0-101: Develop PL/SQL Program Units
- 1Z0-121: Developer/2000: Build Forms I
- 1Z0-122: Developer/2000: Build Forms II
- 1Z0-123: Developer/2000: Build Reports

More Information

The most current information about Oracle certification can be found at http://education.oracle.com. Follow the Certification Home Page link and choose the track that you are interested in. Read the Candidate Guide for the test objectives and test contents, and keep in mind that these can change at any time without notice.

OCP: Database Administrator Track

The Oracle8i Database Administrator certification consists of five tests, and Sybex offers several study guides to help you achieve the OCP Database Administrator Certification. There are three books in this series:

- *OCP: Oracle8i™ DBA SQL and PL/SQL Study Guide*
- *OCP: Oracle8i™ DBA Architecture & Administration and Backup & Recovery Study Guide*
- *OCP: Oracle8i™ DBA Performance Tuning and Network Administration Study Guide*

Additionally, these three books are offered in a boxed set:

- *OCP: Oracle8i™ DBA Certification Kit*

Table F.1 lists the five exams for the DBA track, their scoring (where available), and the Sybex study guides that will help you pass each exam.

Table F.1: OCP Database Administrator Tests and Passing Scores

Exam #	Title	Total Questions	Questions Correct	Passing Score	Sybex Study Guide
1Z0-001	Introduction to Oracle: SQL and PL/SQL	60	43	72%	*OCP: Oracle8i™ DBA SQL and PL/SQL Study Guide*
1Z0-023	Oracle8i: Architecture and Administration	65	38	58%	*OCP: Oracle8i™ DBA Architecture & Administration and Backup & Recovery Study Guide*
1Z0-024	Oracle8i: Performance Tuning	57	38	67%	*OCP: Oracle8i™ DBA Performance Tuning and Network Administration Study Guide*
1Z0-025	Oracle8i: Backup and Recovery	60	34	57%	*OCP: Oracle8i™ DBA Architecture & Administration and Backup & Recovery Study Guide*
1Z0-026	Oracle8i: Network Administration	60	41	60%	*OCP: Oracle8i™ DBA Performance Tuning and Network Administration Study Guide*

Skills Required for DBA Certification

Listed here are some of the skills you must master for DBA certification. Even if you do not have all the skills, you can start taking the exams for which you feel confident. The exams can be taken in any order.

- Understanding RDBMS concepts

- Writing queries and manipulating data

- Creating and managing users and database objects

- Knowledge of PL/SQL programming and constructs

- Oracle Server architecture—database and instance

- Physical and logical storage of database, managing space allocation and growth

- Managing data—storage, loading, and reorganization

- Managing roles, privileges, passwords, and resources

- Backup and recovery options

- Archiving redo log files and hot backups

- Backup and recovery using Recovery Manager (RMAN)

- Creating and managing standby database

- Identifing and tuning database and SQL performance

- Data dictionary views and database parameters

- Configuring Net8 on the server side and the client side

- Using multi-threaded server, connection manager, and Oracle Names

- Backup, recovery, and administration utilities

Tips for Taking the OCP Exam

The following tips will help you prepare for and pass each exam:

- Each OCP test contains about 60–80 questions to be completed in about 90 minutes. Answer the questions that you know first, so that you do not run out of time.

- Many questions on the exam have answer choices that at first glance look identical. Read the questions carefully. Don't just jump to conclusions. Make sure that you are clear about exactly what each question asks.

- Most of the test questions are scenario-based. Some of the scenarios contain non-essential information and exhibits. You need to be able to identify what's important and what's not.

- Do not leave any questions unanswered. There is no negative scoring. You can mark a difficult question or one that you're unsure of and come back to it later.

- When answering questions that you are not sure about, use a process of elimination to get rid of the obviously incorrect answers first. Doing this greatly improves your odds if you need to make an educated guess.

Where Do You Take the Exam?

You may take the exams at any of the more than 800 Sylvan Prometric Authorized Testing Centers around the world. For the location of a testing center near you, call 1-800-891-3926. Outside of the United States and Canada, contact your local Sylvan Prometric Registration Center. The tests can be taken in any order.

To register for an Oracle Certified Professional exam

- Determine the number of the exam you want to take. (The OCP: Introduction to Oracle: SQL and PL/SQL exam number is 1Z0-001.)

- Register with the nearest Sylvan Prometric Registration Center. At this point, you will be asked to pay in advance for the exam. At the time of this writing, the exams are $125 each and must be taken within one year of payment. You can schedule exams up to six weeks in advance or as soon as one working day before the day you wish to take it. If something comes up and you need to cancel or reschedule your exam appointment, contact Sylvan Prometric at least 24 hours in advance.

- When you schedule the exam, you'll get instructions regarding all appointment and cancellation procedures and the ID requirements, and information about the testing-center location.

You can also register for the test online at `http://www.2test.com/register/frameset.htm`. If you live outside the United States, register online at `http://www.2test.com/register/testcenterlocator/ERN_intl_IT&FAA.htm`.

What Does This Book Cover?

This book covers everything you need to pass the OCP: Introduction to Oracle: SQL and PL/SQL exam. This exam is part of the Database Administrator track, as well as the Application Developer track. It teaches you the basics of Oracle, SQL, and PL/SQL. Each chapter begins with a list of exam objectives.

Chapter 1   This chapter starts with the concepts of relational databases, entity-relationship diagrams, and simple queries. This chapter also introduces SQL*Plus, Oracle's tool to interact with the database.

Chapter 2   This chapter discusses the various built-in functions available in Oracle. Single-row and group functions are discussed.

Chapter 3   Chapter 3 introduces you to more complex SQL statements. Subqueries, joins, and set operations are illustrated in detail.

Chapter 4   This chapter covers data manipulation and security in Oracle. You will learn how to insert, update, and delete data; how to control transactions; and how to restrict access to objects through privileges and roles.

Chapter 5   Chapter 5 is dedicated to tables and views. This chapter discusses creating tables with the various datatyp es and options available to store data. Creating and managing views are also covered in this chapter.

Chapter 6   Chapter 6 reviews the other database objects, synonyms, sequences, indexes, and stored SQL. The data dictionary is introduced in this chapter, as well.

Chapter 7   This chapter introduces PL/SQL. The benefits, structure, and writing of simple PL/SQL blocks are discussed. The chapter also introduces you to the language's control structures for iterative programming and conditional processing.

Chapter 8   This chapter covers how to use PL/SQL interactively with the Oracle database. The various SQL commands available in PL/SQL, together with how to declare and use cursors, are discussed in this chapter.

Chapter 9   Chapter 9 discusses composite datatypes. You will read about creating and using PL/SQL collections and record datatypes.

Chapter 10   The final chapter is dedicated to handling errors (called exceptions) in a PL/SQL program. You will learn how to create and customize exceptions and to provide application-specific, meaningful error messages.

Each chapter ends with Review Questions that are specifically designed to help you retain the knowledge presented. To really nail down your skills, read and answer each question carefully.

How to Use This Book

This book can provide a solid foundation for the serious effort of preparing for the Introduction to Oracle: SQL and PL/SQL exam. To best benefit from this book, use the following study method:

1. Take the Assessment Test immediately following this introduction. (The answers are at the end of the test.) Carefully read over the explanations for any question you get wrong, and note which chapters the material comes from. This information should help you plan your study strategy.

2. Study each chapter carefully, making sure that you fully understand the information and the test objectives listed at the beginning of each chapter. Pay extra close attention to any chapter related to questions you missed in the Assessment Test.

3. Complete all hands-on exercises in the chapter, referring to the chapter so that you understand the reason for each step you take. If you do not have an Oracle database available, be sure to study the examples carefully. Answer the Review Questions related to that chapter. (The answers appear at the end of each chapter, after the Review Questions.)

4. Note the questions that confuse or trick you, and study those sections of the book again.

5. Take the Practice Exam in this book. You'll find it in Appendix A. The answers appear at the end of the exam.

6. Before taking the exam, try your hand at the bonus Practice Exam that is included on the CD that comes with this book. The questions on this exam appear only on the CD. This will give you a complete overview of what you can expect to see on the real thing.

7. Remember to use the products on the CD that is included with this book. The electronic flashcards, the Boson Software utilities, and the EdgeTest exam preparation software all have been specifically picked to help you study for and pass your exam. The electronic flashcards can be used on your Windows computer or on your Palm device.

To learn all the material covered in this book, you'll have to apply yourself regularly and with discipline. Try to set aside the same time period every day to study, and select a comfortable and quiet place to do so. If you work hard, you will be surprised at how quickly you learn this material. All the best!

What's on the CD?

We have worked hard to provide some really great tools to help you with your certification process. All of the following tools should be loaded on your workstation when you're studying for the test.

The EdgeTest for Oracle Certified DBA Preparation Software

Provided by EdgeTek Learning Systems, this test-preparation software prepares you to pass the Introduction to Oracle exam. In this test, you will find all of the questions from the book, plus the bonus Practice Exam that appears exclusively on the CD. You can take the Assessment Test, test yourself by chapter, take the Practice Exam that appears in the book or on the CD, or take an exam randomly generated from all of the questions.

Electronic Flashcards for PC and Palm Devices

After you read the *OCP: Oracle8i DBA SQL and PL/SQL Study Guide*, read the Review Questions at the end of each chapter, and study the Practice Exams included in the book and on the CD. But wait, there's more! Test yourself with the flashcards included on the CD. If you can get through these difficult questions and understand the answers, you'll know that you're ready for the *OCP: Introduction to Oracle: SQL and PL/SQL* exam.

The flashcards include more than 100 questions specifically written to hit you hard and make sure that you are ready for the exam. Between the Review Questions, Practice Exam, and flashcards, you should be more than prepared for the exam.

OCP: Oracle 8i DBA SQL and PL/SQL Study Guide in PDF

Sybex is now offering the Oracle certification books on CD, so you can read the book on your PC or laptop. It is in Adobe Acrobat format. Acrobat Reader 4 is also included on the CD.

This will be extremely helpful to readers who fly or commute on a bus or train and don't want to carry a book, as well as to readers who find it more comfortable reading from their computer.

How to Contact the Authors

You can reach Chip Dawes through D & D Technologies, Inc. (www.ddtechnologies.com)—a Chicago-based consultancy—or e-mail him at chip@ddtechnologies.com.

To contact Biju Thomas, you can e-mail him at biju@bijoos.com or visit his Web site for DBAs at www.bijoos.com/oracle.

Assessment Test

1. When creating an ER diagram, what kind of line would you use to represent the following business rules:
   A department may have one or more employees.
   Each employee must belong to one department.

   A. A dotted line with a crowfoot at one end

   B. A solid line with a crowfoot at one end

   C. A dotted line with a crowfoot at each end

   D. A solid line with a crowfoot at each end

2. Which operator will be evaluated first in the following SELECT statement?
   ```
   SELECT (2 + 3 * 4 / 2 - 5) FROM DUAL;
   ```

   A. +

   B. *

   C. /

   D. −

3. Which line of code has an error?
   ```
   SELECT *
   FROM emp
   WHERE comm = NULL
   ORDER BY ename;
   ```

   A. SELECT *

   B. FROM emp

   C. WHERE comm = NULL

   D. There is no error in this statement.

4. The following statement will raise an exception on which line?

```
select dept_name, avg(all salary), count(*)"number of
employees"
from emp , dept
where deptno = dept_no
  and count(*) > 5
group by dept_name
order by 2 desc;
```

A. select dept_name, avg(all salary), count(*)"number of
employees"

B. where deptno = dept_no

C. and count(*) > 5

D. group by dept_name

E. order by 2 desc;

5. Using the following EMP table, you need to increase everyone's salary
by 5% of their combined salary and bonus.

Column Name	emp_id	name	salary	bonus
Key Type	pk	pk		
NULLs/ Unique	NN	NN	NN	
FK Table				
Datatype	varchar2	varchar2	number	number
Length	9	50	11,2	11,2

Which of the following statements will achieve the desired results?

A. UPDATE emp SET salary = (salary + bonus)*1.05;

B. UPDATE emp SET salary = salary*1.05 + bonus*1.05;

C. UPDATE emp SET salary = salary + (salary + bonus)*0.05;

D. A, B, and C all will achieve the desired results.

E. None of these statements will achieve the desired results.

6. The DEPT table has DEPTNO as the primary key and has the following data:

```
SQL> SELECT * FROM dept;
```

```
    DEPTNO DNAME          LOC
---------- -------------- -------------
        10 ACCOUNTING     NEW YORK
        20 RESEARCH       DALLAS
        30 SALES          CHICAGO
        40 OPERATIONS     BOSTON
```

Consider the INSERT statement. Which option is correct?

```
INSERT INTO (SELECT * FROM dept WHERE deptno = 10)
VALUES (50, 'MARKETING', 'FORT WORTH');
```

A. The INSERT statement is invalid; a valid table name is missing.

B. 50 is not a valid DEPTNO value, since the subquery limits the DEPTNO to 10.

C. The statement will work without error.

D. A subquery and a VALUES clause cannot appear together.

7. At a minimum, how many join conditions should there be in the WHERE clause to avoid a Cartesian join if there are three tables in the FROM clause?

A. 1

B. 2

C. 3

D. There is no minimum.

8. Which one of the following statements will succeed?

A. grant create user, alter user to Katrina with admin option;

B. grant grant any privilege to Katrina with grant option;

C. grant create user, alter user to Katrina with grant option;

D. grant revoke any privilege to Katrina with admin option;

9. With regard to the following PL/SQL block, which of the following options is most correct?

```
BEGIN
    UPDATE emp
      SET salary = salary * 1.10
      WHERE class_code = 'A';
    SAVEPOINT ClassA_FloorAdjusted;

    UPDATE emp
      SET  salary = salary * 1.07
      WHERE class_code = 'B';
    SAVEPOINT ClassB_FloorAdjusted;

    UPDATE emp
      SET  salary = salary * 1.05
      WHERE class_code = 'C';
    SAVEPOINT ClassC_FloorAdjusted;

    ROLLBACK TO SAVEPOINT ClassB_FloorAdjusted;

    UPDATE taxes
      SET max_tax = 76200*0.075
      WHERE tax_type = 'FICA';
    SAVEPOINT MaxTax;
```

```
        ROLLBACK to MaxTax;
        ROLLBACK to ClassA_FloorAdjusted;
END;
COMMIT;
```

A. No changes occur to the EMP table, but the TAXES table is changed.

B. Both the EMP and TAXES tables are changed.

C. Only EMP rows with class_code equal to 'A' are changed.

D. Only EMP rows with class_codes equal to 'C' are changed.

E. No changes occur to either the EMP or the TAXES table.

10. What does the following statement do?

```
alter user effie identified by kerberos;
```

A. Creates user account effie.

B. Changes the external authentication service for user effie.

C. Makes effie a globally identified account.

D. Changes user effie's password.

11. Why does the following statement fail?

```
CREATE TABLE FRUITS&VEGETABLES
( NAME VARCHAR2 (40));
```

A. The table should have more than one column defined.

B. NAME is a reserved word, which cannot be used as a column name.

C. The table name is invalid.

D. Column length cannot exceed 30 characters.

12. True or False: A view can only be used to query and update data; you cannot insert into or delete from a view.

A. True

B. False

13. Which option is not available in Oracle when modifying tables?

    A. Add new columns

    B. Rename an existing column

    C. Drop an existing column

    D. All of the above

14. Which of the following statements will remove the primary key constraint pk_books from the table BOOKS? Choose one.

    A. `drop primary key on books;`

    B. `drop constraint pk_books;`

    C. `alter table books drop primary key;`

    D. `alter table books drop pk_books;`

15. The built-in packaged procedure dbms_application_info.set_module has, in the package specification, the following declaration:

    ```
    PROCEDURE DBMS_APPLICATION_INFO.SET_MODULE
    (module_name IN VARCHAR2
    ,action_name IN VARCHAR2);
    ```

    Which of the following statements will successfully call this procedure passing 'Monthly Load' and 'Rebuild Indexes' for the module_name and action_name, respectively? Select all that apply.

    A. ```
       dbms_application_info('Monthly Load'
         ,'Rebuild Indexes');
       ```

    B. ```
       dbms_application_info(
         module_name=>'Monthly Load'
         ,action_name=>'Rebuild Indexes');
       ```

    C. ```
       dbms_application_info('Rebuild Indexes'
         ,'Monthly Load');
       ```

    D. ```
       dbms_application_info(
         module_name->'Monthly Load'
         ,action_name->'Rebuild Indexes');
       ```

16. Which statement will assign the next number from the sequence emp_ seq to the variable *emp_key*? Choose one.

A. `emp_key := emp_seq.nextval;`

B. `emp_key := emp_seq.next_val;`

C. `emp_key := emp_seq.nextvalue;`

D. `emp_key := emp_seq.next_value;`

17. What is value of *V_COUNTER* when the following block is executed?

```
DECLARE
    V_COUNTER NUMBER (2);
BEGIN
    V_COUNTER := V_COUNTER + 1;
END;
```

A. 0

B. 1

C. NULL

D. None of the above

18. What is the value of *V_BONUS* if the value of *V_SALARY* is 500 when the following code is executed?

```
IF V_SALARY > 2000 THEN
   V_BONUS := 300;
ELSIF V_SALARY < 2000 THEN
   V_BONUS := 200;
ELSIF V_SALARY < 1000 THEN
   V_BONUS := 100;
ELSIF V_SALARY < 500 THEN
   V_BONUS := 50;
ELSIF V_SALARY < 200 THEN
   V_BONUS := 20;
ELSE
   V_BONUS := 10;
END IF;
```

A. 20

B. 100

C. 200

D. 300

19. Consider the following PL/SQL block:

```
BEGIN
  FOR x IN 100 .. 108 LOOP

    IF x = 102 THEN

        ROLLBACK;
        EXIT;

    ELSE

        INSERT INTO TABLE_A VALUES (x);
        SAVEPOINT A;

    END IF;
  END LOOP;
END;
```

How many rows will you see added to TABLE_A once you execute this block?

A. 0

B. 2

C. 9

D. 7

20. In the following code snippet, which line has an error?

```
1  FOR rec_c1 IN cur_c1 LOOP
2  FETCH REC_C1 INTO v_x;
3  INSERT INTO TABLE_A VALUES (v_x);
4  END LOOP;
```

A. Line 1

B. Line 2

C. Line 4

D. The code has no error.

21. What is the value of *V_COUNT* when the following PL/SQL block is executed?

```
DECLARE
    V_empno PLS_INTEGER;
    V_count PLS_INTEGER;
    CURSOR c1 IS SELECT empno FROM EMP;
BEGIN
  OPEN C1;
    V_COUNT := C1%ROWCOUNT;
    FETCH C1 INTO v_empno;
  CLOSE C1;
END;
```

A. 0

B. NULL

C. -1

D. 1

22. Which statement will create a record **team_rec** based on the table TEAMS, having a field in each record for each column in the table? Choose one.

A. type team_rec is record like teams;

B. team_rec   teams%tabletype

C. team_rec   teams%type

D. team_rec   teams%rowtype

E. You must list all the columns in the TYPE statement that defines the record.

23. In the following PL/SQL block, what might cause a problem?

```
DECLARE
  customer_rec    customers%rowtype;
BEGIN
  select * into customer_rec where location = '63128';
  approve_payment(customer_rec);
END;
```

A. If a column is added to the CUSTOMERS table, this block will fail.

B. If there is more than one customer with a location of '63128', this block will fail.

C. If there are no customers with a location of '63128', this block will fail.

D. There is no problem with this code.

24. How would you assign the current date and time to the timestamp field in element 3 of the QUOTE_LIST nested table?

A. `quote_list(3).timestamp := sysdate;`

B. `quote_list.timestamp(3) := sysdate;`

C. `quote_list(timestamp).3 := sysdate;`

D. `quote_list.3(timestamp) := sysdate;`

25. In the following PL/SQL block, what does line 2 do?

```
1 declare
2   bad_credit  exception;
3 begin
4   raise bad_credit;
5 exception
6   when bad_credit
7     refuse_order('Nicely');
8 end;
```

A. Raise an exception

B. Declare an exception

C. Associate an exception

D. Handle an exception

26. To which of the following will an exception raised in the exception section of a PL/SQL block pass control?

   A. The current exception section

   B. The executable section of the enclosing PL/SQL block

   C. The exception section of the enclosing PL/SQL block

   D. The operating system will dump a core image.

27. What does the following line of code do?

```
pragma exception_init(max_sessions, -18);
```

   A. The exception max_sessions is associated with error number 18.

   B. The database is instructed to accept a maximum of 18 sessions.

   C. The exception max_sessions is declared.

   D. The stored SQL (function or procedure) containing this directive can be invoked by a maximum of 18 concurrent sessions.

Answers to Assessment Test

1. A.   Because the first rule states "may have," the relationship is optional. Optional relationships are represented by a dotted line. There may be more than one employee in a department; this relationship is represented by a crowfoot. For more about optional and mandatory relationships, see Chapter 1.

2. B.   In the arithmetic operators, unary operators are evaluated first, then multiplication and division, and finally addition and subtraction. The expression is evaluated left to right. For more information about order of evaluation, see Chapter 1.

3. D.   Although there is no error in this statement, the statement will not return the desired result. When a NULL is compared, you cannot use the = or != operators; you must say IS NULL or IS NOT NULL. See Chapter 1 to learn about the comparison operators.

4. C. Group functions cannot appear in the WHERE clause. To learn more about group functions, see Chapter 2.

5. E. These statements don't account for possible NULL values in the bonus column, which is defined as nullable. For more about NULL values, see Chapter 2.

6. C. The statement will work without error. Option B would have been correct if we had used the WITH CHECK OPTION clause in the subquery. See Chapter 3 for more information about subqueries.

7. B. There should be at least $n-1$ join conditions when joining n tables to avoid a Cartesian join. To learn more about joins, see Chapter 3.

8. A. The grant option cannot be used on system privileges, and revoke any privilege is not a valid privilege. For more on privileges, see Chapter 4.

9. C . Only class_code 'A' EMP rows get changed. The furthest we roll back is to the savepoint named ClassA_FloorAdjusted, so the only changes that get committed are those occurring before this savepoint (class_code 'A') or after the rollback to savepoint (nothing). Chapter 4 discusses savepoints and rollbacks.

10. D. Option A would be possible in Oracle6, but the exam is on Oracle8i. The kerberos password is just there to obfuscate. Chapter 4 discusses authentication and user accounts.

11. C. Table and column names can have only letters, numbers, and three special characters: dollar sign ($), underscore (_), and pound sign (#). Chapter 5 discusses table and column names.

12. B. You can insert into and delete from a view. In a joined view (a multiple table/view), you can only insert into or delete from one table at a time. For more about tables and views, see Chapter 5.

13. B. You cannot rename an existing column using the ALTER TABLE command. To rename the column, you must re-create the table with the new name. Turn to Chapter 5 to learn about modifying tables.

14. C. The ALTER TABLE statement is used to create and remove constraints. Option D would work if it included the keyword constraint between drop and pk_books. Chapter 6 discusses constraints.

15. A, B. Option A uses the correct positional notation; Option B uses the correct named notational styles. For more information about positional and named notation, see Chapter 6.

16. A. This kind of question, which quizzes you on precise syntax, really does appear on the exam. Especially for sequences, know the syntactical spelling. You can read about sequences in Chapter 6.

17. C. Since the variable *V_COUNTER* is not initialized in the declaration section, it will assign the default value of NULL. Any arithmetic on NULL results a NULL. For more about variables, see Chapter 7.

18. C. The value of *V_BONUS* is 200. Because the value of *V_SALARY* is 500, when the conditions are evaluated top down, 500 is less than 2000, so the value of *V_BONUS* is 200. Chapter 7 discusses control structures.

19. A. There are two rows inserted into the table when the value of x is 100 and 101, but they are not committed. These two rows are rolled back when the value of x is 102, and the loop is exited. See Chapter 8 for more information about transaction control statements.

20. B. A FOR cursor loop opens the cursor and fetches the first row when you enter the loop. You should not specify explicit OPEN, FETCH, or CLOSE statements. Chapter 8 contains more information on the cursor FOR loop.

21. A. When the cursor is opened, %ROWCOUNT will have a value of 0. After the first successful fetch, it will have a value of 1. For more information about cursors, see Chapter 8.

22. D. The attribute %ROWTYPE is used to create a record based on a table, view, or query. For more about the %ROWTYPE attribute, see Chapter 9.

23. B, C. You can only SELECT INTO when the query returns a single row. Where there is a possibility of either more than one row or no rows being returned, you should not use a SELECT INTO; use a FETCH INTO instead. For more on %ROWTYPE records, see Chapter 9.

24. A. Elements are referenced by subscript notation; they are enclosed in parentheses. Fields are referenced with dot notation, placing a dot between the record name and the field. When records are used in collections, the notation is combined, as shown in answer A. For more on collections, see Chapter 9.

25. B. Line 2 declares the exception, line 4 raises the exception, and line 6 handles the exception. This block does not associate an exception. Chapter 10 discusses exceptions.

26. C. Exceptions raised in an exception handler will propagate to the enclosing block and will pass control to the exception section (since there is an exception condition). To learn more about exception propagation, see Chapter 10.

27. A. The pragma exception_init is used to associate a previously declared exception with a database error number. The error number for "Maximum number of sessions exceeded" just happens to be 18. To learn more about associating exception names with database error numbers, see Chapter 10.

Chapter 1

Relational Technology and Simple SQL SELECT Statements

ORACLE8i SQL AND PL/SQL EXAM OBJECTIVES OFFERED IN THIS CHAPTER:

✓ **Overview of relational databases, SQL, and PL/SQL:**

- Discuss the theoretical and physical characteristics of a relational database
- Describe the Oracle implementation of the RDBMS and ORDBMS
- Describe how SQL and PLSQL are used in Oracle products

✓ **Writing simple queries:**

- Write a basic SELECT statement
- Limit the rows retrieved using a WHERE clause
- Sort the rows retrieved using an ORDER BY clause

✓ **The Oracle SQL environment:**

- Write queries that specify a variable at runtime
- Customize the SQL*Plus environment
- Format data retrieved by a query
- Create and execute script files
- Save customizations
- Differentiate between SQL*Plus commands and SQL statements

Exam objectives are subject to change at any time without prior notice and at Oracle's sole discretion. Please visit Oracle's Training and Certification Web site (http://education .oracle.com/certification/index.html) for the most current exam objectives listing.

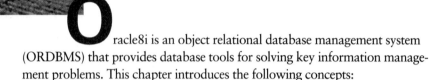

Oracle8i is an object relational database management system (ORDBMS) that provides database tools for solving key information management problems. This chapter introduces the following concepts:

- Relational and object-relational database management systems

- System development phases

- How to write simple queries using structured query language (SQL) to retrieve data stored in the Oracle8i database

You will also learn to format the query output from *SQL*Plus,* Oracle's tool to interact with the database. The first OCP exam emphasizes your understanding of the Oracle SQL usage and structure.

SQL, pronounced *sequel,* has been adopted by most relational database management systems. The American National Standards Institute (ANSI) has been refining standards for the SQL language for the past 20 years. Oracle, like many other companies, has taken the ANSI standard of SQL and extended it to include additional functionality.

Relational Database Systems

Over the years, database management systems have evolved from hierarchical to network to *relational database management systems (RDBMS).* A relational database system is an organized model of subjects and characteristics that have relationships among the subjects. A well-designed relational database provides information about a business or process and is used most widely to store and retrieve information. We see relationships everywhere in our daily lives: parents and children, team and players, doctor and patient, to name a few. Some major advantages of RDBMS are in the way it stores and retrieves information, and in how it maintains data integrity.

RDBMS structures are easy to understand and to build. These structures are logically represented using the *entity-relationship (ER)* model. On the OCP exam, you can expect questions relating to the ER diagram and/or the RDBMS concept. You may be familiar with the RDBMS concepts and ER diagrams already; for those who aren't, we have included a brief introduction here.

Characteristics of a Relational Database

Relational databases have the following three major characteristics that constitute a well defined RDBMS:

Structures   These are objects that store or access data from the database. Tables, views, and indexes are examples of structures in Oracle.

Operations   These are the actions used to define the structures or manipulate data between the structures. SELECT statements or CREATE statements are examples of operations in Oracle.

Integrity rules   These govern the kinds of actions allowed on data and the database structure. Integrity rules protect the data and the structure of the database. The primary keys and foreign keys are examples of integrity rules in Oracle.

Application Development Cycle

A well designed database makes the application programming and tuning much easier. Before going into the details of database design and modeling, let's review the stages involved in application development. Every application, small or large, passes through the stages of the application development cycle (also known as the system development cycle) described in the following paragraphs.

Analysis   Analysis is the first stage of an application development, and it should enable you to answer the following questions: Why is the application being developed? Who is going to use it? How will the application benefit the users? What business rules and needs should be addressed? The complete functionalities of the system should be determined in requirement analysis. Typically, functional-level managers take care of this phase.

Design   Design is the most important phase of application development. After the application requirements are analyzed, the *design phase* begins. In this phase, the database design is performed using ER diagrams. The logical database design is converted to physical structures. You can read about the ER diagram and logical modeling in detail in the next section, "The Logical Model."

Development   In the development phase, coding is done based on the design; you use the end product of the design phase of the life cycle as a building block for the development process. The database design and the designed system requirements provide the basis for the development of the application.

Testing   The developed application is tested against its objectives to ensure that it is doing what it is supposed to do. System/integration testing is done on the entire system. Any errors are corrected, and the application is tested again. Application users do the acceptance testing.

Implementation   Implementation is the final stage in the development cycle. Once the testing is complete, the application is ready to implement. Errors reported after implementation are fixed by going back to the appropriate stages. Following all these steps again carries out enhancements to the application.

Figure 1.1 shows the steps in the application development cycle.

FIGURE 1.1   Application Development Cycle

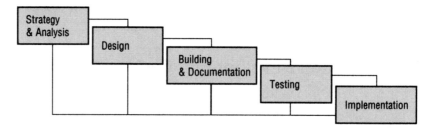

The Logical Model

In the design phase of the system development cycle, a logical model of the database is created. A logical model of an RDBMS is typically a block diagram of entities and relationships, referred to as an ER diagram.

An ER model has

- Entities

- Relationships

- Attributes

An ER model is visual, showing the structure, characteristics, and interactions within and around the data being modeled.

Entities and Attributes   An entity in a logical model is much like a noun in grammar: a person, place, or thing. The characteristics of an entity are known as its attributes. An attribute is detailed information about an entity that qualifies, identifies, classifies, or quantifies the entity. Consider this example: ABC Inc. has many offices in the US; each office has many departments, and each department may have many employees. Looking at ABC Inc. in terms of the ER model, you could identify OFFICE, DEPARTMENT, and EMPLOYEE as entities. Each entity will also have its own characteristics; for instance, when you say "office," you might want to know the city and state where the office is located, as well as how many employees work there. Similarly, you might want to know the department's name, its head, and an employee's name and date of birth. You might also like to know the name of the employee's spouse. In Figure 1.2, OFFICE, DEPARTMENT, and EMPLOYEE are entities, and their attributes are inside the box under each entity.

There are optional and mandatory attributes. For example, in Figure 1.2, under EMPLOYEE, the spouse name is optional, whereas the employee name, department, and date of birth are mandatory. An asterisk along with the attribute name indicates that it is mandatory. The optional attribute may be indicated by a small letter o.

FIGURE 1.2   Entities and Attributes

OFFICE	DEPARTMENT	EMPLOYEE
City State No. of Employees	Manager	Employee Name D.O.B. Spouse Name

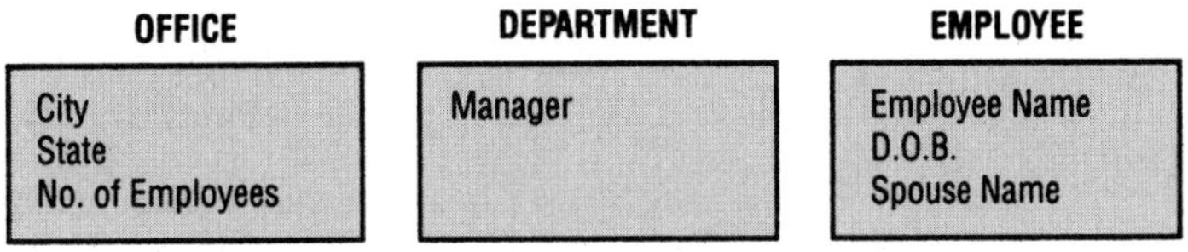

Relationships and Unique Identifiers   In the example of ABC Inc., each office has many departments and each department has many employees. This describes the relationship between the entities. If there is an office in one city, there should be at least one department. So, it is mandatory to have at least one occurrence of department for each location, although there may be many departments. In the ER model, a solid line represents a mandatory relationship and a crowfoot represents the "many." In a department, however, there may not be any employees at all. Optional occurrence is represented by a dotted line.

You should be able to identify each occurrence of an entity uniquely. What happens if there are two employees with the same name—how do you distinguish between them? For office location, the city and state uniquely identify each office; for department, the department name identifies it uniquely. For employee, we can introduce a unique identifier (UID) called employee number. Figure 1.3 is a refined version of Figure 1.2, showing the entities, attributes, relationships, optional and mandatory attributes, and UIDs. UID is represented in the diagram using a pound symbol (#).

FIGURE 1.3 An ER Model

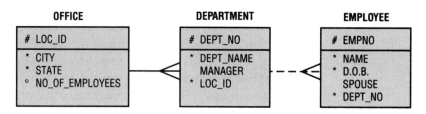

As you can see in Figure 1.4, three types of relationships can be defined between entities.

One-to-One A one-to-one relationship is one in which each occurrence of one entity is represented by single occurrence in another entity. For example, consider an individual and that individual's Social Security number: One person can have only one Social Security number, and a Social Security number can belong to only one person.

One-to-Many A one-to-many relationship is one in which an occurrence of one entity may be represented by many occurrences in another entity. An example is department and employees: One department has one or more employees, and an employee belongs to only one department.

Many-to-Many A many-to-many relationship is one in which an occurrence from one entity may be represented by one or more occurrences in another entity, and an occurrence from the second entity may be represented by one or more occurrences in the first entity. The relationship between doctor and patient is an example: A patient can visit many doctors, and a doctor can have many patients.

Many-to-many relationships should not exist in RDBMS because they cannot be properly joined to represent a single row correctly. To solve this, create another entity that has a one-to-many relationship with the first entity and a one-to-many relationship with the second entity.

FIGURE 1.4 Types of relationships

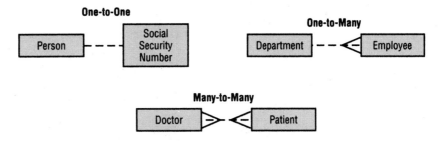

The logical model also provides information known as access paths. These are the common ways in which you query the database to retreive information. For example, you would always query the employee records with the DEPT_NO or EMPNO. Think of access paths as an index into the data, just as the index of a book helps you quickly find the information you need.

When you have established the relationships between entities, it's time to normalize the design. Normalization is the process of eliminating redundant information from the entities until you can uniquely identify each occurrence of the entity. This may not always be practical because of performance and implementation issues. In such cases, you can denormalize, which means you can have some redundant information.

Physical Model

You create a physical model by using the logical model to assist in creating a database and database objects to represent the entities and relationships. In the physical model, each entity becomes a table, and attributes of the entity become columns of the table. The relationship between the entities is part of one or more constraints between the tables. Physical implementations might require you to combine, separate, or create completely new entities in order to best realize the logical model. The unique identifiers of an entity become the primary key of the table. You may create stored procedures, functions, and triggers to enforce business rules.

In an RDBMS, the physical database storage is independent of the logical model.

Oracle's Implementation of RDBMS and ORDBMS

A database server is the key to information management. The Oracle database satisfies the three major characteristics of the relational model:

- Structures

- Operations

- Integrity rules

Oracle lets you define tables, columns, column characteristics like datatype, length, whether the values are mandatory, default, and so on. Defining foreign keys ensures the referential integrity of the data. In addition, you can define primary keys and indexes on the data. In versions 8 and 8i, Oracle has incorporated a variety of components.

Records in a database table can be seen as instances of the entity. Each occurrence of an entity is differentiated by the values of the attributes. Oracle stores these records as rows of the table and the attributes as columns in each row. In its most generic form, a database table can be seen as a single spreadsheet with an unlimited number of columns and rows. The columns are not defined until the user names them and gives them a datatype. Oracle extends the concept of spreadsheets by defining relationships between multiple spreadsheets, defining constraints on columns, and providing mechanisms for multiple users to access the same database table(s) simultaneously.

Data access paths are implemented in Oracle using indexes. Indexing helps to predefine the most common access paths for querying the database. These indexes decrease the time it takes to search for data in a table by using a number of data structures, such as B-trees, bitmaps, and so on.

Oracle implements the RDBMS characteristics using the following set of structures:

- Tables are used for data storage.

- Views and synonyms are created for data access.

- Indexes are used to speed up data access.

- Primary keys, foreign keys, and unique keys are created to enforce data integrity.

- Triggers are created to satisfy the business rules.

- Roles and privileges are used for security.

- Procedures, functions, and packages are used to develop the application and enforce business rules.

Oracle8i is an ORDBMS. It lets you define user-defined object types in the relational database system. Object types are structures that consist of built-in or user-defined datatypes. For example, an address can be defined as an object type and can be referenced in tables:

CUSTOMER_TABLE
```
CUST_NAME   VARCHAR2 (40)
CUST_ADDR   ADDRESS_TYPE
CUST_PHONE  VARCHAR2 (12)
CUST_FAX    VARCHAR2 (12)
```
where ADDRESS_TYPE is an object type defined as

ADDRESS_TYPE
```
STREET   STREET_TYPE
CITY     VARCHAR2 (30)
STATE    CHAR (2)
ZIP      NUMBER (5)
```
where STREET_TYPE is defined as

STREET_TYPE
```
STREET_NUMBER NUMBER    (6)
STREET_NAME1  VARCHAR2 (40)
STREET_NAME2  VARCHAR2 (40)
APARTMENT_NO  VARCHAR2 (5)
```

Now that the ADDRESS_TYPE is defined, it can be used in any number of tables where addresses need to be stored. This small example shows you how objects can be reused.

Oracle uses SQL to access the database. In the following sections, you will learn the basic components of Oracle8i and how to access data.

Oracle Datatypes

When you create a table to store data in the database, you need to specify a datatype for all columns you define in the table. Oracle has different datatypes to suit your requirements. The datatypes are broadly classified into character, number, date, LOB, and RAW datatypes. Oracle8i lets you use user-defined datatypes, but they are constructed from the basic datatypes. In the following sections, you will learn the usage, constraints, and allowable values for each of the Oracle built-in datatypes. See Figure 1.5 for an illustration of the basic datatypes available in Oracle8i.

FIGURE 1.5   Oracle datatypes

Character Datatypes

Character datatypes are used to store alphanumeric data. When you define character data in Oracle, you specify a length for the column, which is the maximum width of the column. Oracle provides the character datatypes described in the following paragraphs.

CHAR(<*size*>)   The CHAR datatype is a fixed-length character string having a maximum length of *size*. Data stored in CHAR columns is space-padded to fill the maximum length. Size can range from a minimum of 1 to a maximum of 2,000.

When you create a column using the CHAR datatype, the database will ensure that all data placed in this column has the defined length. If the data is shorter than the defined length, it is space-padded on the right to the specified length. If the data is longer, an error is raised.

Comparison rules for CHAR types ignore any trailing spaces. See the "Comparison Rules" section that follows for the differences among the character types.

VARCHAR(<*size*>)   A VARCHAR datatype is currently synonymous with the VARCHAR2 datatype.

VARCHAR2(<*size*>)   The VARCHAR2 datatype is a variable-length alphanumeric string having a maximum length of *size* bytes. VARCHAR2 variables only require the amount of space needed to store the data. VARCHAR2 database columns can store up to 4,000 bytes and VARCHAR2 variables up to 32,676 bytes.

An empty VARCHAR2 (2000) column takes up as much room in the database as an empty VARCHAR2(2) column.

The default size of a CHAR datatype is 1. In VARCHAR2, you must always specify the size.

NCHAR(<*size*>) and NVARCHAR2(<*size*>)   NCHAR and NVARCHAR2 datatypes have the same characteristics as the CHAR and VARCHAR2 datatypes and are used to store National Language Support (NLS) data. Oracle's NLS architecture allows you to store, process, and retrieve information in native languages. Database error messages, date, time, calendar, and numeric formats are adapted as in the native language.

LONG   The LONG datatype is a legacy datatype that will no longer be supported in the future. It has been deprecated in favor of *Large Object (LOB)* datatypes. A LONG datatype column is of variable length and can take up to $2^{31}-1$ bytes or 2GB. There are many restrictions on the use of LONG columns and variables. LONG columns cannot appear in WHERE clauses, GROUP BY clauses, ORDER BY clauses, or CONNECT BY clauses, or with the DISTINCT operator in SELECT statements.

Comparison Rules   The VARCHAR and CHAR datatypes have different comparison rules for trailing spaces. With the CHAR datatype, trailing spaces are ignored; with the VARCHAR and VARCHAR2 datatypes, trailing spaces sort higher than no trailing spaces. Here's an example:

```
CHAR datatype:        'Yo'='Yo   '
VARCHAR2 datatype:    'Yo' <'Yo   '
```

Numeric Datatypes

Numeric datatypes are used to store negative and positive integers: fixed-point and floating-point numbers with magnitudes ranging between -1×10^{-130} and $9.999...99 \times 10^{125}$ with a precision of up to 38 digits. Specifying a number outside this range will raise an error.

NUMBER (<*p*>, <*s*>)   The NUMBER datatype stores numbers with a precision of *p* digits and a scale of *s* digits. The precision and scale values are optional.

Precision and Scale   Oracle will round numbers inserted into numeric columns with a scale smaller than the inserted number; see Table 1.1. For example, if a column is defined as NUMBER (4,2) and you insert a value of 12.125 into this column, the resulting number would be rounded to 12.13 before it is inserted into the column.

Specifying the scale and precision does not force all inserted values to be a fixed length. If the number exceeds the precision, however, an Oracle error is returned. If the number exceeds the scale, it is rounded to the scale.

Negative Scale   If the scale is negative, the number is rounded to the left of the decimal. Basically, a negative scale forces *s* number of zeros just to the left of the decimal.

TABLE 1.1   Precision and Scale Examples

Actual Value	Datatype	Stored Value
1234567.89	NUMBER	1234567.89
1234567.89	NUMBER(8)	1234568
1234567.89	NUMBER(6)	Numeric error
1234567.89	NUMBER(9,1)	1234567.9
1234567.89	NUMBER(9,3)	Numeric error
1234567.89	NUMBER(7,2)	Numeric error
1234567.89	NUMBER(5,-2)	1234600
1234511.89	NUMBER(5,-2)	1234500
1234567.89	NUMBER(5,-4)	1230000
1234567.89	NUMBER (*,1)	1234567.9

The Date Datatype

The DATE datatype is used to store date and time information. This datatype can be converted to other forms for viewing, and it has a number of special functions and properties that make date manipulation and calculations simple. The time component of the DATE datatype has a resolution of one second—no less. The DATE datatype occupies a storage space of seven bytes. The following information is contained within each DATE datatype:

- Century
- Year
- Month

- Day

- Hour

- Minute

- Second

Date values are inserted or updated in the database by converting either a numeric or character value into a date datatype using the function TO_DATE. The default format for character dates is defined by the NLS_DATE_FORMAT initialization parameter and can be overridden for the current session. Oracle defaults this format to be DD-MON-YY; this is the format shown whenever a date is selected within SQL*Plus. This format shows that the default date must begin with a two-digit day, followed by a three-character abbreviation for the month, followed by a two-digit year. If you specify the date without including a time component, the time is defaulted to midnight, or 00:00:00 in military time. The SYSDATE function returns the current system date and time from the database server to which you're currently connected.

Comparing Dates   Dates are stored in the database as *Julian numbers* with a fraction component for the time. A Julian date refers to the number of days since Jan. 1, 4712 BC. Due to the time component of the date, comparing dates can result in fractional differences, even though the date is the same. Often dates are added to the system using the SYSDATE function, which includes the time component (the current time on the server). Oracle provides a number of functions that help you to remove the time component when you only want to compare the date portions. The TRUNC function is one of them.

Date Arithmetic   Adding one to the Julian date simply moves the date ahead one day. You can add time to the date by adding a fraction of a day, understanding that one day equals 24 hours or 24×60 minutes or $24 \times 60 \times 60$ seconds. Table 1.2 shows the numbers used to add or subtract time for a DATE datatype.

TABLE 1.2   Date Arithmetic

Time to Add	Fraction	Date Difference
1 Day	1	1
1 Hour	1/24	1/24
1 Minute	$1/(24 \times 60)$	1/1440
1 Second	$1/(24 \times 60 \times 60)$	1/86400

Oracle provides a number of date functions to add or subtract months.

Subtracting two dates gives you the difference between the dates in days. This usually results in a fractional component that represents the time difference. If the time components are the same, there will be no fractional results. The following example shows the current system date (08-Mar-2000 21:24:51) and the difference between system date and 07-Mar-2000 00:00:00. The difference is shown as a fraction: 1.8922564. Using Table 1.2, you can interpret this as one day, 21 hours (0.89225694/24=21.4141536), 24 minutes (0.4141536×60=24.849216), and 51 seconds (0.849216×60=50.9).

```
SQL> select sysdate, to_date('07-MAR-2000','dd-mon-yyyy'),
2   sysdate - to_date('07-MAR-2000','dd-mon-yyyy') diff
3   from dual;
SYSDATE              TO_DATE('07-MAR-200        DIFF
-------------------  -------------------  ----------
2000-03-08-21:24:51  2000-03-07-00:00:00  1.89225694

SQL>
```

LOB Datatypes

Large Object (*LOB*) datatypes store blocks of unstructured data, such as a binary file, a picture, or an external file. Table 1.3 shows a list of LOB datatypes. A LOB can store data up to 4GB. The data may be stored in the database or in an external file. LOB data manipulation is done using the DBMS_LOB package. The LOB locator is stored in the table column, either with or without the actual LOB value. BLOB, NCLOB, and CLOB values can be stored in separate tablespaces. BFILE data is stored in an external file on the server.

TABLE 1.3 LOB Datatypes

Datatype	Purpose	Description
BLOB	Binary Large Object	Can store up to 4GB of binary data in the database.
CLOB	Character Large Object	Can store up to 4GB of character data in the database. Oracle converts the data into Unicode format and stores it in the database.

TABLE 1.3   LOB Datatypes *(continued)*

Datatype	Purpose	Description
BFILE	Binary File	Stores binary data up to 4GB in operating system files outside of the database. The size of the binary file must conform with operating system limitations on file size. A BFILE column stores a file locator that points to an external file containing the data. BFILE datatypes are read-only; you cannot modify them.

There may be more than one LOB datatype column in a table, but there can be only one LONG datatype column.

Other Datatypes

This section covers the datatypes not mentioned previously. Oracle has RAW and ROWID datatypes in addition to the character, numeric, and date datatypes.

RAW   RAW is unstructured, binary data that is not interpreted by the database. This data does not undergo character set conversion during replication or when the client character set differs from the database character set. RAW columns can be up to 2,000 bytes long.

LONGRAW   Like the LONG datatype, LONGRAW is a legacy datatype that has been deprecated in favor of the LOB datatypes BLOB or BFILE. LONGRAWs can store up to 2GB of unstructured data. LONGRAW data cannot be indexed, but RAW data can be indexed.

ROWID   The ROWID datatype is a pseudo-column in the Oracle database that represents the internal unique identifier for each row in a table. Physical ROWIDs store the addresses of rows in ordinary tables (excluding index-organized tables), clustered tables, table partitions and subpartitions, indexes, and index partitions and subpartitions. Logical ROWIDs store the addresses of rows in index-organized tables. Physical ROWIDs provide the fastest possible access to a row of a given table. Versions of Oracle prior to Oracle8 use the restricted ROWID format (block.row.file). Oracle8 uses extended ROWID format, which includes the object ID number (you may select the object number from DBA_OBJECTS view).

UROWID   Universal ROWID, or UROWID, supports both logical and physical ROWIDs, as well as ROWIDs of foreign tables (such as non-Oracle tables accessed through a gateway). A column of the UROWID datatype can store all kinds of ROWIDs.

Literals

Literals are values that represent a fixed value. There are three types of literal values:

- Text
- Integer
- Number

Text literals must be enclosed in single quotes; integer and number literals need not be. You can use literals within many of the SQL functions, expressions, and conditions.

Text   The text literal must be enclosed in single quotation marks. Any character between the quotation marks is considered part of the text value. Oracle treats all text literals as though they were CHAR datatypes. The maximum length of a text literal is 2,000 characters. Single quotation marks can be included in the literal text value by preceding it with another single quotation mark.

Here are some examples:

- 'The Quick Brown Fox'
- 'That man''s suit is black'
- 'And I quote:''This will never do.'' '

Integer   Integer literals can be any number of numerals, excluding a decimal separator and up to 38 digits long.

Examples follow:

- 24
- − 456

Number   Number literals can include scientific notation, as well as digits and the decimal separator.

Here are some examples:

- 24

- –345.65

- 23E–10

SQL Fundamentals

SQL is a simple and powerful language used to create, access, and manipulate data and structure in the database. SQL is like plain English: easy to understand and to write. Oracle divides SQL statements into various categories, which you can see in Table 1.4.

TABLE 1.4 SQL Statement Categories

SQL Category	Description
Data Definition	Data definition language (DDL) statements are used to define, alter, or drop database objects. Examples are CREATE TABLE, ALTER INDEX, GRANT, REVOKE, TRUNCATE, ANALYZE, and so on.
Data Manipulation	Data manipulation language (DML) statements are used to access, create or manipulate data in the existing structures of the database. Examples are SELECT, INSERT, UPDATE, DELETE, LOCK TABLE, EXPLAIN, and so on.
Transaction Control	Transaction control statements manage the changes made by the DML statements, whether to save them or discard them. The COMMIT, ROLLBACK, SAVEPOINT, and SET TRANSACTION commands are all transaction control statements.
Session Control	Session control statements manage the properties of a user's session. The SET ROLE and ALTER SESSION commands are used.
System Control	System control statements are used to manage the properties of the database. The ALTER SYSTEM command is used for this purpose.

In preparing for the Oracle8i SQL and PL/SQL exam, it would be wise to concentrate mainly on simple data definition statements like CREATE TABLE; data manipulation statements like SELECT, INSERT, and UPDATE; and transaction control statements like SAVEPOINT, ROLLBACK, and COMMIT.

Operators and Expressions

An operator is a manipulator that is applied to a data item in order to return a result. Special characters represent different operations in Oracle (+ represents addition, for example). Operators are commonly used in all programming environments, and you should already be familiar with the following operators, which may be classified into two types:

Unary Operator A unary operator has only one operand. +2 and −5 are examples. They have the format *<operator operand>*.

Binary Operator Binary operators have two operands. 5 + 4 and 7 x 5 are examples. They have the format *<operand1 operator operand2>*.

Arithmetic Operators

Arithmetic operators operate on numeric datatypes. Table 1.5 shows you the various arithmetic operators in Oracle and how to use them.

TABLE 1.5 Arithmetic Operators

Operator	Purpose	Example
+ -	Unary operators: Use to represent positive or negative data item. For positive items, the + is optional.	-234.44
+	Addition: Use to add two data items or expressions.	2 + 4
-	Subtraction: Use to find the difference between two data items or expressions.	20.4 - 2
*	Multiplication: Use to multiply two data items or expressions.	5 * 10
/	Division: Use to divide a data item or expression with another.	8.4 / 2

Do not use two hyphens (--) to represent double negation; use a space or parenthesis in between, as in -(-20). Two hyphens represent the beginning of a comment in SQL.

Concatenation Operator

The concatenation operator is used to concatenate or join two character (text) strings. The result of *concatenation* is another character string. If one of the strings is NULL, the result is also NULL. Concatenating a zero-length string ('') with another string results in a string, not a NULL. Two vertical bars (||) are used as the concatenation operator.

Here are a few examples:

- 'Oracle8i' || 'Database' results in 'Oracle8iDatabase'

- 'Oracle8i ' || 'Database' results in 'Oracle8i Database'

- SELECT first_name || ' ' || last_name FROM emp; gives the name of the employees in the EMP table.

Comparison Operators

Comparison operators compare two values or expressions and give a Boolean result of TRUE, FALSE, or NULL. Table 1.6 lists the various comparison operators and how to use them.

TABLE 1.6 Comparison Operators

Operator	Purpose	Example
=	Equality test.	SELECT * FROM emp WHERE last_name = 'SCOTT';
!= \<\> ^=	Inequality test; any of the three operators may be used.	SELECT * FROM emp WHERE first_name != 'TIGER';
<	"Less than" test.	SELECT last_name FROM emp WHERE salary < 2000;

TABLE 1.6 Comparison Operators *(continued)*

Operator	Purpose	Example
>	"Greater than" test.	SELECT first_name, salary FROM emp WHERE salary > 10000;
<=	"Less than or equal to" test.	SELECT last_name FROM emp WHERE salary <= 2000;
>=	"Greater than or equal to" test.	SELECT first_name, salary FROM emp WHERE salary >= 10000;
[NOT] IN	"Equal to any member of" test. If NOT is used, evaluates to TRUE if the value is not in the member list.	SELECT first_name, salary FROM emp WHERE first_name IN ('JOHN', 'SAM', 'MARY', 'LEEZA'); SELECT last_name FROM emp WHERE last_name NOT IN (SELECT last_name FROM emp WHERE dept = 10);
ANY SOME	Compares a value to each value in a list or returned by a query. Must be preceded by =, !=, >, <, <=, >=. Evaluates to FALSE if the query returns no rows.	SELECT last_name FROM emp WHERE salary <= ANY (SELECT salary FROM emp WHERE dept = 10);
ALL	Compares a value to every value in a list or returned by a query. Must be preceded by =, !=, >, <, <=, >=. Evaluates to TRUE if the query returns no rows.	SELECT last_name FROM emp WHERE salary <= ALL (500, 1200, 800);

TABLE 1.6 Comparison Operators *(continued)*

Operator	Purpose	Example
[NOT] BETWEEN a AND b	TRUE if value greater than or equal to a and less than or equal to *b*. If NOT is used, the result is the reverse.	SELECT last_name FROM emp WHERE salary BETWEEN 5000 and 10000;
[NOT] EXISTS	TRUE if a subquery returns at least one row.	SELECT last_name FROM emp A WHERE NOT EXISTS (SELECT 'X' DUMMY FROM emp B WHERE B.dept = 10 AND A.last_name = B.last_name);
a [NOT] LIKE b [ESCAPE 'char']	Used for pattern matching; TRUE if pattern *a* matches pattern *b*. Wild character % is used to match any string of length zero or more characters. Wild character _ is used to match any single character. The keyword ESCAPE is used to cause Oracle to interpret % or _ literally, rather than as a special character.	SELECT last_name FROM emp WHERE last_name NOT LIKE 'THO%'; SELECT last_name FROM emp WHERE last_name LIKE '_HOR%'; SELECT synonym_name FROM dba_synonyms WHERE synonym_name LIKE 'ALL_U%' ESCAPE '\';
IS [NOT] NULL	The only operator used to test for NULL values.	SELECT last_name FROM emp WHERE salary IS NULL;

Comparison operators are mainly used in the WHERE clause of the SQL statement. The result from the condition is evaluated and rows are returned for the TRUE results.

Logical Operators

Logical operators are used to combine the results of two comparison conditions to produce a single result or to reverse the result of a single comparison. Table 1.7 lists the logical operators and how to use them.

TABLE 1.7 Logical Operators

Opera-tor	Purpose	Example
NOT	Used to reverse the result. Evaluates to TRUE if the operand is FALSE. Evaluates to FALSE if the operand is TRUE. Returns NULL if the operand is NULL.	SELECT * FROM emp WHERE NOT (salary < 1000);
AND	Evaluates to TRUE if both operands are TRUE. Evaluates to FALSE if either operand is FALSE. Otherwise returns NULL.	SELECT * FROM emp WHERE last_name = 'JACOB' AND sal > 5000;
OR	Evaluates to TRUE if either operand is TRUE. Evaluates to FALSE if both operands are FALSE. Otherwise returns NULL.	SELECT * FROM emp WHERE last_name = 'JACOB' OR last_name = 'THOMAS';

Set Operators

Set operators are used in compound queries: queries that combine the results of two queries. The number of columns selected in both queries must be the same. Table 1.8 lists the set operators and how to use them.

TABLE 1.8 Set Operators

Operator	Purpose	Example
UNION	Returns all rows from either queries; no duplicate rows.	SELECT last_name from emp UNION SELECT first_ name from emp;
UNION ALL	Returns all rows from either query, including duplicates.	SELECT last_name FROM emp UNION ALL SELECT first_name FROM emp;
INTERSECT	Returns distinct rows that are returned by both queries.	SELECT last_name FROM emp INTERSECT SELECT first_name FROM emp;
MINUS	Returns distinct rows that are returned by the first query but not returned by the second.	SELECT last_name FROM emp MINUS SELECT first_ name FROM emp;

Operator Precedence

If multiple operators are used in the same expression, Oracle evaluates them in the order of precedence set in the database engine. Operators with higher precedence are evaluated before operators with lower precedence.

Operators with same precedence are evaluated from left to right. Table 1.9 lists the precedence.

TABLE 1.9 SQL Operator Precedence

Operator	Purpose
- +	Unary operators, negation
* /	Multiplication, division
+ - ||	Addition, subtraction, concatenation
=, !=, <, >, <=, >=, IS NULL, LIKE, BETWEEN, IN	Comparison
NOT	Logical negation
AND	Conjunction
OR	Disjunction

Using parentheses changes the order of precedence. The innermost parenthesis is evaluated first. In the expression 1+2*3, the result is 7 because 2*3 is evaluated first and the result is added to 1. If the expression had parentheses, (1+2)*3-1+2 is evaluated first, and the result is multiplied by 3, giving 9.

All set operators have equal precedence.

Expressions

An expression is a combination of one or more values, operators, and SQL functions that evaluate to a value. An expression generally assumes the datatype of its components. The simple expression 5 + 6 evaluates to 11 and assumes a datatype of NUMBER. Expressions can appear in the following clauses:

- The SELECT clause of queries
- The WHERE clause
- The VALUES clause of the INSERT statement
- The SET clause of the UPDATE statement

We will review the syntax of using these statements in subsequent chapters. A compound expression specifies a combination of expressions. Here are some examples of compound expressions:

((2 * 4) / (3 + 1)) * 10

LOWER ('JOHN' || ' TAYLOR')

Writing Simple Queries

A query is a request for information from the database tables. Simple queries are those that retrieve data from a single table. The basis of a query is the SELECT statement. Multiple table queries will be discussed in the next chapter.

SELECT Statement

The SELECT statement is the most commonly used statement in SQL and is used to retrieve information already stored in the database. To retrieve data, you can either select all the column values or name specific columns in the SELECT clause to retrieve data. Let's use the EMP table defined in Table 1.10.

TABLE 1.10 EMP Table Definition

Column Name	EMPNO	ENAME	SALARY	COMM	DEPTNO
Key	PK				
Not Null, Unique	NN, U	NN	NN		
FK Table					DEPT
FK Column					DEPTNO
Datatype	NUMBER	VARCHAR2	NUMBER	NUMBER	
Length	4	10	7, 2	7, 2	2

The EMP Table has the following 11 rows of data:

EMPNO	ENAME	SALARY	COMM	DEPTNO
7499	ALLEN	1600	300	30
7521	WARD	1250	500	30
7566	JONES	2975		20
7654	MARTIN	1250	1400	30
7698	K_BLAKE	2850		30
7782	CLARK	2450	24500	10
7788	SCOTT	3000		20
7839	A_EDWARD	5000	50000	10
7844	TURNER	1500	0	30
7876	ADAMS	1100		20
902	FORD	3000		20

The simple form of a SELECT statement is SELECT column_names FROM table_name;.

How do you list the EMPNO and ENAME from this table? If you know the column names and the table name, writing the query is very simple: Execute the query by ending the query with a semicolon. In SQL*Plus, you may enter a slash by itself in a line.

```
SQL> select empno, ename from emp;

    EMPNO ENAME
--------- ----------
     7499 ALLEN
     7521 WARD
     7566 JONES
     7654 MARTIN
     7698 K_BLAKE
     7782 CLARK
     7788 SCOTT
     7839 A_EDWARD
     7844 TURNER
     7876 ADAMS
      902 FORD

11 rows selected.

SQL>
```

Notice that the numeric column (EMPNO) is aligned to the right and the character column (ENAME) is aligned to the left. Does it seem that the column heading ENAME makes no sense? Well, you can provide a column alias. The column alias name is defined next to the column name. The query select empno, ename employee_name from emp; provides an alias name for the column ENAME. Here, the column heading will be displayed as EMPLOYEE_NAME.

If you want a space in the column alias name, you must enclose it in double quotation marks. The case is preserved only when the alias name is enclosed in double quotes; otherwise, the display will be uppercase.

The following example demonstrates using an alias name for the ENAME column:

```
SQL> SELECT empno, ename "Employee Name"
  2  FROM emp
  3  /

    EMPNO Employee N
--------- ----------
     7499 ALLEN
     7521 WARD
     7566 JONES
     7654 MARTIN
     7698 K_BLAKE
     7782 CLARK
     7788 SCOTT
     7839 A_EDWARD
     7844 TURNER
     7876 ADAMS
      902 FORD

11 rows selected.

SQL>
```

In this listing, the column alias name is truncated because the column length is only 10 characters. Later in this chapter, you will learn how to avoid this by using SQL*Plus formatting commands.

The asterisk (*) is used to select all columns in the table. This is very useful when you do not know the column names or when you are too lazy to type all column names.

The DISTINCT keyword followed by the SELECT keyword ensures that the resulting rows are unique. Uniqueness is verified against the complete row, not the first column. If you need to find the unique departments and salaries, issue this query:

```
SQL> SELECT DISTINCT deptno, salary FROM emp;

    DEPTNO    SALARY
    --------- ---------
        10      2450
        10      5000
        20      1100
        20      2975
        20      3000
        30      1250
        30      1500
        30      1600
        30      2850

9 rows selected.

SQL>
```

 DUAL is a dummy table available to all users in the database. It has one column and one row. The DUAL table is used to select system variables or to evaluate an expression. SELECT SYSDATE, USER FROM DUAL; will show the current system date and the connected username.

Limiting Rows

A *WHERE* clause is used to limit the number of rows processed. Any logical conditions of the WHERE clause use the comparison operators. Rows are returned or operated upon where the data satisfies the logical condition(s) of the WHERE clause. You can use column names or expressions in the WHERE clause but not column alias names.

How do you list the employee information for department 10? This example shows how use a WHERE clause to limit the query only to the records belonging to department 10:

```
SQL> SELECT * FROM emp WHERE deptno = 10;
```

EMPNO	ENAME	SALARY	COMM	DEPTNO
7782	CLARK	2450	24500	10
7839	A_EDWARD	5000	50000	10

```
SQL>
```

You need not include the column names in the SELECT clause to use them in the WHERE clause.

Character and range comparisons also can be done in the WHERE clause. To select the rows from the EMP table with enames starting with the literal string A_, you might be tempted to issue this query:

```
SQL> SELECT * FROM emp WHERE ename LIKE 'A_%';
```

EMPNO	ENAME	SALARY	COMM	DEPTNO
7499	ALLEN	1600	300	30
7839	A_EDWARD	5000	50000	10
7876	ADAMS	1100		20

```
SQL>
```

The query returned rows that we did not expect. That is because Oracle treats % and _ as special characters. In pattern matching, % is used to match any number of characters and _ is used to match any one character. To literally query for the character _, use the ESCAPE clause in the LIKE operator:

```
SQL>  SELECT * FROM emp WHERE ename LIKE 'A\_%' ESCAPE
      '\';
```

EMPNO	ENAME	SALARY	COMM	DEPTNO
7839	A_EDWARD	5000	50000	10

```
SQL>
```

To find the NULL values or NOT NULL values, you need to use the IS NULL operator. The = or != operator will not work with NULL values. If you need to find the employees whose commission is NULL, give this query:

```
SQL> SELECT * FROM emp WHERE comm IS NULL;
```

EMPNO	ENAME	SALARY	COMM	DEPTNO
7566	JONES	2975		20
7698	K_BLAKE	2850		30
7788	SCOTT	3000		20
7876	ADAMS	1100		20
902	FORD	3000		20

```
SQL>
```

Sorting Rows

The SELECT statement may include the ORDER BY clause to sort the resulting rows in a specific order based on data in the columns. Without the ORDER BY clause, there is no guarantee that the rows will be returned in any specific order. The rows are returned by ascending order of the columns specified; if you need to sort the rows in descending order, use the keyword DESC next to the column name.

To retrieve all rows from the EMP table, for department 30 and ordered by name, do this:

```
SQL> SELECT * FROM emp WHERE deptno = 30 ORDER BY ename;
```

EMPNO	ENAME	SALARY	COMM	DEPTNO
7499	ALLEN	1600	300	30

```
7698 K_BLAKE              2850                    30
7654 MARTIN               1250        1400        30
7844 TURNER               1500           0        30
7521 WARD                 1250         500         30
```

SQL>

To sort them by salary, highest paid first, and in alphabetical order by name, use this query:

```
SQL> SELECT ename "Employee", SALARY "Salary"
  2  FROM    emp
  3  WHERE   deptno = 30
  4  ORDER BY salary desc, "Employee";


Employee     Salary
----------  ---------

K_BLAKE        2850
ALLEN          1600
TURNER         1500
MARTIN         1250
WARD           1250


SQL>
```

You can use column alias names in the ORDER BY clause.

If the DISTINCT keyword is used in the SELECT clause, you can only use those columns listed in the SELECT clause in the ORDER BY clause. If you have used any operators on columns in the SELECT clause, the ORDER BY clause also should have them, as well. Here is an example:

```
SQL> SELECT 'Name: ' || ename "Employee", SALARY "Salary"
  2  FROM    emp
  3  WHERE   deptno = 30
  4  ORDER BY deptno DESC, "Employee"
SQL> /


Employee          Salary
----------------  ---------
Name: ALLEN         1600
Name: K_BLAKE       2850
```

```
Name: MARTIN              1250
Name: TURNER              1500
Name: WARD                1250

SQL> SELECT DISTINCT 'Name: ' || ename "Employee",
  2    SALARY "Salary"
  3  FROM    emp
  4  WHERE   deptno = 30
  5  ORDER BY deptno DESC, "Employee"
SQL> /
ORDER BY deptno desc, "Employee"
              *
ERROR at line 4:
ORA-01791: not a SELECTed expression

SQL>
```

Not only can you use the column name or column alias to sort the result set of a query, you can also sort the results by position of the column in the SELECT clause. This is very useful if you have a lengthy expression in the SELECT clause and you need the results sorted on this value. For queries that involve the set operators, like UNION or MINUS, the column names cannot be used. In this case, the ordering column(s) must be provided as positions:

```
SQL> SELECT 'Name: ' || ename "Employee", SALARY "Salary"
  2  FROM    emp
  3  WHERE   deptno = 30
  4* ORDER BY 2, 1
SQL> /

Employee          Salary
---------------- ---------
Name: MARTIN        1250
Name: WARD          1250
Name: TURNER        1500
Name: ALLEN         1600
Name: K_BLAKE       2850

SQL>
```

SQL*Plus: Oracle's Native Interface

$S_{QL*Plus}$, widely used by DBAs and developers, is a powerful and straightforward tool from Oracle to interact with the database. SQL*Plus has its own formatting commands to make your queries look better, as well as commands to set up the environment. SQL*Plus is available on all platforms on which Oracle runs. It is provided with the Oracle Client installation software for the client machine. It is also provided at the server level with installation software for the Oracle Server. You can execute any database command or PL/SQL block in SQL*Plus, provided that you have the right privilege to do so. Table 1.11 explains the basic concepts.

TABLE 1.11   SQL*Plus Concepts

Terminology	Description
Command	An instruction you give in SQL*Plus; may be a SQL*Plus command or a SQL command
Block	A logical unit of SQL and PL/SQL statements
Table	The basic unit of data storage in Oracle
Query	A SELECT statement that retrieves data from one or more tables or views
Query results	Also known as a result set, the data retrieved from a query
Report	Query results formatted in a more readable form

PL/SQL is Oracle's procedural extension of the SQL language. In PL/SQL, the SQL commands and procedural statements are considered to be a single block and sent to the Oracle server. You can have programmatic logics built into PL/SQL. You will learn more on PL/SQL concepts and commands in Chapters 7 through 10.

SQL*Plus: Basics

When you start SQL*Plus, it prompts you for the username, password, and connect string. The connect string is the database alias name. If you omit the connect string, SQL*Plus tries to connect you to the local database defined in the ORACLE_ SID variable. Once you are in SQL*Plus, you can connect to another database or change your connection by using the command CONNECT USERNAME/PASSWORD@ CONNECTSTRING. The slash separates username and password; the connect string following @ is the database alias name. If you omit the password, you will be prompted to enter it. You may omit the connect string to connect to a local database.

To exit from SQL*Plus, use the EXIT command. On platforms where a return code is used, you can provide a return code while exiting. You may also use the QUIT command to complete the session. EXIT and QUIT are synonymous.

Entering and Executing Commands

Once you are connected to SQL*Plus, you get the SQL> prompt. This is the default prompt, which can be changed using the SET SQLPROMPT command. Type the command you wish to enter at this prompt. A command can be spread across multiple lines, and the commands are case-insensitive. The previously executed command will always available in the SQL buffer. The buffer can be edited or saved to a file. You can terminate a command in any of the following ways:

- End with a semicolon (;). The command is completed and executed.

- Enter a slash (/) on a new line by itself. The command in the buffer is executed. This method is also used to execute a PL/SQL block.

- Enter a blank line. The command is saved in the buffer.

The RUN command can be used instead of a slash to execute a command in the buffer. The SQL prompt is returned when the command has completed execution. You can enter your next command in the prompt.

Only SQL commands and PL/SQL blocks are stored in the SQL buffer, SQL*Plus commands are not stored in the buffer.

A hyphen (-) is used to indicate command continuation. Although SQL commands can be continued to the next line without a continuation operator, SQL*Plus commands cannot be continued to the next line unless you include a hyphen at the end of the line. For example, the SQL command

```
SQL> SELECT 800 -
> 400 FROM DUAL;
SELECT 800   400 FROM DUAL
              *
ERROR at line 1:
ORA-00923: FROM keyword not found where expected

SQL>
```

gives an error because SQL*Plus treats the minus operator (-) as a continuation character. You may put the minus operator in the next line for the query to succeed:

```
SQL> SELECT 800
  2  - 400 FROM DUAL;

  800-400
----------
      400


SQL>
```

Editing the SQL Buffer

The most recent SQL command executed or entered is stored in the *SQL buffer* of SQL*Plus. You can run this buffer again by simply typing a slash or using the RUN command. SQL*Plus gives you a set of commands to edit the buffer. Suppose that you want to add another column or add an order by condition. You need not type the entire SQL command again; just edit the existing command, which is in the buffer. There are two ways to edit the buffer:

- Use the command EDIT to write the buffer to an operating system file named afiedt.buf (the default file name, which can be changed), then use a system editor to make changes. You can use your favorite text editor by defining it in SQL*Plus. To make Notepad your favorite editor, just issue this command: **DEFINE _EDITOR = NOTEPAD**. You need to provide the entire path if the program is not available in the search path.

- Use the SQL*Plus editing commands. You can make changes, delete lines, and add and list the buffer using these commands. Most editing commands operate on the current line. You can change the current line simply by typing the line number. Table 1.12 shows the editing commands in SQL*Plus.

TABLE 1.12 SQL*Plus Editing Commands

Command	Purpose	Example

LIST
L
LIST m n
LIST LAST
	Lists the contents of the buffer. The asterisk indicates the current line. The abbreviated command for LIST is L. LIST simply used or used with * displays current line. LIST m n displays lines from m through n, if you substitute * for *m* or *n*, it implies the current line. LIST LAST displays the last line.	SQL> L
		  1 SELECT EMPNO, ENAME
		  2* FROM EMP
		SQL> LIST LAST
		  2* FROM EMP
		SQL>

APPEND text A text	Adds text to the end of the last line.	SQL> A WHERE EMPNO <> 7926 2* FROM EMP WHERE EMPNO <> 7926 SQL>

CHANGE /old/new
C /old/new
	Changes old to new. If you omit new, old will be deleted.	SQL> C /<>/=
		  2* FROM EMP WHERE EMPNO = 7926
		SQL> C /7926
		  2* FROM EMP WHERE EMPNO =
		SQL>

TABLE 1.12 SQL*Plus Editing Commands *(continued)*

Command	Purpose	Example

INPUT text
I text
	Adds a line of text. If text is omitted, you can add as many lines you wish.	SQL> I
		  3 7777 AND
		  4 EMPNO = 4354
		  5
		SQL> I ORDER BY 1
		SQL> L
		  1 SELECT EMPNO, ENAME
		  2 FROM EMP WHERE EMPNO =
		  3 7777 AND
		  4 EMPNO = 4354
		  5* ORDER BY 1
		SQL>

DEL
DEL m n
DEL LAST
	Deletes a line. DEL simply used or used with * deletes current line. DEL m n deletes lines from *m* through *n*, if you substitute * for *m* or *n*, it implies the current line. DEL LAST deletes the last line.	SQL> 3
		  3* 7777 AND
		SQL> DEL
		SQL> L
		  1 SELECT EMPNO, ENAME
		  2 FROM EMP WHERE EMPNO =
		  3 EMPNO = 4354
		  4* ORDER BY 1
		SQL> DEL 3 *
		SQL> L
		  1 SELECT EMPNO, ENAME
		  2* FROM EMP WHERE EMPNO =
		SQL>

TABLE 1.12 SQL*Plus Editing Commands *(continued)*

Command	Purpose	Example
CLEAR BUFFER CL BUFF	Clears the buffer. This deletes all lines from the buffer.	SQL> L 1 SELECT EMPNO, ENAME 2* FROM EMP WHERE EMPNO = SQL> CL BUFF buffer cleared SQL> L No lines in SQL buffer. SQL>

Script Files

SQL*Plus provides commands to save the SQL buffer to a file, as well as to run SQL statements from a file. SQL statements saved in a file are called a *script file*. SQL buffer is saved to an operating system file using the command SAVE <filename>. By default, SAVE will not overwrite an existing file; you need to use the keyword REPLACE to overwrite an existing file. If you do not provide an extension, the saved file will have an extension of .sql. You can edit the saved file using the EDIT <filename> command.

You can bring the contents of a *script file* to the SQL buffer using the GET filename command. If you wish to run a script file, you may use the command START <filename>. You can also run a script file using @<filename>. An @@<filename> used inside a script file looks for the filename in the directory where the parent <filename> is saved and executes it. Here are some examples of using the file commands:

```
/* List the SQL buffer */
SQL> L
  1  SELECT EMPNO, ENAME
  2* FROM EMP
/* Save the buffer to a file named myfile. The default
extension will be .SQL */
SQL> save myfile
Created file myfile
/* Edit the file, add a line to the SQL statement, editing
window not shown here */
SQL> edit myfile
```

```
/* List the buffer, the buffer listed is the old buffer,
edited changes not reflected, that is because we edited
the file */
SQL> L
  1  SELECT EMPNO, ENAME
  2* FROM EMP
/* Bring the file contents to the buffer */
SQL> GET MYFILE
  1  SELECT EMPNO, ENAME
  2  FROM EMP
  3* WHERE EMPNO = 1234
/* List the buffer to verify */
SQL> L
  1  SELECT EMPNO, ENAME
  2  FROM EMP
  3* WHERE EMPNO = 1234
/* Save the buffer again to the same file */
SQL> save myfile
File "myfile.SQL" already exists.
Use "SAVE filename REPLACE".
/* Error returned, save using REPLACE keyword */
SQL> save myfile repl
Wrote file myfile
/* Run a file */
SQL> start myfile
  1  SELECT EMPNO, ENAME
  2  FROM EMP
  3* WHERE EMPNO = 1234


no rows selected


SQL>
```

You can use the SPOOL filename command to save the query results to a file. By default, the SPOOL command creates a .lst file. SPOOL OFF stops the writing of output to the file. SPOOL OUT stops the writing of output and sends the output file to the printer.

Having comments in the script file improves the purpose and understanding of the code. You can enter comments in SQL*Plus using the REMARKS command. Lines in the script file beginning with the keyword REM (abbreviated) are comments and are not executed. You can also enter a comment between /* and */.

While executing a script file with comments, the remarks entered using the REMARKS command are not displayed on the screen, but the comments within /* and */ are displayed on the screen.

Environment and Customizations

SQL*Plus has a set of *environment variables* that control the way the SQL*Plus displays data and assigns special characters. The SHOW ALL command lists the current environment. You can customize the environment by using the SET command. Table 1.13 lists the SET commands, highlighting some of the more common commands. The syntax is SET variable value. Most of the variables can be abbreviated (COM for COMPATIBILITY, for example).

In Oracle8i, the database administration commands are also executed from SQL*Plus; earlier administration was done using Server Manager.

TABLE 1.13   SET Commands

Variable Name and Allowed Value	Purpose
APPI[NFO]{ON|OFF|text}	Sets automatic registering of command files through the DBMS_APPLICATION_INFO package.
ARRAY[SIZE] {15|n}	Sets the number of rows—called a batch— that SQL*Plus will fetch from the database at one time.
AUTO[COMMIT] {OFF|ON|IMM[EDIATE]|n}	Controls when Oracle commits pending changes to the database.
AUTOP[RINT] {OFF|ON}	Sets the automatic printing of bind variables from a PL/SQL block after its execution.

TABLE 1.13 SET Commands *(continued)*

Variable Name and Allowed Value	Purpose
AUTORECOVERY {ON|OFF]	ON sets the RECOVER command to automatically apply the default filenames of archived redo log files needed during recovery.
AUTOT[RACE] {OFF|ON|TRACE[ONLY]} [EXP[LAIN]] [STAT[ISTICS]]	Displays a report on the execution of successful SQL DML statements
BLO[CKTERMINATOR] {.|c}	Sets the non-alphanumeric character used to end PL/SQL blocks to *c*.
CMDS[EP] {;|c|OFF|ON}	Sets the non-alphanumeric character used to separate multiple SQL*Plus commands entered on one line to *c*.
COLSEP {_|text}	Sets the text to be printed between selected columns.
COM[PATIBILITY] {V7|V8|NATIVE}	Specifies the version of Oracle to which you are currently connected. Set COMPATIBILITY to V7 for Oracle7, or to V8 for Oracle8 and Oracle8i.
CON[CAT] {.|c|OFF|ON}	Sets the character you can use to terminate a substitution variable reference.
COPYC[OMMIT] {0|n}	Controls the number of batches after which the COPY command commits changes to the database.
COPYTYPECHECK {OFF|ON}	Sets the suppression of the comparison of datatypes while inserting or appending to tables with the COPY command.
DEF[INE] {'&'|c|OFF|ON}	Sets the character used to prefix substitution variables to *c*.

TABLE 1.13   SET Commands *(continued)*

Variable Name and Allowed Value	Purpose
DESCRIBE [DEPTH {1|n|ALL}][LINENUM {ON|OFF}][INDENT {ON|OFF}]	Sets the depth of the level to which you can recursively describe an object.
ECHO {OFF|ON}	Controls whether the START command lists each command in a command file as the command is executed.
EDITF[ILE] file_ name[.ext]	Sets the default filename for the EDIT command.
EMB[EDDED] {OFF|ON}	Controls where each report begins on the page.
ESC[APE] {\\\|c|OFF|ON}	Defines the character you enter as the escape character.
FEED[BACK] {6|n|OFF|ON}	Displays the number of records returned by a query when a query selects at least *n* records.
FLAGGER {OFF|ENTRY|INTERMED[IA TE]|FULL}	Checks to make sure that SQL statements conform to the ANSI/ISO SQL92 standard.
FLU[SH] {OFF|ON}	Controls when output is sent to the user's display device.
HEA[DING] {OFF|ON}	Controls printing of column headings in reports.
HEADS[EP] {||c|OFF|ON}	Defines the character you enter as the heading separator character.
INSTANCE [instance_ path|LOCAL]	Changes the default instance for your session to the specified instance path.
LIN[ESIZE] {80|n}	Sets the total number of characters that SQL*Plus displays on one line before beginning a new line.

TABLE 1.13   SET Commands *(continued)*

Variable Name and Allowed Value	Purpose
LOBOF[FSET] {n|1}	Sets the starting position from which CLOB and NCLOB data is retrieved and displayed.
LOGSOURCE [pathname]	Specifies the location from which archive logs are retrieved during recovery.
LONG {80|n}	Sets maximum width (in bytes) for displaying LONG, CLOB, and NCLOB values; and for copying LONG values.
LONGC[HUNKSIZE] {80|n}	Sets the size (in bytes) of the increments in which SQL*Plus retrieves a LONG, CLOB, or NCLOB value.
NEWP[AGE] {1|n|NONE}	Sets the number of blank lines to be printed from the top of each page to the top title.
NULL text	Sets the text that represents a null value in the result of a SQL SELECT command.
NUMF[ORMAT] format	Sets the default format for displaying numbers.
NUM[WIDTH] {10|n}	Sets the default width for displaying numbers.
PAGES[IZE] {24|n}	Sets the number of lines in each page.
PAU[SE] {OFF|ON|text}	Allows you to control scrolling of your terminal when running reports.
RECSEP {WR[APPED]|EA[CH]|OFF}	Displays or prints record separators.
RECSEPCHAR {_|c}	Defines the record-separating character. A single space is the default.
SERVEROUT[PUT] {OFF|ON} [SIZE n] [FOR[MAT] {WRA[PPED]| WOR[D_ WRAPPED]|TRU[NCATED]}]	Controls whether to display the output (that is, DBMS_OUTPUT.PUT_LINE) of stored procedures or PL/SQL blocks in SQL*Plus.

TABLE 1.13 SET Commands *(continued)*

Variable Name and Allowed Value	Purpose
SHIFT[INOUT] {VIS[IBLE]|INV[ISIBLE]}	Allows correct alignment for terminals that display shift characters.
SHOW[MODE] {OFF|ON}	Controls whether SQL*Plus lists the *old* and *new* settings of a SQL*Plus system variable when you change the setting with SET.
SQLBL[ANKLINES] {ON|OFF}	Controls whether SQL*Plus allows blank lines within a SQL command.
SQLC[ASE] {MIX[ED]|LO[WER]|UP[PER]}	Converts the case of SQL commands and PL/SQL blocks just prior to execution.
SQLCO[NTINUE] {>|text}	Sets the character sequence SQL*Plus displays as a prompt after you continue a SQL*Plus command on an additional line using a hyphen (-).
SQLN[UMBER] {OFF|ON}	Sets the prompt for the second and subsequent lines of a SQL command or PL/SQL block.
SQLPRE[FIX] {#|c}	While entering a SQL command or PL/SQL block, you can enter a SQL*Plus command on a separate line, prefixed by the SQL*Plus prefix character, to execute the command immediately without affecting the SQL command or PL/SQL block that you are entering.
SQLP[ROMPT] {SQL>|text}	Sets the SQL*Plus command prompt.
SQLT[ERMINATOR] {;|c|OFF|ON}	Sets the character used to end and execute SQL commands to *c*.
SUF[FIX] {SQL|text}	Sets the default file extension that SQL*Plus uses in commands that refer to command files.
TAB {OFF|ON}	Determines how SQL*Plus formats white space in terminal output.

TABLE 1.13 SET Commands *(continued)*

Variable Name and Allowed Value	Purpose
TERM[OUT] {OFF|ON}	Controls the display of output generated by commands executed from a command file.
TI[ME] {OFF|ON}	ON displays the current time before each command prompt.
TIMI[NG] {OFF|ON}	ON displays timing statistics on each SQL command or PL/SQL block run.
TRIM[OUT] {OFF|ON}	ON removes blanks at the end of each displayed line.
TRIMS[POOL] {ON|OFF}	ON removes blanks at the end of each spooled line.
UND[ERLINE] {-|c|ON|OFF}	Sets the character used to underline column headings in SQL*Plus reports to *c*.
VER[IFY] {OFF|ON}	Controls whether SQL*Plus lists the text of a SQL statement or PL/SQL command before and after SQL*Plus replaces substitution variables with values.
WRA[P] {OFF|ON}	Controls whether SQL*Plus truncates the display of a selected row if it is too long for the current line width.

You may save the current SQL*Plus environment using the command STORE SET *<filename>*. SQL*Plus creates a .sql file. You may run this file at any time to set up your customized environment.

Wouldn't it be nice to have the environment set the way you like it when you log in to SQL*Plus? Well, there is a way to do this. Create a login.sql file in the current directory of your SQL*Plus executable or in the search path of Oracle. This file will be executed when you log in to SQL*Plus. In this example, let's display the name and username when connected and display the current time on at the prompt. We'll create a login file using the following script:

```
SET HEADING OFF
PROMPT Welcome to SQL*Plus!
```

```
SELECT 'You are connected to ' || GLOBAL_NAME || ' as ' ||
USER
FROM GLOBAL_NAME;
SET TIME ON PAGESIZE 24 LINESIZE 80 HEADING ON
```

More than one SET command can be given in one line.

Producing More Readable Output

Often, the results returned from SQL*Plus wrap to the next line or do not have the proper formatting. You can use simple SQL*Plus formatting commands to produce more readable output and better looking reports. In this section, you will learn how to

- Define the width of a column
- Display meaningful headings
- Format numeric and date datatype values
- Wrap character columns

Imagine that you have been asked to produce a report of all employees in the order of their department and name, using the employee table. You issue this query and get the following output:

```
SQL> SELECT * FROM emp ORDER BY deptno, ename;
```

```
EMPNO ENAME      JOB             MGR HIREDATE      SAL
---------- ---------- ---------- ---------- --------- ----------
      COMM     DEPTNO
---------- ----------
     7782 CLARK      MANAGER        7839 09-JUN-81      2450
      245         10

     7839 KING       PRESIDENT           17-NOV-81      5000
      500         10

7934 MILLER     CLERK          7782 23-JAN-82      1300
```

COMM	DEPTNO
130	10

EMPNO	ENAME	JOB	MGR	HIREDATE	SAL	COMM	DEPTNO
7876	ADAMS	CLERK	7788	23-MAY-87	1100		20
7902	FORD	ANALYST	7566	03-DEC-81	3000		20
7566	JONES	MANAGER	7839	02-APR-81	2975		20
7788	SCOTT	ANALYST	7566	19-APR-87	3000		

EMPNO	ENAME	JOB	MGR	HIREDATE	SAL
----------	----------	----------	----------	---------	----------

COMM	DEPTNO
----------	----------
	20

EMPNO	ENAME	JOB	MGR	HIREDATE	SAL	COMM	DEPTNO
7369	SMITH	CLERK	7902	17-DEC-80	800		20
7499	ALLEN	SALESMAN	7698	20-FEB-81	1600	300	30
7698	BLAKE	MANAGER	7839	01-MAY-81	2850		30
7900	JAMES	CLERK	7698	03-DEC-81	950		30
7654	MARTIN	SALESMAN	7698	28-SEP-81	1250	1400	30

```
    7844 TURNER      SALESMAN        7698 08-SEP-81      1500
       0         30

   EMPNO ENAME      JOB              MGR HIREDATE        SAL
---------- ---------- ---------- ---------- --------- ----------
    COMM     DEPTNO
---------- ----------

    7521 WARD        SALESMAN        7698 22-FEB-81      1250
     500         30
```

```
14 rows selected.
```
Obviously, this is not a pretty format; you certainly cannot present this listing as a report. Let's format this listing to make it more appealing, adjusting the page size and report columns.

First, check the settings, using the SHOW [ALL|parameter] command to find the value of environment variable. You can specify the variable name or ALL to list all variables. To find the values set for the PAGESIZE and LINESIZE parameters, use the SHOW command like this:

```
SQL> show pagesize lines
pagesize 24
linesize 70
SQL>
```
Let's adjust these settings to PAGESIZE of 78 and LINESIZE of 55. You also can turn off the feedback that says, "14 rows selected."

```
SQL> SET PAGESIZE 78 LINESIZE 55
SQL> SET FEEDBACK OFF
```
The COLUMN command can be used to format the heading and display a column's data. To display a heading for the ENAME column, you can use the command COLUMN ENAME HEADING "Employee Name".

Now, we have many columns, but not enough space to display a whole row in one line. Let's make the display of the heading in two lines using the HEADSEP character; the default is "|":

```
COLUMN ENAME HEADING "Employee|Name"
```
To format the displayed data of SALARY column, type **COLUMN SAL FORMAT** "**$999,999.99**".

NOTE The format models used with data are explained in detail in Chapter 2, *Single Row and Group Functions*.

If you format a character column with an insufficient width, the data wraps to the next line. To copy the display format of a column to another with a different heading, use COLUMN COMM LIKE SAL HEADING "Incentive".

You can suppress the display of duplicate column values using the BREAK ON column_name command. The BREAK command has options to skip lines, pages, and so on. You can display our report heading using the TTITLE command.

You have entered all this formatting to produce your report. What about the next time? You can save the formatting and query in a script file and just run the file to produce the report whenever you want to. Here is the script listing:

```
REM Report to display the employee information
REM Created on 05/05/2000
REM
SET PAGES 55 LINES 78 TRIMS ON FEEDBACK OFF ECHO OFF DOCUMENT OFF
/*
   This is an example of multiple line comments.
   Following lines are column formatting commands
*/
COLUMN empno HEADING "Empl|Id" FORMAT 9999
COLUMN ename HEADING "Employee|Name" FORMAT A8
COLUMN job HEADING "Position"
COLUMN mgr LIKE EMPNO HEADING "Mana|-ger"
COLUMN hiredate HEADING "Hire Date"
COLUMN sal FORMAT "$9,999" HEADING "Salary"
COLUMN comm LIKE SAL HEADING "Incentive"
COLUMN deptno HEADING "Dept|Code"
/*
   Save the output to a file, Provide a heading.
*/
SPOOL EMPINFO.LST
TTITLE CENTER "Employee Information" SKIP 2
/* Suppress duplicate department codes */
BREAK ON deptno SKIP 2
REM
REM The query
```

```
REM
SELECT deptno, empno, ename, job, hiredate, sal, comm, mgr
FROM    emp
ORDER BY deptno, ename;
SPOOL OFF
/*
   Clear customizations */
CLEAR COLUMNS
CLEAR BREAKS
SET FEEDBACK ON
```

Executing the script produces the EMPINFO.LST file output.

Employee Information

Dept Code	Empl Id	Employee Name	Position	Hire Date	Salary	Incentive	Mana -ger
10	7782	CLARK	MANAGER	09-JUN-81	$2,450	$245	7839
	7839	KING	PRESIDENT	17-NOV-81	$5,000	$500	
	7934	MILLER	CLERK	23-JAN-82	$1,300	$130	7782
20	7876	ADAMS	CLERK	23-MAY-87	$1,100		7788
	7902	FORD	ANALYST	03-DEC-81	$3,000		7566
	7566	JONES	MANAGER	02-APR-81	$2,975		7839
	7788	SCOTT	ANALYST	19-APR-87	$3,000		7566
	7369	SMITH	CLERK	17-DEC-80	$800		7902
30	7499	ALLEN	SALESMAN	20-FEB-81	$1,600	$300	7698
	7698	BLAKE	MANAGER	01-MAY-81	$2,850		7839
	7900	JAMES	CLERK	03-DEC-81	$950		7698
	7654	MARTIN	SALESMAN	28-SEP-81	$1,250	$1,400	7698
	7844	TURNER	SALESMAN	08-SEP-81	$1,500	$0	7698
	7521	WARD	SALESMAN	22-FEB-81	$1,250	$500	7698

Accepting Values at Runtime

To create an interactive SQL command, define variables in the SQL command. This allows the user to supply values at runtime, further enhancing the ability to reuse your scripts. SQL*Plus lets you define variables in your scripts. An ampersand (&) followed by a variable name prompts for and accepts values at runtime. For example, look at the following SELECT statement that queries the EMP table based on the department number supplied at runtime:

```
SQL> SELECT empno, ename
  2  FROM    emp
  3  WHERE   deptno = &dept;
Enter value for dept: 10
old   3: WHERE   deptno = &dept
new   3: WHERE   deptno = 10

     EMPNO ENAME
---------- ----------
      7782 CLARK
      7839 KING
      7934 MILLER

SQL>
```

You can define a substitution variable in SQL*Plus using the DEFINE command. The variable will always have the CHAR datatype associated with it. Suppose that you have defined DEPT as a variable in your script and used the DEFINE command to provide a value. In this way, you can avoid the prompt for the value at runtime like this:

```
SQL> DEFINE dept = 10
SQL> 1
  1  SELECT empno, ename
  2  FROM    emp
  3* WHERE   deptno = &dept
SQL> /
old   3: WHERE   deptno = &dept
new   3: WHERE   deptno = 10
```

```
    EMPNO ENAME
---------- ----------
     7782 CLARK
     7839 KING
     7934 MILLER
```

SQL>

The old line with the variable and the new line with the substitution are displayed. You can turn off this display by using a SET command: SET VERIFY OFF. To turn off substitution, use SET DEFINE OFF.

When you use substitution variables in a script file, you can submit the substitution variable values while invoking the script (also referred to as supplying command line arguments). The values are assigned to the variables by position. Do this by putting an ampersand (&), followed by a numeral in the script file, in place of a variable name. Each time you run this command file, START replaces each &1 in the file with the first value (called an argument) after START *<filename>*, then replaces each &2 with the second value, and so forth. For example, if the file `query1.sql` contains the following:

```
SELECT empid, ename
FROM   emp
WHERE  deptno = &1
AND    empid = &2;
```

You may execute this file by passing the values in the command line

```
SQL> START query1 10 7326
```

where 10 is substituted for *deptno* and 7326 for *empid*.

SQL*Plus provides the ACCEPT command to accept values from the user. This command is useful to provide the user with a prompt and to get user input. Also, the ACCEPT command lets you define the datatype of the variable. The PROMPT command lets you display text to the user.

Let's see some examples and usage of PROMPT and ACCEPT commands. We'll create a script file named `myscript.sql` and run it:

```
PROMPT This query displays the Employee ID and Name for
PROMPT the employees in the department you supply
PROMPT ===================================================
ACCEPT DEPTNUMB NUMBER PROMPT "Enter Department Number: "
SET VERIFY OFF
SELECT empno, ename "Employee Name"
FROM   emp
```

```
WHERE  deptno = &DEPTNUMB
ORDER BY ename;
SET VERIFY ON
```

Now run this script in SQL*Plus.

```
SQL> @myscript
This query displays the Employee ID and Name for
the employees in the department you supply
======================================================
Enter Department Number: 30


     EMPNO Employee N
---------- ----------
      7499 ALLEN
      7698 BLAKE
      7900 JAMES
      7654 MARTIN
      7844 TURNER
      7521 WARD

6 rows selected.
```

Summary

In this chapter, you have learned about RDBMS and how Oracle implements RDBMS using a variety of objects and structures. The Entity-relationship diagram is a modeling tool used in the beginning stages of application development. The stages of the system development cycle are analysis, design, development, testing, and implementation.

Data in the Oracle database is managed and accessed using SQL. A SELECT statement is used to query data from a table or view. You can limit the rows selected by using a WHERE clause and order the retrieved data using the ORDER BY clause.

SQL*Plus is Oracle's native tool to interact with the database. SQL*Plus supports all SQL commands and has its own formatting and enhancement commands. In Oracle8i, SQL*Plus also supports all database administration commands. Using this tool, you can produce interactive SQL commands and formatted reports.

Key Terms

Before you take the exam, make sure you're familiar with the following terms:

@

@@

Concatenation

Design phase

DUAL

Entity-relationship (ER) model

Environment variables

Julian numbers

LOB

RDBMS

Script file

SQL buffer

SQL*Plus

Structured query language

Review Questions

1. What does a single line with a crowfoot on one end represent in an entity-relationship diagram?

   A. One-to-one relationship

   B. One-to-many relationship

   C. Many-to-many relationship

   D. An access path

2. Look at the following diagram. What kind of relationship exists between Movies and Characters?

   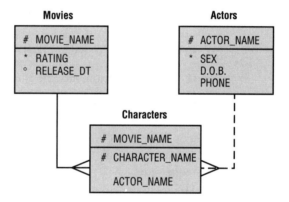

   A. Each movie may have one or more actors.

   B. Each movie must have one or more actors.

   C. Many movies may have many actors.

   D. One movie can have only one actor.

3. When designing the physical model from the logical model, which element from the ER diagram may be attributed as a table?

   A. Relationship

   B. Attribute

   C. Unique identifier

   D. Entity

4. What is wrong with the following query?

   ```
   DEFINE V_DEPTNO = 20
   SELECT ENAME, SALARY
   FROM    EMP
   WHERE DEPTNO = V_DEPTNO;
   ```

   A. It lists the employee name and salary of the employees who belong to Department 20.

   B. The DEFINE statement declaration is wrong.

   C. The substitution variable is not preceded with the & character.

   D. The substitution variable should be preceded with the # character.

5. You issue the following query:
   ```
   SELECT MIN(sal) "Minimum Salary"
   FROM emp;
   ```
   How will the column heading appear in the result?

   A. MINIMUM SALARY

   B. MINIMUM_SALARY

   C. Minimum Salary

   D. minimum_salary

6. Take a look at the EMP table defined in the following table.

Column Name	EMPNO	ENAME	SALARY	COMM	DEPTNO
KEY	PK				
Not Null, Unique	NN, U	NN	NN		
FK Table					DEPT
FK Column					DEPTNO
Datatype	NUMBER	VARCHAR2	NUMBER	NUMBER	NUMBER
Length	4	30	14,2	10,2	2

Imagine that you do the following two queries:

```
1. SELECT DISTINCT empno enumber,  ename FROM emp ORDER
BY 1;
2. SELECT empno,  ename FROM emp ORDER BY  1;
```
Which of the following is true?

A. Statement 1 and 2 will produce the same result.

B. Statement 1 will execute; statement 2 will give an error.

C. Statement 2 will execute; statement 1 will give an error.

D. Statement 1 and 2 will execute but produce different results.

7. You issue the following SELECT statement on the EMP table shown in the preceding table.
```
SELECT (200 + ((salary * 0.1) / 2)) FROM emp;
```
What will happen to the result if all parentheses are removed?

A. No difference because the answer will always be NULL.

B. No difference; the result will be the same.

C. The result will be higher.

D. The result will be lower.

8. Which command in SQL*Plus is used to save the query output to a file?

A. PRINT

B. SAVE

C. REPLACE

D. SPOOL

9. In the following SELECT statement, which component is a literal?
`SELECT 'Employee Name: ' || ename FROM emp where deptno = 10;`

A. 10

B. ename

C. Employee Name:

D. ||

10. When you try to save 34567.2255 into a column defined as NUMBER (7,2) what value is actually saved?

A. 34567.00

B. 34567.23

C. 34567.22

D. 3456.22

11. How would you execute a SQL statement in the SQL buffer of SQL*Plus? Choose all correct answers.

A. Enter a slash (/).

B. Enter an ampersand (&).

C. Enter a hyphen (-).

D. Press Ctrl+D (^D).

12. What is the default display length of the DATE datatype column?

A. 8

B. 9

C. 19

D. 6

13. What will happen if you query the EMP table with the following?
SELECT empno, DISTINCT ename, salary FROM emp;

A. empno, unique values of ename and salary are displayed.

B. empno, unique values of the two columns, ename and salary, are displayed.

C. DISTINCT is not a valid keyword in SQL.

D. No values will be displayed because the statement will give an error.

14. Which clause in a query limits the rows selected?

A. ORDER BY

B. WHERE

C. SELECT

D. FROM

15. You issue the SQL*Plus command SPOOL ON. Which task is accomplished?

A. The next screen output from the SQL*Plus session is saved into a file named afiedt.buf.

B. The next screen output from the SQL*Plus session is saved into a file named ON.lst.

C. The next screen output from the SQL*Plus session is sent to the printer.

D. Nothing happens; a file name is missing from the command.

16. Which SQL*Plus command always overwrites a file?

A. SPOOL

B. RUN

C. EDIT

D. SAVE

17. The following listing shows the records of the EMP table:

EMPNO	ENAME	SALARY	COMM	DEPTNO
7369	SMITH	800		20
7499	ALLEN	1600	300	30
7521	WARD	1250	500	30
7566	JONES	2975		20
7654	MARTIN	1250	1400	30
7698	BLAKE	2850		30
7782	CLARK	2450	24500	10
7788	SCOTT	3000		20
7839	KING	5000	50000	10
7844	TURNER	1500	0	30
7876	ADAMS	1100		20
7900	JAMES	950		30
7902	FORD	3000		20
7934	MILLER	1300	13000	10

When you issue the following query, which value will be displayed in the first row?

```
    SELECT empno
FROM emp
WHERE deptno = 10
ORDER BY ename desc;
```

A. 7782

B. 7934

C. 7876

D. No rows will be returned because ename cannot be used in the ORDER BY clause.

18. Refer to the listing in Question 17. How many rows will the following query return?

```
SELECT * FROM emp WHERE ename BETWEEN 'A' AND 'C'
```

A. 4

B. 2

C. A character column cannot be used in the BETWEEN operator.

D. 3

19. Refer to the EMP table in Question 6. When you issue the following query, which line has an error?

```
1  select empno "Enumber", ename "EmpName"
2  from emp
3  where deptno = 10
4  and   "Enumber" = 7782
5  order by "Enumber"
```

A. 1

B. 5

C. 4

D. No error; the statement will finish successfully.

20. You issue the following query:

```
SELECT empno, ename
FROM emp
WHERE empno = 7782 OR empno = 7876;
```

Which other operator can replace the OR condition in the WHERE clause?

A. IN

B. BETWEEN...AND...

C. LIKE

D. <=

E. >=

Answers to Review Questions

1. B. The crowfoot on one end and single line on the other end rep resents a one-to-many relationship. If the line is solid, the relationship is mandatory; if the line is dotted, the relationship is optional.

2. B. Since the relationship between Movies and Characters is represented by a solid line with a crowfoot at one end, the relationship is mandatory one-to-many: Each movie must have one or more actors.

3. D. When designing the physical structure, you may map an entity in the ER diagram as a table in the database. An attribute may be mapped as a column; a relationship is the referential integrity, and a unique identifier is the primary key.

4. C. The query will return an error, because the substitution variable is used without an & character. In this query, Oracle treats V_DEPTNO as another column name from the table and returns an error.

5. C. The column alias names enclosed in quotes will appear as typed. Spaces and mixed case are displayed in the column alias name only when the alias is enclosed in quotes. If the alias name is not enclosed in quotes, it is displayed in uppercase.

6. A. Statement 1 and 2 will produce the same result. Since EMPNO is the primary key, the rows selected will be unique even if you do not use the keyword DISTINCT. You can use the column name, column alias, or column position in the ORDER BY clause.

7. B. In the arithmetic evaluation, multiplication and division have precedence over addition and subtraction. Even if you do not have the parentheses, salary*0.1 will be evaluated first. The result is then divided by 2, and its result is added to 200.

8. D. The SPOOL command is used to save the query results to a file. Give SPOOL <filename> before the query and SPOOL OFF after the query to save the contents. The SAVE command is used to save the SQL command in the buffer.

9. C. Character literals in the SQL statement are enclosed in single quotes. Literals are concatenated using ||.

10. B. Since the numeric column is defined with precision 7 and scale 2, you can have five digits integer part and two digits after the decimal point. The digits after the decimal are rounded.

11. A. You can execute a command in SQL buffer using the slash. A slash is also used to execute a PL/SQL block.

12. B. The default display format of DATE column is DD-MON-YY, whose length is 9. If the column heading of the default date format column is more than nine characters, it will be truncated.

13. D. DISTINCT is used to display a unique result row, and it should follow immediately the keyword SELECT.

14. B. The WHERE clause is used to limit the rows returned from a query. The WHERE clause condition is evaluated and rows are returned only if the result is TRUE. The ORDER BY clause is used to display the result in certain order.

15. B. The SPOOL command is used to save the SQL*Plus session output in a file. The SPOOL command expects a filename or the keywords OUT or OFF. SPOOL OFF will turn off spooling; SPOOL OUT will turn off spooling and send the output file contents to a printer. If an extension is not specified for the filename, a default extension of .1st is added.

16. A. The SPOOL command always creates a new file; it will not append to an existing file. The SAVE command will give an error if the file exists. To overwrite an existing file, you need to specify the REPLACE option.

17. B. There are three records belonging to deptno 10: empno 7934 (MILLER), 7839 (KING), and 7782 (CLARK). When you sort their names by descending order, MILLER is the first row to display.

18. D. Here, a character column is compared against a string using the BETWEEN operator, which is equivalent to ename >= 'A' AND ename <= 'C'. The name CLARK will not be included in this query, because 'CLARK' is > 'C'.

19. C. Column alias names cannot be used in the WHERE clause. They can be used in the ORDER BY clause.

20. A. The IN operator can be used. You can write the WHERE clause as **WHERE empno IN (7782, 7876);**

Chapter

2

Single-Row and Group Functions

ORACLE8i SQL AND PL/SQL EXAM OBJECTIVES OFFERED IN THIS CHAPTER:

- ✓ Describe the types of single-row functions available in SQL
- ✓ Use character, number, and date functions in SELECT statements
- ✓ Use conversion functions in SELECT statements
- ✓ Identify the group functions
- ✓ Describe the use of group functions
- ✓ Group data using the GROUP BY clause
- ✓ Limit grouped rows using the HAVING clause

Exam objectives are subject to change at any time without prior notice and at Oracle's sole discretion. Please visit Oracle's Training and Certification Web site (http://education.oracle.com/certification/index.html) for the most current exam objectives listing.

Functions are programs that take zero or more arguments and return a single value. Oracle has built a number of functions into SQL, and these functions can be called from SQL or PL/SQL statements. There are two significant classes of functions:

- Single-row functions
- Group *functions* (also known as aggregate functions)

Single-row functions know how many arguments they will have to process before data is fetched from the tables. *Group functions* don't know how many arguments they will have to process until all the data is extracted and grouped into categories. In this chapter, you will discover what single-row and group functions are available, the rules for using them, and what to expect on the exam about functions.

Single-Row Functions in SQL

There are many types of single-row functions built into SQL and PL/SQL. There are character, numeric, date, conversion, and miscellaneous single-row functions, as well as programmer-written stored functions. All can be incorporated into SQL and PL/SQL as single-row functions. These single-row functions can be used in the SELECT, WHERE, and ORDER BY clauses of SELECT statements. For example, the following query includes the TO_CHAR, UPPER, and SOUNDEX single-row functions:

```
SELECT ename, TO_CHAR(hiredate,'Day, DD-Mon-YYYY')
FROM emp
WHERE UPPER(ename) LIKE 'AL%'
ORDER BY SOUNDEX(ename)
```

Single-row functions can appear in other types of statements, as well, such as the SET clause of an UPDATE statement, the VALUES clause of an INSERT statement, or the WHERE clause of a DELETE statement. The certification exam tends to focus on the use of functions in SELECT statements, so we will focus on SELECT statements in this chapter.

The built-in functions presented in this chapter are grouped by class and topic (for example, single-row character functions) and within each topic in alphabetical order. The only exception is the first function, NVL(), which appears first because of its importance.

NULLs and Single-Row Functions

One area in which beginners frequently have difficulty and where even veterans sometimes stumble is the treatment of NULLs. You can expect at least one question on the exam to address the use of NULLs and it probably won't look like a question on the use of NULLs. NULL values represent unknown data or a lack of data. Any arithmetic operation on a NULL results in a NULL. This NULL in/NULL out model is followed for most functions, as well. Only the functions CONCAT, DECODE, DUMP, NVL, and REPLACE can return non-NULL values when called with a NULL argument. Of these, the NVL (for *NullVaLue*) function is most important because it directly deals with the problem of NULLs. It takes two arguments: NVL($x1$, $x2$) where $x1$ and $x2$ are expressions. The NVL function returns $x2$ if $x1$ is NULL; otherwise, $x1$ is returned.

Take a look at the EMP table shown in Table 2.1, which contains salary and bonus columns. Imagine that you need to calculate total compensation; you can

TABLE 2.1 EMP table definition

Column Name	emp_id	Salary	Bonus
Key Type	pk		
NULLs/Unique	NN,U	NN	
FK Table			
Datatype	number	number	number
Length		11,2	11,2

not simply add salary and bonus. If a row has a NULL bonus, then the result of the addition would be NULL. For example, if you wanted to write an UPDATE statement to increase everyone's salary by 10% of their total compensation, the following would not work:

```
UPDATE emp
SET salary = (salary + bonus) * 1.1;
```

In this statement, employees with both salary and bonus would update correctly, but those with no bonus would have salary set to salary + NULL, which adds up to NULL–not the desired result. To write the update statement correctly, use the NVL function to deal with the potential NULLs:

```
UPDATE emp
SET salary = (salary + NVL(bonus,0) ) * 1.1;
```

Now, when you calculate the total compensation, you will add salary + 0 instead of salary + NULL for those employees not getting a bonus. The employees who do get a bonus still get their salary increased correctly, as well.

Be prepared for a possible exam question that tests your knowledge of when to use an NVL function in a calculation, although it probably won't mention NVL and may not look like it is testing your knowledge of NULL.

Single-Row Character Functions

Single-row character functions operate on character data. Most have one or more character arguments, and most return character values.

ASCII(<*c1*>)

Where *c1* is a character string. This function returns the ASCII decimal equivalent of the first character in *c1*. See also CHR( ) for the inverse operation.

```
SELECT ASCII('A') Big_A, ASCII('z') Little_Z FROM dual;

     BIG_A    LITTLE_Z
---------- ----------
        65         122
```

CHR(<i>[USING NCHAR_CS])

Where i is a number. This function returns the character equivalent of the decimal (binary) representation of the character. If the optional USING NCHAR_CS is included, the character from the national character set is returned. The default behavior is to return the character from the database character set.

```
SELECT CHR(65), CHR(122), CHR(223) FROM dual;


CHAR65 CHAR122 CHAR233
------ ------- -------
A      z       ß
```

CONCAT(<c1>, <c2>)

Where $c1$ is a character string, and $c2$ is a character string. This function returns $c2$ appended to $c1$. If $c1$ is NULL, then $c2$ is returned. If $c2$ is NULL, then $c1$ is returned. If both $c1$ and $c2$ are NULL, then NULL is returned. CONCAT returns the same results as using the concatenation operator: $c1||c2$.

```
SELECT CONCAT('Slobo ','Svoboda') UserName FROM dual;


USERNAME
-------------
Slobo Svoboda
```

INITCAP(<c1>)

Where $c1$ is a character string. This function returns $c1$ with the first character of each word in uppercase and all others in lowercase. Words are delimited by white space, control characters, and punctuation symbols.

```
SELECT INITCAP('veni, vedi, vici') Ceasar FROM dual;


CEASAR
----------------
Veni, Vedi, Vici
```

INSTR(*<c1>*, *<c2>*[, *<i>*[, *<j>*]])

Where *c1* and *c2* are character strings and *i* and *j* are integers. This function returns the numeric character position in *c1* where the *j* th occurrence of *c2* is found. The search begins at the *i* th character position in *c1*. INSTR returns a 0 when the requested string is not found. If *i* is negative, the search is performed backwards—right to left—but the position is still counted from left to right. Both *i* and *j* default to 1.

```
SELECT INSTR('Mississippi','i',3,3) FROM dual;


INSTR('MISSISSIPPI','I',3,3)
----------------------------
                          11


SELECT INSTR('Mississippi','i', -2,3) FROM dual;


INSTR('MISSISSIPPI','I',-2,3)
----------------------------
                           2
```

INSTRB(*<c1>*, *<c2>*[, *<i>*[, *<j>*]])

This is the same as INSTR( ), except it returns bytes instead of characters. For single-byte character sets, INSTRB( ) is equivalent to INSTR( ).

LENGTH(*<c>*)

Where *c* is a character string. This function returns the numeric length in characters of *c*. If *c* is NULL, a NULL is returned.

```
SELECT LENGTH('Ipso Facto') ergo FROM dual;


      ERGO
----------
        10
```

LENGTHB(<*c*>)

This function is the same as LENGTH( ), except it returns bytes instead of characters. For single-byte character sets, LENGTHB( ) is equivalent to LENGTH( ).

LOWER(<*c*>)

Where *c* is a character string. This function returns the character string *c* with all characters in lowercase. It frequently appears in WHERE clauses. See also UPPER.

```
SELECT colorname FROM itemdetail
WHERE LOWER(colorname) LIKE '%white%'


COLORNAME
--------------------
Winterwhite
```

LPAD(<*c1*>, <*i*> [, <*c2*>])

Where *c1* and *c2* are character strings and *i* is an integer. This function returns the character string *c1* expanded in length to *i* characters using *c2* to fill in space as needed on the left-hand side of *c1*. If *c1* is over *i* characters, it is truncated to *i* characters. *c2* defaults to a single space. See also RPAD.

```
SELECT LPAD(answer,7,' ') padded, answer unpadded FROM
questions;


PADDED UNPADDED
------- --------
    Yes Yes
     No No
  Maybe Maybe
```

LTRIM(<*c1*>, <*c2*>)

Where *c1* and *c2* are character strings. This function returns *c1* without any leading characters that appear in *c2*. If no *c2* characters are leading characters in *c1*, then *c1* is returned unchanged. *c2* defaults to a single space. See also RTRIM.

```
SELECT LTRIM('Mississippi','Mis') FROM dual;


LTR
---
ppi
```

RPAD(<*c1*>, <*i*>[, <*c2*>])

Where *c1* and *c2* are character strings and *i* is an integer. This function returns the character string *c1* expanded in length to *i* characters using *c2* to fill in space as needed on the right-hand side of *c1*. If *c1* is over *i* characters, it is truncated to *i* characters. *c2* defaults to a single space. See also LPAD.

```
SELECT RPAD(table_name,38,'.'), num_rows FROM user_tables;


RPAD(TABLE_NAME,38,'.')                  NUM_ROWS
-------------------------------------- --------
TEMP_ERRORS...........................        9
CUSTOMERS............................. 367,296
```

RTRIM(<*c1*>, <*c2*>)

Where *c1* and *c2* are character strings. This function returns *c1* without any trailing characters that appear in *c2*. If no *c2* characters are trailing characters in *c1*, then *c1* is returned unchanged. *c2* defaults to a single space. See also LTRIM.

```
SELECT RTRIM('Mississippi','ip') FROM dual;


RTRIM('
-------
Mississ
```

REPLACE(<c1>, <c2>[, <c3>])

Where *c1*, *c2*, and *c3* are all character strings. This function returns *c1* with all occurrences of *c2* replaced with *c3*. *c3* defaults to NULL. If *c3* is NULL, all occurrences of *c2* are removed. If *c2* is NULL, then *c1* is returned unchanged. If *c1* is NULL, then NULL is returned.

```
SELECT REPLACE('uptown','up','down') FROM dual;


REPLACE(
--------
downtown
```

SUBSTR(<c1>, <i>[, < j>])

Where *c1* is a character string and both *i* and *j* are integers. This function returns the portion of *c1* that is *j* characters long, beginning at position *i*. If *j* is negative, the position is counted backwards (that is, right to left). This function returns NULL if *i* is 0 or negative. *j* defaults to 1.

```
SELECT SUBSTR('Message',1,4) from dual;


SUBS
----
Mess
```

SUBSTRB(<c1>, <i>[, <j>])

Where *c1* is a character string and both *i* and *j* are integers. This function is the same as SUBSTR, except *i* and *j* are counted in bytes instead of characters. For single-byte character sets, they are equivalent.

SOUNDEX(<c1>)

Where *c1* is a character string. This function returns the soundex phonetic representation of *c1*. The SOUNDEX function is usually used to locate names that sound alike.

```
SELECT SOUNDEX('Dawes') Dawes, SOUNDEX('Daws') Daws
    , SOUNDEX('Dawson') Dawson
FROM dual;


DAWES DAWS DAWSON
----- ---- ------
D200  D200 D250
```

TRANSLATE(<*c1*>, <*c2*>, <*c3*>)

Where *c1*, *c2*, and *c3* are all character strings. This function returns *c1* with all occurrences of characters in *c2* replaced with the positionally corresponding characters in *c3*. A NULL is returned if any of *c1*, *c2*, or *c3* is NULL. If *c3* has fewer characters than *c2*, then the unmatched characters in *c2* are removed from *c1*. If *c2* has fewer characters than *c3*, then the unmatched characters in *c3* are ignored.

```
SELECT TRANSLATE('fumble','uf','aR') test FROM dual;


TEST
------
Ramble
```

TRIM([[<*c1*>] <*c2*> FROM] <*c3*>)

Where *c2*, and *c3* are all character strings. If present, *c1* can be one of the following literals: LEADING, TRAILING, or BOTH. This function returns *c3* with all *c1* *(leading, trailing, or both)* occurrences of characters in *c2* removed. A NULL is returned if any of *c1*, *c2*, or *c3* is NULL. *c1* defaults to BOTH. *c2* defaults to a space character. This function is new to 8i.

```
SELECT TRIM('  space padded   ') trimmed FROM dual;


TRIMMED
------------
space padded
```

UPPER(<*c*>)

Where *c* is a character string. This function returns the character string *c* with all characters in upper case. UPPER frequently appears in WHERE clauses. See also LOWER.

```
SELECT ename, job, hiredate FROM emp
WHERE UPPER(ename) LIKE 'KI%';


ENAME      JOB        HIREDATE
---------- ---------- --------------------
KING       PRESIDENT  17-Nov-1981 00:00:00
```

Table 2.2 reviews the single-row character functions we have covered.

TABLE 2.2 Character Function Summary

Function	Description
ASCII	Returns the ASCII decimal equivalent of a character
CHR	Returns the character given the decimal equivalent
CONCAT	Concatenates two strings; same as the operator ||
INITCAP	Returns the string with the first letter of each word in uppercase
INSTR	Finds the numeric starting position of a string within a string
INSTRB	Same as INSTR, but counts bytes instead of characters
LENGTH	Returns the length of a string in characters
LENGTHB	Returns the length of a string in bytes
LOWER	Converts string to all lowercase
LPAD	Left-fills a string to a set length using a specified character
LTRIM	Strips leading characters from a string
RPAD	Right-fills a string to a set length using a specified character
RTRIM	Strips trailing characters from a string
REPLACE	Performs substring search and replace
SUBSTR	Returns a section of the specified string, specified by numeric character positions
SUBSTRB	Returns a section of the specified string, specified by numeric byte positions
SOUNDEX	Returns a phonetic representation of a string

TABLE 2.2 Character Function Summary *(continued)*

Function	Description
TRANSLATE	Performs character search and replace
TRIM	Strings leading, trailing, or both leading and trailing characters from a string
UPPER	Converts string to all uppercase

Single-Row Numeric Functions

Single-row numeric functions operate on numeric data and perform some kind of mathematical or arithmetic manipulation. All have numeric arguments and return numeric values. The trigonometric functions all operate on radians, not degrees. Oracle does not provide a built-in conversion function to convert radians to or from degrees.

ABS(<*n*>)

Where *n* is a number. This function returns the absolute value of *n*.

```
SELECT ABS(-52) negative, ABS(52) positive FROM dual;

  NEGATIVE    POSITIVE
---------- ----------
        52          52
```

ACOS(<*n*>)

Where *n* is a number between −1 and 1. This function returns the arc cosine of *n* expressed in radians.

```
SELECT ACOS(-1) pi, ACOS(1) zero FROM dual;

        PI        ZERO
---------- ----------
3.14159265           0
```

ASIN(<*n*>)

Where *n* is a number between –1 and 1. This function returns the arc sine of *n* expressed in radians.

```
SELECT ASIN(1) high, ASIN(0) middle, ASIN(-1) low FROM
dual;
```

```
      HIGH      MIDDLE        LOW
---------- ---------- ----------
1.57079633          0 -1.5707963
```

ATAN(<*n*>)

Where *n* is a number. This function returns the arc tangent of *n* expressed in radians.

```
SELECT ATAN(9E99) high, ATAN(0) middle, ATAN(-9E99) low
    FROM dual;
```

```
      HIGH      MIDDLE        LOW
---------- ---------- ----------
1.57079633          0 -1.5707963
```

CEIL(<*n*>)

Where *n* is a number. This function returns the smallest integer that is greater than or equal to *n*. CEIL rounds up to a whole number. See also FLOOR.

```
SELECT CEIL(9.8), CEIL(-32.85), CEIL(0) FROM dual;
```

```
CEIL(9.8) CEIL(-32.85)    CEIL(0)
---------- ------------ ----------
       10          -32          0
```

COS(<*n*>)

Where *n* is a number in radians. This function returns the cosine of *n*.

```
SELECT COS(-3.14159) FROM dual;
```

```
COS(-3.14159)
-------------
           -1
```

COSH(<*n*>)

Where *n* is a number. This function returns the hyperbolic cosine of *n*.

```
SELECT COSH(1.4) FROM dual;


  COSH(1.4)
----------
2.15089847
```

EXP(<*n*>)

Where *n* is a number. This function returns *e* (the base of natural logarithms) raised to the *n*th power.

```
SELECT EXP(1) "e" FROM dual;


         e
----------
2.71828183
```

FLOOR(<*n*>)

Where *n* is a number. This function returns the largest integer that is less than or equal to *n*. FLOOR rounds down to a whole number. See also CEIL.

```
SELECT FLOOR(9.8), FLOOR(-32.85), FLOOR(137) FROM dual;

FLOOR(9.8) FLOOR(-32.85) FLOOR(137)
---------- ------------- ----------
         9           -33        137
```

LN(<*n*>)

Where *n* is a number greater than 0. This function returns the natural logarithm of *n*.

```
SELECT LN(2.7) FROM dual;


   LN(2.7)
----------
.993251773
```

LOG(<*n1*>, <*n2*>)

Where *n1* and *n2* are numbers. This function returns the logarithm base *n1* of *n2*.

```
SELECT LOG(8,64), LOG(3,27), LOG(2,1024) FROM dual;


 LOG(8,64)  LOG(3,27) LOG(2,1024)
---------- ---------- -----------
         2          3          10
```

MOD(<*n1*>, <*n2*>)

Where *n1* and *n2* are numbers. This function returns *n1* modulo *n2* or the remainder of *n1* divided by *n2*. If *n1* is negative, the result is negative. The sign of *n2* has no effect on the result. This behavior differs from the mathematical definition of the modulus operation.

```
SELECT MOD(14,5), MOD(8,2.5), MOD(-64,7) FROM dual;


 MOD(14,5) MOD(8,2.5) MOD(-64,7)
---------- ---------- ----------
         4         .5         -1
```

POWER(<*n1*>, <*n2*>)

Where *n1* and *n2* are numbers. This function returns *n1* to the $n2^{th}$ power.

```
SELECT POWER(2,10), POWER(3,3), POWER(5,3) FROM dual;


POWER(2,10) POWER(3,3) POWER(5,3)
----------- ---------- ----------
       1024         27        125
```

ROUND(<*n1*>, <*n2*>)

Where *n1* is a number and *n2* is an integer. This function returns *n1* rounded to *n2* digits of precision to the right of the decimal. If *n2* is negative, *n1* is rounded to left of the decimal. This function is similar to TRUNC().

```
SELECT ROUND(12345,-2), ROUND(12345.54321,2) from dual;


ROUND(12345,-2) ROUND(12345.54321,2)
--------------- --------------------
          12300              12345.54
```

SIGN(<*n*>)

Where *n* is a number. This function returns –1 if *n* is negative, 1 if *n* is positive, and 0 if *n* is 0.

```
SELECT SIGN(-2.3), SIGN(0), SIGN(47) FROM dual;


SIGN(-2.3)    SIGN(0)   SIGN(47)
----------  ---------- ----------
        -1           0          1
```

SIN(<*n*>)

Where *n* is a number in radians. This function returns the sine of *n*.

```
SELECT SIN(1.57079) FROM dual;


SIN(1.57079)
------------
           1
```

SINH(<*n*>)

Where *n* is a number. This function returns the hyperbolic sine of *n*.

SQRT(<*n*>)

Where *n* is a number. This function returns the square root of *n*.

```
SELECT SQRT(64), SQRT(49), SQRT(5) FROM dual;

   SQRT(64)    SQRT(49)    SQRT(5)
---------- ---------- ----------
         8          7 2.23606798
```

TAN(<*n*>)

Where *n* is a number in radians. This function returns the tangent of *n*.

```
SELECT TAN(1.57079633/2) "45_Degrees" FROM dual;

45_Degrees
----------
         1
```

TANH(<*n*>)

Where *n* is a number. This function returns the hyperbolic tangent of *n*.

```
SELECT TANH( ACOS(-1) ) hyp_tan_of_pi FROM dual;

HYP_TAN_OF_PI
-------------
   .996272076
```

TRUNC(<*n1*>, <*n2*>)

Where *n1* is a number and *n2* is an integer. This function returns *n1* truncated to *n2* digits of precision to the right of the decimal. If *n2* is negative, *n1* is truncated to left of the decimal. See also ROUND.

```
SELECT TRUNC(123.456,2) pos, TRUNC(123.456,-1) neg
FROM dual;

       POS        NEG
---------- ----------
    123.45        120
```

Take a look at Table 2.3 to review the single-row numeric functions we have discussed.

TABLE 2.3   Numeric Function Summary

Function	Description
ABS	Returns the absolute value
ACOS	Returns the arc cosine
ASIN	Returns the arc sine
ATAN	Returns the arc tangent
CEIL	Returns the next higher integer
COS	Returns the cosine
COSH	Returns the hyperbolic cosine
EXP	Returns the base of natural logarithms raised to a power
FLOOR	Returns the next smaller integer
LN	Returns the natural logarithm
LOG	Returns the logarithm
MOD	Returns modulo (remainder) of a division operation
POWER	Returns a number raised to an arbitrary power
ROUND	Rounds a number
SIGN	Returns an indicator of sign: negative, positive, or zero
SIN	Returns the sine
SINH	Returns the hyperbolic sine
SQRT	Returns the square root of a number

TABLE 2.3 Numeric Function Summary *(continued)*

Function	Description
TAN	Returns the tangent
TANH	Returns the hyperbolic tangent
TRUNC	Truncates a number

Single-Row Date Functions

Single-row date functions operate on date datatypes. Most have one or more date arguments, and most return a date value. Date data is stored internally as numbers: The whole number portion is the number of days since Jan 1, 4712 BC, and the decimal portion is the fraction of a day (for example, .5 = 12 hours). Oracle will implicitly or automatically convert this numeric date data to/from character data using the format model specified with NLS_DATE_FORMAT. This date format model can be changed for each session with the ALTER SESSION SET NLS_DATE FORMAT command. Here's an example:

```
ALTER SESSION SET NLS_DATE_FORMAT='DD-Mon-YYYY
HH24:MI:SS';
```

This ALTER command will set the implicit conversion mechanism to display date data as in 12-Dec-1999 15:45:32. This conversion works both ways, as well; if the character string '30-Nov-1999 20:30:00' were inserted, updated, or assigned to a date column or variable, the correct date would be entered. If the format model were 'DD/MM/YY' or 'MM/DD/YY', there could be some ambiguity in the conversion of some dates, such as 12 April 2000 (04/12/00 or 12/04/00). To avoid problems with implicit conversions, Oracle provides the explicit date/character conversion functions:

- TO_DATE
- TO_CHAR

These explicit conversion functions are covered in the "Single-Row Conversion Functions" section later in this chapter.

ADD_MONTHS(<*d*>, <*i*>)

Where *d* is a date and *i* is an integer. This function returns the date *d* plus *i* months. If *i* is a decimal number, the database will implicitly convert it to an integer by truncating the decimal portion (for example, 3.9 becomes 3).

```
SELECT SYSDATE
      ,ADD_MONTHS(SYSDATE,3)  plus_3
      ,ADD_MONTHS(SYSDATE,-2) minus_2
FROM dual;


SYSDATE       PLUS_3        MINUS_2
-----------   -----------   -----------
30-Nov-1999   29-Feb-2000   30-Sep-1999
```

LAST_DAY(<*d*>)

Where *d* is a date. This function returns the last day of the month for the date *d*.

```
SELECT SYSDATE,LAST_DAY(SYSDATE)+1 FROM dual;


SYSDATE       LAST_DAY(SY
-----------   -----------
23-NOV-1999   01-DEC-1999
```

MONTHS_BETWEEN(<*d1*>, <*d2*>)

Where *d1* and *d2* are both dates. This function returns the number of months that *d2* is later than *d1*. A whole number is returned if *d1* and *d2* are the same day of the month or if both dates are the last day of a month.

```
SELECT MONTHS_BETWEEN('19-Dec-1999','19-Mar-2000')
FROM dual;


MONTHS_BETWEEN('19-DEC-1999','19-MAR-2000')
-------------------------------------------
                                         -3
```

NEW_TIME(<*d*>, <*tz1*>, <*tz2*>)

Where *d* is a date and both *tz1* and *tz2* are one of the time zone constants (shown in Table 2.4). This function returns the date in time zone *tz2* for date *d* in time zone *tz1*.

TABLE 2.4   Time Zone Constants

Code	Time Zone
GMT	Greenwich Mean Time
NST	Newfoundland Standard Time
AST	Atlantic Standard Time
ADT	Atlantic Daylight Time
BST	Bering Standard Time
BDT	Bering Daylight Time
CST	Central Standard Time
CDT	Central Daylight Time
EST	Eastern Standard Time
EDT	Eastern Daylight Time
HST	Hawaii-Alaska Standard Time
HDT	Hawaii-Alaska Daylight Time
MST	Mountain Standard Time
MDT	Mountain Daylight Time
PST	Pacific Standard Time
PDT	Pacific Daylight Time
YST	Yukon Standard Time
YDT	Yukon Daylight Time

```
SELECT SYSDATE Chicago
      ,NEW_TIME(SYSDATE,'CDT','PDT') Los_Angles
FROM dual;


CHICAGO              LOS_ANGLES
-------------------- --------------------
23-Nov-1999 10:00:00 23-Nov-1999 08:00:00
```

NEXT_DAY(<*d*>, <*dow*>)

Where *d* is a date and *dow* is a text string containing the full or abbreviated day of the week in the session's language. This function returns the next *dow* following *d*. The time portion of the return date is the same as the time portion of *d*.

```
SELECT NEXT_DAY('01-Jan-2000','Monday')    "1st Monday"
      ,NEXT_DAY('01-Nov-2004','Tuesday')+7 "2nd Tuesday"
FROM dual;


1st Monday  2nd Tuesday
----------- -----------
03-Jan-2000 09-Nov-2004
```

ROUND(<*d*> [, <*fmt*>])

Where *d* is a date and *fmt* is a character string containing a date-format string. This function returns *d* rounded to the granularity specified in *fmt*.

```
SELECT SYSDATE,ROUND(SYSDATE,'HH24') FROM dual;


SYSDATE              ROUND(SYSDATE,'HH24'
-------------------- --------------------
24-Nov-1999 09:23:56 24-Nov-1999 09:00:00
```

SYSDATE

This function takes no arguments and returns the current date and time to the second. It is one of the most commonly used functions, and there's a good chance you'll see it on the exam.

```
SELECT SYSDATE FROM dual;

SYSDATE
-------------------
24-Nov-1999 09:26:01
```

TRUNC(<*d*>[, <*fmt*>])

Where *d* is a date and *fmt* is a character string containing a date-format string. This function returns *d* truncated to the granularity specified in *fmt*.

```
SELECT TRUNC(last_analyzed,'HH')
FROM user_tables
WHERE table_name='TEST_CASE';

TRUNC(LAST_ANALYZED,
-------------------
28-Nov-1999 11:00:00
```

The single-row date functions we have covered are reviewed in Table 2.5.

TABLE 2.5 Date Function Summary

Function	Description
ADD_MONTHS	Adds a number of months to a date
LAST_DAY	Returns the last day of a month
MONTHS_BETWEEN	Returns the number of months between two dates
NEW_TIME	Returns the date/time in a different time zone
NEXT_DAY	Returns the next day of a week following a given date

TABLE 2.5   Date Function Summary *(continued)*

Function	Description
ROUND	Rounds a date/time
SYSDATE	Returns the current date/time
TRUNCATE	Truncates a date to a given granularity

Single-Row Conversion Functions

Single-row conversion functions operate on multiple datatypes. The TO_CHAR and TO_NUMBER functions have a significant number of formatting codes that can be used to display date and number data in a wide assortment of representations. The exam may include a question that tests your recollection of some of the nuances of these formatting codes. General usage in a professional setting would afford you the opportunity to look them up in a reference. In the test setting, you must recall them.

CHARTOROWID(*<c>*)

Where *c* is a character string. This function returns *c* as a ROWID datatype. No translation is performed; only the datatype is converted.

```
SELECT test_id FROM test_case
WHERE rowid = CHARTOROWID('AAAAoSAACAAAALiAAA');
```

CONVERT(*<c>*, *<dset>*[, *<sset>*])

Where *c* is a character string and *dset* and *sset* are character set names. This function returns the character string *c* converted from the source character set *sset* to the destination character set *dset*. No translation is performed, and the character should exist in both character sets, or the replacement character for the character set is used. *sset* defaults to the database character set.

HEXTORAW(*<x>*)

Where *x* is a hex string. This function returns the hexadecimal string *x* converted to a RAW datatype. There is no translation performed; only the datatype is changed.

```
INSERT INTO printers(printer_nbr, manufacturer, model,
        init_string)
VALUES (12,'HP','LaserJet',HEXTORAW('1B45'));
```

RAWTOHEX(*<x>*)

Where *x* is a raw string. This function returns the raw string *x* converted to hexadecimal. There is no translation performed; only the datatype is changed.

```
SELECT RAWTOHEX(init_string)
FROM printers
WHERE model='LaserJet' AND  manufacturer='HP';


RAWTOHEX(INIT_STRING)
----------------------------------------------------------
1B45
```

ROWIDTOCHAR(*<x>*)

Where *x* is a character string in the format of a ROWID. This function returns the character string *x* converted to a ROWID. There is no translation performed; only the data type is changed.

```
SELECT ROWIDTOCHAR(rowid) FROM test_case
WHERE rownum = 1;


ROWIDTOCHAR(ROWID)
------------------
AAAAoSAACAAAALiAAA
```

TO_CHAR(*<x>* [, *<fmt>* [, *<nlsparm>*]])

Where *x* is either a date or a number, *fmt* is a format string specifying the format that *x* will appear in (see Table 2.6), and *nlsparm* specifies language or location formatting conventions. This function returns *x* converted into a character string.

If *x* is a date, *nlsparm* is an NLS_DATE_LANGUAGE specification, if included. Note that the spelled-out numbers always appear in English, while the day or month may appear in the *NLS* language.

```
SELECT TO_CHAR(SYSDATE,'Day Ddspth,Month YYYY'
               ,'NLS_DATE_LANGUAGE=German') Today_Heute
FROM dual;
```

```
TODAY_HEUTE
----------------------------------------
Samstag    Twenty-Seventh,November   1999


SELECT TO_CHAR(SYSDATE,'"On the "Ddspth" day of "Month,
YYYY')
FROM dual;


TO_CHAR(SYSDATE,'"ONTHE"DDSPTH"DAYOF"MONTH,Y
--------------------------------------------
On the Twenty-Seventh day of November , 1999
```

If x is a number, *nlsparm* can include NLS_NUMERIC_CHARACTERS for specifying decimal and grouping symbols (format symbols D and G respectively), NLS_CURRENCY for specifying the currency symbol (format symbol L), and NLS_ISO_CURRENCY for specifying the ISO international currency symbol (format symbol C). The NLS_CURRENCY symbol and the NLS_ISO_CURRENCY mnemonic are frequently different. For example, the NLS_CURRENCY symbol for U.S. dollars is $, but this symbol is not uniquely American, so the ISO symbol for U.S. dollars is USD.

```
SELECT TO_CHAR(-1234.56,'C099G999D99MI'
              ,'NLS_NUMERIC_CHARACTERS='',.''
              NLS_CURRENCY=''DM''
              NLS_ISO_CURRENCY=''GERMANY''
              ') Balance
FROM dual;


BALANCE
--------------
DEM001.234,56-
```

TABLE 2.6 Date Format Codes

Date Code	Format Code Description	Example
AD or BC	Epoch indicator	'YYYY AD' = 1999 AD
A.D. or B.C.	Epoch indicator with periods	'YYYY A.D.' = 1999 A.D.

TABLE 2.6 Date Format Codes *(continued)*

Date Code	Format Code Description	Example
AM or PM	Meridian indicator	'HH12AM' = 09AM
A.M. or P.M.	Meridian indicator with periods	'HH A.M.' = 09 A.M.
DY	Day of week abbreviated	Mon, Tue, Fri
DAY	Day of week spelled out	Monday, Tuesday, Friday
D	Day of week (1–7)	1,2,3,4,5,6,7
DD	Day of month (1–31)	1,2,3,4...31
DDD	Day of year (1–366)	1,2,3,4...366
J	Julian day (days since 4712BC)	2451514, 2451515, 2451516
W	Week of the month (1–5)	1,2,3,4,5
WW, IW	Week of the year, ISO week of the year	1,2,3,4...53
MM	Two-digit month	01,02,03...12
MON	Month name abbreviated	Jan, Feb, Mar...Dec
MONTH	Month name spelled out	January, February...December
RM	Roman numeral month (I–XII)	I,II,III,IV,V...XII
YYYY, YYY, YY, Y	Four-digit year; last 3 ,2, 1 digits in the year	1999, 999, 99, 9 2000, 000, 00, 0
YEAR	Year spelled out	Nineteen Ninety-Nine

TABLE 2.6 Date Format Codes *(continued)*

Date Code	Format Code Description	Example
SYYYY	If BC, year is shown as negative	-1250
RR	*See description below*	
HH, HH12	Hour of the half-day (1–12)	1,2,3...12
HH24	Hour of the day (0–23)	0,1,2...23
MI	Minutes of the hour (0–59)	0,1,2...59
SS	Seconds of the minute (0–59)	0,1,2...59
SSSSS	Seconds of the day (0–86399)	0,1,2...86399
, . / - ; :	Punctuation	Literal display
'text'	Quoted text	Literal display

The RR code is used for data input with only two digits for the year—it is intended to deal with two-digit years and Y2K. It rounds the century based on the current year and the two-digit year, entered as follows:

- If the current year is >= 50 and the two-digit year is <50, the century is rounded up to the next century.

- If the current year is >= 50 and the two-digit year is >= 50, the century is unchanged.

- If the current year is < 50 and the two-digit year is < 50 the century is unchanged.

- If the current year is < 50 and the two-digit year is >=50, the century is rounded down to the previous century.

So, if the current year is 1999 (>=50) and the two digit year is entered as 03 (<50), the year is interpreted as 2003. If the current year is 2003 (<50) and the two-digit year is entered as 62 (>=50), the year is interpreted as 1962.

For any of the numeric codes, the ordinal and/or spelled-out representation can be displayed with the modifier codes th (for ordinal) and sp (for spelled out). Here is an example:

```
SELECT SYSDATE, TO_CHAR(SYSDATE,'Mmspth'),
       TO_CHAR(SYSDATE,'DDth'), TO_CHAR(SYSDATE,'Yyyysp')
FROM dual;


SYSDATE      TO_CHAR( TO_C TO_CHAR(SYSDATE,'YYYYSP')
-----------  -------- ---- --------------------------------
01-DEC-1999 Twelfth  01ST One Thousand Nine Hundred Ninety-Nine
```

For any of the spelled-out words or ordinals, case follows the pattern of the first two characters in the code. If the first two characters are uppercase, the spelled-out words are all uppercase. If the first two characters are lowercase, then the spelled-out words are all lowercase. If the first two characters are upper- then lowercase, the spelled-out words have the first letter in uppercase and the remaining characters in lowercase, as in INITCAP.

```
SELECT TO_CHAR(SYSDATE,'MONTH'), TO_CHAR(SYSDATE,'Month'),
       TO_CHAR(SYSDATE,'month') FROM dual;


TO_CHAR(S TO_CHAR(S TO_CHAR(S
--------- --------- ---------
DECEMBER  December  december
```

You can see the numeric format codes in Table 2.7.

TABLE 2.7   Numeric Format Codes

Numeric Code	Format Code Description	Example
9	Numeric digits with leading space if positive and a leading – (minus) if negative	9999.9 = 1234.5 9999.9 = -1234.5 9999.9 = .3
0	Leading and/or trailing zeros	0009.90 = 0012.30

TABLE 2.7 Numeric Format Codes *(continued)*

Numeric Code	Format Code Description	Example
,	Comma, for use as a group separator. It cannot appear after a period or decimal code	9,999.9 = 1,234.5
G	Local group separator, could be comma (,) or period (.)	9G999D9 = 1,234.5 9G999D9 = 1.234,5
.	Period, for use as the decimal character. It cannot appear more than once or to the left of a group separator	9,999.9 = 1,234.5
D	Local decimal character, could be comma (,) or period (.)	9G999D9 = 1,234.5 9G999D9 = 1.234,5
$	Dollar-sign currency symbol	$999 = $123
L	Local currency symbol	L999 = $123 L999 = _123
FM	No leading or trailing blanks	FM99.99 = .1
EEEE	Scientific notation	9.9EEEE = 1.2E+05
MI	Negative as a trailing minus	999MI = 137-
PR	Negative in angle brackets (< >)	999PR = <137>
S	Negative as a leading minus	S999 = -137
RN	Uppercase Roman numeral	RN = XXIV
rn	Lowercase Roman numeral	rn = xxiv

```
SELECT TO_CHAR(123456,'9.99EEEE'), TO_
CHAR(123456,'9.9EEEE')
FROM dual;

TO_CHAR(12 TO_CHAR(1
---------- ---------
  1.23E+05    1.2E+05
```

TO_DATE(*<c>* [, *<fmt>* [, *<nlsparm>*]])

Where *c* is a character string, *fmt* is a format string specifying the format that *c* appears in (see Table 2.6), and *nlsparm* specifies language or location formatting conventions. This function returns *c* converted into the DATE datatype.

```
INSERT INTO demo (demo_key, date_col)
VALUES (1,TO_DATE('04-Oct-1957','DD-Mon-YYYY') );
```

TO_MULTI_BYTE(*<c>*)

Where *c* is a character string. This function returns a character string containing *c* with all single-byte characters converted to their multi-byte counterparts. This function is only useful in databases using character sets with both single-byte and multi-byte characters. See also TO_SINGLE_BYTE().

TO_NUMBER(*<c>* [, *<fmt>* [, *<nlsparm>*]])

Where *c* is a character string, *fmt* is a format string specifying the format that *c* appears in, and *nlsparm* specifies language or location formatting conventions. This function returns the numeric value represented by *c*.

TO_SINGLE_BYTE(*<c>*)

Where *c* is a character string. This function returns a character string containing *c* with all multi-byte characters converted to their single-byte counterparts. This function is only useful in databases using character sets with both single-byte and multi-byte characters. See also TO_SINGLE_BYTE().

Table 2.8 lists the single-row conversion functions we have covered.

TABLE 2.8 Conversion Function Summary

Function	Description
CHARTOROWID	Casts a character to ROWID datatype
CONVERT	Converts from one character set to another
HEXTORAW	Casts a hexadecimal to a raw
RAWTOHEX	Casts a raw to a hexadecimal

TABLE 2.8 Conversion Function Summary *(continued)*

Function	Description
ROWIDTOCHAR	Casts a ROWID to a character
TO_CHAR	Converts and format a date into a string
TO_DATE	Converts a string into a date, specifying the format
TO_MULTIBYTE	Converts a single-byte character to its corresponding multi-byte equivalent
TO_NUMBER	Casts a numeric string to a number, specifying the format
TO_SINGLE_BYTE	Converts a multi-byte character to its corresponding single-byte equivalent

Programmer-Written Single-Row Functions

You can use programmer-written single-row functions in your statements, with some restrictions. These restrictions relate to the *purity* of the function—how it interacts with the database. The restrictions do not allow a programmer-written function to violate the database's consistency model. These rules for purity changed between versions 8 and 8.1. In 8 and earlier, programmer-written functions needed to have the compiler directive PRAGMA RESTRICT_REFERENCES declared before those functions could be used in SQL statements (they could always be used in PL/SQL code). There were varying degrees of purity for various uses (SELECT clause, WHERE clause, and so on). In 8.1 (8i), Oracle no longer requires compiler directives, instead checking the purity at runtime by ensuring the following during execution:

- A function called from a query or DML statement cannot end the current transaction, create a save point, roll back to a save point, alter the session, alter the system, or execute DML.

- A function called from a DML statement cannot read or modify the same table that is being modified by the DML statement; this is similar to the mutating tables problem with triggers.

You can read more about creating programmer-written functions in Chapter 7, "PL/SQL Basics."

Other Single-Row Functions

This is the catchall category to include all the single-row functions that don't fit into the other categories. Some are incredibly useful, like DECODE; others are rather esoteric, like DUMP or VSIZE.

BFILENAME(<*dir*>, <*file*>)

Where *dir* is a directory and *file* is a filename. This function returns an empty BFILE locator. This function is used to initialize a BFILE variable or BFILE column in a table. When used, the BFILE is instantiated. Neither *dir* nor *file* needs to exist at the time BFILENAME() is called, but both must exist when the locator is used.

```
DECLARE
    BFILE_LOC  BFILE;
BEGIN
    BFILE_LOC := BFILENAME('C:\DATA\','Foo.dat');
...
```

DECODE(<*x*>, <*m1*>, <*r1*> [, <*m2*>, <*r2...*>] [, <*d*>])

Where *x* is an expression. *m1* is a matching expression to compare with *x*. If *m1* is equivalent to *x*, then *r1* is returned; otherwise, additional matching expressions (*m2*, *m3*, *m4*, and so on) are compared, if they are included, and the corresponding result (*r2*, *r3*, *r4*, and so on) is returned. If no match is found and the default expression *d* is included, then *d* is returned. This function acts like a case statement in C, Pascal, or Ada. DECODE is a very powerful tool that can make SQL very efficient—or very dense and non-intuitive. The following examples will help clarify.

See the examples in "Nesting Functions" section later in this chapter for more advanced uses of DECODE.

In the following example, we query the v$session table to see who is executing which command in the database. The command column displays a numeric code for each command, but we want to report a textual description for a few important commands. We use DECODE in the fourth column to examine the contents of v$session.command. If the command is 0, then we display None; if it is 2, then we display Insert, and so on. If the command is not in our list (0,2,3,6,7,8), then we display the default, Other.

```
SELECT sid ,serial# ,username
      ,DECODE(command
      ,0,'None'
      ,2,'Insert'
      ,3,'Select'
      ,6,'Update'
      ,7,'Delete'
      ,8,'Drop'
      ,'Other') cmd
FROM v$session
WHERE type <> 'BACKGROUND';
```

SID	SERIAL#	USERNAME	CMD
7	147		None
8	147		None
9	24	CHIPD	Other
11	4	CHIPD	Select

DECODE does not have to return a value; it can return NULL. The following example returns NULL if grantable does not equal 'YES'—there is no default specified in the arguments.

```
SELECT owner, table_name, grantor, grantee
```

```
       ,DECODE(grantable,'YES','With Grant Option')
FROM user_tab_privs
WHERE privilege = 'SELECT';
```

```
OWNER TABLE_NAME          GRANTOR   GRANTEE   DECODE(GRANTABLE,
----- ----------------    --------  --------  -----------------
CHIPD ZIP_STATE_CITY      CHIPD     SCOTT     With Grant Option
SYS   V_$INSTANCE         SYS       CHIPD
SYS   DBA_DATA_FILES      SYS       CHIPD
```

DUMP(<x> [, <fmt> [, <n1> [, <n2>]]])

Where x is an expression, *fmt* is a format specification for octal (1008), decimal (1010), hexadecimal (1016), or single characters (1017), and *n1* is the starting byte offset within x; and *n2* is the length in bytes to dump. This function returns a character string containing the datatype of x in numeric notation (for example, 2 = number, 12 = date—see the section on "Oracle Internal Datatypes" in the *OCI Programmer's Guide* for a complete listing), the length in bytes of x, and the internal representation of x. This function is mainly used for troubleshooting data problems.

```
SELECT global_name, DUMP(global_name,1017,8,5) dump_string
FROM global_name;
```

```
GLOBAL_NAME     DUMP_STRING
--------------- -------------------------------------------------
ORACLE.WORLD    Typ=1 Len=12 CharacterSet=WE8ISO8859P1: W,O,R,L,D
```

EMPTY_BLOB()

This function takes no arguments. This function returns an empty BLOB locator. This function is used to initialize a BLOB variable or BLOB column in a table. When used, the BLOB is instantiated but not populated.

```
insert into bclob (pk,clob_col,blob_col)
VALUES (43, empty_clob(), empty_blob() );
```

EMPTY_CLOB()

This function takes no arguments. This function returns an empty CLOB locator. This function is used to initialize a CLOB variable or CLOB column in a table. When used, the CLOB is instantiated but not populated.

```
insert into bclob (pk,clob_col,blob_col)
VALUES (43, empty_clob(), empty_blob() );
```

GREATEST(<*exp_list*>)

Where *exp_list* is a list of expressions. This function returns the expression that sorts highest in the datatype of the first expression. If the first expression is any of the character datatypes, a VARCHAR2 is returned and the *comparison rules* for VARCHAR are used for character literal strings. A NULL in the expression list results in a NULL being returned.

```
SELECT GREATEST('19','24',9) string FROM dual;


STRING
-------
9
```

The comparison rules used by GREATEST and LEAST on character literals order trailing spaces higher than no spaces—this behavior follows the non-padded comparison rules of the VARCHAR datatype. Note the ordering of the leading and trailing spaces—trailing spaces are greatest and leading spaces least. Think, "Leading equals least."

```
SELECT GREATEST(' Yes','Yes','Yes ')
        ,LEAST(' Yes','Yes','Yes ')
FROM dual;

GREA LEAS
---- ----
Yes  Yes
```

LEAST(<*exp_list*>)

Where *exp_list* is a list of expressions. This function returns the expression that sorts lowest in the datatype of the first expression. If the first expression is any of the character datatypes, a VARCHAR2 is returned.

```
SELECT LEAST(SYSDATE,'15-MAR-2000','17-JUN-2000') oldest
FROM dual;


OLDEST
-----------
27-NOV-1999

SELECT ename, sal, LEAST(sal, 3000) FROM emp;


ENAME              SAL LEAST(SAL,3000)
---------- ----------- ----------------
SMITH              800              800
ALLEN             1600             1600
KING              5000             3000
```

UID

This function takes no parameters and returns the integer user_id for the current user. User_ID uniquely identifies each user in a database and can be selected from the view DBA_USERS.

```
SELECT username, account_status FROM dba_users WHERE user_
id=UID;


USERNAME                            ACCOUNT_STATUS
----------------------------------- ---------------------------
CHIPD                               OPEN


INSERT INTO audit_table (who,when,what)
VALUES (UID, SYSDATE, audit_action);
```

USER

This function takes no parameters and returns a character string containing the username for the current user.

```
SELECT USER, UID FROM DUAL;
```

```
USER                                    UID
------------------------------- ----------
CHIPD                                    26
```

USERENV(*<opt>*)

Where *opt* is one of the options listed below. This function returns a VARCHAR2 string containing information corresponding to the option *opt*. The option can appear in upper-, lower-, or mixed case. Valid options follow:

ISDBA

Returns TRUE if the SYSDBA role is enabled in the current session.

```
SELECT USERENV('ISDBA') FROM dual;
```

```
USEREN
------
FALSE
```

SESSIONID

Returns the audsid auditing session identifier.

```
SELECT USERENV('SESSIONID') audsid FROM dual;
```

```
    AUDSID
----------
     47343
```

ENTRYID

Returns the auditing entry identifier if auditing is enabled for the instance (init.ora parm audit_trail = TRUE).

```
SELECT USERENV('ENTRYID') FROM dual;


USERENV('ENTRYID')
------------------
            835641
```

INSTANCE

Returns the instance identifier that the session is connected to. This option is useful only if you are running Parallel Server and have multiple instances.

```
SELECT USERENV('INSTANCE') FROM dual;


USERENV('INSTANCE')
-------------------
                  1
```

LANGUAGE

Returns the language, territory, and database character set. The delimiters are an underscore (_) between language and territory, and a period (.) between the territory and character set.

```
SELECT USERENV('LANGUAGE') FROM dual;


USERENV('LANGUAGE')
------------------------------------------------------
AMERICAN_AMERICA.WE8ISO8859P1
```

LANG

Returns the ISO abbreviation of the session's language.

```
SELECT USERENV('LANG') FROM dual;


USERENV('LANG')
------------------------------------------------------
US
```

TERMINAL

Returns the operating system identifier for the terminal or computer from which the session is operating.

```
SELECT USERENV('TERMINAL') FROM dual;


USERENV('TERMINA
----------------
ttyp04
```

VSIZE(<x>)

Where x is an expression. This function returns the size in bytes of the internal representation of the x.

```
SELECT VSIZE(user), user FROM dual;


VSIZE(USER) USER
----------- ------------------------------
          5 CHIPD
```

Table 2.9 reviews the miscellaneous single-row functions we have discussed.

TABLE 2.9 Miscellaneous Function Summary

Function	Description
BFILENAME	Returns a BFILE locator for the specified file and directory
DECODE	Inline case statement. This is an IF…THEN…ELSE function.
DUMP	Returns raw substring in specified encoding (octal/hex/character/decimal)
EMPTY_BLOB	Returns an empty BLOB locator
EMPTY_CLOB	Returns an empty CLOB locator
GREATEST	Sorts the arguments and returns the largest

TABLE 2.9   Miscellaneous Function Summary *(continued)*

Function	Description
LEAST	Sorts the arguments and returns the smallest
UID	Returns the numeric user ID for the current session
USER	Returns the username for the current session
USERENV	Returns various session based attributes such as auditing session ID, terminal, language, and so on
VSIZE	Returns the internal size in bytes for an expression

Group Functions in SQL

Group functions, sometimes called aggregate functions, return a value based on a number of inputs. The exact number of inputs is not determined until the query is executed and all rows are fetched. This differs from single-row functions, in which the number of inputs is known at parse time—before the query is executed. Because of this difference, group functions have slightly different requirements and behavior from single-row functions. Group functions do not process NULL values and do not return a NULL value. All of the group functions can be applied either to ALL values or to only the DISTINCT values for the specified expression. When ALL is specified, all non-NULL values are applied to the group function. When DISTINCT is specified, only one of each non-NULL value is applied to the group function.

Group (Multi-row) Functions

As with single-row functions, Oracle offers a rich variety of grouping, multi-row functions. These functions can appear in the SELECT or HAVING clauses of SELECT statements. When used in the SELECT clause, they usually require a GROUP BY clause, as well.

AVG([{DISTINCT | ALL}] <*n*>)

Where *n* is a numeric expression. This function returns the mean of the expression *n*. If neither DISTINCT nor ALL is specified in the function call, the default is to use ALL.

```
SELECT AVG(sal), AVG(ALL sal), AVG(DISTINCT sal) FROM
scott.emp;


   AVG(SAL) AVG(ALLSAL) AVG(DISTINCTSAL)
---------- ----------- ----------------
1877.94118  1877.94118       1916.07143
```

COUNT({* | [DISTINCT | ALL] <*x*>})

Where *x* is an expression. This function returns the number of rows in the query. If an expression is given and neither DISTINCT nor ALL is specified, the default is ALL. The asterisk (*) is a special quantity—it counts all rows in the result set, regardless of NULLs.

```
SELECT COUNT(*) emp_count, COUNT(DISTINCT mgr) mgr_count
      ,COUNT(mgr) mgr_count2
FROM scott.emp;

 EMP_COUNT  MGR_COUNT MGR_COUNT2
---------- ---------- ----------
        17          6         16
```

MAX([{DISTINCT | ALL}] <*x*>)

Where *x* is an expression. This function returns the highest value in the expression *x*. If the expression is a character datatype, it returns a VARCHAR2. If the expression *x* is a date datatype, it returns a date. If the expression *x* is a numeric datatype, it returns a number. Although the inclusion of either DISTINCT or ALL is syntactically acceptable, their use does not affect the calculation of a MAX: The largest distinct value is the same as the largest of all values. For dates, the maximum is the latest date. For numbers, the maximum is the largest number. For character strings, the maximum is the one that sorts highest based on the database character set.

```
SELECT MAX(freelists) FROM dba_tables;

MAX(FREELISTS)
--------------
             1
```

MIN([{DISTINCT | ALL}] <x>)

Where x is an expression. This function returns the lowest value in the
expression x. If the expression is a character datatype, it returns a VARCHAR2.
If the expression x is a date datatype, it returns a date. If the expression x is
a numeric datatype, it returns a number. Although the inclusion of either
DISTINCT or ALL is syntactically acceptable, their use does not affect the calculation of a MIN—: The smallest distinct value is the same as the smallest
value. For dates, the minimum is the earliest date. For numbers, the minimum is the smallest number. For character strings, the minimum is the one
that sorts lowest based on the database character set.

```
SELECT MIN(last_analyzed), MIN(blocks), MIN(table_name)
FROM user_tables;

MIN(LAST_AN MIN(BLOCKS) MIN(TABLE_NAME)
----------- ----------- ------------------------------
28-Nov-1999           0 ADDRESS
```

STDDEV([{DISTINCT | ALL}] <x>)

Where x is a numeric expression. This function returns the standard deviation
of the expression x. The standard deviation is calculated as the square root of
the variance.

```
SELECT AVG(latitude),STDDEV(latitude) FROM zip_codes;

AVG(LATITUDE) STDDEV(LATITUDE)
------------- ----------------
   37.7822735       6.96827458
```

SUM([{DISTINCT | ALL}] <x>)

Where x is a numeric expression. This function returns the sum of the expression x.

```
SELECT SUM(blocks) FROM user_tables;


SUM(BLOCKS)
-----------
      12265
```

VARIANCE([{DISTINCT | ALL}] <x>)

Where x is a numeric expression. This function returns the variance of the expression x.

```
SELECT AVG(latitude),VARIANCE(latitude) FROM zip_codes;


AVG(LATITUDE) VARIANCE(LATITUDE)
------------- ------------------
   37.7822735          48.5568507
```

The group functions we have covered are reviewed in Table 2.10.

TABLE 2.10 Group Function Summary

Function	Description
AVG	Returns the statistical mean
COUNT	Returns the number of non-NULL rows
MAX	Returns the largest value
MIN	Returns the smallest value
STD	Returns the statistical standard deviation
SUM	Adds all values and returns the result
VARIANCE	Returns the statistical variance

Grouping Data with GROUP BY

As the name implies, group functions work on data that is grouped. We tell the database how to group or categorize the data with a GROUP BY clause. Whenever we use a group function in the SELECT clause of a SELECT statement, we must place all non-grouping/non-constant columns into the GROUP BY clause. If no GROUP BY clause is specified (only group functions and constants appear in the SELECT clause), then the default grouping is the entire result set. When the query executes and the data is fetched, it is grouped based on the GROUP BY clause and the group function is applied.

```
SELECT state, count(*) zip_count
FROM zip_codes
GROUP BY state;


ST  ZIP_COUNT
--  ----------
AK        360
AL       1212
AR       1309
AZ        768
CA       3982
```

In this example, we categorize (group) the data by state, and apply the group function (COUNT). It returns the number of rows (in our case, zip codes) for each state in our zip_codes table. If we want to order the results by the number of zip codes, our ORDER BY clause can contain either the column number or the grouping function.

```
SELECT state, count(*)
FROM zip_codes
GROUP BY state
ORDER BY COUNT(*) DESC;


ST   COUNT(*)
--  ----------
NY       4315
PA       4296
TX       4123
CA       3982
```

Sometimes, you don't need to group the data in the same way that we report it. If you are interested in how many grouped rows resulted or in the average number of rows for a particular grouping, you can GROUP BY an expression that does not appear in the SELECT list. For example, if we want to know how our sample data loaded into a table, in order to size that table, we will need to know how many rows, on average, fit into a data block. We get this metadata by counting rows that are grouped on the data block portion of the ROWID — the first 15 characters. Then, we take the average of the resulting counts.

```
SELECT AVG(row_count), MAX(row_count), MIN(row_count)
FROM (SELECT COUNT(*) row_count
      FROM zip_codes
      GROUP BY SUBSTR(rowid,1,15));


AVG(ROW_COUNT) MAX(ROW_COUNT) MIN(ROW_COUNT)
-------------- -------------- --------------
    30.7509418             44              6
```

The subquery in the FROM clause returns one count for each data block. We'll cover subqueries in more detail in Chapter 3, "*Displaying Data From Multiple Tables*," but we treat this subquery as if it were a view. Here, we see that we average about 31 rows per data block. It's then a simple extrapolation to approximate how many data blocks we will need to load an arbitrary number of rows.

Limiting Grouped Data with HAVING

You've just seen grouping functions in the SELECT and ORDER BY clauses of queries. These are the only two clauses in which group functions can occur. Group functions cannot be used in the WHERE clause. For example, if we want to query the average sales per sales clerk in the outside sales department and only return those with over $100,000 in gross sales, we would have trouble with the following query:

```
SELECT sales_clerk, SUM(sale_amount)
FROM gross_sales
WHERE sales_dept='OUTSIDE'
  AND  SUM(sale_amount) > 100000
```

```
GROUP BY sales_clerk
```

The database doesn't know what the SUM is when extracting the rows from the table — remember that the grouping is done after all rows have been fetched. We get an exception when we try to use SUM in the WHERE clause. The correct way to get the requested information would be to instruct the database to group all the rows, then limit the output of those grouped rows. We do this with the HAVING clause:

```
SELECT sales_clerk, SUM(sale_amount)
FROM gross_sales
WHERE sales_dept='OUTSIDE'
GROUP BY sales_clerk
HAVING SUM(sale_amount) > 100000
```

As you can see in the previous query, a SQL statement can have both a WHERE clause and a HAVING clause. WHERE filters data before grouping; HAVING filters data after grouping.

You might encounter an exam question that tests whether you will recognize an incorrectly placed group function in the WHERE clause.

Unlike single-row functions, you cannot use programmer-written functions on grouped data.

Nesting Functions

Functions can be *nested* so that the output from one function is used as input to another. Operators have an inherent precedence of execution, but function precedence is based on position only. Functions are evaluated innermost to outermost and left to right. This nesting technique is common with some functions, such as DECODE, and it can be used to implement limited IF...THEN...ELSE logic within a SQL statement. For example, the v$sysstat view contains one row for each of three interesting sort statistics. If you want to report all three statistics on a single line, you can use DECODE combined with SUM to filter out data in the SELECT clause. This filtering operation is usually done in the WHERE or HAVING clause, but if you want all three stats on one line, you can issue this command:

```
SELECT SUM(DECODE(name,'sorts (memory)',value,0)) in_
memory
      ,SUM(DECODE(name,'sorts (disk)',  value,0)) on_disk
      ,SUM(DECODE(name,'sorts (rows)',  value,0)) rows_
sorted
```

```
FROM v$sysstat

IN_MEMORY ON_DISK ROWS_SORTED
--------- ------- -----------
      728      12      326714
```

What happens in the previous statement is a single pass through the v$sysstat table. The pre-summary result set would have the same number of rows as v$sysstat (177, for instance). Of these 177 rows, all rows and columns have zeros, except for one row in each column which has the data of interest (see Table 2.11). The summation operation then adds all the zeros to your interesting data and gives you the results you want.

TABLE 2.11   Pre-Summarized Result Set

in_memory	on_disk	rows_sorted
0	0	0
0	12	0
0	0	0
0	0	326714
728	0	0
0	0	0

Another example of nesting DECODE and a group function is this example, using MAX and nested DECODEs:

```
SELECT owner ,table_name ,grantor ,grantee
,MAX(DECODE(privilege,'SELECT',DECODE(grantable,'YES','g',
'Y'),' '))SEL
,MAX(DECODE(privilege,'INSERT',DECODE(grantable,'YES','g',
'Y'),' '))INS
,MAX(DECODE(privilege,'UPDATE',DECODE(grantable,'YES','g',
'Y'),' '))UPD
```

```
,MAX(DECODE(privilege,'DELETE',DECODE(grantable,'YES','g',
'Y'),' '))DEL
FROM dba_tab_privs
WHERE table_name = UPPER('&TableName')
GROUP BY owner ,table_name ,grantor ,grantee
ORDER BY grantee, table_name;
```

```
OWNER   TABLE_NAME        GRANTOR   GRANTEE   S I U D
------  ----------------  --------  --------  - - - -
CHIPD   ZIP_STATE_CITY    CHIPD     SCOTT     g Y Y
```

In this example, we want to report select, insert, update, and delete privileges
on a table, with a single table per line instead of a single privilege per line. This
statement will report a g if the privilege was granted with the grant option, a Y
if the privilege was granted without the grant option, and a space if the privilege
was not granted. This example takes advantage of the ordinal progression from
space to Y to g: ' '< 'Y'< 'g'.

Nested functions can include single-row functions nested within group
functions, as you've just seen, or group functions nested within either single-
row functions or other group functions. For example, imagine that you need
to report on the departments in the EMP table, showing either the number
of jobs or the number of managers, which ever is greater. You would enter
the following:

```
SELECT deptno, GREATEST(COUNT(DISTINCT job),
COUNT(DISTINCT mgr)) cnt
      ,COUNT(DISTINCT job) jobs
      ,COUNT(DISTINCT mgr) mgrs
FROM emp
GROUP BY deptno;
```

DEPTNO	CNT	JOBS	MGRS
10	4	4	2
20	4	3	4
30	3	3	2

You can also nest group functions within group functions. To report the maximum number of jobs in a single department, you would query:

```
SELECT MAX(COUNT(DISTINCT job))
FROM emp
GROUP BY deptno;


MAX(COUNT(DISTINCTJOB))
-----------------------
                      4
```

Summary

This chapter introduced single-row functions and group functions. You read that single-row functions return a value for each row as it is retrieved from the table, and group functions return a value after all rows have been fetched and grouped. Functions can be nested so that the output of one is the input to another. Single-row functions can be nested in other single row functions or in group functions, and group functions can be nested in single row functions or in other group functions.

Single-row functions can be used in the SELECT, WHERE, and ORDER BY clauses of SELECT statements. We covered the rich assortment of functions available in each datatype and some functions that work on any datatype. When the built-in functions don't quite fit the bill, you can use programmer-written functions, but only with the restrictions we noted.

Group functions can be used in the SELECT, HAVING, and ORDER BY clauses of SELECT statements. Group functions can be applied to all data values or only to the distinct data values. Except for COUNT(*), group functions ignore NULLs. Programmer-written functions cannot be used as group functions.

The topics covered in this chapter that are likely to be on the exam include the following:

- The NVL function—both using it and the effects of failing to use it

- The format models for converting dates to/from character strings

- The DECODE function

- Mistakenly putting a group function in the WHERE clause

Key Terms

Before you take the exam, make sure you're familiar with the following terms:

Aggregate functions

NLS

NULL

ROWID

Single-row functions

Review Questions

1. You want to display each project's start date as the day, week, number, and year. Which statement will give output like the following?

   ```
   Tuesday  Week 23, 1997
   ```

   A. Select proj_id, to_char(start_date, 'DOW Week WOY YYYY') from projects

   B. Select proj_id, to_char(start_date, 'Day'||' Week'||' WOY, YYYY') from projects;

   C. Select proj_id, to_char(start_date, 'Day" Week" WW, YYYY') from projects;

   D. Select proj_id, to_char(start_date, 'Day Week# , YYYY') from projects;

   E. You can't calculate week numbers with Oracle.

2. What will the following statement return?

   ```
   SELECT last_name, first_name, start_date FROM employees
   WHERE hire_date < TRUNC(sysdate) - 5;
   ```

   A. Employees hired in the past 5 years

   B. Employees hired in the past 5 days

   C. Employees hired more than 5 years ago

   D. Employees hired more than 5 days ago

3. Which assertion about the following statements is most true?

```
SELECT name, region_code||phone_number  FROM customers;
SELECT name, CONCAT(region_code,phone_number) FROM
customers;
```

    A. If the region_code is NULL, the first statement will not include that customer's phone_number.

    B. If the region_code is NULL, the second statement will not include that customer's phone_number.

    C. Both statements will return the same data.

    D. The second statement will raise an exception if the region_code is NULL for any customer.

4. Which single-row function could you use to return a specific portion of a character string?

    A. INSTR

    B. SUBSTR

    C. LPAD

    D. LEAST

5. The sales department is simplifying the pricing policy for all products. All surcharges are being incorporated into the base price for all products in the consumer division (code C), and the new base price is increasing by the lesser of 0.5% of the old base price or 10% of the old surcharge. Using the following PRODUCT table, you need to implement this change.

Column Name	sku	name	division	base_price	surcharge
Key Type	pk				
NULLs/Unique	NN	NN	NN	NN	
FK Table					
Datatype	number	varchar2	varchar2	number	number
Length	16	16	4	11,2	11,2

Which of the following statements will achieve the desired results?

A. UPDATE product SET
```
    base_price = base_price + surcharge +
          LEAST(base_price * 0.005 ,surcharge * 0.1)
    ,surcharge = NULL
    WHERE division='C'
```

B. UPDATE product SET
```
    base_price = base_price + NVL(surcharge,0) +
          LEAST(base_price * 0.005 ,surcharge * 0.1)
    ,surcharge = NULL
    WHERE division='C'
```

C. UPDATE product SET
```
    base_price = base_price + NVL(surcharge,0) +
          LEAST(base_price * 0.005 ,NVL(surcharge,0) * 0.1)
    ,surcharge = NULL
    WHERE division='C'
```

D. A, B, and C will all achieve the desired results.

E. None of these statements will achieve the desired results.

6. Which function(s) accept arguments of any datatype? Select all that apply.

   A. SUBSTR

   B. NVL

   C. ROUND

   D. DECODE

   E. SIGN

7. What will be returned from SIGN(ABS(NVL(-32,0)))?

   A. 1

   B. 32

   C. −1

   D. 0

   E. NULL

8. How will the results of the following two statements differ?

```
Statement 1:
SELECT MAX(longitude), MAX(latitude)
FROM zip_state_city;
```

```
Statement 2:
SELECT MAX(longitude), MAX(latitude)
FROM zip_state_city
GROUP BY state;
```

   A. Statement 1 will fail because it is missing a GROUP BY clause.

   B. Statement 2 will return one row, and Statement 1 may return more than one row.

   C. Statement 2 will display a longitude and latitude for each zip_state_city.

   D. Statement 1 will display two values, and Statement 2 will display two values for each state.

9. Which functions could you use to strip leading characters from a character string? Select two.

A. LTRIM

B. SUBSTR

C. RTRIM

D. INSTR

E. MOD

10. Using the following SALES table, you need to report the following:

- Gross, net, and earned revenue

- For the second and third quarters of 1999

- For sales in the states Illinois, California, and Texas (codes IL, CA, and TX)

Column Name	state_code	sales_date	gross	net	earned
Key Type	pk	pk			
NULLs/Unique	NN	NN	NN	NN	NN
FK Table					
Datatype	varchar2	date	number	number	number
Length	2		11,2	11,2	11,2

Which sales data do you report if you issue the following SQL statement?

```
SELECT state_code, SUM(ALL gross), SUM(net),
```

```
SUM(earned)
FROM sales_detail
WHERE TRUNC(sales_date, 'Q') BETWEEN
                  TO_DATE('01-Apr-1999','DD-Mon-YYYY')
              AND TO_DATE('01-Sep-1999','DD-Mon-YYYY')
  AND  state_cd IN ('IL','CA','TX')
GROUP BY state_code
```

A. Data that meets all three requirements

B. Data that meets two of the three requirements

C. Data that meets one of the three requirements

D. Data that meets none of the three requirements

E. You get an exception.

11. Which assertion about the following queries is true?

```
SELECT COUNT(DISTINCT mgr) , MAX(DISTINCT salary) FROM
emp;
SELECT COUNT(ALL mgr) , MAX(ALL salary) FROM emp;
```

A. They will always return the same numbers in columns 1 and 2.

B. They may return different numbers in column 1 but will always return the same number in column 2.

C. They may return different numbers in column 1 and may return different numbers in column 2.

D. They will always return the same number in column 1 but may return different numbers in column 2.

12. What will the following query report?

```
SELECT deptno, COUNT(*) FROM emp GROUP BY deptno;
```

A. The number of employees in each department, including those without a deptno.

B. The number of employees in each department, except those without a deptno.

C. The total number of employees, including those without a deptno.

D. The total number of employees, except those without a deptno.

13. Which of the following is not a group function?

    A. AVG()

    B. COUNT()

    C. LEAST()

    D. STDDEV()

    E. VARIANCE()

14. If it is 5 minutes past noon on 15 Jan 2000, what will the following statement return?

```
SELECT ROUND(SYSDATE) - ROUND(SYSDATE,'Y') FROM dual;
```

    A. 15.5

    B. 15

    C. 0

    D. 16

15. In Oracle, what do trigonometric functions operate on?

    A. Degrees

    B. Radians

    C. Gradients

    D. The default is radians, but degrees or gradients can be specified.

16. Which statement about nested functions is most correct?

    A. Single-row nested functions can be nested in either single-row or group functions.

    B. Group functions can be nested in other group functions.

    C. Group functions can be nested in single-row functions.

    D. A, B, and C

    E. A and B only

17. Why does the following SELECT statement fail?

```
SELECT colorname Colour, MAX(cost)
FROM itemdetail
WHERE UPPER(colorname) LIKE '%WHITE%'
GROUP BY colour
HAVING COUNT(*) > 20;
```

A. A GROUP BY clause cannot contain a column alias.

B. The condition COUNT(*) > 20 should be in the WHERE clause.

C. The GROUP BY clause must contain the group functions used in the SELECT list.

D. The HAVING clause can only contain the group functions used in the SELECT list.

18. What will the following query return?

```
SELECT REPLACE(RTRIM('Anticipation','on'),'ti','shun')
FROM dual;
```

A. Antincipashun

B. Anshuncipashun

C. Anshuncipashunon

D. Anticipashunon

19. Why will the following query raise an exception?

```
select dept_no, avg(distinct salary), count(job) job_
count
from emp
where mgr like 'J%'
   or  abs(salary) > 10
having count(job) > 5
order by 2 desc;
```

A. A HAVING clause cannot contain a group function.

B. The GROUP BY clause is missing.

C. abs() is not an Oracle function.

D. The query will not raise an exception.

20. Which function implements IF..THEN…ELSE logic?

A. INITCAP()

B. REPLACE()

C. DECODE()

D. IFELSE()

Answers to Review Questions

1. C. Double quotes must surround literal strings like " Week".

2. D. The TRUNC function removes the time portion of a date by default, and whole numbers added to or subtracted from dates represent days added or subtracted from that date. TRUNC(sysdate) -5 means five days ago at midnight.

3. C . Both statements are equivalent.

4. B. INSTR returns a number; LPAD adds to a character string; LEAST does not change an input string.

5. C. Statements A and B do not account for NULL surcharges correctly and will set the base price to NULL where the surcharge is NULL.

6. B, D. ROUND does not accept character arguments, SUBSTR only accepts character arguments, and SIGN only accepts numeric arguments.

7. A. The functions are evaluated from the innermost to outermost as follows:
SIGN(ABS(NVL(-32,0))) = SIGN(ABS(-32)) = SIGN(32) = 1

8. D. Option B has the statement numbers transposed. This one was intended to be a trick question. You should read all the answers carefully; the exam may have trick questions like this one.

9. A, B . RTRIM removes trailing (not leading) characters. The others return numbers.

10. A. All requirements are met. The gross, net, and earned revenue requirements are satisfied by the SELECT clause. The second and third quarter sales requirement is satisfied by the first predicate of the WHERE clause: Sales date will be truncated to the first day of a quarter, thus 01-Apr-1999 or 01-Jul-1999 for the required quarters (which are both between 01-Apr-1999 and 01-Sep-1999). The state code's requirement is satisfied by the second predicate in the WHERE clause.

11. B. The first column in the first query is counting the distinct mgr values in the table. The first column in the second query is counting all mgr values in the table. If a manager appears twice, the first query will count her one time, but the second will count her twice. Both the first query and second query are selecting the max salary value in the table.

12. A. COUNT(*) is the only group function that includes NULLs, so all employees will be represented in the grouped data. You will not get a total count for all employees, because the data will be grouped by deptno: There will be one line for each deptno that appears in the EMP table and then one more line for a NULL deptno.

13. C. LEAST is a single-row function.

14. B. The first date will round up to the next day, since its input date is after noon, and the second date will round to the first day of the year. The statement would resolve to 16-Jan-2000 – 01-Jan-2000, which is 15 days (16 – 1).

15. B. Oracle trigonometric functions only operate on radians.

16. D. Any class of function can be nested in any other class of function.

17. A. A GROUP BY clause must contain the column or expressions on which to perform the grouping operation; it cannot use column aliasing.

18. B. First, the RTRIM function removes the trailing *on*, then REPLACE swaps all occurrences of *ti* with *shun*. There are two occurrences of *ti*.

19. B. There is at least one column in the select list that is not a constant or group function, so a GROUP BY clause is mandatory.

20. C. There is no IFELSE function. The INITCAP function capitalizes the first letter in each word. The REPLACE function performs search and replace string operations. The DECODE function is the one that implements IF...THEN...ELSE logic.

Joins and Subqueries

ORACLE8i SQL AND PL/SQL EXAM OBJECTIVES OFFERED IN THIS CHAPTER:

✓ Display data from multiple tables

✓ Write SELECT statements to access data from more than one table using equality and non-equality joins

✓ View data that generally does not meet a join condition by using outer joins

✓ Join a table to itself

✓ Describe the types of problems that subqueries can solve

✓ List types of subqueries

✓ Write single-row and multiple-row subqueries

✓ Write multiple-column subqueries

✓ Describe behavior of subqueries when NULL values are returned

✓ Write subqueries in a FROM clause

Exam objectives are subject to change at any time without prior notice and at Oracle's sole discretion. Please visit Oracle's Training and Certification Web site (http://education.oracle.com/certification/index.html) for the most current exam objectives listing.

A database has many tables that store data. In Chapter 1, you saw how to write simple queries that select data from one table. The ability to join two or more related tables and access information is the core strength of relational databases. Using the SELECT statement, you can write advanced queries that satisfy user requirements. This chapter focuses on querying data from more than one table using table joins and subqueries. A subquery is a query inside another query. Oracle8i has enhanced capabilities for defining the subqueries.

Multiple Table Queries

In Relational Database Management Systems, data stored in different tables is related. You use the power of SQL to relate the information and query data. A SELECT statement has a mandatory SELECT clause and FROM clause. The SELECT clause can have a list of columns, expressions, functions, and so on. The FROM clause tells you which table(s) to look in for the required information. So far, you have seen only one table in the FROM clause; in this chapter, you will learn how to retrieve data from more than one table.

In order to query data from more than one table, you need to identify a common column that relates the two tables. In the WHERE clause, you define the relationship between the tables listed in the FROM clause using comparison operators.

A join is a query that combines rows from two or more tables or views. Oracle performs a join whenever multiple tables appear in the query's FROM clause. The query's SELECT clause can have the columns or expressions from any or all of these tables.

Most of the example queries in this chapter are based on the EMP and DEPT tables. You can see the structure of these tables in Figure 3.1 and the sample data that we will use in Figure 3.2.

FIGURE 3.1   Structure of EMP and DEPT tables

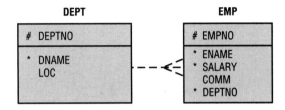

FIGURE 3.2   Data for EMP and DEPT tables

```
SQL> SELECT * FROM dept:
```

DEPTNO	DNAME	LOC
10	ACCOUNTING	NEW YORK
20	RESEARCH	DALLAS
30	SALES	CHICAGO
40	OPERATIONS	BOSTON
50	PAYROLL	DALLAS

```
SQL> SELECT * FROM emp:
```

EMPNO	ENAME	SALARY	COMM	DEPTNO
7566	JONES	2975		20
7654	MARTIN	1250	1400	30
7698	K_BLAKE	2850		30
7788	SCOTT	3000		20
7839	A_EDWARD	5000	50000	10
7844	TURNER	1500	0	30
902	FORD	3000		20

7 rows selected

```
SQL>
```

Take a look at the figures. How would you list the department name and location for each employee, along with his or her salary? The department name and location are in the DEPT table, the employee name and salary are in the EMP table. So, to list the information together in one query, you need to do a join. The DEPTNO column is common to both tables; use this column to relate the rows.

```
SQL> SELECT dname, loc, ename, salary
     FROM   dept, emp
     WHERE  dept.deptno = emp.deptno;


DNAME              LOC               ENAME          SALARY
--------------     --------------    ----------     ----------

RESEARCH           DALLAS            JONES            2975
SALES              CHICAGO           MARTIN           1250
SALES              CHICAGO           K_BLAKE          2850
RESEARCH           DALLAS            SCOTT            3000
ACCOUNTING         NEW YORK          A_EDWARD         5000
SALES              CHICAGO           TURNER           1500
RESEARCH           DALLAS            FORD             3000


7 rows selected.

SQL>
```

Here data is selected from two tables: EMP and DEPT. The department number (DEPTNO) is the relation. Notice that in the WHERE clause, the column names are qualified by the table name; this is required to avoid ambiguity, because the column names are the same in both tables. If the column names are different in each table, you need not *qualify* the column names. Just as you can provide column alias names, you can alias table names, also. Aliases improve the readability of the code, and they can be short names that are easy to type and use as references. The table alias name is given next to the table name. The table can be qualified by specifying its owner (schema). You can use the schema name to qualify a table and the table name to qualify a column. The following example uses alias names d and e for DEPT and EMP tables and uses them to qualify the column names:

```
SQL> SELECT d.dname, d.loc, e.ename, e.salary
     FROM   dept d, emp e
     WHERE  d.deptno = e.deptno
     ORDER BY d.dname;
```

Once table alias names are defined, you cannot use the table name to qualify a column. You should use the alias name to qualify the column. You should not qualify the table or alias name used to qualify the column. For example, the following column qualification is invalid: SELECT scott.emp.ename from EMP;. It should be SELECT emp.ename FROM scott.emp;.

To execute a join of three or more tables, Oracle takes these steps:

1. Oracle joins two of the tables based on the join conditions, comparing their columns.

2. Oracle joins the result to another table, based on join conditions.

3. Oracle continues this process until all tables are joined into the result.

The join query can also contain other conditions in the WHERE clause to restrict rows based on a column in one table. Here's an example:

```
SQL> SELECT dname department, d.loc location, e.ename
name, e.salary
    FROM dept d, emp e
    WHERE d.deptno = e.deptno
  * AND    comm IS NOT NULL
SQL> /
```

DEPARTMENT	LOCATION	NAME	SALARY
SALES	CHICAGO	MARTIN	1250
ACCOUNTING	NEW YORK	A_EDWARD	5000
SALES	CHICAGO	TURNER	1500

```
SQL>
```

Equality and Non-Equality Joins

If the query is relating two tables using an equality operator (=), it is an equality join, also known as an *inner join* or an *equijoin*. If any other operator is used to join the tables in the query, it is a *non-equality join*. You have already seen examples of equality joins; let's consider an example of non-equality join. The EMP table has a column named SALARY; the GRADES table has the range of salary values that correspond to each grade.

```
SQL> SELECT * FROM grades;

GRADE   LOW_SALARY HIGH_SALARY
------- ---------- -----------
P5               0        1200
P4            1201        1400
P3            1401        2000
P2            2001        3000
P1            3001

SQL>
```

To find out which grade each employee belongs to, use this query:

```
SQL> SELECT empno, ename, salary, grade
     FROM    emp e, grades g
     WHERE   e.salary BETWEEN g.low_salary
             AND decode(g.grade, 'P1', 999999, g.high_
salary)
   * ORDER BY salary
SQL> /

    EMPNO ENAME           SALARY GRADE
---------- ---------- ---------- -------
      7654 MARTIN           1250 P4
      7844 TURNER           1500 P3
      7698 K_BLAKE          2850 P2
      7566 JONES            2975 P2
      7788 SCOTT            3000 P2
       902 FORD             3000 P2
      7839 A_EDWARD         5000 P1

7 rows selected.

SQL>
```

Since the upper range of grade P1 is NULL, we have substituted a large value of 999999 in the query using the DECODE function.

Cartesian Joins

A *Cartesian join* occurs when data is selected from two or more tables and there is no common relation specified in the WHERE clause. If you do not specify a join condition for the tables listed in the FROM clause, Oracle joins each row from the first table to every row in the second table. If the first table has three rows and the second table has four rows, the result will have 12 rows. Suppose you add another table with two rows without specifying a join condition; the result will have 24 rows. You should avoid Cartesian joins; for the most part, they happen when there are many tables in the FROM clause and developers forget to include the join condition.

The following example queries the EMP and DEPT tables to illustrate the Cartesian product. For each row in the DEPT table satisfying the WHERE clause, a row from the EMP table is retrieved and joined to.

```
SQL> SELECT d.deptno, e.deptno, e.empno, e.ename
    FROM   dept d, emp e
  * WHERE  e.deptno IN (10, 20)
SQL> /

    DEPTNO     DEPTNO      EMPNO ENAME
---------- ---------- ---------- ----------
        10         20       7566 JONES
        20         20       7566 JONES
        30         20       7566 JONES
        40         20       7566 JONES
        10         20       7788 SCOTT
        20         20       7788 SCOTT
        30         20       7788 SCOTT
        40         20       7788 SCOTT
        10         10       7839 A_EDWARD
        20         10       7839 A_EDWARD
        30         10       7839 A_EDWARD
        40         10       7839 A_EDWARD
```

10	20	902 FORD
20	20	902 FORD
30	20	902 FORD
40	20	902 FORD

16 rows selected.

SQL>

In this example, we have limited the number of rows using the WHERE condition. Because none of the columns in EMP table is joined with DEPT, for each row in DEPT, all rows in EMP are returned.

To avoid a Cartesian join, there should be at least $n - 1$ join conditions when joining n tables.

If a Cartesian join is made between a table having m rows and another table having n rows, the resulting query will have $m \times n$ rows.

Outer Joins

Sometimes, you might want to see the data from one table, even if there is no corresponding row in the joining table. Oracle provides the *outer join* mechanism for this.

The plus symbol surrounded by parentheses ((+)) denotes an outer join in the query. Enter (+) beside the column name of the table, where there may not be a corresponding row. For example, to write a query that performs an outer join of tables A and B and returns all rows from A, apply the outer-join operator (+) to all columns of B in the join condition. For all rows in A that have no matching rows in B, the query returns NULL values for the columns in B.

Consider our example tables EMP and DEPT. There is no employee in the EMP table that belongs to department 40. Let's do an outer join query to display all departments, even if there are no employees:

```
SQL> SELECT D.deptno, E.empno, E.ename
     FROM   dept D, emp E
     WHERE  D.deptno = E.deptno (+);
```

```
  DEPTNO      EMPNO ENAME
---------- ---------- ----------
        10       7839 A_EDWARD
        20       7566 JONES
        20        902 FORD
        20       7788 SCOTT
        30       7654 MARTIN
        30       7698 K_BLAKE
        30       7844 TURNER
        40
```

8 rows selected.

SQL>

The outer-join operator (+) can appear only in the WHERE clause. If there are multiple join conditions between the tables, the outer-join operator should be used against all of the conditions.

An outer join (containing the (+) operator) cannot be combined with another condition using the OR or IN logical operators. For example, the following query is not valid:

```
SQL> SELECT D.deptno, E.empno, E.ename
    FROM    dept D, emp E
    WHERE   D.deptno = E.deptno (+)
  * OR      E.salary > 4000
SQL> /
WHERE  D.deptno = E.deptno (+)
                        *
ERROR at line 3:
ORA-01719: outer join operator (+) not allowed in operand
of OR or IN
```

SQL>

Self-Join

A *self-join* joins a table to itself. The table name appears in the FROM clause twice, with different alias names. The two aliases are treated as two different tables, and they are joined as you would join any other tables, using one or more related columns. The following example lists the president name and predecessor name from the table PRESIDENTS:

```
SQL> DESCRIBE PRESIDENTS
 Name                                   Null?    Type
 ------------------------------------- -------- ----
 INITIALS                                        VARCHAR2(3)
 NAME                                            VARCHAR2(40)
 BIRTH_DATE                                      DATE
 PREDECESSOR                                     VARCHAR2(3)

SQL> SELECT * FROM presidents;

INI NAME                                        BIRTH_DATE  PRE
--- --------------------------------------- ----------- ---
BC  Bill Clinton                                19-AUG-1946 GB
GB  George Bush                                 12-JUN-1924 RR
RR  Ronald Reagan                              06-FEB-1911 JC
JC  Jimmy Carter                               01-OCT-1924 GF

SQL> SELECT a.name "President Name", b.name "Predecessor
Name"
    FROM    presidents a, presidents b
  * WHERE   a.predecessor = b.initials
SQL> /

President Name                    Predecessor Name
------------------------- -------------------------
Bill Clinton                      George Bush
Ronald Reagan                     Jimmy Carter
George Bush                        Ronald Reagan


SQL
```

Using Set Operators

Set operators can be used to select data from multiple tables. Set operators basically combine the result of two queries into one. These queries are known as compound queries. All set operators have equal precedence; when multiple set operators are present in the same query, they are evaluated from left to right unless specified otherwise with parentheses. The datatypes of the resulting columns should match in both queries. Oracle has four set operators, which you can see in Table 3.1.

TABLE 3.1   Oracle Set Operators

Operator	Description
UNION	Returns all unique rows selected by either query
UNION ALL	Returns all rows, including duplicates selected by either query
INTERSECT	Returns rows selected from both queries
MINUS	Returns unique rows selected by the first query but not the rows selected by the second query

Let's consider the tables EAST_ORDERS and WEST_ORDERS as our example to illustrate set operators:

```
SQL> SELECT * FROM EAST_ORDERS;

ORD_DATE    PROD_ID CUSTOMER          QUANTITY
--------- ---------- ---------------- ----------
08-APR-00      1101 BILL                    10
04-APR-00      1102 SCOTT                  210
01-APR-00      1101 SCOTT                   30
08-APR-00      1103 LEEZA                   41
08-APR-00      1103 MARY                    50

SQL> SELECT * FROM WEST_ORDERS;
```

```
ORD_DATE      PROD_ID CUSTOMER          QUANTITY
---------  ----------- ----------------  ----------
18-APR-00     1103 BILL                       15
07-APR-00     1102 MARY                      210
12-APR-00     1101 STEVE                      30
18-APR-00     1103 SCOTT                      50

SQL>
```

The UNION operator is used to return rows from either query. Let's find out the names of the company's customers:

```
SQL> SELECT customer FROM east_orders
       UNION
   * SELECT customer FROM west_orders
SQL> /

CUSTOMER
---------------
BILL
LEEZA
MARY
SCOTT
STEVE

SQL>
```

Notice that even though there are total of nine rows in both tables, the query returned only unique values. The UNION ALL operator does not sort or filter the result set; it returns all rows from both queries. Let's consider this SQL:

```
SQL> SELECT customer FROM east_orders
       UNION ALL
   * SELECT customer FROM west_orders
SQL> /
```

```
CUSTOMER
----------------
BILL
SCOTT
SCOTT
LEEZA
MARY
BILL
MARY
STEVE
SCOTT

9 rows selected.

SQL>
```

The INTERSECT operator is used to return the rows returned by both queries. Let's find the customers who do business in the east as well as in the west:

```
SQL> SELECT customer FROM east_orders
       INTERSECT
    * SELECT customer FROM west_orders
SQL> /

CUSTOMER
----------------
BILL
MARY
SCOTT

SQL>
```

Now, let's find the customers who do business in the east but *not* in the west. We can use the MINUS operator for this:

```
SQL> SELECT customer FROM east_orders
       MINUS
    * SELECT customer FROM west_orders
SQL> /
```

```
CUSTOMER
--------------
LEEZA

SQL>
```

Subqueries

A *subquery* is a query within a query. Typically, subqueries appear in the WHERE clause of the SELECT statement. Oracle supports subqueries in the FROM clause and the HAVING clause. A subquery answers the queries that have multiple parts; the subquery answers one part of the question and the parent query answers the other part. You can have any number of subqueries nested; Oracle does not place a limit. The innermost query is evaluated first. If you have to nest more than six subqueries, performance would be better if you were to write a PL/SQL program involving cursors. Subqueries can be used with SELECT, INSERT, UPDATE, or DELETE statements.

Single-Row and Multiple-Row Subqueries

Single-row subqueries return only one row of result. A single-row subquery uses a single-row operator; the common operator is the equality operator (=). In our example tables, to find the name of the employee with the highest salary, you first need to find the highest salary using a subquery, then execute the parent query with the result from the subquery.

```
SQL> SELECT ename, salary
     FROM    EMP
     WHERE   salary = (SELECT MAX(salary) FROM emp);


ENAME          SALARY
---------- ----------
A_EDWARD         5000

SQL>
```

The parent query of a single-row subquery can return more than one row. For example, to find the names of employees who do not work in the same department as SCOTT, you need to find the department where SCOTT works in a subquery, then execute the parent query.

```
SQL> SELECT ename, deptno
     FROM    emp
     WHERE   deptno != (SELECT deptno FROM emp WHERE ename =
     'SCOTT');
```

```
ENAME          DEPTNO
---------- ----------
MARTIN             30
K_BLAKE            30
A_EDWARD           10
TURNER             30

SQL>
```

Multiple-row subqueries return more than one row of result from the sub-query. It is safer to provide the multiple-row operators in the subqueries if you are not sure of the results. In the previous query, if there is more than one employee named SCOTT, the query will fail. The query will omit all the departments where there is a SCOTT present if you use the multiple-row operator. Here's how to convert the query to a multiple-row subquery:

```
SQL> SELECT ename, deptno
     FROM    emp
     WHERE   deptno NOT IN (SELECT deptno FROM emp WHERE
     ename = 'SCOTT');
```

```
ENAME          DEPTNO
---------- ----------
MARTIN             30
K_BLAKE            30
A_EDWARD           10
TURNER             30

SQL>
```

IN is the most commonly used multiple-row subquery operator. Other operators are EXISTS, ANY, and ALL. You may use NOT with all these operators.

Correlated Subqueries

Oracle performs a *correlated subquery* when the subquery references a column from a table referred to in the parent statement. A correlated subquery is evaluated once for each row processed by the parent statement. The parent statement can be a SELECT, UPDATE, or DELETE statement. In the following example, the highest-paid employee of each department is selected. The subquery is executed for each row returned in the parent query. Notice that the parent table column is used with the alias name inside the subquery.

```
SQL> SELECT deptno, ename, salary
     FROM    emp e1
     WHERE   salary = (SELECT MAX(salary) FROM emp
                              WHERE  deptno = e1.deptno)
     ORDER BY deptno;

    DEPTNO ENAME           SALARY
---------- ---------- ----------
        10 A_EDWARD         5000
        20 SCOTT            3000
        20 FORD             3000
        30 K_BLAKE          2850

SQL>
```

Here is an example of correlated subquery using the EXISTS operator. The EXISTS operator checks for the existence of row in the subquery based on the condition. The SELECT clause in the subquery is ignored when using the EXISTS operator. The query lists the names of employees who work with SCOTT. The subquery selects a dummy value of 'x', which is ignored.

```
SQL> SELECT e1.ename, d.dname
     FROM    emp e1, dept d
     WHERE  e1.deptno = d.deptno
     AND EXISTS
     (SELECT 'x' FROM emp e2
     WHERE  e2.ename = 'SCOTT'
   * AND     e2.deptno = e1.deptno)
```

```
SQL> /

ENAME        DNAME
----------   --------------
JONES        RESEARCH
SCOTT        RESEARCH
FORD         RESEARCH

SQL>
```

The column names in the parent queries are available for reference in subqueries. The column names from the tables in the subquery cannot be used in the parent queries. The scope is only the current query level and its subqueries.

Following are some examples of subqueries in other DML statements.

To update the salary of all employees to the maximum salary in the corresponding department (correlated subquery):

```
SQL> UPDATE emp
    SET    salary = (SELECT MAX(salary)
                        FROM   emp e
                        WHERE  e.deptno = emp.deptno);
```

To delete the records of employees whose salary is below the average salary in the department (correlated subquery):

```
SQL> DELETE FROM emp e
    WHERE salary < (SELECT AVG(salary) FROM emp
                        WHERE  deptno = e.deptno);
```

To insert records into a table using a subquery:

```
SQL> INSERT INTO dept
    SELECT * FROM dallas_dept;
```

In 8i, you can even specify a subquery in the VALUES clause of the INSERT statement.

```
SQL> INSERT INTO dept
        VALUES ((SELECT MAX(deptno)+10 FROM dept), 'EDP');
```

NULL Values in Subqueries

A NULL value returned from the subquery is treated as any other NULL value. No two NULL values are equal. If you need to relate the NULL values returned from the subquery, you may need to manipulate the result set with the NVL or DECODE function.

Multiple-Column Subqueries

A subquery is multiple-column when you have more than one column in the SELECT clause of the subquery. *Multiple-column subqueries* are generally used to compare column conditions or in an UPDATE statement. Let's consider an example. Figure 3.3 shows the columns of the tables CUSTOMERS, PRODUCTS, and ORDERS.

FIGURE 3.3 Customer example

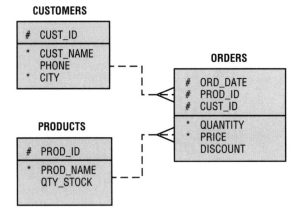

The tables have the following data:

```
SQL> SELECT * FROM customers;

CUST_ CUST_NAME                        PHONE            CITY
----- ------------------------------- ---------------- -----
A0101 Abraham Taylor Jr.                                Fort Worth
B0134 Betty Baylor                     972-555-5555     Dallas
B0135 Brian King                                        Chicago

SQL> SELECT * FROM products;

   PROD_ID PROD_NAME            QTY_STOCK
---------- -------------------- ----------
      1001 Floppy Disk -10 PK        4570
      1002 Floppy Disk -20 PK         324
      1741 CDR - 50 PK                125
      1892 Microsoft Mouse            345
      2001 Oracle 8i EE                 0
      2002 Windows 98
      1045 Zip Disk

SQL> SELECT * FROM orders;

ORD_DATE        PROD_ID CUST_ QUANTITY      PRICE  DISCOUNT
----------- ---------- ----- ---------- ---------- ----------
20-FEB-2000        1741 B0134         5      65.5
02-FEB-2000        1001 B0134        25    2065.85         50
02-FEB-2000        1001 B0135         3                    45

SQL>
```

A multiple-column subquery can be used to find the most recent purchase of a customer whose name starts with Betty. This is also an example of a multiple nested subquery:

```
SQL> SELECT ord_date, cust_name, prod_name, quantity
     FROM   customers c, products p, orders o
     WHERE  o.cust_id = c.cust_id
```

```
    AND    o.prod_id = p.prod_id
    AND    (o.ord_date, o.cust_id) IN
           (SELECT max(ord_date), cust_id
            FROM   orders
            WHERE  cust_id IN (SELECT cust_id FROM customers
                       WHERE upper(cust_name) LIKE 'BETTY%')
  *         GROUP BY cust_id)
SQL>/


ORD_DATE   CUST_NAME                    PROD_NAME            QUANTITY
---------  -------------------------    -------------------  -
20-FEB-00 Betty Baylor                  CDR - 50 PK                5

SQL>
```

The next example updates two columns using a two-column subquery. The objective is to update the ORDERS table for PRICE and DISCOUNT for all records with product 1001, based on the latest price and discount given to customer B0134 for product 1001.

```
SQL> SELECT * FROM orders;

ORD_DATE       PROD_ID CUST_   QUANTITY      PRICE   DISCOUNT
-----------    ----------  -----  ----------  ----------  ----------
20-FEB-2000       1741 B0134          5        65.5
02-FEB-2000       1001 B0134         25     2065.85         50
02-FEB-2000       1001 B0135          3          45

SQL> UPDATE orders o1
SET (price, discount) = (SELECT o1.quantity * o2.price /o2.quantity,
                                o1.quantity * o2.discount /
        o2.quantity
                    FROM   orders o2
              WHERE  (o2.cust_id, o2.prod_id, o2.ord_date) =
             (SELECT o3.cust_id, o3.prod_id, max(o3.ord_date)
                    FROM   orders o3
                    WHERE  prod_id = 1001
```

```
                              AND    cust_id = 'B0134'
                              GROUP BY o3.cust_id, o3.prod_id))
  * WHERE prod_id = 1001
SQL> /

2 rows updated.

SQL> SELECT * FROM orders;

ORD_DATE       PROD_ID CUST_  QUANTITY      PRICE  DISCOUNT
-----------  ---------- -----  ---------- ---------- ----------
20-FEB-2000       1741 B0134          5       65.5
02-FEB-2000       1001 B0134         25    2065.85         50
02-FEB-2000       1001 B0135          3      247.9          6

SQL>
```

Subqueries in the FROM Clause

A subquery can appear in the FROM clause of the SELECT statement. This is similar to defining and using a view. The subquery in the FROM clause is enclosed in parentheses and may be given an alias name. The columns selected in the subquery can be referenced in the parent query, as you would select from any normal table. Let's consider an example. To find the average salary of each department and the difference in salary for each employee respective to the department average, do this:

```
SQL> SELECT e.deptno, e.ename, e.sal salary, a.average,
           e.sal-a.average difference
    FROM    emp e, (SELECT deptno, AVG(sal) average FROM
emp
                 GROUP BY deptno) a
    WHERE  e.deptno = a.deptno
  * ORDER BY 1, 2
SQL> /
```

```
DEPTNO ENAME          SALARY  AVERAGE DIFFERENCE
---------- ----------- ----------- -------- ----------
        10 CLARK          2450    2,917       -467
        10 KING           5000    2,917      2,083
        10 MILLER         1300    2,917     -1,617
        20 ADAMS          1100    2,175     -1,075
        20 FORD           3000    2,175        825
        20 JONES          2975    2,175        800
        20 SCOTT          3000    2,175        825
        20 SMITH           800    2,175     -1,375
        30 ALLEN          1600    1,567         33
        30 BLAKE          2850    1,567      1,283
        30 JAMES           950    1,567       -617
        30 MARTIN         1250    1,567       -317
        30 TURNER         1500    1,567        -67
        30 WARD           1250    1,567       -317

14 rows selected.

SQL>
```

You can have a subquery in the INSERT, UPDATE, and DELETE statements in place of the table name. Here's an example: DELETE FROM (SELECT * FROM dept WHERE deptno < 20) WHERE deptno = 10;

The subquery can have an optional WITH clause. WITH CHECK OPTION specifies that, if the subquery is used in place of a table in an INSERT, UPDATE, or DELETE statement, Oracle will not allow any changes to that table that would produce rows that are not included in the subquery. WITH READ ONLY specifies that the subquery cannot be updated. Let's look at an example:

```
SQL> INSERT INTO (SELECT * FROM dept WHERE deptno < 20)
     VALUES (30, 'MARKETING');

1 row created.

SQL> INSERT INTO (SELECT * FROM dept WHERE deptno < 20
WITH CHECK OPTION)
     VALUES (40, 'EDP');
```

```
INSERT INTO (SELECT * FROM dept WHERE deptno < 20 WITH
CHECK OPTION)
                              *
ERROR at line 1:
ORA-01402: view WITH CHECK OPTION where-clause violation


SQL>
```

You cannot have an ORDER BY clause in the subquery appearing in a WHERE clause. A FROM clause subquery can have an ORDER BY clause.

Summary

Joins are used to relate two or more tables or views. In a relational database, it is common to have a requirement to join data. The tables are joined by using a common column in the tables in the WHERE clause of the query. If the join condition uses the equality operator (= or IN), it is known as an equality join. If any other operator is used to join the tables, it is a non-equality join. If you do not specify any join condition between the tables, the result will be a Cartesian product: each row from the first table joined to every row in the second table. To avoid Cartesian joins, there should be at least $n-1$ join conditions in the WHERE clause when there are n tables in the FROM clause. A table can be joined to itself. If you wish to select the results from a table, even if there are no corresponding rows in the joined table, you can use the outer join operator: (+).

A subquery is a query within a query. Writing subqueries is a powerful way to manipulate data. You can write single-row and multiple-row subqueries. Single-row subqueries must return zero or one row; multiple-row subqueries return zero or more than one row. IN and EXISTS are the most commonly used subquery operators. Subqueries can appear in the WHERE clause or in the FROM clause; they can also replace table names in DELETE, INSERT, and UPDATE statements.

Key Terms

Before you take the exam, make sure you're familiar with the following terms:

Cartesian join

Correlated subquery

Outer join

Qualify

Self-join

Subquery

Review Questions

1. Which line of code has an error?

   A. SELECT dname, ename

   B. FROM   emp e, dept d

   C. WHERE   emp.deptno = dept.deptno

   D. ORDER BY 1, 2;

2. What will be the result of the following query?

   ```
   SELECT c.cust_id, c.cust_name, o.ord_date, o.prod_id
   FROM    customers c, orders o
   WHERE   c.cust_id = o.cust_id (+);
   ```

   A. List all the customer names in the CUSTOMERS table and the orders each customer made from the ORDERS table, even if the customer has not placed an order.

   B. List only the names of customers from the CUSTOMERS table who have placed an order in the ORDERS table.

   C. List all orders from the ORDERS table, even if there is no valid customer record in the CUSTOMERS table.

   D. For each record in the CUSTOMERS table, list the information from the ORDERS table.

3. The CUSTOMERS and ORDERS tables have the following data:

```
SQL> SELECT * FROM customers;

CUST_ CUST_NAME                              PHONE           CITY
----- ------------------------------- --------------- --
A0101 Abraham Taylor Jr.                              Fort Worth
B0134 Betty Baylor                    972-555-5555    Dallas
B0135 Brian King                                      Chicago

SQL> SELECT * FROM orders;

ORD_DATE   PROD_ID CUST_ID QUANTITY   PRICE  DISCOUNT
--------- ---------- ------- ---------- ---------- -------
20-FEB-00     1741 B0134     5        65.5
02-FEB-00     1001 B0134    25        2065.85   50
02-FEB-00     1001 B0135     3        247.9     6
```

When the following query is executed, what will be the value of *PROD_ID* and *ORD_DATE* for the customer "Abraham Taylor Jr."?

```
SELECT c.cust_id, c.cust_name, o.ord_date, o.prod_id
FROM   customers c, orders o
WHERE  c.cust_id = o.cust_id (+);
```

A. NULL, 01-JAN-01

B. NULL, NULL

C. 1001, 02-FEB-00

D. The query will not return customer "Abraham Taylor Jr.".

4. Consider the following query:

```
SELECT dname, ename
FROM    dept d, emp e
WHERE   d.deptno = e.deptno
ORDER BY dname, ename;
```

What type of join is shown?

A. Self-join

B. Equijoin

C. Outer join

D. Non-equijoin

5. When using multiple tables to query information, in which clause do you specify the table names?

A. HAVING

B. GROUP BY

C. WHERE

D. FROM

6. Which two operators are not allowed when using an outer join between two tables?

A. OR

B. AND

C. IN

D. =

7. Which two operators are used to add more joining conditions in a multi-table query?

A. NOT

B. OR

C. AND

D. Comma (,)

8. If you are selecting data from table A (with three rows) and table B (with four rows) using the following query, how many rows will be returned?

```
SELECT A.*, B.*
FROM    A, B;
```

A. 7

B. 1

C. 0

D. 12

9. Refer to the STATE table and its data below.

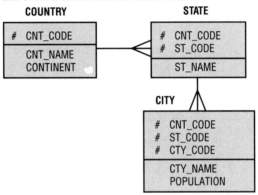

```
SQL> SELECT * FROM country:

    CNT_CODE  CNT_NAME             CONTINENT
----------- -------------------- ---------
          1  UNITED STATES        N. AMERICA
         91  INDIA                ASIA
         65  SINGAPORE            ASIA

SQL> SELECT * FROM state:

    CNT_CODE  ST_CODE  ST_NAME
----------- ------- --------------------
          1  TX      TEXAS
          1  CA      CALIFORNIA
         91  TN      TAMIL NADU
          1  TN      TENNESEE
         91  KL      KERALA

SQL> SELECT * FROM city:

    CNT_CODE  ST_CODE  CTY_CODE  CTY_NAME       POPULATION
----------- ------- ------------------------ ----------
          1  TX          1001  DALLAS
          1  CA          2243  MADRAS
         91  TN          8099  LOS ANGELES

SQL>
```

Consider the following query:

```
SELECT cnt_code
FROM    state
WHERE   st_name = (SELECT st_name FROM state
                           WHERE   st_code = 'TN');
```

A. The query will return the CNT_CODE for the ST_CODE value 'TN'.

B. The query will fail and will not return any rows.

C. The query will display 1 and 91 as CNT_CODE values.

D. The query will fail because an alias name is not used.

10. Refer to the STATE and CITY tables in Question 9. What is the result of the following query?

```
SELECT st_name "State Name"
FROM    state
WHERE   (cnt_code, st_code) = (SELECT cnt_code, st_code
                                    FROM    city
                                    WHERE   cty_name =
'DALLAS');
```

A. TEXAS

B. The query will fail because CNT_CODE and ST_CODE are not in the WHERE clause of the subquery.

C. The query will fail because more than one column appears in the WHERE clause.

D. TX

11. Which line of code has an error?

```
1  SELECT deptno
2  FROM    emp
3  GROUP BY deptno
4  HAVING COUNT(deptno) =
5  (SELECT max(count(deptno))
6    FROM emp
7    GROUP BY deptno);
```

A. Line 3

B. Line 4

C. Line 5

D. Line 7

E. There is no error.

12. Which query is a correlated subquery?

A. `select cty_name from city`

   `where  st_code in (select st_code from state`

   `where st_name = 'TENNESSEE'`

   `and  city.cnt_code = state.cnt_code);`

B. `select cty_name`

   `from   city`

   `where  st_code in (select st_code from state`

   `where st_name = 'TENNESSEE');`

C. `select cty_name`

   `from city, state`

   `where  city.st_code = state.st_code`

   `and    city.cnt_code = state.cnt_code`

   `and    st_name = 'TENNESSEE';`

D. `select cty_name`

   `from city, state`

   `where  city.st_code = state.st_code (+)`

   `and    city.cnt_code = state.cnt_code (+)`

   `and    st_name = 'TENNESSEE';`

13. What value is returned from the subquery when you execute the following query using the data in Question 9's graphic?

```
SELECT CNT_NAME
FROM   country
WHERE  CNT_CODE = (SELECT MAX(cnt_code) FROM country);
```

A. INDIA

B. 65

C. 91

D. SINGAPORE

14. Which line in the following query contains an error?

```
1 SELECT deptno, ename, sal
2 FROM    emp e1
3 WHERE   sal = (SELECT MAX(sal) FROM emp
4                    WHERE   deptno = e1.deptno
5                    ORDER BY deptno);
```

A. Line 2

B. Line 3

C. Line 4

D. Line 5

15. What is the limit on the number of values a subquery using the IN operator can return to the parent query?

A. 1

B. 32,764

C. Unlimited

D. 0

16. Why does the following query fail? (SCOTT and TIGER are valid schema names in the database.)

```
SELECT scott.emp.ename, tiger.dept.dname
FROM    scott.emp, tiger.dept
WHERE   emp.deptno = dept.deptno
ORDER BY 2, 1;
```

A. You cannot query two tables belonging to two different owners.

B. You should not specify the schema name to qualify the column names.

C. The ORDER BY clause should have 1, 2 when specifying by position.

D. An alias name not used to query multiple schema owner tables.

17. Consider the following query:

```
SELECT deptno, ename, salary salary, average,
       salary-average difference
FROM   emp, (SELECT deptno dno, AVG(salary) average
FROM emp
              GROUP BY deptno)
WHERE  deptno = dno
ORDER BY 1, 2;
```

Which of the following statements is correct?

A. The query will fail because no alias name is provided for the subquery.

B. The query will fail because a column selected inside the subquery is referenced outside the scope of the subquery.

C. The query will work without errors.

D. GROUP BY cannot be used inside a subquery.

18. Refer to the COUNTRY table in Question 9. What will be result of the following query?

```
INSERT INTO (SELECT cnt_code FROM country
              WHERE continent = 'ASIA')
VALUES (971, 'SAUDI ARABIA', 'ASIA');
```

A. One row will be inserted into COUNTRY table.

B. WITH CHECK OPTION is missing from the subquery.

C. The query will fail because the VALUES clause is invalid.

D. The WHERE clause cannot appear in the subqueries used in INSERT statements.

19. Choose the most appropriate option.

A. A correlated subquery is evaluated for each row in the parent query.

B. A correlated subquery is evaluated once, and the result is used in the parent query.

C. When a correlated subquery is evaluated, the parent query is evaluated for each row in the subquery.

D. The correlated subquery is executed, and each row from the result is evaluated against the parent query.

20. Which line has an error?

```
1  SELECT EMPLOYEE_ID, EMPLOYEE_NAME
2  FROM    (SELECT empno EMPLOYEE_ID, ename EMPLOYEE_
NAME
3              FROM   emp   WHERE salary > 2500 ORDER BY
ename)
4  WHERE EMPLOYEE_NAME LIKE 'K%';
```

A. Line 4

B. Line 2

C. Line 3

D. No line has an error.

Answers to Review Questions

1. C. When table aliases are defined, you should qualify the column names with the table alias only. In this case, the table name cannot be used to qualify column names.

2. A. A (+) indicates an outer join and is used to display the records, even if there are no corresponding records in the table mentioned. Here, the outer-join operator is given next to the ORDERS table, so even if there are no corresponding orders from a customer, the result set will have the customer name.

3. B. When an outer join returns values from a table that does not have corresponding records, a NULL is returned.

4. B. The DEPTNO columns in both tables are related using the equality operator, so this is an equijoin.

5. D. When querying multiple tables, the table names are given in the FROM clause, the column names to query data are listed in the SELECT clause, and the join conditions are specified in the WHERE clause.

6. A, C. OR and IN are not allowed in the outer-join operations. You can use AND and = in the outer join.

7. B, C. The operators OR and AND are used to add more joining conditions to the query. NOT is a negation operator, and a comma is used to separate column names and table names.

8. D. The query does not have a join condition, so the result is a Cartesian product.

9. Refer to the STATE table and its data below.

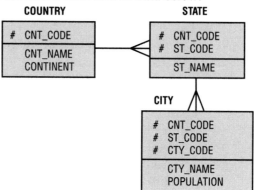

SQL> SELECT * FROM country:

CNT_CODE	CNT_NAME	CONTINENT
1	UNITED STATES	N. AMERICA
91	INDIA	ASIA
65	SINGAPORE	ASIA

SQL> SELECT * FROM state:

CNT_CODE	ST_CODE	ST_NAME
1	TX	TEXAS
1	CA	CALIFORNIA
91	TN	TAMIL NADU
1	TN	TENNESEE
91	KL	KERALA

SQL> SELECT * FROM city:

CNT_CODE	ST_CODE	CTY_CODE	CTY_NAME	POPULATION
1	TX	1001	DALLAS	
1	CA	2243	MADRAS	
91	TN	8099	LOS ANGELES	

SQL>

B. There are two records in the STATE table with the ST_CODE value as 'TN'. Since we are using a single-row operator for the subquery, it will fail. Option C would have been correct if we had used the IN operator instead of = for the subquery.

10. A. The query will succeed, because there is only one row in the city table with CTY_NAME value 'DALLAS'.

11. E. There is no error in the statement. The query will return the department number where the most employees are working.

12. A. A subquery is correlated when a reference is made to a column from a table in the parent statement.

13. C. The subquery returns 91 to the main query.

14. D. You cannot have an ORDER BY clause in the subquery used in a WHERE clause.

15. C. When the IN operator is used, there is no limit on the rows returned by a subquery. If you are using the = operator, only one row can be returned.

16. B. When qualifying the column names, you cannot qualify them with the schema name; only table name or table alias can be used to qualify a column name. The schema name can be used to qualify a table.

17. C. The query will work fine. We do not have to use the alias names because the column names returned from the subquery are different from the parent query.

18. C. Because only one column is selected in the subquery to which we are doing the insert, only one column value should be supplied in the VALUES clause. The VALUES clause can have only CNT_CODE value (971).

19. A. Oracle performs a correlated subquery when the subquery references a column from a table referred to in the parent statement. A correlated subquery is evaluated once for each row processed by the parent statement.

20. D. There is no error in the query. Use of the ORDER BY clause inside the subquery is allowed for subqueries used in the FROM clause.

Chapter

4

Modifying Data and Security

ORACLE8i SQL AND PL/SQL EXAM OBJECTIVES OFFERED IN THIS CHAPTER:

- ✓ Describe each DML statement
- ✓ Insert rows into a table
- ✓ Update rows in a table
- ✓ Delete rows in a table
- ✓ Control transactions with the COMMIT, ROLLBACK, and SAVEPOINT statements
- ✓ Control transactions with the SET TRANSACTION statement
- ✓ Create and modify users
- ✓ Create roles to ease administration of security
- ✓ Describe the difference between system and object privileges
- ✓ Use the GRANT and REVOKE statements to grant and revoke object privileges

Exam objectives are subject to change at any time without prior notice and at Oracle's sole discretion. Please visit Oracle's Training and Certification Web site (http://education.oracle.com/certification/index.html) for the most current exam objectives listing.

In this chapter, we will cover how to

- Change data using SQL and PL/SQL through data manipulation language (DML) statements

- Coordinate multiple changes using transactions

- Allow or prevent changes using privileges and roles

DML Statements

DML is the subset of SQL that is employed to change data. See Table 4.1 for a list of DML *statements* that Oracle supports.

TABLE 4.1 The DML Statements Supported by Oracle

Statement	Purpose
INSERT	Adds rows to a table
UPDATE	Changes the value stored in a table
DELETE	Removes rows from a table
SELECT FOR UPDATE	Prevents other sessions from performing DML on selected rows
LOCK TABLE	Prevents other sessions from performing DML on a table

Inserting Rows into a Table

The INSERT statement is used to add rows to a table. Rows can be added with specific data values, or the rows can be created from existing data using a subquery. Figure 4.1 shows the syntax of the INSERT statement.

FIGURE 4.1 The syntax of the INSERT statement

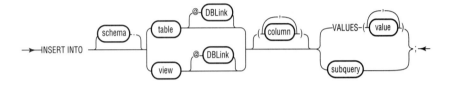

The column list is optional, with the default list of columns being all columns in order of their column_id. The column_id can be seen in the data dictionary views ALL_TAB_COLUMNS, USER_TAB_COLUMNS, or DBA_TAB_COLUMNS. Here are some examples of INSERTs:

```
INSERT INTO checking (account_id, create_date, balance)
    VALUES ('Kiesha' , SYSDATE, 5000);

INSERT INTO brokerage (account_id, create_date, balance)
    SELECT account_id, SYSDATE, 0
    FROM checking
    WHERE account_type = 'C';

INSERT INTO e_checking
    SELECT * from checking
    WHERE account_type = 'C';
```

The number and datatypes of values inserted must match the number and datatype in the column list. Implicit data conversion will be performed if possible to achieve the correct datatypes for the values. A NULL string will implicitly insert a NULL into the appropriate column. The keyword NULL can be used to explicitly assign NULL to a column. The following statements are all equivalent:

```
INSERT INTO customers (cust_id, state, postal_code)
```

```
      VALUES ('Ariel', NULL, '94501');
or

      INSERT INTO customers (cust_id, state, postal_code)
         VALUES ('Ariel',, '94501');
```

Updating Rows in a Table

The UPDATE statement is used to modify existing rows in a table. Figure 4.2 shows the syntax of the UPDATE statement.

FIGURE 4.2 The syntax of the UPDATE statement

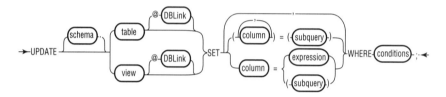

Column_list can be either a single column or a number of columns delimited by commas:

```
UPDATE order_rollup
SET (qty, price) = (SELECT SUM(qty), SUM(price)
                      FROM order_lines
                      WHERE customer_id = 'KOHL')
WHERE customer_id = 'KOHL'
  AND  order_period = TO_DATE('01-Oct-2000');
```

or

```
UPDATE order_rollup
SET phone = '3125551212'
   ,fax   = '7735551212'
WHERE customer_id = 'KOHL';
```

Deleting Rows from a Table

The DELETE statement is used to remove rows from a table. You can see the DELETE statement's syntax in Figure 4.3.

After executing DML, you must execute a COMMIT to make the changes permanent or a ROLLBACK to undo the changes.

FIGURE 4.3 The syntax of the DELETE statement

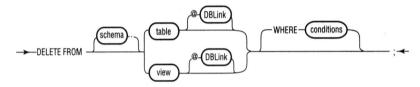

Here are some examples of the DELETE statement:

```
--Remove old orders shipped to some states
DELETE FROM po_lines
WHERE ship_to_state IN ('TX','NY','IL')
 AND  order_date < TRUNC(SYSDATE) - 90

--Remove customer Gomez
DELETE FROM customers
WHERE customer_id = 'GOMEZ';

--Remove duplicate line_detail_ids
--Note keyword FROM is not needed
DELETE line_details
WHERE rowid NOT IN (SELECT MAX(rowid)
                    FROM line_detail
                    GROUP BY line_detail_id)

--Remove all rows from the table order_staging
DELETE FROM order_staging;
```

The WHERE clause is optional; when it is missing, all rows are removed from the table. Removing all rows from a large table can take a long time and require significant rollback segment space. If you are truncating a table, consider using the TRUNCATE statement.

Truncating a Table

If you want to empty a table of all rows, consider the DDL statement TRUNCATE. Like a DELETE statement with no WHERE clause, TRUNCATE will remove all rows from a table. However, TRUNCATE is not DML—it is DDL and therefore has different characteristics from the DELETE statement. Figure 4.4 shows the syntax for TRUNCATE.

FIGURE 4.4 The syntax for the TRUNCATE statement

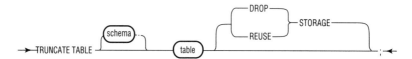

The storage clause is optional, and the default is to DROP STORAGE, which shrinks the table and its indexes down to minextent number of extents and resets the NEXT parameter to the last deallocated extent. In most cases, this space deallocation resets the segments to their original size and original NEXT parameter. REUSE STORAGE will not shrink the table or adjust the NEXT parameter. For example, to remove all rows from the ORDER_STAGING table, shrink the table and indexes to the original size, reset the high-water mark, and commit the change, you could truncate the table as follows:

```
TRUNCATE TABLE order_staging;
```

Alternatively, if you want to keep the storage (so that Oracle doesn't have to reallocate it when you reload the table), remove all rows, reset the high-water mark, and commit the change, you would truncate the table as follows:

```
TRUNCATE TABLE order_staging REUSE STORAGE;
```

The TRUNCATE statement is similar to a DELETE statement without a WHERE clause, except for the following:

- TRUNCATE is very fast on both large and small tables. DELETE will generate undo information, in case a rollback is issued, but TRUNCATE will not generate undo.

- TRUNCATE is DDL and like all DDL, performs an implicit commit—you cannot roll back a TRUNCATE. Any uncommitted DML changes will also be committed with the TRUNCATE.

- TRUNCATE resets the high-water mark in the table and all indexes. Since full table scans and index fast full scans read all data blocks up to the high-water mark, full scan performance after a DELETE will not improve, but after a TRUNCATE it will be very fast.

- TRUNCATE does not fire any DELETE triggers.

- There is no object privilege that can be granted to allow a user to truncate another user's table. The DROP ANY TABLE system privilege is required to truncate a table in another schema. See the "Roles and Privileges" section later in this chapter for more information.

- When a table is truncated, the storage for the table and all indexes can be reset back to the initial size. A DELETE will never shrink the size of a table or its indexes.

- You cannot truncate the parent table from an enabled referential integrity constraint. You must first disable the foreign key constraints that reference the parent table, then you can truncate the parent table.

Compared to dropping and re-creating a table, TRUNCATE does not

- Invalidate dependent objects

- Drop indexes, triggers, or referential integrity constraints

- Require privileges to be regranted again

Understanding the TRUNCATE statement—how it differs from the DELETE statement and especially the fact that it will perform a commit—is important and may appear as an exam question.

Selecting Rows FOR UPDATE

The SELECT...FOR UPDATE statement is used to *lock* specific rows, preventing other sessions from changing or deleting those locked rows. When the rows are locked, other sessions can select these rows, but they cannot change or lock these rows. The syntax for this statement is identical to a SELECT statement, except you append the keywords FOR UPDATE to the statement. The locks acquired for a SELECT...FOR UPDATE will not be released until the transaction ends with a COMMIT or ROLLBACK, even if no data changes.

```
SELECT prod_id, desc, unit_price
FROM   inventory
WHERE  qty < 5
FOR UPDATE;
```

Locking a Table

The LOCK statement is used to lock an entire table, preventing other sessions from performing most or all DML on it. Figure 4.5 shows the LOCK statement's syntax.

FIGURE 4.5 The syntax for the LOCK statement

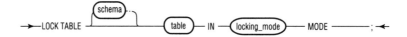

Locking can be in either shared or exclusive mode. Shared mode prevents other sessions from acquiring an exclusive lock but allows other sessions to acquire a shared lock. Exclusive mode prevents other sessions from acquiring either a shared or an exclusive lock.

```
LOCK TABLE inventory IN EXCLUSIVE MODE;
```

Changes to data require an exclusive lock on the rows changed. When table locks are explicitly used, the chances for deadlocks increase. Therefore, use table locks cautiously and sparingly.

Deadlocks

A deadlock occurs when two transactions hold locks and each is waiting for a lock held by the other session. In the example sessions shown in Table 4.2, two users hold clashing locks. Oracle detects this deadlock condition (usually quickly) and raises an exception in one of the sessions. Table 4.2 shows how this works.

TABLE 4.2 Deadlock Detection

Janet's Session	Time Point	Brad's Session
UPDATE customers SET region='H' WHERE state='43' and county='046'; *RX locks acquired for updated rows*	101	

TABLE 4.2 Deadlock Detection *(continued)*

Janet's Session	Time Point	Brad's Session
	102	UPDATE customers SET mgr=4567 WHERE state='47' and county='072'; *RX locks acquired for updated rows*
UPDATE customers SET region='H' WHERE state='47' and county='072'; *Waiting for Brad's transaction to complete*	103	
	104	UPDATE customers SET mgr=4567 WHERE state='43' and county='046'; *Waiting for Janet's transaction to complete*
ERROR at line 1: ORA-00060: dead-lock detected while waiting for resource		

DML Locks in Oracle

Oracle uses DML locks to manage *concurrency*: multiple sessions modifying the same data at the same time. There are two classes of locks:

- Share
- Exclusive

Share locks prevent other exclusive locks; exclusive locks prevent both other share and other exclusive locks. No DML locks, however, prevent read access. Changes to data require an exclusive row-level lock on the rows that are changed. INSERT, UPDATE, and DELETE statements implicitly acquire the necessary row exclusive locks. The five types of locks that Oracle uses are described in the paragraphs that follow and listed in Table 4.3.

Row Share (RS)   This is a row lock, which is acquired implicitly via a SELECT...FOR UPDATE statement or explicitly for no particular row in a table with a LOCK TABLE IN ROW SHARE MODE statement. This lock prevents other sessions from acquiring another RS or an RX lock (INSERT, UPDATE, DELETE) on the rows affected. When acquired on a table, an RS lock does not prevent changes to data rows but does prevent another session from getting an exclusive table lock. An RS lock allows multiple, concurrent RS and RX locks on different rows, as well as table share or SRX locks.

Row Exclusive (RX)   This is a row lock, which is acquired implicitly via an INSERT, UPDATE, or DELETE statement or explicitly for no particular row in a table with a LOCK TABLE IN ROW EXCLUSIVE MODE statement. This lock prevents other sessions from acquiring either an RS or an RX lock (INSERT, UPDATE, DELETE) on the rows affected, as well as preventing all table locks (S, SRX, and X). It allows multiple, concurrent RS and RX locks on different rows.

Share (S)   This is a table lock, which is explicitly acquired with a LOCK TABLE IN SHARE MODE statement. This lock prevents other sessions from acquiring RX locks (INSERT, UPDATE, DELETE) or other table locks (SRX or X). It allows multiple, concurrent RS and S locks on the table. Locking a table in share mode can give your session a transaction-level consistency for the locked table: No other sessions can make changes to the table until you commit and release the table lock.

Share Row Exclusive (SRX)   This is a table lock, which is explicitly acquired with a LOCK TABLE IN SHARE ROW EXCLUSIVE MODE statement. This lock prevents other sessions from acquiring an S, RX, or X lock. It allows other RS locks. It is similar to the S lock, except that only one SRX lock can be placed on a table at a time. If session Y has an SRX lock on a table, session Z can perform a SELECT...FOR UPDATE (RS lock), but session Z will wait if it tries to then update (RX) the rows selected.

Exclusive (X)   This is a table lock, which is explicitly acquired on a table with a LOCK TABLE IN EXCLUSIVE MODE statement. This lock prevents other sessions from acquiring any other share or exclusive locks on the table. It allows only reading operations.

TABLE 4.3   Lock Modes

Lock	Row/ Table	Prevents	Allows	Acquiring Statements
RS (Row Share)	Row or Table	X, RX on the locked rows	RS, S, SRX, RX on the rows not locked	SELECT...FOR UPDATE LOCK TABLE
RX (Row Exclusive)	Row or Table	X, SRX, S, RX on the locked rows	RS, RX on the rows not locked	INSERT UPDATE DELETE LOCK TABLE
S (Share)	Table	X, SRX, RX	RS, S	LOCK TABLE
SRX (Share Row Exclusive)	Table	X, SRX, S, RX	RS	LOCK TABLE
X (Exclusive)	Table	X, SRX, S, RX, RS		LOCK TABLE

Table 4.4 shows two hypothetical sessions: user Alan and user Molly, executing DDL and DML on the same table.

T A B L E 4 . 4 Example Locking Sessions

Molly's Session	Time Point	Alan's Session
UPDATE customers SET region='H' WHERE state='43' and county='046'; *RX locks acquired for updated rows*	201	
	202	TRUNCATE TABLE customers; *ERROR at line 1:* *ORA-00054: resource busy and acquire with NOWAIT specified* **DDL is blocked by the RX lock**
	203	LOCK TABLE customers IN EXCLUSIVE MODE NOWAIT; *...ORA-00054: resource busy...*
	204	LOCK TABLE customers IN EXCLUSIVE MODE; *Waiting for Molly's session*
COMMIT;	205	*Table locked*
UPDATE customers SET region='H' WHERE state='47' and county='072'; *Waiting for Alan's session*	206	
Update complete	207	ROLLBACK;
LOCK TABLE customers IN ROW EXCLUSIVE MODE;	208	

TABLE 4.4 Example Locking Sessions *(continued)*

Molly's Session	Time Point	Alan's Session
	209	LOCK TABLE customers IN SHARE ROW EXCLUSIVE MODE NOWAIT; *...ORA-00054: resource busy...*
	210	LOCK TABLE customers IN ROW EXCLUSIVE MODE;
	211	UPDATE customers SET mgr=4567 WHERE state='43' and county='046';
	212	COMMIT;
UPDATE customers SET region='H' WHERE state='43' and county='046';	213	
COMMIT;	214	
LOCK TABLE customers IN SHARE ROW EXCLUSIVE MODE;	215	
	216	LOCK TABLE customers IN SHARE MODE NOWAIT; *...ORA-00054: resource busy...*
	217	UPDATE customers SET mgr=4567 WHERE state='47' and county='072'; *Waiting on Molly's session*
COMMIT;	218	*Customers updated*

TABLE 4.4 Example Locking Sessions *(continued)*

Molly's Session	Time Point	Alan's Session
SELECT region FROM customers WHERE state='47' and county='072' FOR UPDATE NOWAIT; *...ORA-00054: resource busy...*	219	
	220	COMMIT;
LOCK TABLE customer IN ROW SHARE MODE;	221	
	222	INSERT INTO customer …
	223	COMMIT;
LOCK TABLE customer IN SHARE MODE;	224	
	225	INSERT INTO customer … *Waiting for Molly's session*
COMMIT;	226	
	227	COMMIT;

Transaction Control

Transaction control involves coordinating multiple, concurrent access to the same data. When one session is changing data that another session is accessing, Oracle uses *transactions* to control who has visibility to what changing data, and when they can see that data.

Transactions

Transactions represent an atomic unit of work. All changes to data in a transaction are applied together or rolled back (undone) together. There are a number of statements in SQL and PL/SQL that let the programmer control transactions. The programmer can

- Explicitly begin a transaction, choosing statement-level consistency or transaction-level consistency

- Set undo savepoints and undo changes back to a savepoint

- End a transaction by making the changes permanent or undoing the changes

Table 4.5 explains transaction control statements.

TABLE 4.5 Transaction Control Statements

Statement	Purpose
COMMIT	Ends the current transaction, making data changes permanent and visible to other sessions
ROLLBACK	Undoes all data changes in the current transaction
ROLLBACK TO SAVEPOINT	Undoes all data changes in the current transactions going chronologically backward to the optionally named savepoint
SET TRANSACTION	Enables transaction or statement consistency; specifies named rollback segment for transaction use

Throughout this section, we will use a banking example to clarify transactional concepts and the control statements used to ensure data is changed as designed. In our example, we have a banking customer Kiesha who has a checking account and a brokerage account with her bank. When Kiesha transfers $5,000 from her checking account to her brokerage account, the balance in her checking account is reduced by $5,000, as shown in Figure 4.6, and the cash balance in her brokerage account is increased by $5,000. We cannot allow only one account to change—they must both change or neither must change. To couple these changes, we issued the two update statements and the two log statements in a single transaction. If there is any failure in one of these four statements (say, perhaps, an index on the CHECKING_LOG table hits maxextents), then none of the changes will go through. Only if all four statements succeed will the changes be committed and made permanent.

FIGURE 4.6

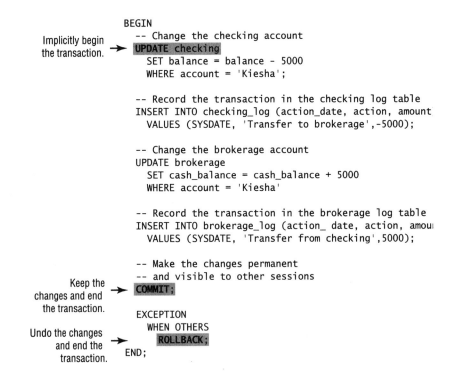

```
                         BEGIN
Implicitly begin           -- Change the checking account
the transaction.    →      UPDATE checking
                             SET balance = balance - 5000
                             WHERE account = 'Kiesha';

                           -- Record the transaction in the checking log table
                           INSERT INTO checking_log (action_date, action, amount
                             VALUES (SYSDATE, 'Transfer to brokerage',-5000);

                           -- Change the brokerage account
                           UPDATE brokerage
                             SET cash_balance = cash_balance + 5000
                             WHERE account = 'Kiesha'

                           -- Record the transaction in the brokerage log table
                           INSERT INTO brokerage_log (action_ date, action, amou
                             VALUES (SYSDATE, 'Transfer from checking',5000);

                           -- Make the changes permanent
       Keep the            -- and visible to other sessions
changes and end     →      COMMIT;
  the transaction.
                         EXCEPTION
                           WHEN OTHERS
Undo the changes             ROLLBACK;
  and end the            END;
  transaction.
```

A transaction will implicitly begin with an INSERT, UPDATE, DELETE, or SELECT...FOR UPDATE statement. The transaction will always end with either an implicit or explicit COMMIT or ROLLBACK statement. A ROLLBACK TO SAVEPOINT will not end a transaction.

Savepoints and Partial Rollbacks

Savepoints are intermediate fallback positions in SQL and PL/SQL code. The ROLLBACK TO SAVEPOINT statement is used to undo changes chronologically back to the last savepoint or to the named savepoint. Savepoints are not used extensively in industry. You must understand them, however, because there will likely be a question related to savepoints on the exam. Savepoints are not labels for GOTO statements, and ROLLBACK TO SAVEPOINT is not a GOTO. The code after a savepoint does not get reexecuted after a ROLLBACK TO SAVEPOINT—only the data changes made since that savepoint are undone.

Again, an example will help clarify. Kiesha tries to withdraw $100 from her checking account. We want to log her request in the ATM activity log, but if she has insufficient funds, we don't want to change her balance and will deny her request:

```
BEGIN
    INSERT INTO ATM_LOG(who, when, what, where)
        VALUES('Kiesha', SYSDATE, 'Withdrawal of
$100','ATM54');
    SAVEPOINT ATM_logged;

    UPDATE checking
      SET balance = balance - 100
      RETURNING balance INTO new_balance;

    IF new_balance < 0
    THEN
      ROLLBACK TO ATM_logged;  -- undo the update statement
      COMMIT;  -- keep the changes prior to the savepoint
(the insert)
      RAISE insufficient_funds;  -- Raise an error / deny
the request
    END IF;
END;
COMMIT;  -- keep the insert and the update
```

The keyword SAVEPOINT is optional, so the following two statements are equivalent:

```
ROLLBACK TO ATM_logged;
ROLLBACK TO SAVEPOINT ATM_logged;
```

Because savepoints are not frequently used, always include the keyword SAVEPOINT in any ROLLBACK TO SAVEPOINT statement. That way, anyone reading the code will be reminded of the keyword SAVEPOINT, making it easier to recognize that a partial rollback has occurred.

Consistency and Transactions

Consistency is one of the key concepts underlying the use of transaction control statements. Understanding Oracle's consistency model will enable you to employ transaction control appropriately and answer exam questions on transaction control correctly. Oracle implements consistency to guarantee that the data seen by a statement or transaction does not change until that statement or transaction completes. This support is only germane to multiuser databases where one database session can change (and commit) data that is being read by another session.

Oracle always uses statement-level consistency, which ensures that the data visible to a statement does not change during the life of that statement. Transactions can consist of multiple statements. When used, transaction-level consistency will ensure that the data visible to all statements in a transaction does not change for the life of the transaction.

Our banking example will help clarify: Matt starts running a total balance report against the checking account table at 10:00; this report takes five minutes. During those five minutes, the data that he is reporting on changes when Kiesha transfers $5,000 from her checking account to her brokerage account. When Matt's session gets to Kiesha's checking account record, it will need to reconstruct what the record looked like at 10:00. Matt's session will, unbeknownst to him, examine the rollback segment that Kiesha used during her account transfer transaction and recreate the image of what the checking account table looked like at 10:00.

Next, at 10:05, Matt runs a total balance report on the cash in the brokerage account table. If he is using transaction-level consistency, his session will re-create what the brokerage account table looked like at 10:00 (and exclude Kiesha's transfer). If Matt's session is using the default statement-level consistency, his session will report on what the brokerage account table looked like at 10:05 (and include Kiesha's transfer).

Oracle never uses locks for reading operations: Reading operations will never block writing operations. Instead, the rollback segments are used to re-create the image needed. Since rollback segments are released for reuse when the transaction writing to them commits, sometimes a consistent image cannot be re-created. When this happens, either a "snapshot too old" exception is raised or a "can't serialize access for this transaction" exception is raised. Using our example, if Matt's transaction can't locate Kiesha's transaction in the rollback segments because it was overwritten, Matt's transaction will not be able to re-create the 10:00 image of the table and will fail.

Oracle implements consistency through the use of *System Change Numbers (SCNs)*. An SCN is a time-oriented, database internal key. The SCN only increases, never decreases, and represents a point in time for comparison purposes. So, in our previous example, Matt's first statement gets the current SCN when it starts reading the checking account table. This starting SCN is compared to each data block's SCN; if the data block SCN is higher (newer), then the rollback segments are examined to find the older version of the data.

Enabling Transaction-Level Consistency

One of the uses of the SET TRANSACTION statement is to enable either transaction-level or statement-level consistency. Oracle uses these terms:

- ISOLATION LEVEL READ COMMITTED indicates statement-level consistency.

- ISOLATION LEVEL SERIALIZABLE indicates transaction-level consistency.

Here are some examples:

```
SET TRANSACTION ISOLATION LEVEL SERIALIZABLE;

SET TRANSACTION ISOLATION LEVEL READ COMMITTED; -- the
default
```

Transaction-level consistency can also be enabled for transactions that only read (do not modify) data, with this statement:

```
SET TRANSACTION READ ONLY;
```

Any attempts to change data in a READ ONLY transaction will raise an exception. Therefore, READ ONLY transactions can only use the following statements:

- SELECT (without a FOR UPDATE clause)

- LOCK TABLE

- SET ROLE

- ALTER SYSTEM

- ALTER SESSION

To end the read-only transaction, you must execute a COMMIT or ROLLBACK statement. The COMMIT or ROLLBACK is necessary to end the transaction, even though no data has changed.

The other use of the SET TRANSACTION statement is to direct Oracle to use a specifically named rollback segment for the transaction. This usage is most common in environments that have mostly small transactions, with a few large transactions that require significant rollback segment space for undo. By default, Oracle allocates rollback segments to transactions using a round-robin algorithm. A particularly large transaction can therefore be assigned to any rollback segment and cause that rollback segment to grow significantly in size. This dynamic space management can have negative performance and disk-space implications. To avoid the random assignment of the large transaction to any rollback segment, begin the large transaction with a SET TRANSACTION statement, such as this one:

```
SET TRANSACTION USE ROLLBACK SEGMENT rb_large;
```

where *rb_large* is the name of the large rollback segment. Now, by specifically assigning the large transaction to a large rollback segment, the other (small) rollback segments will not undergo dynamic space management, and greater efficiency will ensue.

Let's look at an example. We have a rollback segment tablespace 2GB in size and need 10 rollback segments to accommodate our peak online users. These peak online users have only small transactions. Once a week, we have four large transactions run one after another. These large transactions, which delete and load data, require 1GB of undo each. Our rollback segments are sized as follows:

```
rb_large (initial 100M next 100M minextents 2)
rb1 (initial 1M next 1M minextents 5)
rb2 (initial 1M next 1M minextents 5)
rb3 (initial 1M next 1M minextents 5)
rb4 (initial 1M next 1M minextents 5)
rb5 (initial 1M next 1M minextents 5)
rb6 (initial 1M next 1M minextents 5)
rb7 (initial 1M next 1M minextents 5)
rb8 (initial 1M next 1M minextents 5)
rb9 (initial 1M next 1M minextents 5)
```

These all fit nicely in the 2GB tablespace. If we used the default round-robin allocation, our four large transactions would use four separate rollback segments— and would try to grow each of these four to 1GB. Four 1GB segments won't fit in our 2GB tablespace, and the DBA would get paged at 2A.M. when the job fails. Instead, we begin each of our four large transactions with this:

```
SET TRANSACTION USE ROLLBACK SEGMENT rb_large;
```

Now, our four large transactions reuse the same large rollback segment. We can keep our rollback segment tablespace at 2GB—and the DBA can sleep all night.

Creating and Modifying Users

The CREATE USER statement is employed to create a user (sometimes called an account or schema) and optionally to assign additional attributes to that user. When a user connects to an Oracle database, he must be authenticated. Oracle can be configured for one of three types of authentication:

- Database
- External
- Global

The default is database authentication. With database authentication, when a user connects to the database, Oracle checks that the user is a legitimate user for that database and has supplied the correct password. With external authentication, Oracle only checks that the user is a legitimate user for that database; the password is validated by the operating system or network. With global authentication, Oracle only checks that the user is a legitimate user for that database; the password is validated by the Oracle Security Service, a separately licensed and configured service.

Database-Authenticated User Accounts

Database-authenticated accounts are the default type of account, and probably the most common. To create a database-authenticated account for username *piyush* with a password of *welcome*, you would execute the following:

```
CREATE USER piyush IDENTIFIED BY welcome;
```

Piyush can change his password to *saraswati* by executing this:

```
ALTER USER piyush IDENTIFIED BY saraswati;
```

The keywords IDENTIFIED BY *<password>* tell Oracle that the account is a database-authenticated account.

Externally Authenticated User Accounts

User accounts can be configured not to check a password in the database, but instead to rely on password checking from the client's operating system. These externally identified accounts are sometimes called OPS$ accounts because when they were initially introduced in Oracle6, the Oracle account had to be prefixed with the key string OPS$. This is also why the default for the init.ora parameter os_authent_prefix is OPS$–the default behavior is consistent with Oracle6. The os_authent_prefix defines the string that must be prepended to the operating system account name for Oracle externally identified accounts. If this parameter is left as the default of OPS$, then the operating system user *appl* would be created in Oracle as follows:

```
CREATE USER ops$appl IDENTIFIED EXTERNALLY.
```

Frequently, the os_authent_prefix will be set to a blank string (os_ authent_prefix="") so no prefix is required. The same APPL account would then be created like this:

```
CREATE USER appl IDENTIFIED EXTERNALLY.
```

The keywords IDENTIFIED EXTERNALLY tell Oracle that the account is an externally authenticated account. Externally identified accounts are used extensively in cron jobs, batch jobs, or other non-interactive programs where incorporating a password would violate security protocols or result in broken processes when passwords are changed. Externally identified accounts should not be used when client operating systems are inherently insecure (such as MS-DOS, Windows 95, or the Mac OS).

Globally Authenticated User Accounts

User accounts can be configured not to check a password in the database, but instead to rely on password checking from an X.509 enterprise directory service. These types of accounts will be most common in large organizations where a single sign-on system is used. To create a user with global authentication, use the keywords IDENTIFIED GLOBALLY AS *<directory_name>*. Here's an example:

```
CREATE USER scott IDENTIFIED GLOBALLY AS 'CN=scott,
OU=division1, O=sybex, C=US';
```

Creating and Altering User Accounts

The CREATE USER statement is employed to create a user and can also be used to assign any combination of account attributes to the user account. The ALTER USER statement is used to assign any combination of account attributes to the user account, but the account must already exist. The CREATE USER statement must minimally include the username and the password clause.

```
CREATE USER piyush IDENTIFIED BY saraswati;
CREATE USER piyush IDENTIFIED EXTERNALLY;
ALTER  USER manoj  IDENTIFIED BY itsasecret;
```

There are quite a few account attributes that can be assigned with the CREATE or ALTER USER statements. These attributes are described in the following paragraphs.

Assign a Default Tablespace to the User   The default tablespace is where the user's objects (tables, indexes, and clusters) will be placed if an explicit tablespace clause is not included in that object's CREATE statement. The default is the system tablespace, which is generally not a good place to put them.

```
CREATE USER piyush IDENTIFIED BY saraswati
DEFAULT TABLESPACE user_data;

ALTER USER manoj DEFAULT TABLESPACE devl_data;
```

Assign a Temporary Tablespace to the User   The temporary tablespace is where temporary segments from large sorting operations are placed. The default is the system tablespace, which is generally not a good place to put them.

```
CREATE USER piyush IDENTIFIED BY saraswati
TEMPORARY TABLESPACE temp;
```

```
ALTER USER manoj TEMPORARY TABLESPACE temp;
```

Assign Tablespace Quotas to the User   Tablespace quotas limit the amount of disk space that a user can consume within a tablespace. These quotas can be specified in bytes, kilobytes, megabytes, or the special quota *unlimited*, which allows the user to consume any amount of disk space in the specified tablespace. The quota amount is interpreted as bytes if no suffix is included, as kilobytes if the suffix K is included, and as megabytes if the suffix M is included. So 32768, 512K, 8M are 32768 bytes, 512 kilobytes (524,288 bytes), and 8 megabytes (8,225,568 bytes), respectively.

```
CREATE USER piyush IDENTIFIED BY saraswati
DEFAULT TABLESPACE user_data
QUOTA UNLIMITED ON user_data
QUOTA 20M ON tools;
```

```
ALTER USER manoj QUOTA 2500K ON tools;
```

Assign a Profile to the User   Profiles can be used to limit the resources that a user's session can consume. Some of these limiting resources include connect time, idle time, logical reads per session, failed login attempts, and the password verification function. The default profile allows unlimited resource usage. Before using profiles to limit resource consumption, the `init.ora` parameter `resource_limit` must be set to TRUE.

```
CREATE USER piyush IDENTIFIED BY saraswati
PROFILE instructor;
```

```
ALTER USER manoj PROFILE engineer;
```

Make Roles Assigned to a User Enabled or Disabled, by Default This attribute can only be set with the ALTER USER statement. Attempts to set this attribute with a CREATE USER statement will raise an exception.

```
ALTER USER manoj DEFAULT ROLE ALL EXCEPT salary_adm;
```

Expire the User's Password so that It Will Need to be Changed on the Next Login When a user's password expires, the user will be forced to change passwords on the next connection to the database. Oracle will first prompt the user for the old password, then for the new password, and finally for the new password a second time in order to confirm it. This functionality is frequently used for new accounts when a default password is assigned and the new user must change her password immediately. Another common use is when the user forgets her password. The DBA changes and expires it, then lets the user know the temporary password. With the expired password, the user must change her password on the next login.

```
ALTER USER manoj IDENTIFIED BY welcome;
ALTER USER manoj PASSWORD EXPIRE;
```

Lock the Account so the User Cannot Log in to the Database This capability is frequently used for application schema accounts where no one actually logs into the database as that user, but that user owns tables used by an application.

```
ALTER USER gl ACCOUNT LOCK;
```

Unlock the Account so the User Can Again Log in to the Database When account locking is performed on an application schema account, this attribute would need to be unlocked for upgrades, then locked again after the maintenance operation.

```
ALTER USER gl ACCOUNT UNLOCK;
```

Privileges and Roles

Privileges allow a user account to access objects or execute programs that are owned by another user. Oracle has three types of privileges:

- Object
- System
- Role

These privileges can be granted (assigned) to a user, to the special user public, or to a role. We discussed users in the previous section, "Creating and Altering User Accounts." Granting a privilege to the special user "public" implicitly grants that privilege to any user who connects to the database. Granting a privilege to public is analogous to granting that privilege to everyone, without having to specify who everyone is.

A role is an instrument for administering privileges. Privileges can be granted to a role, then that role can be granted to another role or to a user. Users can thus inherit privileges via roles. Roles serve no other purpose than to administer privileges. Once granted, privileges can be revoked (cancelled) in the same manner in which they were granted.

Creating and Using Roles

As you just read, roles exist only to ease the administration of privileges. To take advantage of the administrative relief that a role may provide, you must first create it with the CREATE ROLE statement. Figure 4.7 shows the CREATE ROLE statement's syntax.

FIGURE 4.7 The syntax for the CREATE ROLE statement

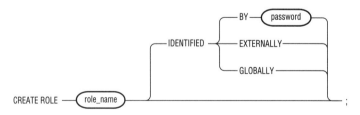

By default, a role will be created without a password or other identification. If a role is created with the IDENTIFIED BY clause, that role is disabled by default. To enable the role, use the SET ROLE statement:

```
SET ROLE role_name IDENTIFIED BY password;
```

Externally and globally identified roles are authenticated by the operating system and by Oracle Security Service, respectively. Often, users will need privileges to modify data in application tables, but only when running the application, not when using *ad hoc* tools. This context-sensitive security can be achieved by a role that has a password. When a user connects to the database inside the application, the application code, without the user's knowledge, will execute a SET ROLE statement, passing the secret password to the database. The user does not have to know the role's password and therefore may not be able to manually execute the SET ROLE with password while inside an ad hoc tool, such as SQL*Plus.

The SET ROLE statement can be used to enable or disable any combination of roles that have been granted to a user.

Object Privileges

Object privileges are permissions on schema objects, such as tables, views, programmer-defined functions, and libraries. There are nine different types of object privileges that can be granted to a user or role. These privileges are shown here.

Privilege Object	Alter	Delete	Execute	Index	Insert	Read	Reference	Select	Update
Directory	No	No	No	No	No	Yes	No	No	No
Function	No	No	Yes	No	No	No	No	No	No
Procedure	No	No	Yes	No	No	No	No	No	No
Package	No	No	Yes	No	No	No	No	No	No
DB Object	No	No	Yes	No	No	No	No	No	No
Library	No	No	Yes	No	No	No	No	No	No

Operator	No	No	Yes	No	No	No	No	No	No
Sequence	Yes	No	No	No	No	No	No	Yes	No
Table	Yes	Yes	No	Yes	Yes	No	Yes	Yes	Yes
Type	No	No	Yes	No	No	No	No	No	No
View	No	Yes	No	No	Yes	No	No	Yes	Yes

For objects that can have more than one privilege, the special privilege ALL can be granted or revoked. For tables, ALL includes SELECT, INSERT, UPDATE, and DELETE, as well as INDEX, ALTER, and REFERENCE. Take care before granting ALL on a table; you might not wish to grant the INDEX, ALTER, and REFERENCE privileges.

The ALTER Privilege on a Table   This privilege allows the grantee to execute the ALTER TABLE or LOCK TABLE statement on the table. An ALTER TABLE statement can do the following:

- Rename the table

- Add columns

- Drop columns

- Change the datatype and size of columns

- Convert the table to a partitioned table

The ALTER privilege on a sequence allows the grantee to execute the ALTER SEQUENCE statement on the sequence, which lets the grantee do such things as reset the minvalue, increment, and cache size.

The DELETE Privilege on a Table or View   This privilege allows the grantee to execute a DELETE statement to remove rows from the table or view. The SELECT privilege must be granted together with the DELETE privilege, or the grantee will be unable to select the rows and therefore unable to delete them. DELETE also allows the grantee to lock the table.

The EXECUTE Privilege on a Function or Procedure   This privilege gives the grantee the permission to execute the specified program. The EXECUTE privilege on a package allows the grantee to execute or use any program or program object (such as a record type or cursor) declared in the package specification. The EXECUTE privilege on an operator or type will allow the grantee to use that operator in SQL or PL/SQL. On a DB Object, EXECUTE will allow the grantee to use that DB Object and invoke its methods.

The INDEX Privilege on a Table   This privilege allows the grantee to create indexes on or to lock that table. Confusion can arise when one schema owns a table but another schema owns the indexes. Use care when granting this privilege.

The INSERT Privilege on a Table or View   This privilege gives the grantee the ability to create rows in that table or view. If the INSERT privilege is on specific columns of the table or view, the grantee will only be able to populate the columns on which he has been granted INSERT privileges. INSERT also implicitly gives the grantee the ability to lock the table.

The READ Privilege   This privilege can only be granted on a directory and lets the grantee read BFILEs in the specified directory. This privilege should not be confused with SELECT, which allows a user to read a table or view.

The REFERENCE Privilege   This privilege can only be granted on a table to a user (not a role). It allows the grantee to create integrity constraints that reference that table. The grantee can also lock the table. SELECT does not have to be granted with REFERENCE for the database to enforce referential integrity constraints. However, this can give rise to situations in which the parent schema cannot read the child records and the child schema cannot read the parent records, but the database will enforce the parent-child relationship. Use care when granting this privilege.

The SELECT Privilege on a Table or View   This privilege gives the grantee permission to execute SELECT statements on the table or view, allowing the grantee to read the table's, or view's contents. The SELECT privilege on a sequence allows the grantee to obtain the current value (CURRVAL) or to increment the value by selecting NEXTVAL.

The UPDATE Privilege   This privilege allows the grantee to change data values in the table or view. The SELECT privilege must be granted together with the UPDATE privilege, which implicitly gives the grantee the ability to lock the table.

At a finer granularity, you can grant the privileges INSERT, UPDATE, and REFERENCES on specific columns of tables. On views, you can grant INSERT and UPDATE on specific columns. Revoking column privileges, however, must be done table-wide. For example, Norman grants UPDATE on the columns surname, address, and city, then later needs to revoke UPDATE on address and city, leaving UPDATE on surname. Norman must first revoke UPDATE on the whole table, then grant UPDATE on the column surname again.

System Privileges

System privileges give the grantee the ability to perform system-level activities, such as connecting to the database, altering the user session, creating tables, or creating users. A complete list of system privileges can be obtained from the data dictionary view SYSTEM_PRIVILEGE_MAP. Like object privileges, system privileges are assigned with the GRANT statement. A notable syntactical difference between system and object privileges is how you pass along the ability for the recipient to grant that privilege in turn. With object privileges, you use the WITH GRANT OPTION clause, but with system privileges you use the WITH ADMIN OPTION clause. The functionality is identical, but the syntax is different. This syntax difference is trivial in practice, because if you try to grant system privileges using WITH GRANT OPTION, the error message says, "Only the ADMIN OPTION can be specified." On the exam, however, you must know the syntax and not rely on an error message.

Roles and Role Privileges

Role privileges are those privileges that a user owns by way of a role. Any combination of system privileges, object privileges, and role privileges may be granted to a role. As with system privileges, passing along the ability for the recipient to grant the privilege in turn requires the WITH ADMIN OPTION clause. Role privileges can be enabled and disabled during a session with the SET ROLE statement. Therefore, role privileges cannot be relied upon for privileges in stored SQL. If a function, procedure, package, trigger, or method uses an object owned by another schema, privileges on that object must be granted directly to the owner of the stored SQL. Since granted privileges cannot vary from session to session, they will always be in effect and can be relied upon.

Assigning and Rescinding Privileges

Earlier in this chapter, we covered object, system, and role privileges. When you want to assign one or more of these privileges to a user or a role, use the GRANT statement. You can see the GRANT statement's syntax in Figure 4.8.

FIGURE 4.8 The syntax for the GRANT statement

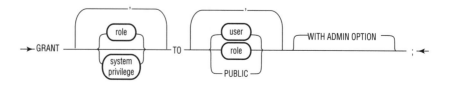

Object privileges can be granted WITH GRANT OPTION, which gives the grantee permission to grant those privileges in turn to any other user or role, or to public. For example, in Figure 4.9 Oliver grants SELECT on sales to Bill with the grant option. Bill can then grant SELECT on sales to Bonnie.

FIGURE 4.9 Granting privileges

Oliver grants to Bill, and Bill grants to Bonnie.

If user Bill is dropped, however, as shown in Figure 4.10, the chain is broken and Bonnie loses her SELECT privilege, as you can see in Figure 4.11.

FIGURE 4.10 The chain is broken.

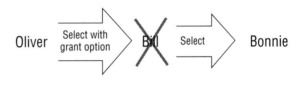

User Bill is dropped.

FIGURE 4.11 The privileges are lost.

Oliver   Bonnie

Bonnie loses the privileges that Bill had granted to her.

Because both grantor and grantee for object privileges are kept in the data dictionary, a user or role can be granted the same privilege from multiple grantees. When this happens, all grantors must revoke the privilege before the grantee actually loses the ability to exercise the privilege. Let's take our previous example of Oliver, Bill, and Bonnie, but this time add another user, Dennis. Oliver has granted to Bill who has granted to Bonnie. Oliver has also granted to Dennis, and Dennis has granted to Bonnie, as well. You can see this in Figure 4.12.

FIGURE 4.12 Receiving a privilege from multiple grantors

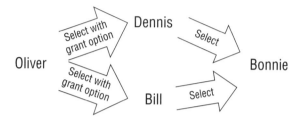

Oliver grants to both Bill and Dennis;
Bill and Dennis both grant to Bonnie.

Now, when user Bill is dropped, Bonnie only loses one of her two privileges. She can still execute SELECT statements on the sales table, as shown in Figure 4.13.

FIGURE 4.13 Bonnie retains her privilege if any granted path remains.

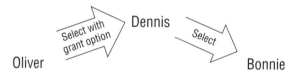

Bill is dropped, but Bonnie still has the privilege from Dennis.

A notable difference between object privileges and system or role privileges is that the grantor of the system or role privilege is not kept. Thus, if Oliver grants DBA to Bill with admin option then Bill grants DBA to Bonnie, the database does not record that Bill granted to Bonnie—only that Bonnie has the role privilege. If Bill is dropped, Bonnie still retains the system and role privileges that Bill granted to her. See Figure 4.14 for an illustration of how this works.

FIGURE 4.14 System and role privileges remain when the grantor is dropped.

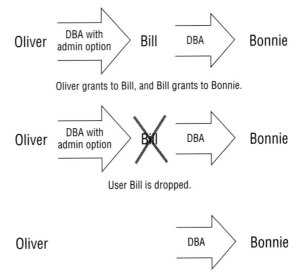

Oliver grants to Bill, and Bill grants to Bonnie.

User Bill is dropped.

Bonnie retains the role that Bill granted to her.

To rescind privileges, use the REVOKE statement, whose syntax is shown in Figure 4.15.

FIGURE 4.15 The syntax for the REVOKE statement

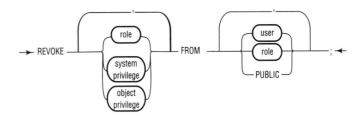

The WITH GRANT OPTION and the WITH ADMIN OPTION of the GRANT statement confer upon the recipient the ability to grant the privileges to other users or roles. To rescind only the grant or admin option, the entire privilege must be dropped and granted again. However, this can have unintended consequences. For example, if Joshua has used his grant option and granted David object privileges, then when Joshua's privilege is revoked, David's is revoked along with Joshua's.

Privileges and the Data Dictionary

The data dictionary can be examined to see what privileges have been granted. DBA_TAB_PRIVS contains the object privileges that have been granted from any user to any user and shows whether it was granted with the grant option. Don't let the name confuse you: DBA_TAB_PRIVS is not for just tables; it also includes privileges granted on functions, packages, sequences, libraries, and so on. Other data dictionary views and their contents are listed in Table 4.6. Rote memorization is not much fun, but knowing the contents of these dictionary views is very important, because you are likely to encounter one or more questions about them on the exam. In a professional setting, you can simply look up the view definitions in a reference or describe them in a tool like SQL*Plus. On the exam, however, you must rely on your memory of this material.

You can help yourself to memorize these views by closing this book, pulling out a sheet of paper, and seeing how many of the privilege views in Table 4.6 you can write down. The very act of writing them down will stimulate your memory and help you to recall them later.

TABLE 4.6 Data Dictionary Views on Privileges

Dictionary View	View Description
ALL_COL_PRIVS	The column privileges that have been granted to the user or to public or for which the user is the owner
ALL_COL_PRIVS_MADE	The column privileges that have been granted on tables and views where the user is either the owner or the grantor
ALL_COL_PRIVS_RECD	The column privileges that have been granted to the user or to public
ALL_TAB_PRIVS	The object privileges that have been granted to the user or to public or for which the user is the owner
ALL_TAB_PRIVS_MADE	The object privileges in which the user is either the owner of the object or the grantor of the privilege
ALL_TAB_PRIVS_RECD	The object privileges that have been granted to the user or to public

TABLE 4.6 Data Dictionary Views on Privileges *(continued)*

Dictionary View	View Description
DBA_COL_PRIVS	All column privileges that have been granted
DBA_ROLE_PRIVS	All roles that have been granted to users or to other roles
DBA_SYS_PRIVS	All system privileges that have been granted to users or to roles
DBA_TAB_PRIVS	All object privileges that have been granted
ROLE_ROLE_PRIVS	Roles that have been granted to the user both directly and indirectly
ROLE_SYS_PRIVS	System privileges that have been granted to the user via roles directly and indirectly
ROLE_TAB_PRIVS	Object privileges that have been granted to the user via roles directly and indirectly
SESSION_PRIVS	All system privileges that are available to the user in the current session
USER_COL_PRIVS	The column privileges that have been granted for which the user is owner, grantor, or grantee
USER_COL_PRIVS_MADE	The column privileges that have been granted for which the user is owner or grantor
USER_COL_PRIVS_RECD	The column privileges that have been granted for which the user is owner or grantee
USER_ROLE_PRIVS	The roles that have been granted directly to the user
USER_SYS_PRIVS	The system privileges that have been granted directly to the user
USER_TAB_PRIVS	The object privileges that have been granted directly to the user

TABLE 4.6 Data Dictionary Views on Privileges *(continued)*

Dictionary View	View Description
USER_TAB_PRIVS_MADE	The object privileges that have been granted to others
USER_TAB_PRIVS_RECD	The object privileges that have been granted to the user

Summary

In this chapter, you saw how to modify data, who can modify data, and under what conditions a user can modify data. This includes the DML statements INSERT, UPDATE, and DELETE, along with SELECT FOR UPDATE and LOCK TABLE. The DDL statement TRUNCATE has similarities to DELETE, but the two statements also have important differences. We discussed concurrency and how to use locks to manage concurrent changes, as well as what causes deadlocks. We also discussed consistency and how to use transactions to manage consistency. The SET TRANSACTION statement is usually used to set statement-level or transaction-level consistency, but it can also be used to assign a transaction explicitly to a specific rollback segment. You read about how to create and manage user accounts and set the various attributes of those accounts. We also looked at the three types of privileges and how they differ. Finally, we reviewed the data dictionary tables that contain the various privileges.

Key Terms

Before you take the exam, make sure you're familiar with the following terms:

Consistency

Concurrency

Statement

Transaction

Lock

SCN

Review Questions

1. When a program executes a SELECT... FOR UPDATE statement, which of the following must it do?

    A. Execute a COMMIT or ROLLBACK to end the transaction, even if no data has changed

    B. Change the data values in the rows selected, then commit or roll back to end the transaction

    C. Execute a COMMIT or ROLLBACK to end the transaction, but only if data has changed

    D. Because a transaction doesn't start until data has actually changed, no COMMIT or ROLLBACK needs to be executed

2. Which of the following statements will not implicitly begin a transaction?

    A. INSERT

    B. UPDATE

    C. DELETE

    D. SELECT FOR UPDATE

    E. None of the above; they all implicitly begin a transaction.

3. If Julio executes a LOCK TABLE IN SHARE ROW EXCLUSIVE MODE statement, with which of the following statements will Marisa *not* wait for Julio's commit or rollback? Select all that apply.

    A. INSERT

    B. SELECT FOR UPDATE

    C. LOCK TABLE IN SHARE MODE

    D. LOCK TABLE IN EXCLUSIVE MODE

    E. None of the above; all will wait.

4. Which of the following statements end a transaction? Select all that apply.

A. `LOCK TABLE IN EXCLUSIVE MODE`

B. `COMMIT`

C. `ROLLBACK TO SAVEPOINT`

D. `ALTER USER`

E. `CREATE INDEX`

5. Which of the following queries will display the privileges on another user's procedure that you have granted to a third party? Select one.

A. `SELECT owner, proc_name, grantor, grantee`
   `FROM all_sql_privs`

B. `SELECT owner, sql_name, grantor, grantee`
   `FROM all_sql_privs`

C. `SELECT owner, table_name, grantor, grantee, privilege`
   `FROM all_tab_privs_made`

D. `SELECT owner, sql_name, grantor, grantee`
   `FROM user_table_privs`

6. Can you execute an `ALTER INDEX REBUILD` while there are uncommitted updates on a table from other sessions?

A. No, it will always fail with a resource busy error.

B. Yes, but you have to specify the keyword `WAIT` to wait for the commit or rollback.

C. Yes, the row exclusive locks from the `UPDATE` statements only block other changes to the same rows.

D. Yes, but only if the updates do not change the indexed columns.

7. Which of the following actions can you *not* do with an `ALTER USER` statement?

A. Expire a password

B. Enable DBA privileges

C. Set the default tablespace for tables

D. Set the default tablespace for indexes

8. Which of the following statements will improve the performance of a full table scan on table ORDERS?

A. `delete from orders;`

B. `truncate table orders;`

C. `create index ord_idx2 on orders (customer_id);`

D. `alter session set hash_area_size 16613376;`

9. The following table shows two concurrent transactions. What happens at time point 9?

Session A	Time	Session B
UPDATE customers SET region='H' WHERE state='43' and county='046';	6	
	7	UPDATE customers SET mgr=4567 WHERE state='47' and county='072';
UPDATE customers SET region='H' WHERE state='47' and county='072';	8	
	9	UPDATE customers SET mgr=4567 WHERE state='43' and county='046';

A. Session B will wait for session A to commit or roll back.

B. Session A will wait for session B to commit or roll back.

C. A deadlock will occur, and both sessions will hang until the DBA kills one or until one of the users cancels their statement.

D. A deadlock will occur, and Oracle will cancel one of the statements.

E. Both sessions are not updating the same column, so no waiting or deadlocks will occur.

10. The following table shows two concurrent transactions. Which statement about the result returned in Session A at time point 16 is most true?

Session A	Time	Session B

`SELECT SUM(deposit_amt)`
`FROM transaction_log`
`WHERE deposit_date >`
`TRUNC(SYSDATE);`
	12	

	13	`INSERT INTO`
		`transaction_log`
		`(deposit_date,`
		`deposit_amt) VALUES`
		`(SYSDATE, 6247.00);`

	14	`COMMIT;`
Table scan for the active SELECT reaches the datablock where Session B's row was inserted.	15	
Table scan complete; results returned.	16	

A. The results would include the changes committed by transaction B at time point 14.

B. The results would not include the changes committed by transaction B at time point 14.

C. The results would include the changes committed by transaction B at time point 14 if the two sessions were connected to the database as the same user.

D. Session A would raise a "snapshot too old" exception.

11. The following table shows two concurrent transactions. Which statement about the results returned in Session A at time points 16 and 18 is most true?

Session A	Time	Session B
SET TRANSACTION ISOLATION LEVEL READ CONSISTENT;	11	
SELECT SUM(deposit_amt) FROM transaction_log WHERE deposit_date > TRUNC(SYSDATE);	12	
	13	INSERT INTO transaction_log (deposit_date, deposit_amt) VALUES (SYSDATE, 6247.00);
	14	COMMIT;
Table scan for the active SELECT reaches the datablock where Session B's row was inserted.	15	
Table scan complete; results returned.	16	
SELECT SUM(deposit_amt) FROM transaction_log WHERE deposit_date > TRUNC(SYSDATE);	17	
Table scan complete; results returned.	18	

    A. The results would be identical.

    B. The results would be different.

    C. The results would only be identical if the two seesions were connected to the database as the same user.

    D. Both statements would include the data committed by transaction B at time point 14.

12. The following table shows two concurrent transactions. Which statement about the results returned in Session A at time points 16 and 18 is most true?

Session A	Time	Session B
SET TRANSACTION ISOLATION LEVEL SERIALIZABLE;	11	
SELECT SUM(deposit_amt) FROM transaction_log WHERE deposit_date > TRUNC(SYSDATE);	12	
	13	INSERT INTO transaction_log (deposit_date, deposit_amt) VALUES (SYSDATE, 6247.00);
	14	COMMIT;
Table scan for the active SELECT reaches the datablock where Session B's row was inserted.	15	
Table scan complete; results returned.	16	
SELECT SUM(deposit_amt) FROM transaction_log WHERE deposit_date > TRUNC(SYSDATE);	17	
Table scan complete; results returned.	18	

A. The results would be identical.

B. The results would be different.

C. The results would only be identical if the two seesions were connected to the database as the same user.

D. Both statements would include the data committed by transaction B at time point 14.

13. You have a DELETE statement that will generate a large amount of undo. One rollback segment, named `rb_large`, is larger than the others. How would you force the use of this rollback segment for the DELETE operation?

A. `alter session use rollback segment rb_large;`

B. `set transaction use rollback segment rb_large;`

C. `begin work using rollback segment rb_large`

D. You cannot force the use of a specific rollback segment.

14. Oracle user applmgr has granted SELECT on table PO_DETAILS with grant option to Philippe. Philippe has granted SELECT on `applmgr.po_details` to Naomi. When Philippe leaves the company and the DBA drops user Philippe, what happens to Naomi's privilege on `applmgr.po_details`?

A. Naomi retains the SELECT privilege; the grantor follows the chain and reverts to applmgr.

B. Naomi's SELECT privilege is revoked.

C. Naomi retains the SELECT privilege, and the grantor is still shown in the data dictionary as Philippe; nothing about Naomi's privilege changes.

D. Naomi's SELECT privilege is revoked only if Philippe was the only grantor to grant her the privilege.

15. Which of the following statements will give user Zachary the privilege to modify only the column "comments" on the customer table?

A. `grant update on customer(comments) to zachary;`

B. `grant update (comments) on customer to zachary;`

C. `grant update on customer.comments to zachary;`

D. `grant update on customer columns(comments) to zachary;`

16. Mary has granted INSERT, UPDATE, DELETE on chart_of_accounts to
    Charlie with the grant option. Charlie is changing jobs and should not
    have the grant option. How can Mary rescind the grant option from
    Charlie, leaving the INSERT, UPDATE, DELETE privilege, but without
    the grant option? You also want to ensure that whomever Charlie
    granted the privileges to will retain the privileges.

    A. Grant the privileges on chart_of_accounts without the grant option,
       then revoke the privileges "with grant option."

    B. Simply revoke the grant option.

    C. Revoke the privileges, so that the grant option goes away,
       then grant the privileges without the grant option.

    D. Extract all the grants that Charlie made from the data dictionary,
       revoke the privileges on chart_of_accounts, grant the privileges on
       chart_of_accounts without the grant option,
       regrant all the extracted privileges.

17. You need to report on all of the column privileges that you have made
    on your BONUS table. All this information must be included: the name
    of the account receiving the privilege, which column, and which privi-
    lege. Which of the following statements will accomplish this task?

    A. `select grantor, table_name, column_name, privilege`
       `from user_col_privs_recd where table_name ='BONUS';`

    B. `select * from all_col_privs_made where table_`
       `name='BONUS';`

    C. `select table_name, column_name, privilege, grantee`
       `from user_col_privs_made where table_name ='BONUS';`

    D. `select grantee, table_name, column_name, privilege`
       `from all_tab_col_privs where owner=user and table_`
       `name='BONUS';`

18. EMP is a table. Mary is a user. Sales_mgr is a role. Which one of the
    following statements will fail?

    A. `grant sales_mgr to mary with admin option;;`

    B. `grant read on emp to mary;`

    C. `grant insert,update,delete on emp to mary with`
       `grant option;`

    D. `grant reference on emp to mary;;`

19. Which of the following table privileges cannot be granted to a role (can only be granted to a user)?

A. INDEX

B. ALTER

C. REFERENCE

D. TRUNCATE

20. If Judy grants ALL on her table FORMAT_CODES to public, which operation will user Jerry not be able to perform?

A. create index on judy.format_codes

B. alter table judy.format_codes

C. delete from table judy.format_codes

D. truncate table judy.format_codes

Answers to Review Questions

1. A. SELECT...FOR UPDATE implicity begins a transaction and so must execute a COMMIT or ROLLBACK to end the transaction, even if no data has changed. Data does not have to change after a SELECT...FOR UPDATE.

2. E. If a transaction is not currently open, any DML will implicitly begin a transaction.

3. B. The row share exclusive mode will block other table locks and row exclusive locks, but not row share locks.

4. B, D, E. COMMIT, ROLLBACK, and any DDL end a transaction—DDL is automatically committed. ROLLBACK TO SAVEPONT is only a partial undo; it does not end the transaction.

5. C. All of the other data dictionary tables are fictitious.

6. A. The row exclusive locks from the update will block all DDL, including DDL on the indexes—it does not matter which columns the index is on. You cannot specify WAIT on DDL.

7. D. It would be nice, but Oracle does not (yet) let you set a default tablespace for indexes. DBA privileges could be enabled by default with an ALTER USER statement if the role was granted to the user previously and set to disabled.

8. B. A truncate will reset the high-water mark on a table, so when a full table scan (that scans to the high-water mark) is executed against the table, it will run very fast. Deletes do not affect the high-water mark or full scan performance. Indexes and hash_area_size do not affect full scan performance.

9. D. At time point 8, session A will wait for session B; at time point 9, a deadlock will occur, and Oracle will recognize it and cancel one of the statements. Oracle locks to the granularity of a row, so even though the columns are different, the locks will still block each other.

10. B. Statement-level read consistency would ensure that the data visible to each statement does not change while the statement is executing. The "snapshot too old" exception might be raised if there were a lot of other transactions committing to the database between time points 12 and 16, but if this exception were raised, the table scan would neither complete nor return results.

11. B. The `read consistent` isolation level is statement-level read consistency, so each statement sees the committed data that existed at the beginning of the statement. The committed data at time point 17 includes Session B's `COMMIT` at time point 14.

12. A. The serializable isolation level is transaction-level read consistency, so both of Session A's `SELECT` statements see the same data image. Neither would include the changes committed at time point 14.

13. B. The `SET TRANSACTION` statement can be used to force the use of a specific rollback segment, provided the `SET TRANSACTION` statement begins the transaction.

14. D. This one is tricky; B is correct, but D is more correct. When a user is dropped, all object privileges that the user had granted are implicitly revoked. But a user can get a privilege from more than one grantor. When a grantee has the privilege from more than one grantor, all grantors must revoke the privilege before the grantee actually loses the privilege.

15. B. Any additional columns would appear as a comma-delimited list within the parentheses.

16. D. There is no simple and easy way to remove the grant option while retaining the privilege. Revoking a privilege from someone will cascade through and revoke it from all grantees, so it would be crucial to first extract these privileges before revoking them.

17. C. The grantee is the recipient of the privilege. Every one of the ALL_ DATA dictionary views contains not only the user's own objects, but also those that they have access to, so ALL_COL_PRIVS_MADE may contain privileges on other schemas' tables. ALL_TAB_COL_PRIVS is not a valid data dictionary view.

18. B. The READ privilege is only valid on directories.

19. C. TRUNCATE is not a table privilege. INDEX and ALTER can be granted to either a user or a role, but REFERENCE can only be granted to a user.

20. D. TRUNCATE is not a table privilege.

Chapter 5

Creating and Managing Tables and Views

ORACLE8i SQL & PL/SQL EXAM OBJECTIVES OFFERED IN THIS CHAPTER:

✓ **Creating and managing tables:**

- Create tables
- Describe the datatypes that can be used when specifying column definition
- Alter table definitions
- Drop, rename, and truncate tables

✓ **Creating and managing views:**

- Describe a view
- Create a view
- Retrieve data through a view
- Insert, update, and delete data through a view
- Drop a view

Exam objectives are subject to change without prior notice and at Oracle's sole discretion. Please visit Oracle's Training and Certification Web site (http://education.oracle.com/certification/index.html) for the most current exam objective listing.

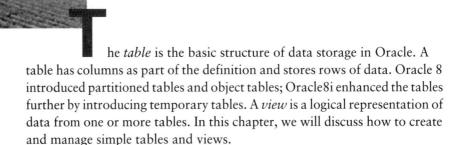

he *table* is the basic structure of data storage in Oracle. A table has columns as part of the definition and stores rows of data. Oracle 8 introduced partitioned tables and object tables; Oracle8i enhanced the tables further by introducing temporary tables. A *view* is a logical representation of data from one or more tables. In this chapter, we will discuss how to create and manage simple tables and views.

Managing Tables

Y ou can think of a table as a spreadsheet having columns and rows. It is a structure that holds data in a relational database. The table is created with a name to identify it, and columns are defined with valid column names. The column attributes, such as the *datatype* and size, should be specified when creating tables. CREATE TABLE is a comprehensive command with many options. Here is the simplest way to create a table:

```
SQL> CREATE TABLE products
  2  ( PROD_ID    NUMBER (4),
  3    PROD_NAME  VARCHAR2 (20),
  4    STOCK_QTY  NUMBER (15,3)
  5  );

Table created.

SQL>
```

A table named PRODUCTS has been created under the *user (schema)* connected to the database. Let's see the basic components of this command. You use the keywords CREATE TABLE, followed by the table name. The table name can be qualified with the username; you must qualify the table when creating a table in another user's schema. The column definitions are enclosed in parentheses. The table has three columns, each identified by a name and datatype. Commas separate the column definitions. This table has two columns with the NUMBER datatype and one column with the VARCHAR2 datatype. A datatype must be specified for each column.

See Chapter 1, *Relational Technology and Simple SQL SELECT Statements*, for the different datatypes available in Oracle.

Table 5.1 summarizes the built-in data types that can be used while creating tables. Immediately following the datatype, you specify the width of the column. For NUMBER datatypes, you also have the option of specifying a precision. DATE datatypes do not have a width specified. Each DATE column stores the date and time component.

TABLE 5.1 Oracle Built-in Datatypes

Datatype	Description
CHAR (*<size>*)	Fixed-length character data of length in bytes specified inside parentheses. Size defaults to 1 if not defined.
VARCHAR (*<size>*)	Same as VARCHAR2 datatype.
VARCHAR2 (*<size>*)	Variable-length character data. Maximum allowed length is specified in parentheses. You must specify a size; there is no default value.
NCHAR (*<size>*)	Same as CHAR, stores National Language Support (NLS) character data.
NVARCHAR2 (*<size>*)	Same as VARCHAR2, stores NLS character data.
LONG	Stores variable-length character data up to 2GB. Use CLOB or NCLOB datatypes instead. Provided in Oracle8i for backward compatibility.

TABLE 5.1 Oracle Built-in Datatypes *(continued)*

Datatype	Description
NUMBER (*<preci-sion>, <scale>*)	Stores fixed and floating-point numbers. You can specify a precision (total length including decimals) and scale (digits after decimal point).
DATE	Stores date data. Has century, year, month, date, hour, minute, seconds internally. Can be displayed in various formats.
RAW (*<size>*)	Variable-length datatype used to store unstructured data, without a character set conversion. Provided for backward compatibility. Use BLOB and BFILE instead.
LONG RAW	Same as RAW, can store up to 2GB of binary data.
BLOB	Stores up to 4GB of unstructured binary data.
CLOB	Stores up to 4GB of character data.
NCLOB	Stores up to 4GB of NLS character data.
BFILE	Stores unstructured binary data in operating system files outside the database.
ROWID	Stores binary data representing a physical row address of table's row.
UROWID	Stores binary data representing any type of row address: physical, logical or foreign.

You can specify constraints at the table level, as well as at the column level, while creating tables. The most commonly used column-level constraint is the NOT NULL constraint. Constraints are discussed in detail in Chapter 6, *Other Database Objects and the Data Dictionary*.

When creating or altering a table, you can specify *default values* for columns. The default value specified will be used when the inserted value for the column is NULL. The default value specified in the definition should satisfy the datatype and length of the column. If a default value is not explicitly set, the default for the column is implicitly set to NULL. Default values cannot refer to another column, and they cannot have the pseudo-columns LEVEL, NEXTVAL, CURRVAL, ROWNUM, or PRIOR. The default values can include SYSDATE, USER, USERENV, and UID.

In the following example, the table ORDERS is created with a column STATUS that has a default value PENDING. The column ORDER_NUMBER is created as a NOT NULL column. Oracle gives an error if you try to insert NULL values into this column.

```
CREATE TABLE ORDERS (
ORDER_NUMBER NUMBER (8) NOT NULL,
STATUS       VARCHAR2 (10) DEFAULT 'PENDING');

SQL> INSERT INTO ORDERS (ORDER_NUMBER) VALUES (4004);

1 row created.

SQL> SELECT * FROM orders;

ORDER_NUMBER STATUS
------------ ----------
        4004 PENDING

SQL>
```

The following dictionary views provide information about the table and its columns:

- DBA_TABLES
- DBA_ALL_TABLES
- USER_TABLES
- USER_ALL_TABLES
- ALL_TABLES
- ALL_ALL_TABLES
- DBA_TAB_COLUMNS
- USER_TAB_COLUMNS
- ALL_TAB_COLUMNS

You can use the DESCRIBE (SQL*Plus) command to list all of the columns, their datatype, size, nullity, and order.

Naming Conventions

Table names are used to identify each table. You should make table names as descriptive as possible; table/column names are called identifiers and can be up to 30 characters long. An identifier name should begin with a letter and may contain numeric digits. The only special characters allowed in an identifier name are the dollar sign ($), the underscore (_), and the pound sign (#). The underscore can be used for meaningful separation of the words in an identifier name. These names are case insensitive. If, however, you enclose the identifier names in double quotes (""), it will be case-sensitive in the Oracle dictionary.

Creating table names enclosed in quotes can cause serious problems when you do a query if you do not know the exact case of the table name.

The case sensitivity of names is illustrated in the following example:

```
SQL> CREATE TABLE MyTable (
  2    Column_1  NUMBER,
  3    Column_2  CHAR);
Table created.

SQL> desc mytable
 Name                                      Null?    Type
 ----------------------------------------- -------- ------
 COLUMN_1                                            NUMBER
 COLUMN_2                                            CHAR(1)

SQL> select table_name from user_tables
  2  WHERE  table_name = 'MyTable';
no rows selected

SQL>CREATE TABLE "MyTable" (
  2    "Column1" number,
  3    "Column2" char);
```

```
Table created.

SQL> desc "MyTable"
 Name                                      Null?    Type
 ----------------------------------------- -------- ------
 Column1                                             NUMBER
 Column2                                             CHAR(1)

SQL> select table_name from user_tables
  2   WHERE  upper(table_name) = 'MYTABLE';

TABLE_NAME
------------------------------
MYTABLE
MyTable
SQL>
```

It is a good practice to have the other objects directly related to the table also reflect the table name. For example, consider the EMPLOYEE table. The primary key of the table might be named PK_EMPLOYEE, indexes might be EMPLOYEE_NDX1 and EMPLOYEE_NDX2, check constraints might be CK_EMPLOYEE_STATUS, triggers might be TRG_EMPLOYEE_HIRE, and so on.

The purpose of the table and the column can be documented in the database using the COMMENT command. Let's provide comments for our example table:

```
SQL> COMMENT ON TABLE MYTABLE IS 'Oracle8i Study Guide
Example Table';
Comment created.

SQL> COMMENT ON COLUMN MYTABLE.COLUMN_1 is 'First column
in MYTABLE';
Comment created.
SQL>
```

WARNING SQL reserved words cannot be used as table or column names. You can use them only if you enclose the reserved words in double quotes.

Creating from Another Table

You can create a table using a query based on one or more existing tables. The column datatype and width will be determined by the query result. A table created in this fashion can select all the columns from another table (you may use *), or a subset of columns or expressions and functions applied on columns (these are called derived columns). Consider a simple query: You need to duplicate the structure and data of the EMP table to the EMPLOYEES table. Use the keyword AS to specify a query in the CREATE TABLE statement, like this:

```
SQL> CREATE TABLE employees
  2  AS SELECT * FROM emp;

Table created.

SQL>
```

You can have complex query statements in the CREATE TABLE statement. The table is created with no rows if the query returned no rows. If you just want to copy the structure of the table, make sure that the query returns no rows:

```
CREATE TABLE Y AS SELECT * FROM X WHERE 1 = 2;
```

You can provide column alias names to have different column names in the newly created table. The following example shows a table structure, displays the data, then creates a new table with the data and displays it:

```
SQL> DESCRIBE CITY
 Name                                      Null?     Type
 ----------------------------------------- --------  ------
 CNT_CODE                                  NOT NULL  NUMBER(4)
 ST_CODE                                   NOT NULL  VARCHAR2(2)
 CTY_CODE                                  NOT NULL  NUMBER(4)
 CTY_NAME                                            VARCHAR2(20)
```

```
POPULATION                                              NUMBER

SQL> SELECT COUNT(*) FROM city;

  COUNT(*)
----------
         3

SQL> CREATE TABLE new_city AS
  2  SELECT cty_code CITY_CODE, cty_name CITY_NAME FROM
city;

Table created.

SQL> SELECT COUNT(*) FROM new_city;

  COUNT(*)
----------
         3

SQL> DESC NEW_CITY
 Name                                     Null?    Type
 ---------------------------------------- -------- ------
 CITY_CODE                                         NUMBER(4)
 CITY_NAME                                         VARCHAR2(20)

SQL>
```

CREATE TABLE...AS SELECT... will not work if the query refers to columns of LONG datatype.

When you create a table using the subquery, only the NOT NULL constraints associated with the columns are copied to the new table. Other constraints and column default values are not copied.

Modifying Table Definitions

After you've created a table, there are several reasons that you might want to modify it. You can modify a table to change its column definition or default values, add a new column, or drop an existing column. You cannot rename columns. You might also modify a table if you need to change or add constraint definitions. The ALTER TABLE command is used to change table definitions.

Adding a Column

Here is the syntax to add a new column to an existing table:

```
ALTER TABLE [schema.]table_name ADD column_definitions;
```

Let's add a new column, ORDER_DATE, to the ORDERS table. When a new column is added, it is always at the bottom of the table. For the existing rows, the new column value will be NULL.

```
SQL> DESCRIBE orders
 Name                                      Null?    Type
 ----------------------------------------- -------- ------
 ORDER_NUMBER                              NOT NULL NUMBER(8)
 STATUS                                             VARCHAR2(10)


SQL> SELECT * FROM orders;

ORDER_NUMBER STATUS
------------ ----------
        4004 PENDING
        5005 COMPLETED


SQL> ALTER TABLE orders ADD order_date DATE;

Table altered.
```

```
SQL> DESC orders
 Name                                            Null?    Type
 ---------------------------------------------   -------- ------
 ORDER_NUMBER                                    NOT NULL NUMBER(8)
 STATUS                                                   VARCHAR2(10)
 ORDER_DATE                                               DATE

SQL> SELECT * FROM orders;

ORDER_NUMBER STATUS      ORDER_DAT
------------ ----------  ---------
        4004 PENDING
        5005 COMPLETED

SQL>
```

If you are adding more than one column, the column definitions should be enclosed in parentheses and separated by commas. If you specify a DEFAULT value for a newly added column, all the rows in the table would have the default value automatically assigned. For example, to add two more columns to the ORDERS table, you would do this:

```
SQL> ALTER TABLE orders ADD (quantity NUMBER (13,3),
  2                          update_dt DATE DEFAULT
sysdate);

Table altered.

SQL> SELECT * FROM orders;

ORDER_NUMBER STATUS      ORDER_DAT  QUANTITY UPDATE_DT
------------ ----------  ---------  -------- ---------
        4004 PENDING                         23-MAR-00
        5005 COMPLETED                       23-MAR-00

SQL>
```

When adding a new column, you cannot specify the NOT NULL constraint if the table already has rows. To add a NOT NULL column, you need to follow three steps: Modify the table to add the column, update the column with values for all the existing rows, and then add a NOT NULL constraint.

Modifying a Column

The syntax to modify an existing column in a table follows:

```
ALTER TABLE [schema.]table_name MODIFY column_name new_
attributes;
```

If you omit any of the parts of the column definition (datatype, default value, or column constraint), the omitted parts remain unchanged. If you are modifying more than one column at a time, enclose the column definitions in parentheses. For example, to modify the ORDERS table, increasing the STATUS column to 15 and reducing the QUANTITY column to 10,3, do this:

```
ALTER TABLE orders MODIFY (quantity number (10,3),
                           status varchar2 (15));
```

These are the rules for modifying column definitions:

- You can increase the length of the character column and the precision of the numeric column.

- To decrease the length of the column, the column should not contain any values; all rows for the column should be NULL.

- You can increase or decrease the decimal places of a NUMBER column without decreasing the precision, even if the column values are not NULL.

- The column must be NULL to change its datatype. If you do not change the length, you can change the datatype from CHAR to VARCHAR2 or vice versa, even if the column is not empty.

Dropping a Column

Prior to Oracle8i, the only way to remove a column was to re-create the table without the column name. In Oracle8i, you have the much awaited option of dropping a column. You can drop a column that is not used immediately, or you can mark the column as not used and drop it later.

Here is the syntax for dropping a column:

```
ALTER TABLE [schema.]table_name
```

```
DROP {COLUMN column_name | (column_names)}[CASCADE
CONSTRAINTS]
```

DROP COLUMN drops the column name specified from the table. You can provide more than one column name separated by commas inside parentheses. The *indexes* and constraints on the column are also dropped. You must specify CASCADE CONSTRAINTS if the dropped column is part of a multicolumn constraint; the constraint will be dropped.

The syntax for marking a column as unused follows:

```
ALTER TABLE [schema.]table_name
SET UNUSED {COLUMN column_name | (column_names)}[CASCADE
CONSTRAINTS]
```

You usually mark a column as unused and not dropped if the table is very large and takes a lot of resources at peak hours. In such cases, you would mark the column as unused and drop it later. Once the column is marked as unused, you will not see it as part of the table definition. Let's mark the UPDATE_DT column in the ORDERS table as unused:

```
SQL> ALTER TABLE orders SET UNUSED COLUMN update_dt;

Table altered.

SQL> DESCRIBE orders
 Name                                      Null?    Type
 ----------------------------------------- -------- ------
 ORDER_NUMBER                              NOT NULL NUMBER(8)
 STATUS                                             VARCHAR2(15)
 ORDER_DATE                                         DATE
 QUANTITY                                           NUMBER(10,3)

SQL>
```

The syntax for dropping a column already marked as unused is

```
ALTER TABLE [schema.]table_name
DROP {UNUSED COLUMNS | COLUMNS CONTINUE}
```

Use the COLUMNS CONTINUE clause to continue a DROP operation that was previously interrupted. To clear data from the UPDATE_DT column from the ORDERS table, do this:

```
ALTER TABLE orders DROP UNUSED COLUMNS;
```

The data dictionary views DBA_UNUSED_COL_TABS, ALL_UNUSED_COL_TABS, and USER_UNUSED_COL_TABS provide the names of tables in which you have columns marked as unused.

Dropping/Renaming Tables

Dropping a table is simple. Once you drop a table, the action cannot be undone. The syntax follows:

```
DROP TABLE [schema.]table_name [CASCADE CONSTRAINTS]
```

When you drop a table, the data and definition of the table are removed. The indexes, constraints, triggers, and privileges on the table are also dropped. Oracle does not drop the views, materialized views, or other stored programs that reference the table, but it marks them as invalid. You must specify the CASCADE CONSTRAINTS clause if there are referential integrity constraints referring to the primary key or unique key of this table. Here's how to drop the table TEST owned by user SCOTT:

```
DROP TABLE scott.test;
```

Renaming a Table

The RENAME command is used to rename a table and other database objects, such as views or private *synonyms*. Oracle automatically transfers integrity constraints, indexes, and grants on the old table to the new table. Oracle invalidates all objects that depend on the renamed table, such as views, synonyms, stored procedures, and functions. The syntax for the RENAME command follows:

```
RENAME old_name TO new_name;
```

Here, old_name and new_name are names of a table, view, private synonym, or *sequence*.

To rename the ORDERS table to PURCHASE_ORDERS, you would use this syntax:

```
SQL> RENAME orders TO purchase_orders;

Table renamed.

SQL> DESCRIBE purchase_orders
 Name                                      Null?     Type
 ----------------------------------------- --------- ------
 ORDER_NUMBER                              NOT NULL  NUMBER(8)
 STATUS                                              VARCHAR2(15)
 ORDER_DATE                                          DATE
 QUANTITY                                            NUMBER(10,3)

SQL>
```

You can rename only the objects you own; you cannot rename an object owned by another user.

Truncating a Table

The *TRUNCATE* statement is similar to the DROP command, but it does not remove the structure of the table, so none of the indexes, constraints, triggers, or privileges on the table are dropped. By default, the space allocated to the table and indexes is freed. If you do not wish to free up the space, include the REUSE STORAGE clause. You cannot roll back a truncate operation. Also, you cannot selectively delete rows using the TRUNCATE command. The syntax of TRUNCATE command is

```
TRUNCATE {TABLE|CLUSTER} [schema.]name [{DROP|REUSE}
STORAGE]
```

You cannot truncate the parent table of an enabled referential integrity constraint. You must first disable the constraint and then truncate the table, even if the child table has no rows. The following example demonstrates this:

```
SQL> CREATE TABLE t1 (t1f1 NUMBER CONSTRAINT pk_t1 PRIMARY
KEY);
Table created.
```

```
SQL> CREATE TABLE t2 (t2f1 NUMBER CONSTRAINT fk_t2
                                REFERENCES t1 (t1f1));
Table created.

SQL> TRUNCATE TABLE t1;
truncate table t1
            *
ERROR at line 1:
ORA-02266: unique/primary keys in table referenced by
enabled foreign keys


SQL> ALTER TABLE t2 DISABLE CONSTRAINT fk_t2;
Table altered.

SQL> TRUNCATE TABLE t1;
Table truncated.

SQL>
```

Use the TRUNCATE command to delete all rows from a large table; it does not write the rollback entries and is much faster than the DELETE command when deleting a large number of rows.

Managing Views

A *view* is a customized representation of data from one or more tables. The view takes the result of a query and stores it in the database. A view can be considered as a stored query or a virtual table. Only the query is stored in the *Oracle data dictionary*; the actual data is not copied anywhere. So, creating views does not take any storage space, other than the space in the data dictionary. A view can also hide query complexity. You may have multiple table joins in the query, but the user sees only the view. The views can have different column names than the base table. You may create a view to limit the data accessible to other users. In most cases, a view can be used wherever a table is used. All operations performed on the view affect the underlying base table or tables and are subject to firing triggers defined in the base table (if any), as well as integrity checks.

When you issue a query against a view, most of the time Oracle merges the query with the query that defines the view, then executes the resulting query as if the query were issued directly against the base tables. This helps to use the indexes if there are any defined on the table.

The maximum number of columns that can be defined in a view is 1,000, just like a table.

Creating a View

Use the CREATE VIEW command to create a view. The query that defines the view can refer to one or more tables, to materialized views, or to other views. The query cannot have a FOR UPDATE clause; an ORDER BY clause was not permitted in versions prior to Oracle8i. In 8i, the query can have an ORDER BY clause. Let's begin by creating a simple view. The view named TOP_EMP has the employee information for employees whose salary is above 2999. Note that the empno and ename columns are renamed by using alias names in the view definition.

```
SQL> CREATE VIEW TOP_EMP AS
  2  SELECT empno EMPLOYEE_ID, ename EMPLOYEE_NAME, salary
  3  FROM    emp
  4  WHERE   salary > 2999;

View created.

SQL> DESCRIBE top_emp
 Name                             Null?    Type
 -------------------------------- -------- ----
 EMPLOYEE_ID                               NUMBER(4)
 EMPLOYEE_NAME                             VARCHAR2(10)
 SALARY                                    NUMBER(7,2)

SQL>
```

You can also specify the column names immediately following the view name to have different column names in the view. Let's re-create the view using defined column names. The OR REPLACE clause is used to modify a view; basically, you are re-creating the view.

```
SQL> CREATE OR REPLACE VIEW TOP_EMP
  2  (EMPLOYEE_ID, EMPLOYEE_NAME, SALARY) AS
  3  SELECT empno, ename, salary
  4  FROM    emp
  5  WHERE   salary > 2999;

View created.

SQL>
```

WARNING If you use an asterisk (*) to select all columns from a table in the query to create a view and you later modify the table to add columns, you should re-create the view to reflect the new columns.

You can create views that manipulate data or that join more than one table. In this example, the view is created with employee name, salary, bonus, and department name. Note that the derived column has NUMBER datatype, but no length is derived.

```
SQL> CREATE VIEW EMP_BONUS AS
  2  SELECT dname, empno, ename, salary, salary * .15
bonus
  3  FROM    emp a, dept b
  4  WHERE   a.deptno = b.deptno;

View created.

SQL> DESC EMP_BONUS
```

Name	Null?	Type
DNAME		VARCHAR2(14)
EMPNO		NUMBER(4)
ENAME		VARCHAR2(10)
SALARY		NUMBER(7,2)
BONUS		NUMBER

```
SQL>
```

You can create views with errors using the FORCE option. Normally, if the view has errors, the view will not be created. If, however, you need to create the view with errors (for example, if the underlying table is not created yet), you can do so. The view will be invalid. Later, you can fix the error, such as creating the underlying table, and then the view can be recompiled. Oracle recompiles invalid views when the view is accessed.

```
SQL> CREATE FORCE VIEW ORDER_STATUS AS
  2  SELECT * FROM PURCHASE_ORDERS
  3* WHERE  STATUS = 'APPROVED'
SQL> /
Warning: View created with compilation errors.

SQL>
```

When you use the CREATE OR REPLACE option instead of dropping and re-creating the view, the privileges granted on the view are preserved. The dependent stored programs and views become invalid.

Retrieving Data

You can query data from a view as you would query a table. You can use views in joins and subqueries. You can use all SQL functions and all the clauses of the SELECT statement when querying against a view, as you would query against a table. Let's query the results of the EMP_BONUS view we just created:

```
SQL> SELECT * FROM EMP_BONUS ORDER BY dname, empno;
```

```
DNAME                     EMPNO ENAME          SALARY        BONUS
--------------       ----------  ----------   ----------   ----------
ACCOUNTING             7839 A_EDWARD            5000          750
RESEARCH                902 FORD                3000          450
RESEARCH               7566 JONES               2975       446.25
RESEARCH               7788 SCOTT               3000          450
SALES                  7654 MARTIN              1250        187.5
SALES                  7698 K_BLAKE             2850        427.5
SALES                  7844 TURNER              1500          225

7 rows selected.

SQL>
```

Inserting, Updating, and Deleting Data

You can update, insert, and delete rows through a view with restrictions. If the view is joining more than one table, you can update only one base table at a time. For updating or inserting into a view, all the columns that are part of a constraint should be in the view definition. The columns that can be updated in a view can be queried from the data dictionary USER_UPDATABLE_COLUMNS.

```
SQL> SELECT TABLE_NAME, COLUMN_NAME, UPDATABLE,
    INSERTABLE, DELETABLE
  2  FROM    USER_UPDATABLE_COLUMNS
  3* WHERE   TABLE_NAME = 'EMP_BONUS'
SQL> /
```

TABLE_NAME	COLUMN_NAME	UPD	INS	DEL
EMP_BONUS	DNAME	NO	NO	NO
EMP_BONUS	EMPNO	YES	YES	YES
EMP_BONUS	ENAME	YES	YES	YES
EMP_BONUS	SALARY	YES	YES	YES
EMP_BONUS	BONUS	NO	NO	NO

```
SQL>
```

We created the EMP_BONUS view by joining the DEPT and EMP tables. Since the primary key of DEPT table, DEPTNO, is not part of the view definition, the DEPT table cannot be updated, deleted, or inserted.

You can create views with an optional WITH clause. WITH READ ONLY specifies that the view cannot be updated or deleted and that new rows cannot be inserted. WITH CHECK OPTION specifies that inserts and updates done through the view should satisfy the WHERE clause of the view. For example, if you create the TOP_EMP view WITH CHECK OPTION, you cannot add new rows through the view whose salary is below 3000. WITH CHECK OPTION creates a constraint with constraint type "V". If you do not provide a name, the constraint is created with a SYS_ name.

```
SQL> CREATE OR REPLACE VIEW TOP_EMP
  2  (EMPLOYEE_ID, EMPLOYEE_NAME, SALARY) AS
  3  SELECT empno, ename, salary
  4  FROM    emp
  5  WHERE   salary > 2999
  6* WITH CHECK OPTION CONSTRAINT TOP_EMP_SAL
SQL> /
View created.

SQL> INSERT INTO TOP_EMP VALUES (1234, 'ADAMS', 1200);
INSERT INTO TOP_EMP VALUES (1234, 'ADAMS', 1200)
                 *
ERROR at line 1:
ORA-01402: view WITH CHECK OPTION where-clause violation

SQL> INSERT INTO TOP_EMP VALUES (1234, 'ADAMS', 3500);
1 row created.

SQL>
```

Any INSERT, UPDATE, or DELETE operation on a join view can modify only one underlying base table at a time.

If a view is defined by a query that contains SET or DISTINCT operators, a GROUP BY clause, or a group function, then rows cannot be inserted into, updated in, or deleted from the base tables using the view.

Dropping a View

Drop a view using the DROP VIEW command. The view definition is dropped from the dictionary, and the privileges and grants on the view are also dropped. Other views and stored programs that refer to the dropped view become invalid.

```
DROP VIEW TOP_EMP;
```

A view can be recompiled using the ALTER VIEW command. The objects dependent on the view are invalidated. Here's an example: ALTER VIEW MY_ VIEW COMPILE;.

Summary

This chapter discussed how to create and maintain tables and views. Tables are the basic structure of data storage. You can also store data in clusters and materialized views. A view does not take any data storage space.

The CREATE TABLE command is used to create a new table. A table should have at least one column, and a datatype should be assigned to the column. Oracle has character, numeric, raw, LOB, and ROWID datatypes. The table name and column name should begin with a letter and may contain letters, numbers, or special characters. You can create a new table from an existing table using the CREATE TABLE...AS SELECT... command. You can add, modify, or drop columns from an existing table. To change the datatype of a column or to reduce its size, make sure the column is empty. You can use the TRUNCATE TABLE command to delete all rows from a table.

A view is a tailored representation of data from one or more tables or views. The view is a stored query. Views can be used to present a different perspective of data, to limit the data access, or to hide a complex query. You can update, delete, and insert into the base tables through the view (with restrictions), but the operation can affect only one table at a time if there is more than one table in the view definition.

Key Terms

Before you take the exam, make sure you are familiar with the following terms:

Datatype

Default column values

Index

Oracle data dictionary

Owner

Schema

Sequence

Synonym

SYS

Table

Truncate

User

View

Review Questions

1. The table STATE is defined as in the following table.

Column Name	CNT_CODE	ST_CODE	ST_NAME
Key Type	PK, FK	PK	
Nulls/Unique			NN
FK Table	COUNTRY		
FK Column	CNT_CODE		
Datatype	NUMBER	VARCHAR2	VARCHAR2
Length	4	2	20

If you execute the statement that follows, how many constraints will the STATE_COPY table have?

```
CREATE TABLE STATE_COPY AS SELECT * FROM STATE
```

A. 4

B. 1

C. 0

D. 2

2. Refer to the table in Question 1. Which of the following lines of code has an error?

```
1   CREATE OR REPLACE VIEW US_STATES
2   AS SELECT ST_CODE ST_CODE,
3          ST_NAME STATE_NAME
4   FROM    STATE
5   WHERE   CNT_CODE = 1
6   ORDER BY ST_CODE;
```

A. Line 5

B. Line 2

C. Line 6

D. There is no error.

3. Which line of code has an error?

```
1   CREATE TABLE FRUITS_VEGETABLES
2   (FRUIT_TYPE VARCHAR2,
3    FRUIT_NAME CHAR (20),
4    QUANTITY   NUMBER);
```

A. Line 1

B. Line 2

C. Line 3

D. Line 4

4. Which statement successfully adds a new column ORDER_DATE to the table ORDERS?

A. ALTER TABLE ORDERS ADD COLUMN ORDER_DATE DATE;

B. ALTER TABLE ORDERS ADD ORDER_DATE (DATE);

C. ALTER TABLE ORDERS ADD ORDER_DATE DATE;

D. ALTER TABLE ORDERS NEW COLUMN ORDER_DATE TYPE DATE;

5. Refer to the table in Question 1. What's wrong with the following statement?

```
CREATE TABLE USA_STATES
SELECT * FROM STATE
WHERE  CNT_CODE = 1;
```

   A. A keyword is missing.

   B. The WHERE condition cannot be specified in the subquery creating tables.

   C. The column names should be defined.

   D. There is no error; a new table USA_STATES will be created.

6. What are the special characters allowed in a table name? Choose two answers.

   A. &

   B. #

   C. @

   D. $

7. Consider the following statement and choose the most appropriate option.

```
CREATE TABLE MY_TABLE
(1ST_COLUMN NUMBER,
  2ND_COLUMN VARCHAR2 (20));
```

   A. Tables cannot be created without defining a primary key. The table definition here is missing the primary key.

   B. The reserved word COLUMN cannot be part of the column name.

   C. Numbers are not allowed in the leading position of the column name.

   D. There is no maximum width specified for the first column definition. You must always specify a maximum width when defining columns.

8. Which dictionary view would you query to list only the tables you own?

   A. ALL_TABLES

   B. DBA_TABLES

   C. USER_TABLES

   D. USR_TABLES

9. Refer to the STATE table in Question 1. The table has six rows. If you issue the following command, which statement is correct?

   `ALTER TABLE STATE ADD UPDATE_DT DATE DEFAULT SYSDATE;`

   A. A new column, UPDATE_DT, is added to the STATE table and its contents for the existing rows are NULL.

   B. Since the table is not empty, you cannot add a new column.

   C. The DEFAULT value cannot be provided if the table has rows.

   D. A new column, UPDATE_DT, is added to STATE and is populated with the current system date and time.

10. Choose two correct statements:

    A. The TRUNCATE statement is used to selectively remove rows from table.

    B. The TRUNCATE statement is used to remove all rows from a table.

    C. Rows removed using the TRUNCATE command cannot be undone.

    D. The TRUNCATE command drops the constraints and triggers associated with the table.

11. Views created with which option make sure that rows added to the base table through the view are accessible to the view?

A. WHERE

B. WITH READ ONLY

C. WITH CHECK OPTION

D. CREATE OR REPLACE VIEW

12. A view is created using the following code. What operations are permitted on the view?

```
CREATE VIEW USA_STATES
AS SELECT * FROM STATE
WHERE  CNT_CODE = 1
WITH READ ONLY;
```

A. SELECT

B. SELECT, UPDATE

C. SELECT, DELETE

D. SELECT, INSERT

13. How do you remove the view USA_STATES from the schema?

A. ALTER VIEW USA_STATES REMOVE;

B. DROP VIEW USA_STATES;

C. DROP VIEW USA_STATES CASCADE;

D. DROP USA_STATES;

14. Refer to the STATE definition in the table in Question 1 and to the COUNTRY definition in the following table.

Column Name	CNT_CODE	CNT_NAME
Key Type	PK	
Nulls/Unique		NN
FK Table		
FK Column		
Datatype	NUMBER	VARCHAR2
Length	4	20

A view is created as follows:

```
CREATE OR REPLACE VIEW COUNTRY_STATE AS
SELECT a.CNT_NAME, b.CNT_CODE, b.ST_CODE, b.ST_NAME
FROM   COUNTRY a, STATE b
WHERE  a.CNT_CODE = b.CNT_CODE;
```

Which options are valid statements?

A. INSERT INTO country_state (cnt_code, st_code, st_name) VALUES (1, 'AZ', 'ARIZONA');

B. INSERT INTO country_state VALUES (NULL, 1, 'AZ', 'ARIZONA');

C. DELETE FROM country_state WHERE cnt_code = 1;

D. UPDATE country_state set cnt_name = 'USA' WHERE cnt_name = 'UNITED STATES';

15. Which data dictionary view has information on the columns that can be updated in a view?

   A. USER_VIEWS

   B. USER_UPDATABLE_COLUMNS

   C. USER_COLUMNS

   D. USER_COLUMNS_UPDATABLE

16. Which two of the following statements are correct?

   A. The DESCRIBE command is used to view the structure of objects in the database.

   B. The DESCRIBE command can be used only against tables.

   C. The DESCRIBE command issued against a procedure displays the arguments to the procedure.

   D. The DESCRIBE command shows the primary key and foreign key information of the table.

17. Which option in the view creation creates a view even if there are syntax errors?

   A. CREATE FORCE VIEW…

   B. CREATE OR REPLACE VIEW…

   C. CREATE VIEW FORCE…

   D. FORCE VIEW…

18. What is the default length of a CHAR datatype column, if no length is specified in the table definition?

   A. 256

   B. 1,000

   C. 64

   D. 1

19. What is the command for dropping a column UPDATE_DT from table STATE?

A. ALTER TABLE STATE DROP COLUMN UPDATE_DT;

B. ALTER TABLE STATE REMOVE COLUMN UPDATE_DT;

C. DROP COLUMN UPDATE_DT FROM STATE;

D. You cannot drop a column from the table.

20. Choose one invalid datatype from the following options:

A. CLOB

B. VARCHAR

C. TIME

D. BFILE

Answers to Review Questions

1. B. When you create a table using another table, only the NOT NULL constraints are created.

2. D. There is no error. Prior to Oracle8i, the ORDER BY clause was not allowed in the view definition. In 8i, however, using an ORDER BY clause is acceptable.

3. B. A VARCHAR2 datatype should always specify the maximum length of the column.

4. C. The correct statement is C. When adding only one column, the column definition need not be enclosed in parentheses.

5. A. The keyword AS is missing before the subquery.

6. B, D. Only three special characters ($_#) are allowed in the table names along with letters and numbers.

7. C. Column names (all identifiers) should begin with a letter and may contain numbers or special characters such as $,#, and _. You cannot use a reserved word for column names (any identifier); here, the word 1ST_COLUMN is not a reserved word.

8. C. The USER_TABLES view provides information on the tables owned by you. DBA_TABLES will have all the tables in the database, and ALL_TABLES will have the tables owned by you as well as the tables to which you have access. USR_TABLES is not a valid dictionary view.

9. D. When a default value is specified in the new column added, the column values for the existing rows are populated with the default value.

10. B, C. You cannot specify a WHERE clause in the TRUNCATE statement; it removes all the rows in the table, releases the storage space (this is the default), and does not drop or invalidate any of the dependent objects.

11. C. WITH CHECK OPTION makes sure that the new rows added or the rows updated are accessible to the view. The WHERE in the view definition limits the rows selected in the view from the base table.

12. A. When the view is created with the READ ONLY option, only reads are allowed from the view.

13. B. A view is dropped using the DROP VIEW view_name; command.

14. A, C. Since the view contains a join, in order to do INSERT or UPDATE to the base table, all the keys in the base table should be part of the view. In this view, only the keys of STATE table are included. Option B fails because it is using a column from COUNTRY table, although the value supplied is NULL.

15. B. The USER_UPDATABLE_COLUMNS view shows the columns that can be updated.

16. A, C. The SQL*Plus command DESCRIBE can be used to view the structure of a table, a view, a materialized view, and the arguments of procedures, functions, and packages.

17. A. The CREATE FORCE VIEW statement creates an invalid view even if there are syntax errors. Normally, a view will not be created if there are compilation errors.

18. D. If you do not specify length for a CHAR datatype column, the default length of 1 is assumed.

19. A. There is no DROP COLUMN command or a REMOVE clause in the ALTER TABLE.

20. C. TIME is an invalid datatype. The correct datatype is DATE, which stores date and time components.

Chapter

6

Other Database Objects and the Data Dictionary

ORACLE8i SQL AND PL/SQL EXAM OBJECTIVES OFFERED IN THIS CHAPTER:

- ✓ Describe other database objects and their uses
- ✓ Describe constraints
- ✓ Create and maintain a primary key constraint
- ✓ Create and maintain a referential integrity constraint
- ✓ Create and maintain a check constraint
- ✓ Create, maintain, and use sequences
- ✓ Describe the different types of indexes
- ✓ Create and maintain indexes
- ✓ Create private and public synonyms
- ✓ Describe some of the more common data dictionary views a user may access
- ✓ Query from the data dictionary
- ✓ Write a query to generate SQL from the data dictionary

Exam objectives are subject to change at any time without prior notice and at Oracle's sole discretion. Please visit Oracle's Training and Certification Web site (http://education.oracle.com/certification/index.html) for the most current exam objectives listing.

In this chapter, we will cover all of the database objects except tables and views, which are covered in Chapter 5, *Creating and Managing Tables and Views*. We will also go over some of the more commonly used data dictionary views, how to extract information from them, and how to write SQL to generate SQL—easing the administrative drudgery of mass changes.

Other Database Objects

An Oracle database can have far more than simply tables and views. Constraints enforce integrity rules. Sequences can be used to generate artificial keys and synonyms, alias objects. You can create stored SQL to implement business or integrity rules in a number of forms: functions, procedures, packages, and triggers. Some types of indexes can be deployed to enhance the performance of queries.

Throughout this chapter, we will use automobile insurance examples. In this scenario, we have a POLICIES table that contains information on the insurance policies issued, such as the policy holder's name and address. We also have an INSURED_AUTOS table that contains information on the individual automobiles insured on our policies and an AUTOMOBILES table that contains information on all makes and models of automobiles manufactured. See Figure 6.1 for an entity-relationship diagram of these three tables.

FIGURE 6.1 Entity-relationship diagram for examples

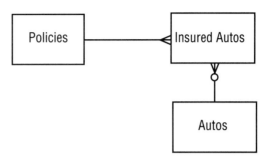

Constraints

Constraints are used to enforce data integrity. There are five varieties of constraints:

- Check
- NOT NULL
- Unique
- Primary key
- Foreign key

Constraints are rules and as such don't take up space in a database as a table does. Instead, constraints exist only in the data dictionary and are applied during the execution of SQL and PL/SQL. When constraints are enabled, they are enforced. When constraints are disabled, they are not enforced, but they still exist in the data dictionary. To disable a constraint, for example, in order to improve the performance of a bulk load operation, execute an ALTER TABLE statement:

```
ALTER TABLE table_name DISABLE CONSTRAINT constraint_name;
```

or

```
ALTER TABLE policies DISABLE CONSTRAINT chk_gender;
```

To re-enable the disabled constraint after the bulk load, again use the ALTER TABLE statement:

```
ALTER TABLE table_name ENABLE CONSTRAINT constraint_name;
```

or

```
ALTER TABLE policies  ENABLE CONSTRAINT chk_gender;
```

To drop a constraint that is no longer needed, you once again use the ALTER TABLE statement:

```
ALTER TABLE table_name DROP CONSTRAINT constraint_name;
```

or

```
ALTER TABLE policies DROP CONSTRAINT chk_gender;
ALTER TABLE AUTOMOBILES DROP PRIMARY KEY;
```

Knowing that the ALTER TABLE statement is used to drop a constraint, especially a primary key, is important and frequently appears on the exam.

Check Constraints

Check constraints require a specific Boolean condition on a column or set of columns to be true or at least one of the column values to be NULL. Check contraints are used to enforce simple business rules about the content of data in your table. For example, our POLICIES table has columns for the gender and marital_status of the policy holder. The gender can be only M or F, and the marital_status can only be one of S, M, D, or W. We use check constraints to ensure that our data conforms to these rules. Check constraints can reference other columns in the row being checked but cannot reference other rows or other tables, or call the functions SYSDATE, UID, USER, or USERENV. If your business rules require this kind of data checking, use triggers. Check constraints cannot protect columns of datatype LOB, object, nested table, VARRAY, or ref. A single column can be protected by more than one check constraint, and a check constraint protects one or more columns.

Create a check constraint along with the table, using the CREATE TABLE statement; after the table is created, use the ALTER TABLE statement. If the check protects a single column, it can be created inline with the column in the CREATE TABLE statement. The general syntax of a check constraint follows:

```
CONSTRAINT [constraint_name] CHECK( condition );
```

A check constraint can also be created or added as a table constraint. When it protects two or more columns, you must use the table constraint syntax. The constraint name is optional and, if this name is not present, Oracle will generate a unique name that begins with SYS_. The following example shows check constraints with both the inline column syntax and the table constraint syntax:

```
CREATE TABLE policies
(policy_id      NUMBER
,holder_name    VARCHAR2(40)
,gender         VARCHAR2(1) constraint chk_gender CHECK
  (gender in ('M','F'))  --inline syntax
,marital_status VARCHAR2(1)
,date_of_birth  DATE
-- table constraint syntax
,constraint chk_marital CHECK (marital_status in ('S' ,'M'
  ,'D' ,'W'))
);
```

You should not rely on system-generated names for constraints. If you want to compare table characteristics, such as between production and acceptance test, the inconsistent system-generated names will make this comparison more difficult.

NOT NULL Constraints

A *NOT NULL constraint* applies to a single column and requires data values for the column it protects. By default, Oracle allows a NULL value in any column. Where business rules require data in specific columns, a NOT NULL constraint on those specific columns will ensure that the protected columns always contain data. For example, each row in our POLICIES table must have the name and date_of_birth columns populated, so we modify the CREATE TABLE statement as follows:

```
CREATE TABLE policies
(policy_id      NUMBER
,holder_name    VARCHAR2(40) NOT NULL
,gender         VARCHAR2(1)
,marital_status VARCHAR2(1)
,date_of_birth  DATE         NOT NULL
);
```

The ALTER TABLE syntax for NOT NULL constraints is slightly different than for the other constraints. You must modify the column to add a NOT NULL constraint to it. Alternatively, you can add a check constraint that specifies the NOT NULL condition. Examples follow:

```
ALTER TABLE policies
MODIFY holder_name NOT NULL;
```

or

```
ALTER TABLE policies
ADD CONSTRAINT chk_holder (holder_name NOT NULL);
```

NOT NULL constraints appear in the data dictionary view DBA_CONSTRAINTS as check constraints. When created inline, NOT NULL constraints also appear in the data dictionary view DBA_TAB_COLUMNS as a column attribute. To drop a NOT NULL constraint, use the ALTER TABLE MODIFY statement, like this:

```
ALTER TABLE policies MODIFY holder_name NULL;
```

Unique Constraints

A *unique constraint* protects one or more columns in a table, ensuring that no two rows contain duplicate data in the protected columns. For example, in our INSURED_AUTOS table we need to ensure that the combination of policy_id and the auto's VIN number is unique. Create a unique constraint together with the table, using the CREATE TABLE statement; after the table is created, use the ALTER TABLE statement. If the constraint is on a single column, it can be created inline with the CREATE TABLE statement. Using our insurance example, a policy may have a rider, and if it does, the rider_id must be unique. Here's the general syntax:

```
,column_name data_type CONSTRAINT constraint_name UNIQUE
```

For our POLICIES table, the code would look like this:

```
,rider_id       NUMBER     CONSTRAINT uniq_rider UNIQUE
```

If the unique constraint protects two or more columns, the constraint needs to be added as a table constraint with the syntax shown in Figure 6.2.

FIGURE 6.2   Unique constraint syntax

Unique constraints are enforced with a B-tree index, so the USING clause may be exploited to specify characteristics for the index, such as the tablespace or storage parameters. The CREATE TABLE statement that includes a unique constraint will create a unique index on the protected columns. The CREATE TABLE statement for POLICIES would look like this:

```
CREATE TABLE insured_autos
(policy_id       NUMBER
,vin             VARCHAR2(40)
,coverage_begin  DATE
,coverage_term   NUMBER
,CONSTRAINT uniq_auto UNIQUE (policy_id ,vin)
  USING INDEX TABLESPACE indx
  STORAGE (INITIAL 1M NEXT 10M PCTINCREASE 0)
);
```

You can disable a unique constraint so that it is not enforced but still exists. This technique is frequently used for bulk loads on a table where constraint checking on each row as the row is inserted can degrade performance significantly from a single check after all rows are inserted. To disable a unique constraint, use the ALTER TABLE statement:

```
ALTER TABLE insured_autos DISABLE CONSTRAINT uniq_auto;
```

To remove a unique constraint entirely, use the ALTER TABLE...DROP CONSTRAINT statement with the constraint name, like this:

```
ALTER TABLE insured_autos DROP CONSTRAINT uniq_auto;
```

You will not be able to drop a unique constraint on a table that has foreign keys pointing to it. You must disable or drop the foreign key constraints first.

Disabling or dropping a unique constraint usually drops the enforcing index, thus depriving any SQL of the performance benefits it may have provided. If you frequently disable or drop a unique constraint, you can avoid the performance problems caused by the missing index by following these steps:

1. Create a non-unique index on the columns that the unique constraint will protect.

2. Add the unique constraint.

The unique constraint will not create a second index and will still enforce uniqueness. If the constraint were dropped, a unique index would be dropped along with the constraint, but the non-unique index will remain. With our INSURED_AUTOS example, we could do this:

```
CREATE INDEX insured_autos_u1-- non-unique index
ON insured_autos (policy_id ,vin)
TABLESPACE indx
STORAGE (INITIAL 1M NEXT 10M PCTINCREASE 0);


ALTER TABLE insured_autos
ADD CONSTRAINT uniq_auto UNIQUE (policy_id ,vin);
```

There is a tradeoff involved in using a non-unique index to enforce a unique constraint. The optimizer can perform a unique scan on a unique index, but it can perform only a range scan on a non-unique index. Using our non-unique index trick will result in one additional logical read for every index access that must be done in range scan mode, as opposed to unique scan mode.

Primary Key Constraints

Tables can have only a single *primary key constraint*. A table's primary key can protect one or more columns and incorporates NOT NULL constraints on each column in the key, as well as a unique constraint on all columns in the key. This combination of NOT NULL and unique will ensure that the primary key uniquely identifies each and every row. As with the unique constraint, the primary key is enforced with a B-tree index.

You can create a primary key constraint together with the table using the CREATE TABLE statement; after the table is created, use the ALTER TABLE statement. If the primary key is on a single column, it can be created inline with the CREATE TABLE statement:

```
CREATE TABLE policies
(policy_id NUMBER CONSTRAINT pk_policies PRIMARY KEY
,holder_name    VARCHAR2(40)
,gender         VARCHAR2(1)
,marital_status VARCHAR2(1)
,date_of_birth  DATE
);
```

As with unique constraints, if the primary key protects two or more columns, it must be created as a table constraint:

```
CREATE TABLE insured_autos
(policy_id       NUMBER
,vin             VARCHAR2(40)
,coverage_begin  DATE
,coverage_term   NUMBER
,CONSTRAINT pk_insured_autos PRIMARY KEY (policy_id ,vin)
   USING INDEX TABLESPACE indx
   STORAGE (INITIAL 1M NEXT 10M PCTINCREASE 0)
);
```

To disable or drop a primary key constraint, you must do so with the ALTER TABLE statement, like this:

```
ALTER TABLE policies DROP PRIMARY KEY;
```

or

```
ALTER TABLE policies DISABLE PRIMARY KEY;
```

You will not be able to drop a primary key on a table that has foreign keys pointing to it. You will have to disable or drop the foreign key constraints first. As with a unique constraint, dropping or disabling a primary key constraint will usually drop the enforcing index. You can use the same trick of creating a non-unique index before creating the primary key to avoid dropping the index with the primary key. As with the unique constraint, using a non-unique index costs you the ability to perform a unique index scan.

Foreign Key Constraints

A *foreign key constraint* protects one or more columns in a table by ensuring that each row's data values contains one or more null values or that all the data values in the protected columns exist in a primary or unique constraint. The referenced (primary or unique) constraint can protect the same table or a different one. Unlike unique or primary keys, foreign keys do *not* implicitly create a B-tree index to enforce the constraint. When dealing with foreign key constraints, we often use the terms *parent table* and *child table*. The parent table is the referenced table, that is, the one with the primary or unique key. The child table is the referencing table, that is, the one whose data values are checked for existence elsewhere. Foreign key constraints are often called referential integrity constraints because they enforce referential data integrity.

You can create a foreign key constraint in the CREATE TABLE statement; after the table is created, use the ALTER TABLE statement. As with the primary key, if the foreign key protects a single column (like policy_id the following example), it can be created inline with the column definition; otherwise, it is created with table constraint syntax:

```
CREATE TABLE insured_autos
(policy_id      NUMBER        CONSTRAINT policy_fk
   REFERENCES policies(policy_id)
   ON DELETE CASCADE
,vin            VARCHAR2(40)
,coverage_begin DATE
,coverage_term  NUMBER
,make           VARCHAR2(30)
,model          VARCHAR2(30)
,year           NUMBER(4)
,CONSTRAINT auto_fk FOREIGN KEY (make, model, year)
   REFERENCES automobiles (make, model, year)
   ON DELETE SET NULL
);
```

A foreign key constraint that protects two or more columns must be created using the table constraint syntax shown in Figure 6.3.

FIGURE 6.3   Foreign key constraint syntax

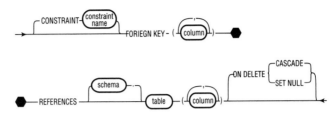

The ON DELETE clause tells Oracle what to do with the child records if a parent record is deleted. The default is to prohibit deletes on the parent table if child records exist. You can configure the foreign key constraint to *on delete cascade*, which causes deletes on the parent record to cascade, deleting any child records automatically. Alternatively, the constraint can be set to *on delete set NULL*, which causes deletes on the parent table to update the child table setting any referencing rows to NULL. So, using our INSURED_AUTOS table, you can see that a delete on the POLICIES table will cascade and delete rows in the INSURED_AUTOS table, as well. Deletes in the AUTOMO-BILES table, however, will cause rows in the INSURED_AUTOS table to be updated, setting the columns make, model, and year to NULL.

Foreign Keys and NULLs

The treatment of NULL values in columns protected by a foreign key constraint can produce unanticipated results. Oracle uses the ISO standard Match None rule for enforcing foreign key constraints. This rule states that if any column in a foreign key contains a NULL value, any remaining key columns do not have to match values in the parent. For example, our parent table, AUTOMOBILES, has a primary key on make, model, year, and our dependent table, INSURED_AUTOS, has a foreign key constraint pointing to the AUTOMOBILES table. Notice the row in the INSURED_AUTOS table that contains a NULL model. This row has passed the constraint check, even though the make (Tucker) does not appear in the parent table AUTO-MOBILES, as you can see in Tables 6.1 and 6.2.

TABLE 6.1   AUTOMOBILES Table Data

make	model	year
Ford	Taurus	2000
Toyota	Camry	1999

TABLE 6.2 INSURED_AUTOS Table Data

policy_id	make	model	year
576	Ford	Taurus	2000
577	Ford	Taurus	2000
578	Tucker	NULL	1949

Deferred Constraint Checking

By default, constraints are checked during the execution of a statement that changes data under constraint protection. This is called immediate constraint checking because the constraint is checked immediately at the end of each statement. You have the option of performing constraint checks at the end of a transaction by enabling deferred constraint checking. This deferred constraint checking can be useful if your application changes tables protected by foreign key constraints and does so in an order that, within the transaction, temporarily violates the constraint. For example, the first statement in a transaction inserts a row into a child table that would violate a foreign key constraint. But the second statement inserts a row into the parent table that will satisfy the constraint. The third statement commits the changes. If immediate constraint checking were used, the first statement would fail, but with deferred constraint checking, both statements would succeed since the constraint check is not performed until the commit.

By default, constraints are *deferrable* and checked *initially immediate*. They can be set to *nondeferrable* and checked *initially deferred*. The deferrable and nondeferrable settings control the ability of a session to change when the constraint will be checked. The initially immediate and initially deferred settings control the default constraint checking for a particular constraint.

To enable deferred constraint checking, use the SET CONSTRAINTS statement, whose syntax is shown in Figure 6.4.

FIGURE 6.4   Set constraints syntax

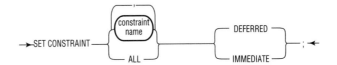

Constraints in Practice

Oracle employs an optimistic model when enforcing constraint checking. This model assumes that most checks will succeed and is appropriate for most environments. The constraint check is made after the rollback segment is allocated, the undo is recorded, the table data is changed, and any index entries are modified. While this optimistic model is best for most applications, if your application and data are such that a pessimistic model is more appropriate, you may want to check the constraint conditions in the application code prior to executing the DML; this will save the database the work of making all the changes, then rolling them back when the constraint fails. You will still want the constraints on the table for data hygiene and documentation purposes, but you might not want to rely on the database's constraint enforcement to filter large amounts of unwanted data.

Sequences

An Oracle *sequence* is a named sequential number generator. Sequences are often used for artificial keys or to order rows that otherwise have no order. Like constraints, sequences exist only in the data dictionary. Sequences can be configured to increase or decrease without bound or to repeat (cycle) upon reaching a bounding value. Sequences are created with the CREATE SEQUENCE statement. Figure 6.5 shows the syntax of the CREATE SEQUENCE statement.

FIGURE 6.5 Create sequence syntax

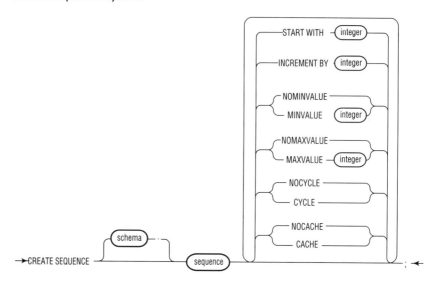

Keyword	Description
START WITH	Defines the first number that the sequence will generate. The default is one.
INCREMENT BY	Defines the increase or decrease for subsequently generated numbers. To specify a decreasing sequence, use a negative INCREMENT BY.
MINVALUE	The lowest number the sequence will generate. This is the bounding value in a decreasing sequence. The default MINVALUE is the keyword NOMINVALUE, which translates to 1 for an increasing sequence and to -10^{26} for a decreasing sequence.

MAXVALUE	The largest number that the sequence will generate. This is the bounding value in the default, increasing sequence. The default MAXVALUE is the keyword NOMAXVALUE which translates to 10^{27} for an increasing sequence and to -1 for a decreasing sequence.
CYCLE	Configures the sequence to repeat numbers after reaching the bounding value.
NOCYCLE	Configures the sequence to not repeat numbers after reaching the bounding value. This is the default. When you try to generate the MAXVALUE+1, an exception will be raised.
CACHE	Defines the size of the block of sequence numbers held in memory. The default is 20.
NOCACHE	Forces the data dictionary to be updated for each sequence number generated, guaranteeing no gaps in the generated numbers.

When you create the sequence, the START WITH value must be equal to or greater than MINVALUE. Sequence numbers can be configured so that a set of numbers is fetched from the data dictionary and cached or held in memory for use. Caching the sequence improves its performance because the data dictionary table does not have to be updated for each generated number, only for each set of numbers. The negative aspects of caching the sequence can result when the database is bounced (shut down and restarted)—any unused, cached values are lost.

To access the next number in the sequence, you simply select from it, using the pseudo-column *nextval*. To get the last sequence number that your session has generated, you select from it using the pseudo-column *currval*. If your session has not yet generated a new sequence number, currval will be undefined.

Know the precise syntax for and how to use sequence_name.nextval and sequence_name.currval. This syntax is important and frequently appears on the exam.

Sequences are removed with the DROP SEQUENCE statement:

```
DROP SEQUENCE sequence_name
```

In the following transcript, we create a sequence, then use it to generate column values in INSERT statements and an UPDATE statement:

```
create sequence policy_seq nomaxvalue nocycle;


Sequence created.


select policy_seq.currval from dual;  --no current value


ERROR at line 1:
ORA-08002: sequence POLICY_SEQ.CURRVAL is not yet defined
in this session



select policy_seq.nextval from dual;


   NEXTVAL
----------
         1


select policy_seq.currval from dual;


   CURRVAL
----------
         1


-- update an existing table with the sequence

select * from old_acme_policies;
```

```
POLICY_ID ACME_ID          HOLDER_NAME
---------- ---------------- ------------------------------
          C23              Joshua
          C24              Elizabeth
          D31              David
          D34              Sara
          A872             Jamie
          A891             Jeff
          A884             Jennie

update old_acme_policies
   set policy_id = policy_seq.nextval;

7 rows updated.

select * from old_acme_policies;

POLICY_ID ACME_ID          HOLDER_NAME
---------- ---------------- ------------------------------
        5 C23              Joshua
        6 C24              Elizabeth
        7 D31              David
        8 D34              Sara
        9 A872             Jamie
       10 A891             Jeff
       11 A884             Jennie

rollback;

update old_acme_policies set
   policy_id = policy_seq.nextval;

7 rows updated.

-- the rollback does not undo the generation of the
-- sequence numbers
```

```
select * from old_acme_policies;

POLICY_ID ACME_ID          HOLDER_NAME
---------- ----------------  ----------------------------
       12 C23               Joshua
       13 C24               Elizabeth
       14 D31               David
       15 D34               Sara
       16 A872              Jamie
       17 A891              Jeff
       18 A884              Jennie

commit;
```

Indexes

Indexes are data structures that can offer improved performance in obtaining specific rows over the default full-table scan. Indexes do not always improve performance, however, and in this section we will review the indexing technologies covered on the exam, as well as look at when and how indexes can improve performance. Oracle offers

- B-tree, hash, and bitmap index types

- Index-organized tables

- Function-based indexes

- Domain indexes

The certification exam tends to focus primarily on B-trees and may have a question about bitmap indexes, so we'll concentrate on these two types only.

Oracle retrieves rows in a table in one of two ways:

- By ROWID

- By full-table scan

Both B-tree and bitmap indexes map column data to ROWIDs for the columns of interest, but they do so in different ways. When one or more indexes are used, Oracle will use the known column values to find the interesting ROWIDs. The rows can then be retrieved by ROWID. While indexes can improve the performance of data retrieval, indexes degrade performance for data changes (DML), because the indexes must be modified in addition to the table.

It's important to know that indexes degrade the performance of DML operations; this is frequently a question on the exam.

The B-Tree Index

B-tree indexes are the most common index type, as well as the default. They can be either unique or non-unique and either simple (one column) or concatenated (multiple columns). B-tree indexes provide the best performance on high-cardinality columns, that is, on columns having many distinct values. B-tree indexes offer a more efficient method to retrieve a small number of interesting rows than does a full table scan, but they do not improve retrieval performance if more than about 10 percent of the table must be examined. As the name implies, a *B-tree index* is based on a binary tree, constructed with branch blocks and leaf blocks. Branch blocks contain the index columns (the key) and an address to another index block. Leaf blocks contain the key and the *ROWID* for each matching row in the table. Additionally, the leaf blocks are a doubly linked list, so they can be range-scanned in either direction. Figure 6.6 shows how the B-tree index key values are constructed into a binary tree.

FIGURE 6.6 Index structure of B-tree index on name

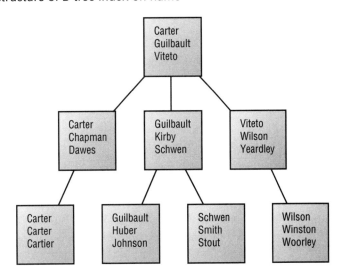

B-tree indexes may be used if any combination of the leading columns of the index are used in the SQL statement. For example, our INSURED_ AUTOS table has an index on the make, model, and year columns:

```
CREATE TABLE insured_autos
(policy_id       NUMBER
,vin             VARCHAR2(40)
,coverage_begin  DATE
,coverage_term   NUMBER
,make            VARCHAR2(30)
,model           VARCHAR2(30)
,year            NUMBER(4)
);


CREATE INDEX auto_idx ON insured_autos (make, model,
year);
```

We could use the auto_idx index if we ran the following query, to see how many Ford Taurus autos we have issued policies on. Since make and model are a leading subset of columns in the index, the index may be used:

```
SELECT COUNT(*)
FROM insured_autos
WHERE make = 'Ford'
  AND  model = 'Taurus';
```

We would not be able to use the auto_idx index if we ran the following query, since model is *not* a leading subset of columns in the index:

```
SELECT COUNT(*)
FROM insured_autos
WHERE model = 'Taurus';
```

The Bitmap Index

Bitmap indexes are primarily used for decision support systems or static data; they do not support row-level locking. Bitmap indexes can be simple (one column) or concatenated (multiple columns), but in practice bitmap indexes are almost always simple. Bitmap indexes are best used for low- to medium-cardinality columns where multiple bitmap indexes can be combined with AND and OR conditions. Each key value has a bitmap, which contains a TRUE, FALSE, or NULL value for every row in the table. The bitmap index is constructed by storing the bitmaps in the leaf nodes of a B-tree structure. The B-tree structure makes it easy to find the bitmaps of interest quickly. Additionally, the bitmaps are stored in a compressed format, so they take up significantly less disk space than B-tree indexes. Figure 6.7 shows how a bitmap index on the state column of the INSURED_AUTOS table would be structured. The bitmaps are in the leaf blocks of a B-tree structure. Each row (ROWID) in the table has an entry in each bitmap. These entries are either TRUE or FALSE (1 or 0).

FIGURE 6.7 Index structure of bitmap index on state of residence

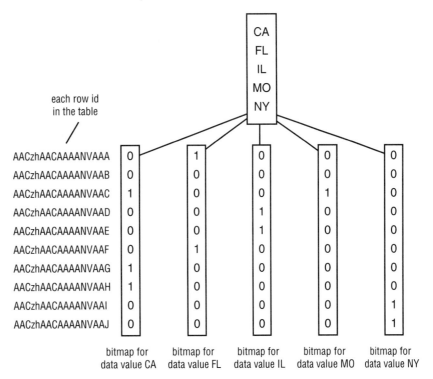

When a query references a number of bitmap-indexed columns, the bitmaps can be combined with AND and OR operations to find the interesting data. For example, an insurance company that offers policies for automobiles has a large table of insured autos named, appropriately, INSURED_ AUTOS. This table contains a number of low- to medium-cardinality attributes of the insured autos, including year, make, model, color, body style, engine size, and so on. The actuarial department needs to do some analysis of insured autos based on various combinations of these attributes in order to set rates appropriately, so we create bitmap indexes on each of these columns. We are interested in getting the VIN# for certain insured autos with the following query:

```
SELECT vin
FROM insured_autos
WHERE body_style='HATCH'
  AND  make in ('Ford', 'Dodge', 'Honda')
  AND  year BETWEEN 1990 AND 1993
  AND  color IN ('red', 'white', 'blue')
```

To combine the bitmaps, Oracle will perform a bitwise OR for the four year bitmaps of interest, a bitwise OR for the three make bitmaps of interest, a bitwise OR for the three color bitmaps of interest, then AND the three derived bitmaps to locate the ROWIDs of interest. Figure 6.8 illustrates this bitmap merge operation.

FIGURE 6.8 Bitmap merge

ROWIDs	Ford		Dodge		Honda		1995		1996		1997		1998		Red		White		Blue
AA..AC	0	or	1	or	0	and	1	or	0	or	0	or	0	and	0	or	0	or	1
AA..AD	0		0		1		0		0		0		0		1		0		0
AA..AE	1		0		0		0		1		0		0		0		0		0
AA..AF	0		0		0		0		0		0		0		0		0		0
AA..AG	0		0		0		0		0		0		1		0		1		0
AA..BD	0		0		0		0		0		0		1		0		0		0
AA..BE	1		0		0		0		0		1		0		0		0		0
AA..BF	0		0		1		0		0		0		0		0		0		0
AA..CA	0		0		0		0		1		0		0		1		0		0

The bitmaps above evaluate to the following:

ROWIDs				
AA..AC	1		1		1
AA..AD	1		0		1
AA..AE	1		1		0
AA..AF	0		0		0
AA..AG	0	and	1	and	1
AA..BD	0		1		0
AA..BE	1		1		0
AA..BF	1		0		0
AA..CA	0		1		1

Next, the three bitmaps evaluate to the following single bitmap

ROWIDs	
AA..AC	1
AA..AD	0
AA..AE	1
AA..AF	0
AA..AG	0
AA..BD	0
AA..BE	0
AA..BF	0
AA..CA	0

The times that bitmap indexes really stand out are when various combinations of multiple indexed columns are specified. A single bitmap index usually will not afford improved performance over a full-table scan. In the AUTOS example, if we had one B-tree index on the three columns year, make, and color, it would perform slightly better than the combination of the bitmap indexes, but if the queries did not always use all three of these columns or used other combinations of columns, the number of B-tree indexes required would grow to be quite large, especially if we had many of these attribute columns.

Indexes in Practice

Indexes may improve the performance of SELECT, UPDATE, and DELETE operations. An index can be used if a leading subset of the indexed columns appear in the SELECT or WHERE clause. Additionally, if all the columns needed to satisfy a query appear in an index, Oracle need only access the index and not the table. For example, we have our INSURED_AUTOS table, which has an index on the columns (make, model, year). If we run the following query to get a count of the number of 1999 Ford Taurus autos that we have issued policies against, Oracle only needs to access the index and not the table. All necessary columns are in the index:

```
SELECT COUNT(*)
FROM insured_autos
WHERE make = 'Ford'
  AND model = 'Taurus'
  AND year = 1999;
```

Knowing that the table does not need to be accessed if the index contains all needed information is important and is frequently a question on the exam.

Synonyms

A *synonym* is an alias for another database object. A *public synonym* is available to all users, while a *private synonym* is available only to the owner or to the accounts to whom that owner grants privileges. A synonym can point to a table, view, sequence, procedure, function, or package in the local database, or, via a database link, to an object in another database. Synonyms are frequently used to simplify SQL by giving a universal name (public synonym) to a local or remote object. Synonyms also can be used to give different or multiple names to individual objects. Unlike views or stored SQL, synonyms don't become invalid if the object they point to is dropped. Likewise, you can create a synonym that points to an object that does not exist or that the owner does not have permissions on.

For example, user SCOTT owns a table EMP. All users log in to the database under their own userID and so must reference the table with the owner as SCOTT.EMP. But when we create a public synonym EMP for SCOTT.EMP, then anyone who has privileges on the table can simply reference it in their SQL or PL/SQL as EMP, without having to specify the owner. When the statement is parsed, Oracle will resolve the name EMP via the synonym to SCOTT.EMP.

When Oracle performs name resolution for references to tables, stored procedures, stored functions, or packages, there are three places that Oracle will look for the referenced object, in this order:

1. An object owned by the current user

2. A private synonym

3. A public synonym

The syntax for creating a synonym follows:

```
CREATE [PUBLIC] SYNONYM synonym_name FOR
[schema.]object[@db_link];
```

Here's an example:

```
CREATE PUBLIC SYNONYM policies FOR poladm.policies@prod;
```

or

```
CREATE SYNONYM plan_table FOR system.plan_table;
```

The public synonym policies would then refer to the POLICIES table owned by user poladm in the prod database. The synonym plan_table would point to the table named PLAN_TABLE that is owned by user system.

To remove a synonym, use the DROP SYNONYM statement:

```
DROP [PUBLIC] SYNONYM synonym_name;
```

Procedures and Functions

Procedures and *functions* are named PL/SQL programs that are stored in a compiled form in the database. Functions take zero or more parameters and return a value. Procedures take zero or more parameters and return no values. Both functions and procedures can receive or return zero or more values through their parameter lists. The primary difference between procedures and functions, other than the return value, is how they are called. Procedures are called as stand-alone executable statements:

```
pay_invoice(invoice_nbr,30,due_date);
```

Functions are called anywhere an expression is valid:

- In an assignment:

```
order_volume := open_orders(SYSDATE, 30);
```

- In a Boolean expression:

```
IF (open_orders(SYSDATE, 30) < 500 )
THEN …
```

- In a default value assignment:

```
DECLARE
    order_volume NUMBER DEFAULT open_orders(SYSDATE, 30);
BEGIN …
```

- In a SQL statement:

```
SELECT vendor_name
FROM vendors
WHERE open_orders(SYSDATE, 30, vendor_id) = 0;
```

- In the parameter list of another program:

```
process_vendor(vendor_id,open_orders(vendor=>vendor_id));
```

The syntax for creating a procedure follows:

```
CREATE [OR REPLACE] PROCEDURE [schema.]procedure_name
[ parameter_list ]
{AS | IS}
  declaration_section
BEGIN
  executable_section
[EXCEPTION
  exception_section]
END [procedure_name];
```

The declaration, executable, and exception sections are all covered in greater detail in Chapter 7, *PL/SQL Basics*. The parameter_list is a comma-delimited list of zero or more parameters. Each parameter has the following syntax:

```
paramter_name mode datatype [(:= | DEFAULT) value]
```

The mode describes whether the parameter can be read from or written to. Valid modes are IN for read-only access, OUT for write-only access and IN OUT for read-write access. The datatype is the parameter's datatype, but not the size. The size is determined by the calling program. You have the option of assigning a default value to a parameter, so the calling program does not have to supply it. Specifying the default value can be performed either with the assignment operator (:=) or with the keyword DEFAULT. Therefore, the following two statements are equivalent:

```
today DATE :=       SYSDATE;
today DATE DEFAULT SYSDATE;
```

Sometimes extracting information from the data dictionary is clumsy, because LONG datatypes are sometimes used and these LONG datatypes impose a number of restrictions on their use from SQL*Plus. You have greater flexibility in working with LONGs from PL/SQL. For example, we want to extract ALTER TABLE statements from the data dictionary to assign default values to table columns, but the data_default column is a LONG, so we create the following procedure that uses dbms_output. A caveat for this procedure is that dbms_output has a limit of 255 characters per line, so if we have really long default values, we'll need to add a loop to the output part of the program to chop up the data_default into smaller pieces. But most defaults are things like Y, N, or SYSDATE.

```
CREATE OR REPLACE PROCEDURE Get_col_defaults
(ownr IN VARCHAR2 ,tabl IN VARCHAR) IS
    CURSOR def_col_cur IS
    SELECT 'ALTER TABLE'||LOWER(ownr)||'.'||
        LOWER(tabl)||' MODIFY '||
        column_name||' DEFAULT ' part1, data_default
    FROM  dba_tab_columns
    WHERE owner=ownr
     AND  table_name=tabl
     AND  data_default IS NOT NULL;

  BEGIN
    FOR def_col_rec IN def_col_cur
    LOOP
       dbms_output.put(def_col_rec.part1);
       dbms_output.put(def_col_rec.data_default);
       dbms_output.put_line(';');
    END LOOP;
  END;
```

The syntax for creating a function is almost identical to that of a procedure. Note that the required RETURN clause is the only difference:

```
CREATE [OR REPLACE] FUNCTION [schema.]function_name
[ parameter_list ]
RETURN returning_datatype
{AS | IS}
  declaration_section
BEGIN
  executable_section
[EXCEPTION
  exception_section]
END [procedure_name];
```

Functions must have one or more RETURN statements in their executable section.

You might recall from Chapter 2, *Single-Row and Group Functions*, that Oracle's trigonometric functions only operate on radians. If we want a SIN function that takes degrees, we can write it ourselves and simply put a wrapper around Oracle's built-in function:

```
CREATE OR REPLACE FUNCTION my_sin(DegreesIn IN NUMBER)
RETURN NUMBER
IS
  pi                   NUMBER := ACOS(-1);
  RadiansPerDegree     NUMBER;

BEGIN
  RadiansPerDegree := pi/180;

  RETURN(SIN(DegreesIn*RadiansPerDegree));
END;
```

This function can be called just like the built-in function:

```
SELECT my_sin(90) FROM dual;


MY_SIN(90)
----------
         1
```

When we try 180 degrees, however, we notice that we get some rounding errors:

```
SELECT my_sin(180) FROM dual;


MY_SIN(180)
-----------
 1.0000E-38
```

So, we add the ROUND function to round the result to the 37th decimal, which should be sufficient as long as we are not calculating trajectories for Mars space probes:

```
CREATE OR REPLACE FUNCTION my_sin(DegreesIn IN NUMBER)
RETURN NUMBER
```

```
IS
  pi                  NUMBER := ACOS(-1);
  RadiansPerDegree    NUMBER;

BEGIN
  RadiansPerDegree := pi/180;

  RETURN(ROUND(SIN(DegreesIn*RadiansPerDegree),37));
END;
```

Now, we get the 0 that we expected from 180 degrees:

```
SELECT my_sin(180) FROM dual;

MY_SIN(180)
-----------
          0
```

Parameter Passing

When calling procedures and functions, there are two techniques that you can use to pass parameters to the programs:

- Positional notation

- Named notation

As the name implies, *positional notation* passes parameters based on their position in the parameter list, regardless of name. With *named notation*, the programmer specifically assigns a value to a named parameter; the order in which the parameters appear does not matter. The names of the parameters are available from the package specification. As you can see in the example below, the named notation is more verbose, but it is also more self-documenting. For our example, we want to use the packaged procedure DBMS_UTILITY.ANALYZE_SCHEMA to analyze user Scott's schema, estimating the statistic by sampling 10 percent of each table:

```
-- positional notation
dbms_utility.analyze_schema('SCOTT','ESTIMATE',NULL,10);
```

```
--named notation
dbms_utility.analyze_schema(schema=>'SCOTT'
  ,method=>'ESTIMATE',estimate_percent=>10);
--named notation with parms in different order
dbms_utility.analyze_schema(estimate_percent=>10,
  schema=>'SCOTT',method=>'ESTIMATE');
```

There are some additional, advanced options that procedures and functions can use, such as deterministic, parallel enabled, and authid. These advanced concepts are not typically addressed on the exam and are not covered in this text. See the language reference for the exhaustive details.

Packages

Packages are containers that bundle together procedures, functions, and data structures. They consist of an externally visible package specification, which contains the function headers, procedure headers, and externally visible data structures. The package also consists of a package body, which contains the declaration, executable, and exception sections of all the bundled procedures and functions.

There are a number of differences between packaged and non-packaged PL/SQL programs. Package data is persistent for the duration of the user's session. Package data thus exists across commits in the session. When you grant the execute privilege on a package, it is for all programs and data structures in the package specification. You cannot grant privileges on only one procedure or function within a package. Packages can overload procedures and functions, declaring multiple programs with the same name. The correct program to be called is decided at runtime, based on the number or datatypes of the parameters. An example of an overloaded function is the TRUNC function declared in the package STANDARD. There is one TRUNC function for a date datatype and another for numeric data. The PL/SQL engine decides which to call at runtime based on which datatype gets passed to TRUNC. A package body can also be wrapped, or delivered in compiled form (PCODE), so that the source code is not readable.

To create a package, you must first create the package specification, using the following syntax:

```
CREATE [OR REPLACE] PACKAGE [schema.]package_name
{AS | IS}
```

```
      public_variable_declarations     |
      public_type_declarations         |
      public_exception_declarations    |
      public_cursor_declarations       |
      function_specifications          |
      procedure_specifications
   END [package_name];
```

To create the package body, use the CREATE PACKAGE BODY statement after creating the package specification. (You will raise an exception if you try to create the body before the spec.) The syntax for the package body follows:

```
CREATE [OR REPLACE] PACKAGE BODY [schema.]package_name
{AS | IS}
      private_variable_declarations    |
      private_type_declarations        |
      private_exception_declarations   |
      private_cursor_declarations      |
      function_specifications          |
      procedure_specifications
   END [package_name];
```

The private data structures are those used within the package body, which are not visible to the calling program.

For our example, we want to collect a series of database statistics from V$ tables and include a timestamp in the data. We write the five SELECT statements, using SYSDATE and discover that sometimes the time portion changes from the first statement to the last. It doesn't change enough to throw our statistics off by a meaningful amount, only by a couple of seconds, but sometimes those couple of seconds cross a minute or hour boundary, and we want a consistent timestamp reported. The call to SYSDATE to get the timestamp is a function call and does not obey database read consistency. We can't use SET TRANSACTION ISOLATION LEVEL SERIALIZABLE or SET TRANSACTION READ ONLY to get SYSDATE to report the same time across multiple statements. We can use a package, however, to grab a timestamp at the beginning of the collection interval, and then use the saved timestamp in our SELECTs:

```
CREATE OR REPLACE PACKAGE timestamp IS    -- package spec
    FUNCTION GetTimestamp RETURN DATE;
    PRAGMA RESTRICT_REFERENCES (GetTimestamp, WNDS);
    PROCEDURE ResetTimestamp;
END timestamp;

CREATE OR REPLACE PACKAGE BODY timestamp IS
    /* Global data structures */
    StartTimeStamp   DATE := SYSDATE;

    FUNCTION GetTimestamp RETURN DATE IS
    BEGIN
        RETURN StartTimeStamp;
    END GetTimestamp;

    PROCEDURE ResetTimestamp IS
    BEGIN
        StartTimeStamp := SYSDATE;
    END ResetTimestamp;
END timestamp;
```

Now the first call to `timestamp.GetTimestamp` will set the package variable to the current time. In the five collection statements, we substitute `timestamp.GetTimestamp` for SYSDATE, and the timestamps are then consistent.

Triggers

Triggers are programs that are executed automatically in response to a change in the database. Triggers can be configured to fire, or execute, either before or after the triggering event. The events that can be hooked with triggers include the following:

- DML events
- DDL events
- Database events

DML event triggers can be statement or row triggers. The DML statement trigger fires before or after the triggering statement. The DML row trigger fires before or after each row affected by the statement is changed. You can define multiple triggers for a single event and type (for example, two or more before-statement triggers), but there is no way to enforce the order in which these multiple triggers will fire. Table 6.3 lists the trigger events that you can use.

TABLE 6.3 Trigger Events

Event	Trigger Description
insert	Fires whenever a row is inserted into the table or view.
update	Fires whenever a row is updated in the table or view.
delete	Fires whenever a row is deleted from a table or view.
create	Fires whenever a CREATE statement adds a new object to the database or a specific schema.
alter	Fires whenever an ALTER statement changes an object in the database or a specific schema.
drop	Fires whenever a DROP statement removes an object from the database or a specific schema.
startup	Fires when the database is opened. Can only be an after-event trigger.
shutdown	Fires when the database is closed via either the normal or immediate option, but not the abort option. Can only be a before-event trigger.

TABLE 6.3 Trigger Events *(continued)*

Event	Trigger Description
logon	Fires when a session is created, that is, when a user connects. Can only be an after-event trigger.
logoff	Fires when a session disconnects from the database. Can only be a before-event trigger.
servererror	Fires when a server error occurs. Can only be an after-event trigger.

The syntax for creating a trigger follows:

```
CREATE [OR REPLACE] TRIGGER trigger_name
{BEFORE | AFTER | INSTEAD OF} event
ON {table_or_view_name | DATABASE}
[FOR EACH ROW [WHEN condition]]
trigger_body
```

Only DML triggers (INSERT, UPDATE, DELETE) on views can be INSTEAD OF triggers and only DML triggers on tables can be BEFORE or AFTER triggers.

To create a trigger that populates the who_last and when_last columns of our POLICIES table with the current user and SYSDATE for the last change to a policy, you could create the following trigger:

```
CREATE OR REPLACE TRIGGER policy_who BEFORE insert or
update
ON policies
FOR EACH ROW
BEGIN
  :new.who_last  := USER;
  :new.when_last := SYSDATE;
END
```

The :new in this example refers to a record containing the new, post-change data. The :old would refer to a record containing the old, pre-change data. The trigger can have visibility to both old and new values. However, the :old on an insert and the :new on a delete have no meaning; they contain all NULLs.

Like constraints, triggers may be disabled or enabled to turn off or turn on their execution. Triggers are bit different from constraints when it comes to enabling or disabling. To enable or disable a single trigger, use the ALTER TRIGGER statement:

```
ALTER TRIGGER trigger_name ENABLE;
ALTER TRIGGER trigger_name DISABLE;
```

or

```
ALTER TRIGGER policy_who ENABLE;
ALTER TRIGGER policy_who DISABLE
```

To enable or disable all triggers on a table, use the ALTER TABLE statement:

```
ALTER TABLE table_name DISABLE ALL TRIGGERS;
ALTER TABLE table_name ENABLE  ALL TRIGGERS;
```

or

```
ALTER TABLE policies DISABLE ALL TRIGGERS;
ALTER TABLE policies ENABLE  ALL TRIGGERS;
```

Remove triggers with the DROP TRIGGER statement:

```
DROP TRIGGER trigger_name;
```

or

```
DROP TRIGGER policy_who;
```

Triggers in Practice

Triggers are often used to bolt on functionality to a purchased application. These applications generally do not include the source code; therefore, customizations are not otherwise feasible. Even if you do have the source code (as with Oracle Financials or SAP), you might want to implement the customizations as a different program unit (the trigger) rather than the purchased program. That way, you won't have to re-customize it with every patch applied. The bolt-on functionality may be something like auditing or logging that does not change the business rules that the purchased application has implemented. You don't want to modify and test changes to the business rule code if you don't have to.

`After` DML triggers are slightly more efficient than `before` triggers, since the row must be fetched twice with a `before` trigger: once for the trigger and again for the DML. An `after` row trigger only has to fetch the row once for the DML.

A Quick 'n' Dirty Review of the Data Dictionary

The Oracle data dictionary contains metadata on your database. The underlying tables have names like OBJ$, UET$, and SOURCE$. These tables are created from the `sql.bsq` script during execution of the CREATE DATABASE statement. Rarely, if ever, do you need to access these underlying tables, however. The script `catalog.sql`, usually located in $ORACLE_HOME/ rdbms/admin, is typically run right after the CREATE DATABASE statement. The `catalog.sql` script creates the data dictionary views that everyone normally uses.

For most data dictionary views, there are three similar views with different contents:

- There are those prefixed with USER_, which contain information about objects owned by your schema or privileges granted to or from your schema.

- The next, more comprehensive, views are those prefixed by ALL_, which contain objects and privileges that you own or have privileges on.

- The most comprehensive views are those prefixed by DBA_, which include all objects and privileges in the database.

A family of views, such as DBA_TABLES, ALL_TABLES, and USER_TABLES, exists for most dictionary views. There are more than 100 such view families, so a comprehensive listing here would be long, tedious, and of little value. Most are unlikely to appear on the exam, such as views for replication, function-based indexes, programmer-defined operators, and so on. Table 6.4 includes some of the more important view families: Each family will have a DBA_ , an ALL_, and a USER_ view. You are likely to encounter questions on the exam that will test your general knowledge of these views. If you have worked with Oracle for a year or more, you will probably be familiar with many of these views.

If you're relying on this book to learn everything about Oracle that may appear on the exam, crack open a pack of sticky notes, make up some flashcards with the following data dictionary families, and trudge through the rote memorization of them. You can stick them on the mirror for review while you're brushing your teeth, stick them to the back of your favorite cereal box for some light breakfast reading, stick them to your computer monitor—get creative. Just *don't* stick them inside the windshield of your car or to your spouse's forehead.

TABLE 6.4 Important Data Dictionary View Families

View family	Description
COL_PRIVS	Column privileges, such as grantee, grantor, and privilege
EXTENTS	Extent information, such as datafile, segment_name, and size
INDEXES	Index information, such as type, uniqueness, and referenced table
IND_COLUMNS	Index column information, such as column order in index
OBJECTS	Object information, such as status and DDL time
ROLE_PRIVS	Role privileges, such as grantee and admin option
SEGMENTS	Segment (table and index) information, such as tablespace and storage
SEQUENCES	Sequence information, such as cache, cycle, and last_number
SOURCE	Source code for all stored SQL except triggers
SYNONYMS	Synonym information, such as referenced object and db_link
SYS_PRIVS	System privileges, such as grantee, privilege, and admin option
TAB_COLUMNS	Table and view column information, including column datatype

TABLE 6.4 Important Data Dictionary View Families *(continued)*

View family	Description
TAB_PRIVS	Table privileges, such as grantor, grantee, and privilege
TABLES	Table information, such as tablespace, storage parms, and row count
TRIGGERS	Trigger information, such as type, event, and trigger body
USERS	User information, such as temp and default tablespace
VIEWS	View information, including the view definition

There are some data dictionary tables that may appear on the exam but aren't really in a dictionary family. Table 6.5 shows these important single views.

TABLE 6.5 Important Individual Data Dictionary Views

View name	Description
USER_COL_PRIVS_MADE	Column privileges that you have granted to others
USER_COL_PRIVS_RECD	Column privileges that you have received from others
USER_TAB_PRIVS_MADE	Table privileges that you have granted to others
USER_TAB_PRIVS_RECD	Table privileges that you have received from others

The other major group of dictionary views are the V$ views, so called because they all start with V$ or GV$ (for global V$). The V$ views are based on the X$ virtual tables. These V$ views are owned by user SYS and by default are only available to users with DBA privileges. These views give visibility to a wealth of instance-oriented information, as opposed to the database-oriented information in the DBA_, ALL_, and USER_ views. Shared memory, latch, lock and wait statistics all appear in V$ views. The SQL and PL/SQL exam probably won't have extensive questions on these views, but understanding that they exist and provide tuning data might be tested.

The Inside Hack to X$ Tables

The X$ tables are really data structures in memory that have a table-based interface, so they are available to be queried with SQL. You can get a listing of all of them from V$FIXED_TABLE. They typically have cryptic table and column names, but you can gain insight into what they contain by examining the V$ view definitions in V$FIXED_VIEW_DEFINITION. Once you get a feel for the naming conventions, they don't seem as cryptic:

- KG = Kernel Generic
- KS = Kernel Services
- KT = Kernel Transactions
- KC = Kernel Cache

If you try to grant privileges on an X$ table, you will get the exception "ORA-02030: can only select from fixed tables/views." The way to work around this is to follow these steps:

1. Create a view on the X$ table.

2. Grant select on the view to whoever needs to read it.

3. Create a public synonym on the view with the same name as the base table.

For example, all the init.ora parameters are listed in X$KSPPI. To give public access to this information, you could do the following as user SYS:

```
CREATE VIEW x_$ksppi AS SELECT  * FROM x$ksppi;
GRANT SELECT ON x_$ksppi TO PUBLIC;
CREATE PUBLIC SYNONYM x$ksppi FOR sys.x_$ksppi;
```

Now, when anyone references X$KSPPI, the public synonym will direct them to the view SYS.X_$KSPPI, which directs them to the fixed table SYS.X$KSPPI.

Be careful with some of the X$ tables: Oracle does not support direct access to them and reserves the right to change them from release to release, but like the rest of the data dictionary, parts have changed little if at all since Oracle6. Use them at your own risk (as do many DBAs), and the X$ tables more than likely will not appear on the exam.

Querying the Data Dictionary

One of the most powerful techniques that a DBA can employ is to use the data dictionary to generate SQL. For example, if we want to change the temporary tablespace for all users (except SYS) to TEMP, we have a few choices:

- Manually key in each statement, and be typing for weeks on a large system

- Manually key in the statement once with a variable for the username, then key in the username once for each user, and be at it for hours on a large system

- Write a SQL statement to generate the necessary ALTER USER statements and be done in minutes

The obvious choice is to generate the SQL as follows:

```
SELECT 'ALTER USER '||username||
  ' TEMPORARY TABLESPACE temp;'
FROM DBA_USERS
WHERE username <> 'SYS'
  AND temporary_tablespace <> 'TEMP';
```

The results of this query can be spooled to a file then executed. They will look like this:

```
ALTER USER SYSTEM TEMPORARY TABLESPACE temp;
ALTER USER OUTLN TEMPORARY TABLESPACE temp;
ALTER USER DBSNMP TEMPORARY TABLESPACE temp;
ALTER USER SCOTT TEMPORARY TABLESPACE temp;
ALTER USER DEMO TEMPORARY TABLESPACE temp;
```

Let's look at another example of when this technique can be used. You re-created an important package and now virtually every function, procedure, trigger, and package in your application schema is invalid. Since you don't want to key in ALTER COMPILE statements until next February, you decide to use SQL to generate SQL. You cleverly write the following to generate the ALTER COMPILE statements:

```
SELECT 'ALTER '||DECODE(object_type,'PACKAGE BODY'
  ,'PACKAGE',object_type)
      ||' '||object_name||' COMPILE'
```

```
        ||decode(object_type,'PACKAGE BODY',' BODY;',';')
FROM user_objects
WHERE status = 'INVALID'
```

You run this SQL, spooling the output to a file, then execute the spooled SQL—job done. You even have time to go to lunch, while everything compiles. Life is good.

Summary

In this chapter, we reviewed the five types of constraints, how to create and drop them via the CREATE TABLE or ALTER TABLE statements, and the fact that an index is used to enforce unique and primary key constraints. We covered sequence number generators and how to use them with the NEXTVAL and CURRVAL keywords.

Oracle has many index types, and we looked at B-tree and bitmap indexes: how they are constructed and when they can be used. You saw when indexes can speed up access to data and also that they slow down inserts, updates, and deletes.

Oracle synonyms are a mechanism to alias other objects, either local or in another database accessed through database links. Synonyms can be globally available (public) or restricted to limited users (private). You saw that functions can return multiple values through the parameter list, must contain a return statement, and can be used in any expression. Procedures, on the other hand, return values through their parameter list only and are executed as stand-alone statements. Triggers are PL/SQL programs that have no parameter lists or return values and execute in response to database events. Packages are constructed of a specification and a body and may contain functions, procedures, and data structures. You read about named and positional notation for passing parameters to procedures and functions. Finally, we touched on a number of the data dictionary view families and how to use them to generate SQL.

Key Terms

Before you take the exam, make sure you're familiar with the following terms:

Cardinality

Child table

Currval

Deferrable

Foreign key constraint

Function

Initially deferred

Initially immediate

Key

Named notation

Nextval

Nondeferrable

NOT NULL constraint

On delete cascade

On delete set NULL

Package

Parent table

Procedure

Primary key constraint

Positional notation

Private synonym

Public synonym

ROWID

Sequence

Synonym

Unique constraint

Review Questions

1. Which of the following statements will create a primary key constraint pk_books on the table BOOKS, column ISBN? Choose one.

   A. `create primary key on books(ISBN);`

   B. `create constraint pk_books primary key`
      `on books(ISBN);`

   C. `alter table books`
      `add constraint pk_books primary key (ISBN);`

   D. `alter table books`
      `add primary key (ISBN);`

2. Which of the following check constraints will raise an exception? Choose all that apply.

   A. `CONSTRAINT gender_chk`
      `CHECK (gender in 'M','F')`

   B. `CONSTRAINT no_old_order`
      `CHECK (order_date > SYSDATE - 30)`

   C. `CONSTRAINT vendor_chk`
      `CHECK (vendor_id in (select vendor_id from vendors))`

   D. `CONSTRAINT profit_chk`
      `CHECK (gross > net)`

3. Which data dictionary view(s) will contain information about NOT NULL constraints? Select all that apply.

   A. `DBA_TAB_COLUMNS`

   B. `DBA_IND_COLUMNS`

   C. `DBA_CONSTRAINTS`

   D. `DBA_COL_CONSTRAINTS`

4. The table ANIMALS has a unique constraint on the two nullable columns genus and species. How many rows can contain genus = 'Smiladon' and NULL species?

A. 0

B. 1

C. Any number up to all rows −1

D. Any number up to all rows

5. You have a large job that will load many thousands of rows into your BOOK_AUTHORS table. To speed up the loading process, you want to temporarily stop enforcing the foreign key constraint book_fk. Which of the following statements will satisfy our requirement? Choose all that apply.

A. `alter constraint book_fk disable;`

B. `alter table book_authors direct insert mode;`

C. `alter table book_authors disable constraint book_fk;`

D. `alter table book_authors disable all constraints;`

6. Which statement will force the constraint checks to occur at the end of the transaction? Choose one.

A. `set transaction defer constraints;`

B. `set transaction delay constraints;`

C. `set constraints transaction level;`

D. `alter session set constraints deferred;`

7. Which named PL/SQL program must return a value? Choose one.

A. Procedure

B. Function

C. Trigger

D. Method

8. How do you return multiple values from a procedure?

   A. Use IN parameters.

   B. Use OUT parameters.

   C. Use pointers.

   D. You can't.

9. You have a large job that will load many thousands of rows into your ANI-MALS table. To speed up the loading process, you want to temporarily stop firing the trigger `location_trigr`. Which of the following statements will satisfy your requirement? Choose all that apply.

   A. `alter trigger location_trigr disable;`

   B. `alter table animals direct insert mode;`

   C. `alter table animals disable trigger location_trigr;`

   D. `alter table book_authors disable all triggers;`

10. Which of the following events is not a trigger event? Choose one.

    A. `before insert`

    B. `after create`

    C. `before logon`

    D. `after startup`

    E. `after delete`

11. A power user is running some reports and has asked you to put two new B-tree indexes on a large table so that her reports will run faster. You acknowledge that the indexes would speed up the reports. Can the proposed indexes slow other processes? Choose one.

    A. No, indexes only speed up queries.

    B. Yes, the indexes will make the optimizer take longer to decide the best execution plan.

    C. Yes, DML will run more slowly.

    D. Yes, table reorgs will be slower.

12. Examine the following table instance exhibit. Which index could be used to speed up the following query?

```
SELECT emp_id FROM emp WHERE sur_name LIKE 'DAW%S';
```

Column Name	emp_id	surname	first_name	hire_date
Key Type	pk			
NULLs/ Unique	NN	NN		NN
FK Table				
Datatype	varchar2	varchar2	varchar2	date
Length	9	50	40	

A. B-tree index on (surname, hire_date)

B. B-tree index on (emp_id)

C. B-tree index on (emp_id, surname)

D. No index would help; a full-table scan is the best access method.

13. Examine the following table instance exhibit. Which index could be used to speed up the following query?

```
select gender, avg(salary)
from emp
where marital_status = 'S'
group by gender;
```

Column Name	emp_id	gender	marital_status	state_residence
Key Type	pk			
NULLs/ Unique	NN	NN	NN	NN
FK Table				
Datatype	varchar2	varchar2	varchar2	varchar2
Length	9	1	1	2

    A. Bitmap index on (marital_status)

    B. Bitmap index on (marital_status, gender)

    C. Two separate bitmap indexes on (marital_status) and (gender)

    D. No indexes would help; a full-table scan is the best access method.

14. In which clauses in a SELECT statement can an index be used? Choose all that apply.

    A. SELECT

    B. FROM

    C. WHERE

    D. HAVING

15. What order does Oracle use in resolving a table or view referenced in a SQL statement?

 A. Table/view within user's schema, public synonym, private synonym

 B. Table/view within user's schema, private synonym, public synonym

 C. Public synonym, table/view within user's schema, private synonym

 D. Private synonym, public synonym, table/view within user's schema

16. Which statement will display the last number generated from the emp_seq sequence? Choose one.

 A. `select emp_seq.curr_val from dual;`

 B. `select emp_seq.currval from dual;`

 C. `select emp_seq.lastval from dual;`

 D. `select last_number from all_sequences where sequence_name ='EMP_SEQ';`

 E. You can't get the last sequence number generated.

17. Which data dictionary table would you look in to find which tablespace you would use for temporary segments in large sorting operations?

 A. MY_SORT_SEGMENTS

 B. USER_USERS

 C. USER_SORT_SEGMENTS

 D. USER_SORT_SPACE

18. Which data dictionary table can be queried to determine the unique B-tree indexes that you own? Choose one.

 A. USER_IND_COLUMNS

 B. DBA_INDICES

 C. USER_INDEXES

 D. USER_TAB_INDEXES

19. Which of the following can you *not* do with a package?

A. Overload procedures and functions

B. Hide data

C. Retain data across commits

D. Grant execute privileges on one procedure in a package

20. Which of the following calls to the stored function my_sine() will raise an exception?

A. Theta := my_sine(45);

B. IF (my_sine(45) > .3) THEN

C. DECLARE
    Theta   NUMBER DEFAULT my_sine(45);
  BEGIN …

D. my_sine(45);

Answers to Review Questions

1. C. The ALTER TABLE statement is used to create and remove constraints. Option D would work if it included the keyword constraint between add and primary.

2. B, C. Check constraints cannot reference the function SYSDATE or other tables.

3. A, C. NOT NULL constraints appear in two separate areas of the data dictionary. They appear as column attributes in DBA_TAB_COLUMNS and as check constraints in DBA_CONSTRAINTS.

4. D. A unique constraint will ensure that data is not duplicated in the protected columns, but a NULL is not data; it is the lack of data. A NULL value in one column protected by a unique constraint basically allows any data to appear in the other columns protected by that constraint.

5. C. To temporarily suspend the checking of constraints, you disable them. To disable constraints on a table, you need to disable them one at a time with the ALTER TABLE statement. There is no direct insert mode.

6. D. The ALTER SESSION statement is used to defer constraint checks or to set them to immediate.

7. B. Functions must include a RETURN statement and must return a value.

8. B. OUT parameters pass values out of a procedure. IN parameters pass values into the procedure. You cannot declare pointers in PL/SQL.

9. A, D. Triggers can be disabled in two ways: singly, with the ALTER TRIGGER statement, or *en masse* with the ALTER TABLE statement.

10. C. An after logon trigger is valid, but not a before logon trigger.

11. C. This one's a little tricky. B, C, and D are all true, but C is the best answer. Two additional indexes should not appreciably slow the optimizer, and table reorgs in Oracle (unlike other databases) are usually not needed. DML (insert, update, delete) operations will definitely be slowed as the new indexes will need to be maintained.

12. A. An index can be used if a leading subset of the columns is used. In our case, the first column in the index is on surname, so the (sur_name, hire_date) index could be used to perform a range scan on surname.

13. D. Bitmap indexes only improve performance when more than one is used and the combination of all of them returns a small portion of the table. This example requires a full-table scan because only one column (marital_status) is a candidate for using bitmap indexes.

14. A, C. The obvious answer is C, but an index can be used for the SELECT clause, as well. If an index contains all of the columns needed for the query, the table does not need to be accessed.

15. B. Private synonyms override public synonyms, and tables or views owned by the user always resolve first.

16. B. D is close, but it shows the greatest number in the cache, not the latest generated. The correct answer is from the sequence itself using the pseudo-column currval.

17. B. USER_USERS is in the dictionary family _USERS, which contains temporary and default tablespaces for user accounts. The USER_PREFIX tells you that USER_USERS will contain information on your account.

18. C. USER_IND_COLUMNS can tell you which indexes you own and which columns are in them, but not if the index type is B-tree or bitmap. DBA_INDICES and USER_TAB_INDEXES do not exist.

19. D. You can only grant execute on the entire package, not on any individual packaged programs.

20. D. Functions cannot be called as stand-alone statements; procedures are called that way.

PL/SQL Basics

ORACLE8i SQL AND PL/SQL EXAM OBJECTIVES OFFERED IN THIS CHAPTER:

✓ **Declaring Variables:**

- List the benefits of PL/SQL
- Describe the basic PL/SQL block and its sections
- Describe the significance of variables in PL/SQL
- Declare PL/SQL variables

✓ **Writing executable statements:**

- Describe the significance of the executable section
- Write statements in the executable section
- Describe the rules of the nested blocks
- Execute and test a PL/SQL block

✓ **Writing control structures:**

- Identify the uses and types of control structures
- Construct an IF statement
- Construct and identify different loop statements
- Control block flow using nested loops and labels

Exam objectives are subject to change at any time without prior notice and at Oracle's sole discretion. Please visit Oracle's Training and Certification Web site (http://education.oracle.com/certification/index.html) for the most current exam objectives listing.

In the previous chapters, you have seen how to use structured query language (SQL) and to interact with Oracle. In this chapter, we will begin programming in Oracle. PL/SQL is Oracle's procedural extension to SQL, the standard database access language. PL/SQL is integrated into the Oracle server and other tools. In recent years, more developers and DBAs have started to use PL/SQL. This chapter will show you the basics of PL/SQL, its structure and components. You will also learn how to write and execute a PL/SQL program, use control structures and loops, and create stored programs like procedures, functions, packages, and triggers.

Benefits of PL/SQL

PL/SQL has been available in Oracle since version 6. Once you have learned PL/SQL's benefits and ease of data management, it is difficult to imagine Oracle without PL/SQL. PL/SQL is not a separate product; it is a technology integrated into the server and certain Oracle tools like Forms. Think of PL/SQL as an engine inside the Oracle server. The SQL statement executor processes the individual SQL statements, and the *PL/SQL engine* handles the PL/SQL program as a single unit. Figure 7.1 shows how PL/SQL works from inside the Oracle server. When the PL/SQL block is passed to the PL/SQL engine, the Oracle server SQL statement executor processes the SQL statements inside the PL/SQL block, and the PL/SQL engine processes the procedural statements.

FIGURE 7.1   The PL/SQL engine

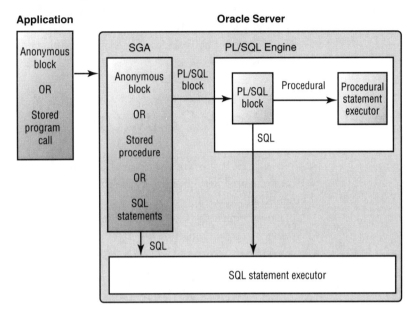

The benefits of PL/SQL follow:

- PL/SQL is a high-performance transaction-processing language. It is portable to any Oracle environment and supports all SQL data manipulation commands. Data-definition and data-control elements of SQL can also be handled by PL/SQL using special PL/SQL program units supplied by Oracle.

- PL/SQL supports all SQL datatypes and all SQL functions; it also lets you use all Oracle object types.

- PL/SQL blocks can be named and stored in the Oracle server and reused as required in another PL/SQL program or from the SQL command line. The small unit of code is more manageable and reusable. PL/SQL programs stored in the Oracle server can be accessed from any client/server tools.

- Security on PL/SQL structures stored in the server can be managed using the Oracle database objects syntax. You can grant and revoke privileges on these stored PL/SQL programs to and from other users in the database.

- PL/SQL code can be written using any ASCII text editor, so it is portable to any operating environment in which Oracle runs.

- With SQL, Oracle must process each SQL statement one at a time. In a networked environment, this means that a separate call must be made to the Oracle server each time a SQL statement is issued, which involves network traffic. With PL/SQL, the entire block of statements is sent to the Oracle server at one time, reducing network traffic.

The PL/SQL Block Structure

P L/SQL is a block-structured language. The units that constitute a PL/SQL program are logical blocks. A PL/SQL program may contain one or more blocks (called sub-blocks). Each block may be divided into three sections. As in many programming languages, the variables are declared before they are used. PL/SQL provides a separate section for error handling. The following paragraphs describe the different sections of a PL/SQL block.

Declaration section   The *declaration section* contains the datatype and initial value of all variables and constants used in the executable section of the block. This section begins with the keyword DECLARE. If you don't need to declare a variable, you can omit this section. This section also declares cursors and user-defined exceptions that are referenced in the other block sections.

Executable section   The *executable section* is a mandatory section in the PL/SQL block. This section begins with the keyword BEGIN. All the executable statements are given in this section. This section can also have other PL/SQL blocks inside.

Exception section   The *exception section* is an optional section, which has executable statements to handle an exception or error. Exceptions are discussed in detail in Chapter 10, *Exception Handling*.

Here is the syntax of a block:

```
[DECLARE]
    -- declaration statements
BEGIN
    -- executable statements
[EXCEPTION]
    -- exception statements
END;
```

Each statement or declaration in a PL/SQL block is terminated with a semicolon. In other words, a semicolon is the statement *delimiter* in PL/SQL. A statement may be broken down into multiple lines for readability, and the semicolon marks the end of the statement. More than one statement can appear in one line, separated by a semicolon. Each PL/SQL block begins with the keyword DECLARE or BEGIN and ends with the keyword END. A single line of comment is preceded by two hyphens (--). A set of comments can be enclosed in /* and */. Figure 7.2 shows an example of a PL/SQL block.

FIGURE 7.2 A PL/SQL block

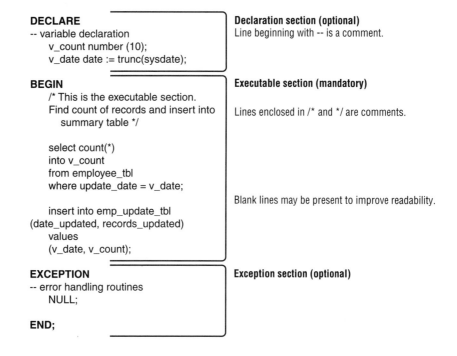

As you can see in Figure 7.2, data-manipulation SQL statements are used in the executable section, along with PL/SQL variables. A block within a block is called a nested block or a *sub-block*. In the following sections, we will discuss the components of each section.

Named and Anonymous Blocks

A PL/SQL block can be a named block or an *anonymous block*. The block shown in Figure 7.2 is an anonymous block. Anonymous blocks can be used in the server side or client side. There are two types of *named blocks*, shown in Table 7.1.

TABLE 7.1 PL/SQL Named Blocks

Block Type	Properties
Function	Takes zero or more parameter values and returns one value
Procedure	Takes zero or more parameter values and may return value through parameters

A named block may appear in the declaration part of another block. This is known as a subprogram. A subprogram may be referenced in the executable or the exception section of the block.

PL/SQL blocks may be compiled separately and stored in the database. Any application that connects to the database can access these stored programs (the user should have the appropriate privileges). Oracle provides four types of stored programs:

- Function
- Procedure
- Package
- Trigger

The stored programs are another example of how well PL/SQL is integrated to the Oracle server. Once created, these units can be managed as other database objects. Execute privileges can be controlled by grants. Changes to the stored program made in the server are immediately available to all clients. The following paragraphs describe each kind of stored program.

Function A *function* is a named PL/SQL block that is stored in the database. A function accepts zero or more input parameters and returns one value. The datatype of the return value is defined when the function is created. User-defined functions can be used in the same way as Oracle built-in single-row functions. The syntax for defining a function follows:

```
FUNCTION name [(parameter[, parameter, …])] RETURN
datatype IS
    [local declarations]
BEGIN
    executable statements
[EXCEPTION
    exception handlers]
END [name];
```

The following function accepts the length and width as parameters and returns the area. A function is created in the database using a CREATE OR REPLACE command.

```
create or replace function find_area
    (vlength in number, vwidth in number)
    return number
as
    varea number;
begin
    varea := vlength * vwidth;
    return varea;
end;

SQL> select find_area (10, 30) area from dual;

    AREA
---------
    300
```

Procedure   A stored *procedure* is a PL/SQL block that accepts zero or more parameters as input (IN), output (OUT), or both (INOUT). Unlike functions, procedures do not return a value; the INOUT parameter or OUT parameter may be used instead to pass a value from the procedure. Procedures cannot be used in

SQL statements; they can be invoked using the EXECUTE command or called inside a PL/SQL block. Here is the syntax for defining a procedure:

```
PROCEDURE name [(parameter[, parameter, …])] IS
   [local declarations]
BEGIN
   executable statements
[EXCEPTION
   exception handlers]
END [name];
```

In the following example, the procedure is created with the length and width as parameters and returns the area in the third parameter:

```
create or replace procedure get_area
(vlength in number, vwidth in number, varea out number)
as
begin
  varea := vlength * vwidth;
end;

SQL> variable warea number;
SQL> execute get_area (10, 30, :warea);

PL/SQL procedure successfully completed.

SQL> print warea

    WAREA
---------
      300
```

Package   A *package* is nothing but a collection of related objects that are grouped together. When any of the functions or procedures in the package is referenced, the package is loaded into memory. Subsequent access of any of the procedures or functions in the package will be faster.

Packages have two parts: the specification and the body. The specification declares the variables, constants, cursors, and subprograms. The body fully defines the subprograms and cursors.

Trigger   A *trigger* is associated with a table or a database event. The trigger defined on a table is fired when a triggering event, such as INSERT, UPDATE, or DELETE, occurs on the table.

For more information on functions, procedures, packages, and triggers, see Chapter 6, *Other Database Objects and the Data Dictionary*.

Variables and Constants

V*ariables* are storage locations in the memory to hold values that can be referenced inside the block. Think of a variable as a container to store things. You can change the contents of the container.

Declaring Variables

Variables are always declared in the declaration section of the PL/SQL block. PL/SQL is a strongly typed language, which means that you cannot forward-reference a variable. You must declare a variable before referencing it in other statements or other declarations. To use a variable in the executable or exception section of the block, it must be defined in the declaration section.

Variables are declared with the following syntax:

```
Variable_name [CONSTANT] datatype [NOT NULL] [:= | DEFAULT
expression]
```

To declare a variable of the same datatype as the database column, use the %TYPE declaration, for example, V_EMP_ID EMPLOYEE.EMP_ID%TYPE;. Here, EMPLOYEE is a table, and EMP_ID is a column in the table.

Multiple variables cannot be declared in the same statement.

Assigning Values to Variables

There are two methods you can use to assign value to a variable:

- Assign values directly to the variable. The assignment is done using the assignment operator (:=), and each declaration is delimited by a semicolon (;):

```
X := 200;
Y := Y + (X * 20);
```

- Assign values through SQL SELECT INTO or FETCH INTO:

```
SELECT SUM(SALARY), SUM(SALARY * 0.1)
INTO    TOTAL_SALARY, TOTAL_COMMISSION
FROM    EMPLOYEE
WHERE   DEPT = 10;
```

You can assign initial value to a variable at the time of declaration. Here's an example:
```
TOTAL_SALARY NUMBER (10,2) := 0;
TOTAL_SALARY NUMBER (10,2) DEFAULT 0;
```

Constants

A *constant* is similar to a variable, but its value cannot be changed inside the program. The value to a constant is assigned when the constant is defined. Its declaration is the same as a variable declaration, but the keyword CONSTANT is included. Both constants and variables can be defined as any SQL or user-defined datatype. Here's an example:

```
ZERO_VALUE  CONSTANT   NUMBER := 0;
```

In this example, a constant named ZERO_VALUE is defined as NUMBER and assigned a value of 0. You may use this constant anywhere inside the program.

Declarations can impose a NOT NULL constraint on variables. These variables should always be initialized with a value, such as COUNTER_VALUE NUMBER (4) NOT NULL := 0;.

Every variable and constant has a datatype that specifies the storage format and valid range of values. PL/SQL has scalar, composite, reference, and LOB datatypes. In this chapter, we discuss scalar and LOB datatypes.

Scalar Datatypes

A scalar datatype has no internal components and falls into any of four categories:

- Number
- Character
- Date/time
- Boolean

The following tables illustrate the different scalar datatypes available in PL/SQL. Table 7.2 shows the numeric datatypes, Table 7.3 shows the character datatypes, and Table 7.4 shows the date and Boolean datatypes.

TABLE 7.2 Scalar Types: Numeric

Datatype	Range	Subtypes	Description
BINARY_ INTEGER	− 214748 3647 214748 3647	NATURAL NATURALN POSITIVE POSITIVEN SIGNTYPE	Used to store signed integers. Requires less storage than NUMBER values. Using the subtypes can restrict range. NATURAL: Only non-negative values (>=0). POSITIVE: Only positive values (>0). NATURALN: Only non-negative, non-NULL values. POSITIVEN: Only positive non-NULL values. SIGNTYPE: Only the values 1, 0, or 1.
NUMBER	1.0E− 130 9.99E1 25	DEC DECIMAL DOUBLE PRECISION FLOAT INTEGER INT NUMERIC REAL SMALLINT	Used to store numbers of virtually any range and precision. This is the most commonly used numeric datatype. You can optionally specify a precision (total number of digits) and scale (digits after the decimal point). The syntax is NUMBER [(<*precision*> [, <*scale*>])] The default value for precision is 38 and for scale is 0. The subtypes are mainly provided for compatibility with ANSI/ISO and IBM types.
PLS_ INTEGER	− 214748 3647 214748 3647		Same as BINARY_INTEGER but uses machine arithmetic for faster performance. NUMBER and BINARY_INTEGER use library arithmetic. Use PLS_INTEGER for better performance.

When a precision and a scale are defined in a NUMBER datatype, the value is rounded to the scale. For example, if COMMISSION is defined as NUMBER (10,2), a value of 300.34678 would be rounded to 300.35. If the scale is not defined, the number is rounded to the integer.

TABLE 7.3 Scalar Types: Character

Datatype	Range	Subtypes	Description
CHAR	Max length is 32767 bytes.	CHARACTER	Used to store fixed-length alpha numeric data. If length is not defined, it defaults to 1.
LONG	Max width is 2147483647 bytes.		Used to store variable-length alpha-numeric data.
RAW	Max length is 32767 bytes.		Used to store binary data or byte strings, like graphics or digitized pictures. PL/SQL does not interpret RAW data.
LONGRAW	Max width is 2147483647 bytes.		Same as LONG, but PL/SQL does not interpret RAW data.
ROWID	18 bytes.		Used to store ROWID values of the table pseudo-column.

TABLE 7.3 Scalar Types: Character *(continued)*

Datatype	Range	Subtypes	Description
VARCHAR2	Max length is 32767 bytes.	STRING VARCHAR	Used to store variable-length alpha-numeric data. The length is a required parameter, for example: VARCHAR2 (20). This is a commonly used datatype.

Many databases use the 7-bit ASCII character set. The lengths for the datatypes given in Table 7.3 are specified in bytes. If a multibyte character set like Japanese is used, VARCHAR2 (10) may not hold 10 characters.

TABLE 7.4 Date and Boolean

Data type	Range	Description
BOOLEAN	TRUE FALSE	Use to store logical values TRUE or FALSE. Takes no parameters.
DATE	01/01/4712 BC 12/31/4712 AD	Use to store fixed-length date and time values. DATE values always include the time up to the precision of seconds.

BOOLEAN values cannot be inserted to a database column. Also, you cannot select column values into a BOOLEAN variable.

LOB Datatypes

LOB (large object) datatypes are used to store blocks of unstructured data like video, sound clip, graphic, and so on, up to 4GB in size. LOB supports random access, whereas LONG supports only sequential access. LOB types store values called locators, which specify the location of the large object. The large object may be stored inline (stored along with the row) or out-of-line (stored outside of the row). To manipulate the LOB objects in PL/SQL, use the Oracle-supplied package DBMS_LOB. These are the LOB datatypes available:

- BFILE
- BLOB
- CLOB
- NCLOB

Variables declared in the declaration section are always initialized to *NULL* if no initial value is specified.

Operators

As in any other programming language, PL/SQL has a set of operators. The operators can be classified as follows:

- Arithmetic operators
- Relational operators
- Comparison operators
- Logical operators

Arithmetic operators, shown in Table 7.5, are used in expressions.

Relational operators are mainly used in the conditional structures (IF) or in the WHERE clause of the SQL statement. Relational operators check for a condition and the result is always Boolean: TRUE or FALSE. You can see the relational operators in Table 7.6.

Comparison operators, shown in Table 7.7, supplement the relational operators by adding more operators. Comparison operators also check for a condition, and the result is Boolean.

Table 7.8 shows the logical operators, which are used to group multiple relational and comparison operators. PL/SQL supports all the operators used in SQL. The operators are explained in detail in Chapter 1, *Relational Technology and Simple SQL SELECT Statements.*

TABLE 7.5 Arithmetic Operators

Operator	Operation
+	Addition
-	Subtraction
/	Division
*	Multiplication
**	Exponentiation

TABLE 7.6 Relational Operators

Operator	Operation
<	Less than
<=	Less than or equal to
>	Greater than
>=	Greater than or equal to
=	Equal to
!=	Not equal to
<>	Not equal to

TABLE 7.6 Relational Operators *(continued)*

Operator	Operation
:=	Assignment
||	Concatenation

TABLE 7.7 Comparison Operators

Operator	Purpose
IS NULL	Returns TRUE if the operand is NULL
LIKE	Compares character value to a pattern
BETWEEN	Checks if the value is in a specified range
IN	Tests for operand in a set of values

TABLE 7.8 Logical Operators

Operator	Purpose
AND	Both conditions satisfy
OR	Either condition satisfies
NOT	Negation

Questions involving logical operators are very likely to appear on the test. The following tables can be used as truth tables for the three logical operators.

This table shows the AND truth table:

AND	TRUE	FALSE	NULL
TRUE	TRUE	FALSE	NULL
FALSE	FALSE	FALSE	FALSE
NULL	NULL	FALSE	NULL

This second table shows the OR truth table:

OR	TRUE	FALSE	NULL
TRUE	TRUE	TRUE	TRUE
FALSE	TRUE	FALSE	NULL
NULL	TRUE	NULL	NULL

The last table shows the NOT truth table:

NOT	
TRUE	FALSE
FALSE	TRUE
NULL	NULL

The Executable Section

The executable section contains all the statements and expressions that need to be executed. This is the only mandatory section in a block. The executable section begins with the keyword BEGIN and ends with the keyword EXCEPTION, or, if an exception section is not present, it ends with the keyword END. A semicolon delimits each statement. Variables are assigned values using the assignment operator (:=), a SELECT INTO statement, or a FETCH INTO statement. The errors in the executable section are handled in the exception section. An executable section can have another PL/SQL block inside. This is known as a *nested block*. Calls to other procedures or functions inside an executable section are also treated as nested blocks.

All SQL data manipulation statements can be used in the executable section. A PL/SQL block cannot display output to the screen from a SELECT statement. SELECT statements must contain an INTO clause or be part of a cursor. The variables and constants used in this section must be declared in the declaration section. The executable section must contain at least one executable statement. A NULL is a valid executable statement. Transaction control statements, such as COMMIT and ROLLBACK, can be used in the executable section. No data definition statements, such as CREATE TABLE or ALTER TABLE, are allowed in the PL/SQL block. Data definition language statements must be executed with an EXECUTE IMMEDIATE statement or with a call to DBMS_SQL.

Executing a Block

You have written a block; now, how do you execute it? An anonymous PL/SQL block can be executed from SQL*Plus by typing a slash (/) in the line after the block. Here is an example:

```
1  declare
2     v_comm_percent constant number := 10;
3  begin
4     update emp
5     set    comm = sal * v_comm_percent
6     where  deptno = 10;
7* end;
SQL> /

PL/SQL procedure successfully completed.

SQL>
```

Named programs are executed differently. A procedure is executed by specifying its name and required parameters inside another block. From the SQL*Plus command line, a procedure is executed by using the keyword

EXECUTE. To make the previous example a stored procedure and execute it from SQL*Plus, do the following:

```
  1  create or replace procedure update_commission
  2     (v_dept in number, v_percent in number default 10)
is
  3  begin
  4     update emp
  5     set    comm = sal * v_percent
  6     where  deptno = v_dept;
  7* end;
SQL> /

Procedure created.

SQL> execute update_commission (10, 15);

PL/SQL procedure successfully completed.

SQL>
```

To execute this procedure from another stored program or anonymous block, you need not specify the keyword EXECUTE. Here's an example:

```
  1  declare
  2     v_dept number;
  3  begin
  4     select a.deptno
  5     into   v_dept
  6     from   emp a
  7     where  job = 'PRESIDENT';
  8     update_commission (v_dept);
  9* end;
SQL> /

PL/SQL procedure successfully completed.

SQL>
```

A function is executed like any other SQL built-in function:

```
1  create or replace function calculate_area
(v_length in number, v_width in number)
2  return number
3  is
4     v_area number;
5  begin
6     v_area := v_length * v_width;
7     return v_area;
8* end;
SQL> /

Function created.

SQL> select calculate_area (10, 14) from dual;

CALCULATE_AREA(10,14)
---------------------
                  140

SQL>
```

Functions are called inside a PL/SQL block by assigning the return value to a variable:

```
V_AREA := calculate_area (10, 14);
```

The functions and procedures inside a package are executed by qualifying the function or procedure with the package name. Here's an example:

```
EXECUTE SALARY_PACKAGE.CALCULATE_COMMISSION;
```

where SALARY_PACKAGE is a package and CALCULATE_COMMISSION is a procedure.

Control Structures

*C*ontrol structures are lines of code that control the flow of the PL/SQL program. PL/SQL supports both conditional and iterative control structures.

Conditional or decision-control structures are used to perform an operation or statement based on the outcome of another statement or expression. IF...THEN...ELSE...END IF statements let you say, "If this is true, then do this; otherwise, do that." For example, imagine that you must calculate bonuses for employees according to the following criteria: If an employee is in the HR department, his bonus is 20 percent; if he is in the IT department, he will get a 25 percent bonus; otherwise, he gets a 10 percent bonus. *Iterative control* structures perform one or more statements repeatedly, either a certain number of times or until a condition is met. There are three forms of iterative structures:

- LOOP
- WHILE...LOOP
- FOR...LOOP

To calculate the bonuses for all employees in the company, you need to execute the bonus-calculating procedure for each employee; that is, the same steps must be performed again and again until all employees have been done.

Branching control structures are used to switch the program flow to a different part of the program. A GOTO statement is used for branching unconditionally. You can use branching to skip a set of statements unconditionally. Branching destroys the flow of the program; it is not recommended to use branching and move the program flow to a different part of the program.

Syntax and Usage

The following sections give you the syntax and usage of the different control structures available in Oracle.

IF...THEN

The IF statement evaluates a condition, and if the condition is satisfied, a set of statements are executed. The statements are enclosed in keywords THEN and END IF, like this:

```
IF condition THEN
   Statement 1;
   Statement 2;
   ... ... ...
END IF;
```

The statements are executed only if the result of the condition is TRUE. The condition always evaluates to a Boolean result of TRUE or FALSE. If the condition results in FALSE or NULL (when a Boolean variable is not initialized, its value will be NULL), the statements between THEN and END IF are skipped and the statements after END IF are executed. Here's an example:

```
A := 10;
IF A <= 20 THEN
    B := A + 20;
END IF;
B := B + 10;
```

In this example, the condition in the IF statement is TRUE, so the statement B := A + 20 will be executed, and then control passes to B := B + 10.

The keyword to end a conditional control structure is END IF; note the space between END and IF.

IF...THEN...ELSE

This is similar to IF...THEN, but a set of statements can be executed if the condition evaluates to FALSE or NULL. The syntax for the IF...THEN...ELSE statement is this:

```
IF condition THEN
    Statement 1;
    Statement 2;
    ... ... ...
ELSE
    Statement 3;
    Statement 4;
    ... ... ...
END IF;
```

The statements between THEN and ELSE are executed only if the condition is TRUE, and the statements between ELSE and END IF are executed only if the condition is FALSE, as you can see in the following example:

```
1  create or replace function greatest (a in number, b
in number)
2  return number is
3    g number;
4  begin
```

```
 5     if a > b then
 6         g := a;
 7     else
 8         g := b;
 9     end if;
10     return g;
11* end;
SQL> /

Function created.

SQL> select greatest (2, 5) from dual;

GREATEST(2,5)
-------------
            5

SQL>
```

Nested IF statements are allowed. An IF statement or an IF...ELSE statement can appear inside another IF or IF...ELSE statement.

For example, to find the greatest number among three numbers, do this:

```
if (a > b) and (a > c) then
    g := a;
else
    g := b;
    if c > g then
        g := c;
    end if;
end if;
```

IF...THEN...ELSIF

Use this structure if you need to select an action from several mutually exclusive conditions. This form of IF uses the keyword ELSIF. Here's the syntax for an IF...THEN...ELSIF statement:

```
IF condition1 THEN
    Statement 1;
ELSIF condition2 THEN
    Statement 2;
```

```
ELSIF condition3 THEN
    Statement 3;
ELSE
    Statement 4;
END IF;
Statement 5;
```

If condition1 is TRUE, Statement 1 is executed and control passes to Statement 5. If condition1 is FALSE, condition2 is evaluated; if this condition is TRUE, Statement 2 is executed and then Statement 5. If none of the conditions in the ELSIF clause is met, Statement 4 is executed and then Statement 5.

For example, let's say that you want to find the bonus amount based on salary. If salary is less than 1000, the bonus is 200. For salary between 1000 and 2999, the bonus is 300. Each condition in the IF structure is evaluated top down; if a condition matches, the statements inside the IF clause are executed and the IF statement is completed. The next condition will not be matched. In this example, if the salary is 3500, the first and second condition fail; the third condition, salary < 5000, is true, so the statement bonus := 400 is executed and the control passes to the end of the IF structure.

```
IF salary < 1000 THEN
    bonus := 200;
ELSIF salary < 3000 THEN
    bonus := 300;
ELSIF salary < 5000 THEN
    bonus := 400;
ELSIF salary < 7000 THEN
    bonus := 500;
ELSE
    bonus := 0;
END IF;
```

The keyword in IF...THEN...ELSIF control structure is ELSIF-not ELSEIF or ELSE IF.

LOOP

The basic form of iterative control is the LOOP statement. The statements between LOOP and END LOOP are executed infinitely. The syntax for the basic LOOP is this:

```
LOOP
    Statements;
END LOOP;
```

Since the default for a basic loop is to execute infinitely, you must use an EXIT statement to force a loop to complete unconditionally and pass control to the statement following the END LOOP, as you can see in this example:

```
X := 100;
LOOP
   X := X + 10;
   IF X > 1000 THEN
       EXIT;
   END IF;
END LOOP;
Y := X;   -- the value of Y would be 1010
```

The EXIT statement cannot be used outside the loop. To complete a PL/SQL block before its end is reached, you may use the command RETURN.

The EXIT WHEN statement completes an infinite loop conditionally. If the condition is evaluated to TRUE, the loop is terminated and the statement next to END LOOP is processed. Here is an example:

```
X := 100;
LOOP
   EXIT WHEN X > 1000;
   X := X + 10;
END LOOP;
Y := X;   -- the value of Y would be 1010
```

WHILE...LOOP

WHILE...LOOP has a condition associated with the loop. The condition is evaluated, and, if the result is TRUE, the statements inside the loop are executed. If the condition is FALSE, execution continues from the next statement to END LOOP. Here's an example:

```
X := 100;
WHILE X <= 1000 LOOP
    X := X + 10;
END LOOP;
Y := X;    -- the value of Y would be 1010
```

If the condition in the WHILE...LOOP is evaluated to FALSE the very first time, the loop will never be executed. To execute the loop at least once, irrespective of the result of the condition, use the basic loop with a conditional EXIT toward the end of the loop, like this:

```
LOOP
... ... ...
EXIT WHEN ...;
END LOOP;
```

FOR...LOOP

Use the FOR...LOOP if you need the iterations to occur a fixed number of times. In the basic loop and WHILE...LOOP, the number of iterations is unknown. The FOR...LOOP is executed for a range of values. The syntax for the FOR...LOOP follows:

```
FOR counter IN [REVERSE] start_range .. end_range LOOP
        Statements;
END LOOP;
```

Here, *counter* is a variable known as the index variable (this need not be declared in the declaration section; it is implicitly declared as INTEGER), which will have the value of start_range for the first iteration, start_range+1 for the second, start_range+2 for the third, and so on, until end_range. Therefore, if the start_range and end_range are equal, the loop will execute once. The index variable is available only for reference inside the loop. Both range values are inclusive. The two dots (..) serve as a range operator. If the REVERSE keyword is used, the range is decremented. The ranges can be expressions or variables. The following shows an example:

```
X := 100;
FOR V_COUNTER in 1 .. 10 LOOP   -- executes 10 times
    X := X + 10;
END LOOP;
Y := X;   -- the value of Y would be 200
```

To exit a FOR...LOOP prematurely, you may use the EXIT statement. You cannot assign a new value to the counter variable.

If the lower bound is larger than the upper bound in a FOR...LOOP, the loop will not be executed at all. Use the REVERSE keyword to assign values in the descending order to the index variable.

Labels

You may use *labels* for better readability. A block or a loop may be labeled. The label precedes a block or a loop and is enclosed in double angle brackets (<< and >>). The END statement or the END LOOP statement can refer to the label.

Labeled Blocks

A block followed by a label name is known as a labeled block. Do not confuse a labeled block with a named block; each is different, and labeled blocks can appear inside a named block. Here is an example of block syntax using the labels:

```
<<label_name>>
[DECLARE]
```

```
… … …
BEGIN
… … …
[EXCEPTION]
… … …
END label_name;
```

Labeling a block is especially useful if there are nested blocks and you do not know which END belongs to which block, for example:

```
declare
  v_dept       number (2);
  v_emp_count number (4);
begin
  for v_counter in 1 .. 6 loop
      <<select_block>>
      BEGIN
        select deptno
        into    v_dept
        from    dept
        where   deptno = v_counter * 10;
        <<count_block>>
        BEGIN
          select count(*)
          into    v_emp_count
          from    emp
          where   deptno = v_dept;
        END count_block;
        dbms_output.put_line ('There are ' || v_emp_count || '
                              employees in dept ' || v_
dept);
      EXCEPTION
        when no_data_found then null;
      END select_block;
  end loop;
end;
```

DBMS_OUTPUT.PUT_LINE is an Oracle-supplied procedure used to display output to the screen from a PL/SQL program. You should set the SQL*Plus parameter SERVEROUTPUT to ON before using this procedure.

Labeled Loops

Similar to labeled blocks, loops can also be labeled. Apart from improving readability, the advantage of labeled loops is that you can exit to any level of the loop in a nested loop structure.

For example, here all the three loops are exited when the *v_condition* variable is 0. Note that the label name appears after the keyword EXIT:

```
<<outer_loop>>
LOOP

    ... ... ...
    <<inner_loop>>
    LOOP

        ... ... ...
        <<innermost_loop>>
        LOOP

            ... ... ...
            EXIT outer_loop WHEN v_condition = 0;
        END LOOP innermost_loop;

        ... ... ...
    END LOOP inner_loop;
END LOOP outer_loop;
```

The GOTO Statement

A GOTO statement with a label may be used to pass control to another part of the program. GOTO statements in the program are not very widely used and are not recommended. If you do use a GOTO statement with a label, the label should precede an executable statement and must be unique.

Remember, NULL is a valid executable statement. A GOTO statement can branch to a statement farther up or down in the block. Here is an example:

```
X := 100;
FOR V_COUNTER in 1 .. 10 LOOP
    IF V_COUNTER = 4 THEN
        GOTO end_of_loop;
    END IF;
    X := X + 10;
    <<end_of_loop>>
    NULL;
END LOOP;
Y := X;
```

A GOTO statement can branch out of an IF statement, a loop, or a sub-block. A GOTO statement cannot branch into an IF statement, a loop, or a sub-block. Branching from one IF statement clause to another and from the exception section to the executable section is also illegal.

The NULL statement specifies "no action." The control passes to the next statement doing nothing. The NULL statement can be used when an executable statement is mandatory, as in the IF clause or GOTO label, and you have no action to do. If NULL is used in the IF statements to specify alternative actions, it tells the reader that the associated alternative is not overlooked, but no action is required.

Nested Blocks

A block inside another block is called a *nested block*. The variables defined inside the PL/SQL block are local to the block. The scope is available to all sub-blocks. If the same variable name is defined in the sub-block, the variable defined in the sub-block gets precedence. A variable defined in the sub-block cannot be referenced in the parent block. A GOTO statement can pass control to a parent block, but it cannot do so from a block into the sub-block. The following example shows the scope of the variables when using nested blocks. Notice that the blocks are labeled in this example.

```
<<OUTER_BLOCK>>
DECLARE
```

```
      A_NUMBER INTEGER;
      B_NUMBER INTEGER;
   BEGIN
      -- A_NUMBER and B_NUMBER are available here
      <<SUB_BLOCK>>
      DECLARE
         C_NUMBER INTEGER;
         B_NUMBER NUMBER (20);
         -- B_NUMBER is declared here again. reference to B_
   NUMBER
         -- in this block will refer to the number datatype
   variable.
      BEGIN
         -- C_NUMBER is available only to this block.
         -- A_NUMBER is available in this block
         C_NUMBER := A_NUMBER;
         -- reference to the outer_block's b_number can be made
         -- by using the block label name
         C_NUMBER := OUTER_BLOCK.B_NUMBER;
      END SUB_BLOCK;
      -- C_NUMBER is not available here
   END OUTER_BLOCK;
```

Similar to blocks, a control structure enclosed in another is called a nested loop. All nested structures (IF THEN, LOOP, or SUB-BLOCK) should be completely enclosed in the parent structure. The following code is illegal:

```
BEGIN
   IF X < 10 THEN
      WHILE Y < 20 LOOP
         NULL;
   END IF;
      END LOOP;
END;
```

Summary

This chapter showed how to write simple and nested PL/SQL blocks and how well PL/SQL is integrated with the Oracle server. PL/SQL blocks may be named and stored in the database as functions and procedures. A package is a collection of objects, and a trigger is a PL/SQL block that executes automatically when an event occurs.

Variables are declared in the declaration section, SQL and PL/SQL statements are written in the executable section, and any error handling routines are written in the exception section. Program flow can be controlled using IF...THEN, IF...THEN...ELSE, and IF...THEN...ELSIF structures. Iterations are performed using the basic loop, WHILE...LOOP, and FOR...LOOP. Blocks and control structures can be nested.

Key Terms

Before you take the exam, make sure you're familiar with the following terms:

Anonymous block

Constant

Control structures

Declaration section

Exception section

Executable section

Function

Iterative control

Delimiter

Labels

Named block

Nested block

NULL

Package

PL/SQL engine

Procedure

Sub-block

Trigger

Variable

Review Questions

1. Which section of the PL/SQL block handles errors and abnormal conditions?

   A. Declaration section

   B. Exception section

   C. Executable section

   D. Anonymous block

2. What is the mandatory clause in a SELECT statement when used inside a PL/SQL block?

   A. INTO

   B. WHERE

   C. ORDER BY

   D. GROUP BY

3. Which line of the code has an error?

   ```
   1   declare
   2     X1 number := 0;
   3     1Y number := 0;
   4   begin
   5     X := 10;
   6     1Y := X + 1Y;
   7   end;
   ```

   A. Line 2

   B. Line 3

   C. Line 5

   D. The code has no error.

4. In which section of the PL/SQL block is a constant assigned value?

   A. Executable section

   B. Declaration section

   C. Exception section

   D. Declaration section or executable section

5. What is the name of the PL/SQL block that is associated with a table and executes automatically when an event occurs?

   A. Function

   B. Procedure

   C. Package

   D. Trigger

6. Which data dictionary view will have the stored program (named block) code?

   A. USER_PROCEDURES

   B. USER_OBJECTS

   C. USER_SOURCE

   D. DBA_VIEWS

7. Why does the following statement in the declaration section fail?

   `PRODUCT_IN_STOCK BOOLEAN := 'TRUE';`

   A. Assignment operation is not permitted in the declaration section.

   B. The size/width for the PRODUCT_IN_STOCK variable is not defined.

   C. BOOLEAN is not a valid datatype supported by PL/SQL.

   D. A Boolean variable cannot be assigned a character string value.

8. What is the value of *X* when the following block is executed?

```
declare
 X number := 0;
begin
  X := 10;
  FOR V_COUNTER in 1 .. 10 LOOP
    X := X + 10;
  END LOOP;
end;
```

A. 10

B. 110

C. 100

D. 1

9. Which control structure evaluates the condition in the beginning of the loop and does not even enter into the loop if the condition evaluates to FALSE?

A. FOR...LOOP

B. WHILE...LOOP

C. LOOP

D. GOTO

10. Why does the following declaration fail?

```
MY_NUMBER POSITIVEN;
```

A. A variable declared as POSITIVEN should always be initialized to a non-NULL value.

B. POSITIVEN is not a PL/SQL datatype.

C. The variable name is invalid.

D. The statement is missing a keyword.

11. What type of constraint can be defined when you declare a variable?

A. Check constraint.

B. NOT NULL constraint.

C. Check constraint and NOT NULL constraint.

D. No constraints can be defined on a variable.

12. What will the value of *V_STATUS* be when the following code is executed?

```
DECLARE
    V_BONUS        BOOLEAN;
    V_COMMISSION BOOLEAN := FALSE;
    V_STATUS       BOOLEAN;
BEGIN
    V_STATUS := V_BONUS AND V_COMMISSION;
END;
```

A. TRUE

B. FALSE

C. NULL

13. What will the value of *V_STATUS* be when the following code is executed?

```
DECLARE
    V_BONUS        NUMBER DEFAULT 10;
    V_COMMISSION NUMBER DEFAULT 30;
    V_STATUS       BOOLEAN;
BEGIN
    V_STATUS := V_BONUS < V_COMMISSION;
END;
```

A. TRUE

B. FALSE

C. NULL

D. This is an incorrect usage of a Boolean variable.

14. What is the value of *X* when the following block of code is executed?

```
DECLARE
    X NUMBER := 0;
BEGIN
    FOR I in 5 .. 5 LOOP
        X := I;
    END LOOP;
END;
```

A. NULL

B. 5

C. 0

D. Unknown

15. Choose two answers that are true: A variable is defined as %TYPE.

A. If the underlying table column datatype changes, the PL/SQL code needs to be changed.

B. You do not have to know the datatype or the precision of that column.

C. Only character variables can be defined using %TYPE.

D. You need not be concerned about changes that may be made to column definitions.

16. Why does the following code fail?

```
DECLARE
    V_BONUS NUMBER;
BEGIN
    SELECT SALARY V_SALARY
    FROM    EMPLOYEE
    WHERE   EMP_ID = 101;
    V_BONUS := V_SALARY * 0.1;
END;
```

A. The *V_BONUS* variable is not initialized.

B. The SELECT statement cannot have an alias name.

C. The exception section is missing.

D. None of the above

17. Which line of the following code has an error?

```
1  X := Y + 200;
2  IF X < 10 THEN
3     Y := 30;
4  ELSEIF X < 40 THEN
5     Y := 20;
6  END IF;
```

A. Line 2

B. Line 3

C. Line 4

D. Line 5

18. Fill in the blank: A _____ is a PL/SQL stored program that fires when an event occurs.

A. Function

B. Trigger

C. Procedure

D. Package

19. Which control structure would be most appropriate to use if you want to perform the following task:

- Increase by 25 percent the salaries of employees who were born before 1980

- Increase by 10 percent the salaries of those who were born between 1980 and 1990

- Not increase the salaries of those who were born after 1990

A. IF...THEN...ELSIF...ELSE

B. IF...THEN...ELSE

C. WHILE...LOOP

D. FOR...LOOP

Answers to Review Questions

1. B. The exception section handles the errors and abnormal conditions raised from the executable section of the block.

2. A. The SELECT statement used in the PL/SQL block must have an INTO clause. Since PL/SQL cannot display output to the screen directly from a SELECT statement, an INTO clause is mandatory.

3. B. PL/SQL identifiers cannot begin with a numeral; variable names begin with a letter.

4. B. A constant has to be assigned a value when it is declared. A constant's value cannot be changed after the initial assignment.

5. D. A trigger is defined on a table and is fired (executed) when a triggering event like INSERT, UPDATE, or DELETE occurs on the table.

6. C. The dictionary view USER_SOURCE will have the source code for stored programs like procedures, functions, or packages created by the user. The column TYPE identifies the type of the stored program.

7. D. Anything enclosed in single quotes is treated as a character string. A Boolean variable cannot be assigned a character value. The Boolean variable can accept only a TRUE, FALSE, or NULL value.

8. B. The answer is 110. Although X is initialized to 0, it is assigned a value of 10 in the beginning of the block. The loop executes 10 times, incrementing by 10 each time.

9. B. The WHILE...LOOP evaluates the condition in the beginning of the loop. A FOR...LOOP does not have a condition; it iterates a set number of times. A basic loop is an infinite loop; it should come out of the loop using the EXIT statement. The GOTO statement is used to branch control to a different part of the program.

10. A. The datatype POSITIVEN declares the variable as NOT NULL, so a value should be assigned at the time of declaration.

11. A. NOT NULL is the only constraint that can be attached to a variable in PL/SQL. The constraint is defined as follows:

```
MY_VARIABLE NUMBER (3) NOT NULL := 0;
```

When you define a NOT NULL constraint, the variable should always be initialized with a value.

12. B. Since *V_BONUS* is not initialized, its value is NULL. NULL and FALSE with an AND operator results in FALSE.

13. A. The expression V_BONUS < V_COMMISSION is evaluated to TRUE and is assigned to *V_STATUS*.

14. B. Although the upper and lower bounds of the FOR loop are the same, the loop executes once. Hence, the value is *5*.

15. B, D. When you declare a variable to a database column with the %TYPE attribute, you do not have to know what the datatype or precision of that column is, nor do you need to be concerned about changes that may be made to column definitions.

16. D. The SELECT statements used in PL/SQL should always have the INTO clause.

17. C. ELSEIF is not a valid keyword; the keyword is ELSIF with only one *E*.

18. B. Triggers are associated with events, and they fire automatically when the event occurs.

19. A. Since you have three conditions, using IF...THEN...ELSIF...ELSE would be most appropriate. Here is the code:

```
IF TO_CHAR(DOB, 'YYYY') < 1980 THEN
    SALARY := SALARY + SALARY * 1.25;
ELSIF TO_CHAR(DOB, 'YYYY') <= 1990 THEN
    SALARY := SALARY + SALARY * 1.1;
    ELSE
        NULL;
END IF;
```

Chapter

8

Interacting with the Database

ORACLE8i SQL & PL/SQL EXAM OBJECTIVES OFFERED IN THIS CHAPTER:

✓ **Interacting with the Oracle Server:**

- Write a successful SELECT statement in PL/SQL
- Declare dynamically the datatype and size of a PL/SQL variable
- Write DML statements in PL/SQL
- Control transactions
- Determine the outcome of SQL DML statements

✓ **Writing explicit cursors:**

- Distinguish between an implicit and an explicit cursor
- Use a PL/SQL record variable
- Write a cursor FOR loop

✓ **Advanced explicit cursor concepts:**

- Write a cursor that uses parameters
- Determine when a FOR UPDATE clause in a cursor is required
- Determine when to use the WHERE CURRENT OF clause
- Write a cursor that uses a subquery

Exam objectives are subject to change at any time without prior notice and at Oracle's sole discretion. Please visit Oracle's Training and Certification Web site (http://education .oracle.com/certification/index.html) for the most current exam objectives listing.

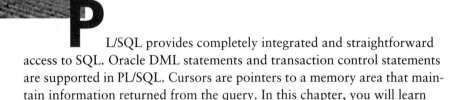

PL/SQL provides completely integrated and straightforward access to SQL. Oracle DML statements and transaction control statements are supported in PL/SQL. Cursors are pointers to a memory area that maintain information returned from the query. In this chapter, you will learn

- How to access an Oracle database from PL/SQL

- How to use cursors

- When to use implicit cursors and explicit cursors

Accessing the Database

SQL is the language used to access the Oracle database. PL/SQL extends the functionality of SQL and also introduces advanced procedural logic. Data manipulation language (DML) commands and transaction control language (TCL) statements of SQL are supported in PL/SQL. Data definition language (DDL) statements are not supported in PL/SQL. This means that you cannot create tables or any other objects inside a PL/SQL block. Advanced PL/SQL programming using built-in packages like DBMS_SQL or the EXECUTE IMMEDIATE command allows you to build dynamic SQL statements that execute DDL statements inside a PL/SQL block. SQL statements are compiled before they are executed; the PL/SQL compiler makes sure that the objects referenced in the block are defined and that the user has privileges on them.

In the following sections, we will discuss the various DML and TCL statements that can be used for Oracle database access from PL/SQL.

The DML statement EXPLAIN PLAN cannot be used inside a PL/SQL block.

Queries

The SELECT statement is used to *query* data from the database. When using this statement in PL/SQL, always make sure that the INTO clause is present. The values returned from the query are assigned to the variables in the INTO clause. The variables should be defined earlier, in the DECLARE section. For variables and the different sections in a PL/SQL block, see Chapter 7, *PL/SQL Basics*. Here is the syntax of a simple SELECT INTO statement:

```
SELECT [DISTINCT | ALL] {* | column [, column, … ]}
INTO {variable [, variable, …] | record }
FROM {table | (sub-query) } [alias]
WHERE … … …
```

The SELECT statements used in the PL/SQL block cannot return more than one row. If more than one row is to be processed, you need to use an explicit cursor. Cursors are discussed later in this chapter. The INTO clause should have the same number of variables as the columns selected in the SELECT clause. A record variable also can be specified in the INTO clause.

The example shown in Listing 8.1 queries data from the EMP table for the highest-paid employee and displays it to the screen using the DBMS_OUTPUT built-in package. There are three columns selected in the SELECT statement, and there are three variables used in the INTO clause. The variables in the INTO clause should be declared in compatible datatypes of the column values selected.

LISTING 8.1: Highest-paid employee

```
SQL> SET SERVEROUTPUT ON
SQL> LIST
    DECLARE

        v_empno      NUMBER (4);
        v_ename      VARCHAR2 (20);
        v_salary     NUMBER (10,2);
```

```
      BEGIN

        SELECT empno, ename, salary
        INTO   v_empno, v_ename, v_salary
        FROM   emp
        WHERE  salary = (SELECT MAX(salary)
                         FROM    EMP);

        DBMS_OUTPUT.PUT_LINE ('Highest Paid Employee is ' ||
      v_ename);
        DBMS_OUTPUT.PUT_LINE ('Id is ' || v_empno || ' Salary

                                    || to_char(v_salary,
      '999,999.99'));

       * END;
      SQL> /
      Highest Paid Employee is A_EDWARD
      Id is 7839 Salary     5,000.00

      PL/SQL procedure successfully completed.
```

The DBMS_OUTPUT package is very useful when debugging PL/SQL programs. Basically, the DBMS_OUTPUT.PUT_LINE procedure takes a VARCHAR2 input and copies the line to a private buffer for the session. You must set SERVEROUTPUT to ON to display the buffer contents to the screen. The buffer contents are displayed when the program (procedure, function, trigger, or anonymous block) completes.

The %TYPE Attribute

In addition to the built-in and user-defined datatypes, you can also declare variables and constants in a PL/SQL program referencing a column name to inherit its datatype and length. This dynamic datatype assignment is very useful; you need not change the program code if the datatype or length of the column in the table is changed, where the variable is referenced.

The following are all valid declarations using *%TYPE*. Optionally, you can specify the schema name of the table.

```
v_empno     SCOTT.EMP.EMPNO%TYPE;
c_comm      CONSTANT EMP.COMM%TYPE := 100;
v_ename     EMP.ENAME%TYPE NOT NULL := 'NO NAME';
v_salary    EMP.SALARY%TYPE;
```

In the %TYPE, you can specify not only column names but also variable, record, cursor, or constant declarations. This helps to define the same type of variables in the program. In the following example, a variable *V_A* is defined, and its attributes are copied to variables *V_B* and *V_C*. The initialization values are not copied; only the datatype and length are copied.

```
1  DECLARE
2    V_A  NUMBER (5) := 10;
3    V_B  V_A%TYPE := 15;
4    V_C  V_A%TYPE;
5  BEGIN
6  DBMS_OUTPUT.PUT_LINE
7        ('V_A='||V_A||'  V_B='||V_B||'  V_C='||V_C);
8* END;
SQL> /
V_A=10  V_B=15  V_C=

PL/SQL procedure successfully completed.

SQL>
```

SQL functions, pseudo-columns, and all operators can be used in PL/SQL.

Other DML Statements

The other DML statements that you can use to manipulate data are INSERT, UPDATE, DELETE, and LOCK TABLE. The syntax of these statements inside PL/SQL is the same as the syntax you would use for these statements in SQL. These DML statements are discussed in Chapter 4, *Modifying Data and Security*. You can reference any variable declared in the DECLARE section inside the SELECT, INSERT, DELETE, and UPDATE statements, as long as they are in the scope of the block, if there are nested blocks.

Use the INSERT statement to add new rows to a table, DELETE to remove rows from a table, and UPDATE to change existing row values. LOCK TABLE temporarily limits access to data.

The example shown in Listing 8.2 creates a procedure to delete an employee from the EMP table. The steps of this procedure follow:

1. The employee number is passed to the procedure as a parameter.

2. The employee number and name of the employee in the deleted record are saved in another table called FORMER_EMP.

3. The record is deleted from the EMP table.

4. The DELETE_DATE column in the FORMER_EMP table is updated with the current system date.

This example uses the SELECT statement to get the employee name, the INSERT statement to create a record in the FORMER_EMP table, the UPDATE statement to set the DELETE_DATE column, and finally the DELETE statement to remove the row from the EMP table.

LISTING 8.2: FIRE_EMPLOYEE procedure

```
CREATE OR REPLACE PROCEDURE FIRE_EMPLOYEE (p_empno in
number)
AS
   v_ename   EMP.ENAME%TYPE;

BEGIN

   SELECT ename
   INTO   v_ename
   FROM   emp
```

```
   WHERE   empno = p_empno;

   INSERT INTO former_emp (empno, ename)
   VALUES (p_empno, v_ename);

   DELETE FROM emp
   WHERE   empno = p_empno;

   UPDATE former_emp
   SET     date_deleted = SYSDATE
   WHERE   empno = p_empno;

EXCEPTION
   WHEN NO_DATA_FOUND THEN
        DBMS_OUTPUT.PUT_LINE('Employee Number Not Found!');
END;
/
```

To delete the employee number 7654, you invoke the procedure with the employee number as the parameter:

```
SQL> EXEC fire_employee (7654);

PL/SQL procedure successfully completed.

SQL> SELECT * FROM former_emp;

    EMPNO ENAME                     DATE_DELE
---------- -------------------- ---------
     7654 MARTIN                    29-MAR-00

SQL>
```

A function cannot modify data in a table, that is, you cannot use the DML statements INSERT, UPDATE, or DELETE in a function.

Outcome of DML Statements

When a DML statement (SELECT, INSERT, UPDATE, or DELETE) is executed, the outcome of the statement is saved in four *cursor attributes*. These attributes can be used to control the program flow or just to know the status. When performing these DML statements, PL/SQL opens a cursor internally and processes the result. The cursor is an area in the memory that maintains information from the query. The cursor is opened for performing the DML statement and is closed when the statement completes. The status of the implicit cursor just executed is available in SQL%FOUND, SQL%NOTFOUND, and SQL%ROWCOUNT attributes. SQL%FOUND and SQL%NOTFOUND are Boolean values, and SQL%ROWCOUNT is an integer.

SQL%FOUND and SQL%NOTFOUND Before executing any DML statement, the value of SQL%FOUND and SQL%NOTFOUND will be NULL. After the DML statement, the SQL%FOUND attribute will be

- TRUE for INSERT
- TRUE for DELETE and UPDATE if at least a row is deleted or updated
- TRUE for SELECT INTO if a row is returned

When SQL%FOUND is TRUE, the value of SQL%NOTFOUND will be FALSE.

SQL%ROWCOUNT SQL%ROWCOUNT has the number of rows processed by the last DML statement. Before any DML statement, the SQL%ROWCOUNT value will be NULL. For a SELECT INTO statement, the SQL%ROWCOUNT value will be 1 if successful; SQL%ROWCOUNT will have a value of 0 if not successful, which also raises the NO_DATA_FOUND exception.

SQL%ISOPEN SQL%ISOPEN is a Boolean result, which is TRUE if the cursor is open and FALSE if the cursor is closed. The SQL%ISOPEN attribute is always FALSE because the implicit cursor is opened for a DML statement and closed immediately after the statement.

The example shown in Listing 8.3 illustrates how to use the implicit cursor attributes. We count the number of records in the EMP table with salary above

3000 and increase the salary by 10 percent. The value of SQL%ROWCOUNT and SQL%FOUND are displayed.

LISTING 8.3: Using cursor attributes

```
DECLARE

    v_count        PLS_INTEGER;
    v_rowcount     PLS_INTEGER;

BEGIN

    SELECT COUNT(*)
    INTO   v_count
    FROM   emp
    WHERE  salary > 3000;

    v_rowcount := SQL%ROWCOUNT;

    DBMS_OUTPUT.PUT_LINE ('Total rows from table     : ' ||
v_count);
    DBMS_OUTPUT.PUT_LINE ('%ROWCOUNT value from SELECT: ' ||
v_rowcount);

    IF SQL%FOUND THEN

        DBMS_OUTPUT.PUT_LINE ('Records Found For Update');

        UPDATE emp
        SET    salary = salary * 1.10
        WHERE  salary > 3000;

        v_rowcount := SQL%ROWCOUNT;

        DBMS_OUTPUT.PUT_LINE ('SQL%ROWCOUNT value after
update: ' || v_rowcount);

        IF SQL%NOTFOUND THEN
```

```
                    DBMS_OUTPUT.PUT_LINE ('No rows updated');

        END IF;

    END IF;

END;

SQL> /
Total rows from table    : 2
%ROWCOUNT value from SELECT: 1
Records Found For Update
SQL%ROWCOUNT value after update: 2

PL/SQL procedure successfully completed.

SQL>
```

Transaction Control Statements

A *transaction* is a logical unit of work that may include one or more DML statements. Transactions help in ensuring data integrity. For example, in Listing 8.2, there are various DML statements involved in removing an employee. If any of the statements fail, the entire transaction will be rolled back. You can use explicit COMMIT, ROLLBACK, SAVEPOINT, and SET TRANSACTION statements inside a PL/SQL block. A transaction begins when you start a session (or when another transaction ends) and you issue the first DML statement. Issuing a COMMIT or ROLLBACK command ends a transaction. SQL*Plus commits the transaction when you exit.

COMMIT terminates the current transaction, saves all database changes permanently, and releases all locks. *ROLLBACK* terminates the current transaction and releases locks but does not make the changes permanent—the changes are undone. Setting an intermediate point to go back to inside a transaction is useful when the transaction involves many database operations. The *SAVEPOINT* command is used to mark the intermediate points. The SET TRANSACTION statement is used to set transaction properties such as read-write access and isolation level.

WARNING   The transaction control statements COMMIT, ROLLBACK, SAVEPOINT, and ROLLBACK TO SAVEPOINT cannot be used in a trigger.

Explicit Cursors

When the query returns more than one row, you need to define an explicit cursor; you cannot use a SELECT INTO statement. An implicit cursor is managed by PL/SQL; the implicit cursor is opened when the query begins and closed automatically when the query ends. An explicit cursor is defined in the declare section of the PL/SQL block and is opened, fetched and closed in the executable or exception section. An explicit cursor can be deemed an array with no upper limit. It can have any number of rows. Table 8.1 summarizes the differences between implicit and explicit cursors.

TABLE 8.1   Implicit versus Explicit Cursors

Implicit Cursor	Explicit Cursor
Maintained internally by PL/SQL. Opened and closed automatically when the query is executed.	Defined, opened, and closed explicitly in the program. The cursor has a name.
The cursor attributes are prefixed with SQL (for example, SQL%FOUND).	The cursor attributes are prefixed with the cursor name (for example, C1%FOUND).
The cursor attribute %ISOPEN is always FALSE, because the implicit cursor is closed immediately when the query completes.	The %ISOPEN attribute will have a valid value depending upon the status of the cursor.
Only one row can be processed; the SELECT statement with the INTO clause is used.	Any number of rows can be processed. Iterative routines should be set up in the program, and each row should be fetched explicitly (except for a cursor FOR loop).

Using Cursors

The term *cursor* usually refers to an explicit cursor. From now on, we will simply say "cursor" for an explicit cursor. The cursor to be used in the program is defined in the DECLARE section. The cursor has a name and a SELECT statement. WHERE, ORDER BY, GROUP BY, subqueries, and so on, are all permitted in a cursor definition.

Declaring a Cursor

A cursor declaration defines the SELECT statement for the query you need to process in the body of the block. In its simple form, a cursor declaration has the following syntax:

```
CURSOR cursor_name IS select_statement;
```

The *cursor name* is an undeclared PL/SQL variable. You cannot assign values to a cursor name or use it in an expression. The following example opens a cursor on the EMP table for records with SALARY above 2000. If there is no WHERE clause, all rows from the EMP table will be processed.

```
DECLARE
CURSOR C_EMP IS SELECT empno, ename, salary
FROM emp
WHERE salary > 2500
ORDER BY ename;
... ... ...
BEGIN
```

You can use a view or select from multiple tables/views in the cursor definition. You can select all columns by using the asterisk (*) instead of column names.

Opening a Cursor

The cursor should be opened before its row values can be used. Opening the cursor initiates the query processing. Here is the syntax for opening a simple cursor:

```
OPEN cursor_name;
```

where *cursor_name* is the name of the cursor defined in the declaration section. For example, to open the cursor defined on EMP table, do this:

```
OPEN C_EMP;
```

Closing a Cursor

Explicitly opened cursors should be closed explicitly. The syntax for closing a cursor follows:

```
CLOSE cursor_name;
```

For example, to close the cursor defined on the EMP table, do this:

```
CLOSE C_EMP;
```

Fetching a Cursor

A cursor is *fetched* to retrieve a row at a time; use the FETCH command for this. After each fetch, the cursor advances to the next row in the result set. Here is the syntax of the FETCH command:

```
FETCH cursor_name INTO variable [, variable]…;
```

For each column in the cursor definition SELECT, there should be a corresponding variable in the FETCH variable list. The variables should be declared with the appropriate datatype in the declaration section. Consider the following example: The cursor is defined to select ENAME and SALARY from EMP table. The variables to hold the result from the cursor fetch are also defined. Each time, we fetch into the same variables (you can also fetch into different variables, if required). There are three rows in the EMP table (because there is no WHERE clause, all rows in the table are processed), so we fetch three times from the cursor and display the output to the screen:

```
SET SERVEROUTPUT ON
DECLARE
  V_enameEMP.ENAME%TYPE;
  V_salaryEMP.SALARY%TYPE;
  CURSOR c_emp IS SELECT ename, salary FROM emp;
BEGIN
  OPEN c_emp;
  FETCH c_emp INTO v_ename, v_salary;
  DBMS_OUTPUT.PUT_LINE ('Salary of Employee '|| v_ename
|| ' is '|| v_salary);
  FETCH c_emp INTO v_ename, v_salary;
```

```
        DBMS_OUTPUT.PUT_LINE ('Salary of Employee '|| v_ename
||' is '|| v_salary);
    FETCH c_emp INTO v_ename, v_salary;
        DBMS_OUTPUT.PUT_LINE ('Salary of Employee '|| v_ename
||' is '|| v_salary);
    CLOSE c_emp;
END;
```

What if there are more than three rows returned, or what if there are not three rows in the table? You can use the iterative control structures and the cursor attributes to loop through all the records in the cursor. Similar to the implicit cursor attributes, there are four explicit cursor attributes. The cursor attributes are prefixed with the cursor name. The purpose and functionalities of the cursor attributes for explicit cursors are the same as they are for implicit cursors.

Let's now rewrite the previous example to use a loop to manage the number of fetches. The program exits the loop when there are no more rows to fetch.

```
SET SERVEROUTPUT ON
DECLARE
  V_ename   EMP.ENAME%TYPE;
  V_salary  EMP.SALARY%TYPE;
  CURSOR c_emp IS SELECT ename, salary FROM emp;
BEGIN
  OPEN c_emp;
  LOOP
    FETCH c_emp INTO v_ename, v_salary;
    EXIT WHEN c_emp%NOTFOUND;
    DBMS_OUTPUT.PUT_LINE ('Salary of Employee '|| v_ename
||
                          ' is '|| v_salary);
  END LOOP;
  CLOSE c_emp;
END;
```

Record Variables

Defining a record variable using the TYPE command and using *%ROWTYPE* are discussed in Chapter 9, *Working with Composite Datatypes and Collections*.

A record variable can be used to fetch the rows from a cursor. It is easier to define and to use than declaring each variable separately when selecting all columns from a table or referring to the columns in a cursor—especially if the cursor is selecting a lot of columns or if you do not want to declare each variable for the cursor to fetch into. The following example defines a cursor using the %ROWTYPE and uses it in the program.

When you are using %ROWTYPE on a table and fetching into a record, it is always safer to select all the columns in the table using an asterisk (*) than to list column names. Another caveat is that you might select the columns in a different order than in the table definition. By using an asterisk (*) in the SELECT clause, you eliminate this problem. In the example, although we selected all columns from the table, we did not use them all in the program. The record elements will have the same name as the table columns.

```
SET SERVEROUTPUT ON
DECLARE
   R_emp   EMP%ROWTYPE;
   CURSOR c_emp IS SELECT * FROM emp;
BEGIN
   OPEN c_emp;
   LOOP
     FETCH c_emp INTO r_emp;
     EXIT WHEN c_emp%NOTFOUND;
     DBMS_OUTPUT.PUT_LINE ('Salary of Employee '|| r_
emp.ename ||
                           ' is '|| r_emp.salary);
   END LOOP;
   CLOSE c_emp;
END;
```

You can also define the %ROWTYPE on a cursor name. Since forward declaration is not allowed in PL/SQL, you must declare the cursor first and then use the cursor name to define the record variable. Consider this example:

```
DECLARE
   CURSOR c_emp IS SELECT ename, salary FROM emp;
   R_emp   c_emp%ROWTYPE;
BEGIN
```

```
      OPEN c_emp;
      LOOP
        FETCH c_emp INTO r_emp;
        EXIT WHEN c_emp%NOTFOUND;
        DBMS_OUTPUT.PUT_LINE ('Salary of Employee '|| r_
  emp.ename ||
                            ' is '|| r_emp.salary);
      END LOOP;
      CLOSE c_emp;
  END;
```

The example uses a record variable r_emp, which is defined based on the cursor c_emp. For PL/SQL to recognize this record variable, the cursor must be declared previously. The example will display the employee names and their salary from the EMP table.

Cursors with Parameters

As with a procedure or a function, you can pass parameters into a cursor and use them in the query. This is very useful when you have to open the cursor based on a certain condition or when you need to fetch the records that satisfy a condition derived elsewhere. The syntax for declaring a cursor with parameters follows:

```
CURSOR cursor_name [(parameter [,parameter]…)] IS select_
statement;
```

Here is the syntax for defining a parameter:

```
Parameter_name  [IN] data_type [{:= | DEFALUT} value]
```

Unlike using procedures, you can only pass values to the cursor; you cannot pass values out of the cursor through parameters. Only the datatype of the parameter is defined, not its length. Optionally, you can provide a default value for the parameter, which will take effect if no value is passed to the cursor. The parameter name defined in the cursor declaration is only a placeholder; the parameter is not available elsewhere for reference and need not be declared elsewhere in the program.

You can also use a %TYPE instead of a datatype in the parameter declaration for a cursor, for example, CURSOR c1 (p_name EMP.ENAME%TYPE) IS SELECT....

The actual values are applied to the parameter when you open a cursor. The syntax for opening a cursor with parameters is this:

```
OPEN cursor_name [(value [,value]...)];
```

where *value* can be a literal or a variable.

If you have not defined default values for a parameter (when it is declared in the cursor), opening the cursor without a parameter will cause an error. Each formal parameter in the cursor definition should have a corresponding actual value when opening the cursor. Formal parameters defined with a default value need not have a corresponding actual value.

Consider an example: In preparing a report, you need to print each department number and name in one line followed by the employees working in that department (name and salary); you also need to print the total department salary, then proceed to the next department, and so on. This is shown in Listing 8.4. Here, you define two cursors: one for department and one for employee. The employee cursor uses a parameter to select only the employees belonging to a department. Notice that the employee cursor is opened and closed for each department with a new parameter value. This example also uses %TYPE and %ROWTYPE variables.

LISTING 8.4: Cursors with parameters

```
DECLARE

    CURSOR c_dept IS SELECT * FROM dept ORDER BY deptno;

    CURSOR c_emp (p_dept VARCHAR2) IS
                SELECT ename, salary
                FROM    emp
                WHERE   deptno = p_dept
                ORDER BY ename;
```

```
        r_dept    DEPT%ROWTYPE;

        v_ename   EMP.ENAME%TYPE;
        v_salary EMP.SALARY%TYPE;

        v_tot_salary   NUMBER (10,2);

    BEGIN

      OPEN c_dept;
      LOOP
        FETCH c_dept INTO r_dept;
        EXIT WHEN c_dept%NOTFOUND;

        DBMS_OUTPUT.PUT_LINE ('Department : ' || r_dept.deptno
    || ' - '
                             || r_dept.dname);
        v_tot_salary := 0;

        OPEN c_emp (r_dept.deptno);
        LOOP
          FETCH c_emp INTO v_ename, v_salary;
          EXIT WHEN c_emp%NOTFOUND;

          DBMS_OUTPUT.PUT_LINE ('Name: ' ||v_ename || '
    Salary:'
                                ||v_salary);
          v_tot_salary := v_tot_salary + v_salary;

        END LOOP;
        CLOSE c_emp;

        DBMS_OUTPUT.PUT_LINE ('Total Salary for Dept: ' || v_
    tot_salary);

      END LOOP;
      CLOSE c_dept;

    END;
    /
```

Cursor FOR Loops

In most situations, we follow this procedure:

1. Open a cursor

2. Start a loop

3. Fetch the cursor

4. Check whether rows are returned

5. Process

6. Close the loop

7. Close the cursor

You can simplify this type of coding by using a *cursor FOR loop*. You declare the cursor as you normally would, and in the body of the block, instead of opening and closing the cursor explicitly, you can use the FOR loop. The loop automatically processes all records returned from the query. You can even define the query in the cursor FOR loop itself. The syntax of the cursor FOR loop follows:

```
FOR record_name IN
{cursor_name [(parameter [,parameter]…)]
| (query_definition)}
LOOP
statements
END LOOP;
```

Let's rewrite the example in Listing 8.4 using a cursor FOR loop; you can see this revision in Listing 8.5. Notice that when using a cursor FOR loop, you need not define the record variables. The record variables are implicitly declared and are only available inside the loop. The sequence of statements between LOOP and END LOOP is executed once for each row returned by the cursor.

LISTING 8.5: Using a cursor FOR loop
```
DECLARE

    CURSOR c_dept IS SELECT deptno, dname
                    FROM dept ORDER BY deptno;
```

```
            CURSOR c_emp (p_dept VARCHAR2) IS
                    SELECT ename, salary
                    FROM    emp
                    WHERE   deptno = p_dept
                    ORDER BY ename;


        v_tot_salary  NUMBER (10,2);

BEGIN

  FOR r_dept IN c_dept LOOP

    DBMS_OUTPUT.PUT_LINE ('Department : ' || r_dept.deptno
|| ' - '
                            || r_dept.dname);
    v_tot_salary := 0;

    FOR r_emp IN c_emp (r_dept.deptno) LOOP

      DBMS_OUTPUT.PUT_LINE ('Name: ' ||r_emp.ename || '
Salary:'
                            ||r_emp.salary);
      v_tot_salary := v_tot_salary + r_emp.salary;

    END LOOP;

    DBMS_OUTPUT.PUT_LINE ('Total Salary for Dept: ' || v_
tot_salary);

  END LOOP;

END;
/
```

When using expressions in the cursor declaration, you should specify an alias name for the declaration. The alias name can be used for referencing the cursor column.

Cursor FOR Loop Using a Query

A query can be defined in the cursor FOR loop. The cursor does not have a name because it is not declared explicitly. The record name is defined with the cursor query. Listing 8.6 is the same as Listing 8.5, using the query definition (subquery) in the cursor FOR loop instead of defining it in the declaration section.

LISTING 8.6: Query in a cursor FOR loop

```
DECLARE

   v_tot_salary  NUMBER (10,2);

BEGIN

   FOR r_dept IN (SELECT deptno, dname
                   FROM dept ORDER BY deptno) LOOP

     DBMS_OUTPUT.PUT_LINE ('Department : ' || r_dept.deptno
|| ' - '
                            || r_dept.dname);
     v_tot_salary := 0;

     FOR r_emp IN (SELECT ename, salary
                   FROM    emp
                   WHERE   deptno = r_dept.deptno
                   ORDER BY ename) LOOP

        DBMS_OUTPUT.PUT_LINE ('Name: ' ||r_emp.ename || '
Salary:'
                              ||r_emp.salary);
        v_tot_salary := v_tot_salary + r_emp.salary;
```

```
        END LOOP;

        DBMS_OUTPUT.PUT_LINE ('Total Salary for Dept: ' || v_
tot_salary);

    END LOOP;

END;
/
```

 You can terminate a cursor FOR loop before its completion by using the EXIT or GOTO statement. When the loop terminates, the associated cursor is closed.

Subqueries in a Cursor

A *subquery* is a query that appears inside a query, usually enclosed in parentheses. You can use subqueries in the cursor definition as you would use them in any SELECT statement. Most commonly, the subquery is defined in the WHERE clause or in the FROM clause. Subqueries can also be used in the query defined inside the cursor FOR loop. Writing subqueries is discussed in Chapter 3, *Joins and Subqueries*.

Let's consider few examples of using subqueries in a cursor. The following example defines a subquery in the WHERE clause. Let's define a cursor to process the employee records that do not belong to the ACCOUNTING department:

```
CURSOR c1 IS SELECT * FROM emp
            WHERE  deptno NOT IN (SELECT deptno
                                  FROM    dept
                                  WHERE   dname !=
'ACCOUNTING');
```

The example shown in Listing 8.7 uses a subquery in the FROM clause. The script gets the total tablespace size from the DBA_DATA_FILES view and total free space size from the DBA_FREE_SPACE view in the subquery; it selects the tablespace name, total size, and total free space in the cursor. The cursor also uses alias names.

LISTING 8.7: Cursor using subquery

```
DECLARE

  CURSOR C1 IS SELECT a.tablespace_name TSNAME,
      SUM(a.tots) Tot_Size, SUM(a.sumb) Tot_Free
    FROM   (SELECT tablespace_name, 0 tots, SUM(bytes) sumb
  FROM   dba_free_space a
      GROUP BY tablespace_name
      UNION
      SELECT tablespace_name, SUM(bytes) tots, 0
      FROM   dba_data_files
      GROUP BY tablespace_name) a
    GROUP BY a.tablespace_name;

  v_pctfree PLS_INTEGER;

BEGIN

  FOR R1 IN C1 LOOP

    v_pctfree := r1.tot_free / r1.tot_size * 100;
    DBMS_OUTPUT.PUT_LINE (r1.tsname ||' has '|| r1.tot_
free ||
                          ' bytes free out of total '||
r1.tot_size ||
                          ' ('||v_pctfree||'%)');
  END LOOP;

END;
/
```

Updating and Deleting in a Cursor

UPDATE and DELETE statements can be used in PL/SQL to update or delete multiple rows. (The INSERT statement can insert multiple rows simultaneously by using a subquery.) An explicit cursor needs to be used only when you want to query multiple rows from a table or tables. PL/SQL provides options to delete or to update the record you just fetched using the explicit cursor.

The *WHERE CURRENT OF* clause in an UPDATE or DELETE statement specifies that the most recent row fetched from the table should be updated or deleted. To use this feature, you must declare the cursor with the *FOR UPDATE clause*. When the session opens a cursor with the FOR UPDATE clause, all rows in the return set will hold row-level exclusive locks. Other sessions can only query the rows, but they cannot update, delete, or select with FOR UPDATE.

Here is the syntax of the FOR UPDATE clause in the SELECT statement:

```
FOR UPDATE [OF [schema.]table.column [,[schema.]table.column] …
    [NOWAIT]
```

Use the OF clause to lock only the tables mentioned in a multiple-table query. The column names improve readability, the rows are locked, and there is no column-level lock. If you omit the OF clause, selected rows of all tables in the query are locked. If the rows are already locked by another session, NOWAIT specifies, "Do not wait; return an error." Normally, Oracle waits until the rows are available (that is, until the other user issues a COMMIT or ROLLBACK).

The syntax of using the WHERE CURRENT OF clause in UPDATE and DELETE statements follows:

```
WHERE {CURRENT OF cursor_name | search_condition}
```

The example shown in Listing 8.8 opens a cursor for employees and updates the commission, if there is no commission assigned based on the salary level.

LISTING 8.8: Cursor using FOR UPDATE and WHERE CURRENT OF

```
DECLARE

  CURSOR c1 IS SELECT empno, salary
               FROM    emp
               WHERE   comm IS NULL
               FOR UPDATE OF comm;


  v_comm NUMBER(10,2);


BEGIN

  FOR r1 IN c1 LOOP

    IF r1.salary < 500 THEN
```

```
        v_comm := r1.salary * 0.25;
   ELSIF r1.salary < 1000 THEN
        v_comm := r1.salary * 0.20;
   ELSIF r1.salary < 3000 THEN
        v_comm := r1.salary * 0.15;
   ELSE
        v_comm := r1.salary * 0.12;
   END IF;

   UPDATE emp
   SET    comm = v_comm
   WHERE CURRENT OF c1;

 END LOOP;
END;
/
```

The FOR UPDATE clause in the SELECT statement can only be specified in the top level; subqueries cannot have this clause.

Summary

In this chapter, you read how PL/SQL interacts with the Oracle database and how DML statements can be used inside a PL/SQL block. For queries returning only one row, you can use the SELECT INTO statement; for queries returning more than one row, you must define an explicit cursor. Implicit cursors are opened for DML statements and closed when the statement completes. Implicit cursors are managed by PL/SQL.

Explicit cursors should be defined, opened, and closed explicitly in the program. A cursor FOR loop is an exception to this: You need not open or close the cursor explicitly. You declare the cursor in the declaration section of the block and manipulate the cursor using OPEN, FETCH, and CLOSE statements. There are four cursor attributes associated with an explicit or implicit cursor: %ISOPEN, %FOUND, %NOTFOUND, and %ROWCOUNT.

You can pass parameters to the cursor. The cursor parameter can only pass a value into the parameter; it cannot pass a value out. You can lock the rows that the cursor returns for later program updates. You also can use subqueries in the cursor definition.

Key Terms

Before you take the exam, make sure you are familiar with the following terms:

%ROWTYPE

%TYPE

COMMIT

Cursor attributes

Cursor FOR loop

Fetch

FOR UPDATE clause

Query

ROLLBACK

SAVEPOINT

Subquery

Transaction

WHERE CURRENT OF

Review Questions

1. What is wrong with the following cursor declaration?

```
CURSOR c1 (pempno IN NUMBER (4)) IS
SELECT EMPNO, ENAME
FROM    EMP
WHERE   EMPNO = pempno;
```

   A. The INTO clause is missing.

   B. Inside the cursor definition, the variable should be preceded with a colon (:pempno).

   C. IN cannot be specified in the cursor definition.

   D. The size of the datatype should not be specified in the cursor definition.

2. Take a look at the following listing of EMP table data.

EMPNO	ENAME	SALARY	COMM	DEPTNO
1234	ADAMS	3500		
7566	JONES	2975		20
7654	MARTIN	1250	1400	30
7698	K_BLAKE	2850		30
7788	SCOTT	3000		20
7839	A_EDWARD	5000	50000	10
7844	TURNER	1500	0	30
902	FORD	3000		20

Consider the following block. What will be value of V_EMPNO when the block is executed? (EMPNO is the primary key of EMP.)

```
DECLARE
  v_empno  EMP.EMPNO%TYPE := 800;
  CURSOR   c_emp (p_empno EMP.EMPNO%TYPE := 1234) IS
           SELECT empno FROM emp
           WHERE empno = p_empno;
BEGIN
 OPEN c_emp (NULL);
 FETCH c_emp INTO v_empno;
 CLOSE c_emp;
END;
```

A. 1234

B. 800

C. NULL

D. 0

3. What is the value of V_A when the following block is executed? The table EMP has the rows listed in Question 2.

```
DECLARE
    V_A NUMBER;
    V_E NUMBER;
    CURSOR c1 IS SELECT empno FROM EMP;
BEGIN
    OPEN c1;
    LOOP
        FETCH c1 INTO V_E;
        V_A := C1%ROWCOUNT;
        EXIT WHEN C1%NOTFOUND;
    END LOOP;
    CLOSE C1;
END;
```

A. 8

B. 9

C. 6

D. 0

4. An EMP table has the data shown in Question 2. What will be value of *v_count* when the following block is executed?

```
DECLARE
    v_count  NUMBER;
    r_emp EMP%ROWTYPE;
BEGIN
    SELECT * INTO r_emp FROM EMP
    WHERE empno < 7700;
    v_count := SQL%ROWCOUNT;
END;
```

A. The block will fail with errors.

B. 4

C. 8

D. 0

5. What will the output be from the following PL/SQL block? The contents of the EMP table are shown in Question 2.

```
SET SERVEROUTPUT ON
DECLARE
    v_ename  EMP.ENAME%TYPE := 'NO NAME';
BEGIN
    SELECT ename INTO v_ename
    FROM EMP
    WHERE  empno = 9999;
    IF SQL%NOTFOUND THEN
        DBMS_OUTPUT.PUT_LINE('No Such Employee Number');
    ELSE
        DBMS_OUTPUT.PUT_LINE(v_ename);
    END IF;
EXCEPTION
    WHEN NO_DATA_FOUND THEN
        DBMS_OUTPUT.PUT_LINE('Invalid Employee Number');
END;
```

A. The block will return an error.

B. No Such Employee Number

C. NO NAME

D. Invalid Employee Number

6. What will the output be from the following PL/SQL block? The contents of the EMP table are shown in Question 2.

```
SET SERVEROUTPUT ON
DECLARE
   v_ename   EMP.ENAME%TYPE := 'NO NAME';
   CURSOR c1 IS
      SELECT ename
      FROM EMP
      WHERE  empno = 9999;
BEGIN
   OPEN C1;
   FETCH c1 INTO v_ename;
   IF C1%NOTFOUND THEN
      DBMS_OUTPUT.PUT_LINE('No Such Employee Number');
   ELSE
      DBMS_OUTPUT.PUT_LINE(v_ename);
   END IF;
EXCEPTION
   WHEN NO_DATA_FOUND THEN
      DBMS_OUTPUT.PUT_LINE('Invalid Employee Number');
END;
```

A. The block will return an error.

B. No Such Employee Number

C. NO NAME

D. Invalid Employee Number

7. Consider the following PL/SQL block. Which line of code has an error? The contents of the EMP table are shown in Question 2.

```
1   DECLARE
2     v_ename   EMP.ENAME%TYPE := 'NO NAME';
3     CURSOR c1 IS
4        SELECT ename
5        FROM EMP;
6   BEGIN
7     OPEN C1;
8     LOOP
9       FETCH c1 INTO v_ename;
10      IF C1%NOTFOUND THEN
11          EXIT;
12      ELSE
13          DBMS_OUTPUT.PUT_LINE(v_ename);
14      END IF;
15      CLOSE C1;
16    END LOOP;
END;
```

A. Line 3

B. Line 7

C. Line 11

D. Line 9

8. Consider the following PL/SQL block. What is the value of *V_COUNT* when the block is executed and no rows are deleted?

```
DECLARE
    V_COUNT NUMBER;
BEGIN
    DELETE FROM EMP
    WHERE  EMPNO < 0;
    V_COUNT := SQL%ROWCOUNT;
END;
```

A. NULL

B. TRUE

C. 0

D. FALSE

9. In a PL/SQL block, what is the value of SQL%NOTFOUND before executing any DML statements?

A. NOTFOUND

B. TRUE

C. NULL

D. FALSE

10. Which of the following statements require an explicit cursor if processing more than one row?

A. SELECT

B. UPDATE

C. DELETE

D. INSERT

11. Which commands are allowed inside a PL/SQL block? Choose all that apply.

A. TRUNCATE

B. DELETE

C. SAVEPOINT

D. ALTER TABLE

12. Which line of code has an error? EMPNO is the primary key of the EMP table.

```
1  DECLARE
2  v_empno NUMBER (4);
3  v_ename VARCHAR2 (20);
4  BEGIN
5  SELECT empno, ename, salary
6  INTO    v_empno, v_ename
7  FROM    emp
8  WHERE   empno = 1234;
9  END;
```

A. Line 3

B. Line 5

C. Line 6

D. The code has no error.

13. Consider the following SELECT statement. What happens if there are no rows satisfying the WHERE condition?

```
SELECT COUNT(*)
INTO    V_COUNT
FROM    EMP
WHERE   SALARY < 10;
```

A. A NO_DATA_FOUND exception is raised.

B. The SELECT statement executes successfully.

C. A TOO_FEW_ROWS exception is raised.

D. COUNT(*) is not valid to use in PL/SQL.

14. Consider the following PL/SQL block. Which line has an error?

```
1  DECLARE
2     v_empno    PLS_INTEGER := 1234;
3  BEGIN
4     GRANT DELETE TO BILL;
5     DELETE FROM EMP
6     WHERE  EMPNO = 1234;
7     ROLLBACK;
8  END;
```

A. Line 2

B. Line 4

C. Line 7

D. The code has no error.

15. Consider the following PL/SQL block. Which line has an error?

```
1  DECLARE
2     CURSOR c_emp IS SELECT empno, ename, salary
3     FROM emp
4     WHERE salary < 3500;
5  BEGIN
6     FOR r_emp IN c_emp LOOP
7        UPDATE emp
8        SET salary = salary * 1.25
9        WHERE CURRENT OF c_emp;
10     END LOOP;
11  END;
```

A. Line 2

B. Line 6

C. Line 9

D. The code has no error.

16. Consider the following PL/SQL block and choose the most appropriate answer.

```
DECLARE
  CURSOR c_emp IS SELECT empno, ename
  FROM emp
  WHERE salary < 3500
  FOR UPDATE;
BEGIN
  FOR r_emp IN c_emp LOOP
    UPDATE emp
    SET salary = salary * 1.25
    WHERE CURRENT OF c_emp;
  END LOOP;
END;
```

A. The block will give a salary raise by 25 percent for each employee whose salary is below 3500.

B. The block will fail because there is no column name specified in the FOR UPDATE clause.

C. You cannot use a WHERE CURRENT OF clause with the cursor FOR loop.

D. The SALARY column used in the WHERE clause in not appropriate because it is not in the SELECT clause.

17. Consider the following PL/SQL block, and choose the most appropriate answer.

```
DECLARE
   r_c1   c1%rowtype;
   CURSOR c1 IS SELECT empno FROM emp;
BEGIN
   OPEN c1;
   FETCH c1 INTO r_c1;
   CLOSE c1;
END;
```

   A. The code block has no error.

   B. The declaration of r_c1 is illegal.

   C. The declaration of r_c1 cannot use %ROWTYPE because the cursor has only one column selected. %TYPE should be used instead.

   D. The FETCH statement is malformed; you cannot use the INTO clause.

18. What is the value of *v_status* when the following code block is executed?

```
DECLARE
   v_status BOOLEAN;
   v_date   DATE;
BEGIN
   SELECT SYSDATE INTO v_date FROM DUAL;
   v_status := SQL%ISOPEN;
END;
```

   A. 0

   B. TRUE

   C. FALSE

   D. 1

19. Which of the following cursor attributes are invalid? Choose two.

   A. %NOTOPEN

   B. %NOTFOUND

   C. %FOUND

   D. %OPEN

20. If C1 is the cursor that is opened in a PL/SQL block, which attribute will have the number of rows fetched so far?

   A. C1%COUNT

   B. C1%ROWCOUNT

   C. COUNT%C1

   D. C1%COUNTROW

Answers to Review Questions

1. D. The size of the parameter should not be specified; only the datatype must be specified.

2. B. The cursor is opened with a NULL value as a parameter; hence, the fetch will fail to return any row. So, the initialized value for V_EMPNO remains the same. If the cursor had been opened without any parameter, it would have taken the default value of 1234.

3. A. The %ROWCOUNT value is incremented when a row is fetched. Since there are eight rows in the table, eight fetches are made. This means that the value of %ROWCOUNT is 8. The ninth fetch did not return any row, so the value of %ROWCOUNT remains the same.

4. A. Since there are four rows satisfying the WHERE condition, the SELECT statement will fail with a TOO_MANY_ROWS exception. The SELECT INTO clause can only select one row.

5. D. The SELECT INTO clause raises a NO_DATA_FOUND exception if there are no rows selected. Although the value of SQL%NOTFOUND is TRUE, control does not pass to the next statement when an exception is raised.

6. B. When the cursor does not return any row, the value of C1%NOTFOUND will be TRUE after the first fetch. A NO_DATA_FOUND exception will not be raised when using explicit cursors.

7. D. There are eight rows in the EMP table, so the loop will try to execute eight times. The cursor is closed inside the loop, however, so trying to fetch the second row inside the loop will return an error. The cursor should be closed outside the loop.

8. C. When no rows are deleted from the table, the value of %ROWCOUNT will be 0.

9. C. SQL%NOTFOUND will have a Boolean value, and before executing any DML statement, it will be NULL.

10. A. You can update, delete, or insert any number of rows in PL/SQL without an explicit cursor. If your query is selecting more than one row, you must use an explicit cursor. SELECT INTO can process only one row.

11. B, C. DDL statements are not allowed inside a PL/SQL block. TRUNCATE and ALTER TABLE are DDL statements.

12. B. There are only two variables defined. The INTO clause has only two variables, but the SELECT clause has three columns.

13. B. The SELECT statement executes successfully, and the *V_COUNT* variable will have a value of 0 assigned.

14. B. Data control language statements are not allowed in PL/SQL. GRANT and REVOKE are DCL statements.

15. C. The WHERE CURRENT OF clause can only be used if the cursor is defined with a FOR UPDATE clause.

16. A. The block will execute without any error. Use of FOR UPDATE without any table or column name is allowed.

17. B. The declaration of r_c1 references the cursor c1, which is declared only in the next line. Forward declaration is not allowed in PL/SQL.

18. C. The value of SQL%ISOPEN is always FALSE. The implicit cursor is opened and closed when the DML statement completes.

19. A, D. %NOTOPEN and %OPEN are invalid. To check the open status of the cursor, the valid attribute is %ISOPEN.

20. B. C1%ROWCOUNT will have the number of records fetched so far from the cursor C1. %COUNT and %COUNTROW are not valid cursor attributes. There are four cursor attributes that can be used to check the cursor status: C1%ROWCOUNT, C1%NOTFOUND, C1%FOUND, and C1%ISOPEN.

Chapter
9

Working with Composite Datatypes and Collections

ORACLE8i SQL AND PL/SQL EXAM OBJECTIVES OFFERED IN THIS CHAPTER:

- ✓ Create user-defined PL/SQL records
- ✓ Create a record with the %ROWTYPE attribute
- ✓ Describe the types of PL/SQL collections
- ✓ Create PL/SQL collections
- ✓ Add and remove elements from a collection
- ✓ Manage collections with the collection methods

Exam objectives are subject to change at any time without prior notice and at Oracle's sole discretion. Please visit Oracle's Training and Certification Web site (http://education .oracle.com/certification/index.html) for the most current exam objectives listing.

Up to this point, we have worked primarily with atomic data structures. PL/SQL not only supports these atomic structures but also composite structures. PL/SQL has two types of composite structures: records and collections. Records are composed of heterogeneous fields, and collections are composed of homogeneous elements. In this chapter, we will learn about the types of records and collections, how to define records and collections, and how to use these composite structures in your programs.

PL/SQL Records

Records are a PL/SQL composite datatype, which is in contrast to scalar datatypes, such as VARCHAR2, NUMBER, or DATE. Scalar datatypes and other language primitives come predefined in the package standard, but composite datatypes, like records, must be defined before they can be used. A *record* is called a composite datatype because it is composed of a logical group of data elements called fields. A *field* can be either a scalar datatype or another record type. If you've done any C programming, a record is similar to a struct. Conceptually, a record is also similar to a row in a database table, with a record's fields being analogous to a table's columns. They are so similar that PL/SQL makes it easy to define and use records based on a database table or on a virtual table (view or query). As with a table, each column/field within a row/record can be referenced and assigned values individually, or all fields within the record can be referenced in a single statement. Records can also be used as parameters to a procedure or function, giving you a simple and elegant way to pass complex data structures among your PL/SQL programs.

In this chapter, our examples will use a model that includes stock quotes and portfolios of stocks and mutual funds. Stock quotes include a number of data elements, such as stock symbol, bid price, ask price, and volume. Portfolios contain a number of holdings, which can be either a stock, a bond, or a mutual fund. Each holding has attributes, such as the security, purchase date, price, and quantity.

Creating Records

To use a record, you must define its structure, then declare variables of that defined type. PL/SQL gives you explicit and implicit techniques for defining records. You explicitly define a record based on the fields in the definition. Then, once the record type is defined, you declare or create record variables of that type for use. The other technique is to implicitly declare a record variable based on the structure of a table or query using the *%ROWTYPE* attribute. These implicit record variables are a more powerful technique because they are created dynamically at runtime.

Explicitly Defined Records

Explicitly defined records are defined in the declaration section of a PL/SQL block before creating any variable of that record type. Use the *TYPE* statement to define a record, then create variables of that record's type. The general syntax for defining a record is

```
TYPE record_type IS RECORD (field_definition_list);
```

where *field_definition_list* is a comma-delimited list of field definitions. The syntax for each field definition is

```
field_name  data_type_and_size  [NOT NULL] [{:= | DEFAULT}
default_value]
```

Field names must obey the same naming rules as tables or columns (that is, no leading numbers, maximum of 30 characters, and so on). So, our stock quote record could be defined and a variable created like this:

```
DECLARE
  TYPE stock_quote_rec IS RECORD
    (symbol    stocks.symbol%TYPE
    ,bid       NUMBER(10,4)
```

```
,ask        NUMBER(10,4)
,volume     NUMBER      NOT NULL := 0   -- default
,exchange VARCHAR2(6) DEFAULT 'NASDAQ' -- default
);
```

```
real_time_quote   stock_quote_rec;   -- declare the
variable
```

Studying our example, you can see that the fields *bid*, *ask*, and *volume* are defined as NUMBER datatypes. The exchange field is defined with a default value of 'NASDAQ'. Default values can be assigned with either the keyword DEFAULT or with the assignment operator in the field definition. The volume field is defined with the NOT NULL restriction and a default value of 0, using the assignment operator technique. The NOT NULL restriction on a field in a record works in the same way as a NOT NULL constraint on a column in a table: The field must contain a value. If you use a NOT NULL restriction, you must use a default value.

The *%TYPE* attribute on the definition of the field symbol is used to reference the datatype and size of a table or view in the database. Your program doesn't have to know that type and size ahead of time. It's a way of saying, "Use whatever the database uses for this field." In our example, the record field will be defined at compile time to be the same datatype and size as the column symbol in our table STOCKS. Whenever your code will be using data from the database, you should use the %TYPE attribute for variable or field definitions. The reasons are twofold:

- You can't goof and key in the wrong datatype or size, because you're referencing the source.

- More significantly, changes to the size or type in the table are automatically reflected in your program—increasing the width of a column will not automatically break your program code.

The datatype for each field's definition can be a scalar type, as seen in the stock_quote_rec example, or the field can be a previously defined record. Expanding our stock trading example, we want to build a record for a detailed quote, containing the basic information found in the stock_quote_rec, as well as some additional information, such as the timestamp for the quote, the bid and ask size, and the last few ticks. We define our detailed quote record as follows:

```
DECLARE
   TYPE stock_quote_rec IS RECORD
     (symbol   stocks.symbol%TYPE
     ,bid      NUMBER(10,4)
     ,ask      NUMBER(10,4)
```

```
      ,volume   NUMBER        NOT NULL := 0
      ,exchange VARCHAR2(6) DEFAULT 'NASDAQ' -- default

   );

   TYPE detailed_quote_rec IS RECORD
      (quote            stock_quote_rec   -- nested record
      ,timestamp        date
      ,bid_size         NUMBER
      ,ask_size         NUMBER
      ,last_ticks       VARCHAR2(4)
      );

   real_time_detail   detailed_quote_rec;
```

Implicitly Defined Records

An implicitly defined record is one in which we don't have to describe each field in the record definition. Since we don't define the structure of the record, we don't need to use the TYPE statement. Instead, we use the %ROWTYPE attribute on the variable declaration statement to implicitly define a record to have the same structure as a database table, view, or cursor. Like the %TYPE attribute for a field, the %ROWTYPE attribute is a great way to define records that will hold database data. Since we don't hard-code the record description, changes to the underlying record structure result in automatic changes to the record. For example, we will be working with data from the ACCOUNTS table and want a record defined with the same attributes as this table:

```
DECLARE
   account_info   accounts%ROWTYPE;  -- a record

   CURSOR xactions_cur (acct_no IN VARCHAR2) IS
     SELECT action, timestamp, holding
     FROM portfolios
     WHERE account_nbr = 'acct_no'
   ;

   xaction_info  xactions_cur%ROWTYPE;  -- a record
variable
```

Knowing how to define and use a record with the %ROWTYPE attribute is important and is frequently the topic of a question on the exam.

Some other PL/SQL constructs with which you may have experience use implicitly defined records without using the %ROWTYPE attribute, such as the record in a cursor FOR loop or the :old and :new records in a trigger.

```
DECLARE
   CURSOR xactions_cur IS
      SELECT action, timestamp, holding
      FROM portfolios
      WHERE account_nbr = '37'
   ;
BEGIN
   FOR xactions_rec in xactions_cur
   LOOP
      IF xactions_rec.holding = 'ORCL'  -- implicit record
      THEN
         notify_shareholder;
      END IF;
   END LOOP;
```

Using Records

You can use records to assign values, pass values to other PL/SQL programs, or compare values. Records, being composite data structures, have meaning on two levels and can be used at those levels. You can reference the whole record, populating all fields with a single SELECT INTO or FETCH. You can pass the whole record to a program or assign all of its fields values to another record—again, with a single statement. At a lower, more detailed level, you can deal with the individual fields within the record. You can assign values to an individual field or perform a Boolean comparison on an individual field. You can also pass one or more individual fields to another program.

Referencing Records

Records are composed of fields, and we often want to manipulate the contents of these individual fields. To access a field in a record, use *dot notation*—that is, use a dot to delimit the record structure drilling down to the field. Using our detailed_quote_rec record example from earlier in this chapter, we want to assign 1000 to the bid_size field and 156700 to the volume field:

```
DECLARE
  TYPE stock_quote_rec IS RECORD
    (symbol   stocks.symbol%TYPE
    ,bid      NUMBER(10,4)
    ,ask      NUMBER(10,4)
    ,volume   NUMBER       NOT NULL := 0   -- default
    ,exchange VARCHAR2(6) DEFAULT 'NASDAQ' -- default

    );

  TYPE detailed_quote_rec IS RECORD
    (quote             stock_quote_rec   -- nested record
    ,timestamp         date
    ,bid_size          NUMBER
    ,ask_size          NUMBER
    ,last_tick         VARCHAR2(4)
    );

  real_time_detail   detailed_quote_rec;
BEGIN

  -- assign a value to a field
  real_time_detail.bid_size := 1000;

  -- next assign a value to a field in a nested record
  real_time_detail.quote.volume := 156700;

  -- pass a data structure to a procedure
  log_quote(real_time_detail.quote);
```

Notice how we simply string together the component names in the nested record until we reach the field we want. Real_time_detail is the top-level record, quote is a field in real_time_detail, and volume is the field in quote: thus, real_time_detail.quote.volume. Additional levels of nesting will necessitate additional components in the reference.

One of the more powerful capabilities of records comes from our ability to pass whole data structures to PL/SQL programs with a single reference. In our last example, we pass the quote field, which is also a record, to the procedure log_quote. By passing a record, instead of each individual field, we can streamline our code, making it easier to understand and maintain.

Assigning Values to Records

There are several ways to assign values to a record or to fields within a record. You can use the SELECT INTO or FETCH statements to populate the entire record or individual fields, you can assign one record's values to another *en masse*, or you can populate the record piecemeal by assigning values to each field. We will examine each method with an example.

To assign values with the SELECT INTO statement, place your record or fields in the INTO clause of a SELECT statement. The variables in the INTO clause get populated with the positionally corresponding column from the SELECT list. In the following example, the first column in the SELECT list, symbol, gets loaded into the first field in the INTO list, stock_info1.symbol. The second column in the SELECT list gets loaded into the second variable in the INTO list, and so on:

```
DECLARE
   stock_info1   stocks%ROWTYPE;
   stock_info2   stocks%ROWTYPE;
BEGIN
   -- Populate the specific fields in a record
   SELECT symbol, exchange
   INTO stock_info1.symbol, stock_info1.exchange
   FROM stocks
   WHERE symbol = 'ORCL';

   -- Populate the whole record in one statement
   SELECT * INTO stock_info2 FROM stocks
   WHERE symbol = 'ORCL';
```

This technique of defining a record based on a table, then selecting * from the table into the record using the primary key, is a simple and elegant way to get one row of information from the database into your PL/SQL programs, with a minimum of coding effort and no knowledge of the number of columns, their datatypes, or sizes. But beware! If the statement returns more than one row, Oracle won't be able to stuff two or more rows into your record and you'll get a nasty runtime error.

If you have more than one row that may be returned from your SQL statement or you want to parameterize your cursor for reuse, you can open the cursor, then use FETCH instead of the SELECT INTO statement. You still get the simple, elegant technique, but in a safer package. The FETCH statement has the following syntax:

```
FETCH cursor_name INTO variable;
```

Using our STOCK_INFO example, we could do this:

```
DECLARE
   CURSOR stock_cur (symbol_in VARCHAR2) IS
     SELECT symbol, exchange, begin_date
     FROM stocks
     WHERE symbol = UPPER(symbol_in);

   stock_info  stock_cur%ROWTYPE;
BEGIN
   -- we have to open before we can fetch
   OPEN stock_cur('ORCL');
   FETCH stock_cur INTO stock_info;  -- populate the record
```

One useful technique that you can use with records is to copy an entire record to another with a single statement. The records must be declared of the exact same type in order for this to work. The records can't be based on two different TYPE statements that happen to have the same structure; they must be defined with the same type:

```
DECLARE
   TYPE stock_quote_rec IS RECORD
     (symbol   stocks.symbol%TYPE
     ,bid      NUMBER(10,4)
     ,ask      NUMBER(10,4)
     ,volume   NUMBER
     );
```

```
TYPE stock_rec_too IS RECORD
  (symbol   stocks.symbol%TYPE
  ,bid      NUMBER(10,4)
  ,ask      NUMBER(10,4)
  ,volume   NUMBER
  );    -- looks the same but is not

stock_one    stock_quote_rec;
stock_two    stock_quote_rec;
-- These fields have the same type and size as
stock_also  stock_rec_too; -- stock_quote_rec, but it's a
different datatype
BEGIN
  stock_one.symbol := 'ORCL';
  stock_one.volume := 1234500;

  stock_two  := stock_one;  -- works OK
  stock_also := stock_one;  -- error, datatype mismatch
  stock_also.symbol := stock_one.symbol;
  stock_also.volume := stock_one.volume;
```

There are two things that you might want to do with records but cannot: use them in INSERT statements or in record-level comparisons, like this:

```
INSERT INTO stocks VALUES (stock_record);  -- ERROR
```

or

```
IF stock_rec1 > stock_rec2 THEN    -- ERROR
```

The INSERT trick with a %ROWTYPE record would be cool, but it's not supported—beware of it on the exam. The problem with the comparison of records relates to sorting them. Since Oracle does not have knowledge of what would make one record sort higher or lower than another, it can't compare them. So, to compare records, you have two options:

- You can write a function that will return a scalar datatype (which Oracle knows how to sort) and use this function for the comparison:

```
IF sort_rec(stock_one) > sort_rec(stock_two) THEN
```

- You can use database objects. Database objects can be defined with an ORDER or MAP method, allowing Oracle to do comparisons on composite data structures. Database objects are beyond the scope of this book. If you need to compare complex structures, check them out in the Oracle manuals.

PL/SQL Collections

*C*ollections are similar to arrays in other languages. In Oracle release 7.3 and earlier, there was only one kind of collection, called a PL/SQL table. This type of collection is still supported but is now known as an index-by table. A collection is an ordered group of elements. Like records, collections must be defined with the TYPE statement, then variables of that type can be created and used. Collections are typically a lightly covered topic on the exam; they are presented here in greater detail than what you might need strictly for the exam. To actually use collections, however, you will need the level of detail presented in this section. So, if you need only to pass the exam, study the tables to know the differences in the collections. If you want to make use of collections, read this whole section.

Types of Collections

There are three types of PL/SQL collections:

- Index-by tables

- Nested tables

- VARRAYs

There are a number of differences among the collection types, including bounding, sparsity, and the ability to store each in the database. Bounding refers to a limit in the number of elements that a collection can have. VARRAYs have a limit and are thus bounded, while index-by and nested tables are unbounded, having no limit to the number of elements they may contain. Sparsity describes whether or not there can be gaps in the subscripts. Index-by tables can always be sparse, nested tables can become sparse if elements are deleted, and VARRAYs can never be sparse. Figure 9.1 illustrates sparsity in collections and how nested tables can become sparse.

FIGURE 9.1 Sparsity in collections

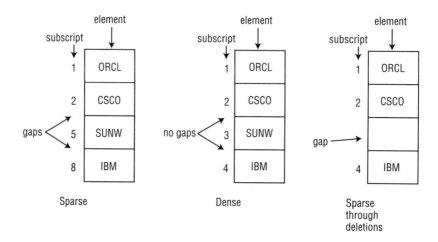

Index-by tables cannot be stored in the database, but nested tables and VARRAYs can be stored in the database.

While the three types of collections have differences, they also have a number of similarities, which is why they are all called collections. They are all single-dimensional, array-like structures and have built-in programs called methods, accessed via dot notation. Table 9.1 describes a number of properties and how they vary among the collection types.

TABLE 9.1 Collection Properties

Property	Index-by Table	Nested Table	VARRAY
Syntax to define a collection	Type table index-by binary integer	Type table	Type VARRAY
Legal datatypes	Any PL/SQL datatype	Only database datatypes	Only database datatypes
Initialization	Automatic	Via constructor	Via constructor
Uninitialized collection	Empty, elements are undefined but referenceable	NULL, illegal to reference the elements	NULL, illegal to reference the elements

TABLE 9.1   Collection Properties *(continued)*

Property	Index-by Table	Nested Table	VARRAY
Can be stored in a database	No	Yes, but element order is not preserved	Yes, and element order is preserved
Bounding	Not bounded	Not bounded, because it can be extended	Bounded; cannot be extended
Sparsity	Sparse	Can become sparse after deletions	Never sparse
Subscript range	$-2^{31}+1$ to $2^{31}-1$	1 to $2^{31}-1$	1 to max_size (max_size $< 2^{31}$)
Can you always assign a value to an element?	Yes	No, the collection may need to be extended first	No, the collection may need to be extended first and cannot be extended past the upper bound

Index-by Tables

Index-by tables are the granddaddy of collections; they were introduced in Oracle7 (in which they were called PL/SQL tables) and continue to exist in Oracle8 and 8i. Index-by table collections are defined with the TYPE statement:

```
TYPE type_name IS TABLE OF element_type [NOT NULL] INDEX
   BY BINARY_INTEGER;
```

The important wording here is INDEX BY BINARY INTEGER. Without it, the collection is a nested table. The *element_type* can be any valid PL/SQL datatype, including PLS_INTEGER, SIGNTYPE, and BOOLEAN. The other collection types are restricted to database datatypes, but since index-by tables cannot be stored in the database, they are not bound by this restriction.

While collections can be only one-dimensional, you can create them with an *element_type* that is a record, achieving pseudo–two-dimensional structures. When using a collection of records, however, you can only build the record using scalar datatypes (no nesting of records in collections). The NOT NULL keyword works in the same way in an index-by table as it does for fields in records or columns in a database table: This keyword tells Oracle to require a value for any element in the collection. Once the index-by table type is defined, you can create collections of this type in the same manner as other variables or records:

```
DECLARE
  -- define the index-by table type
  TYPE symbol_tab_typ IS TABLE OF VARCHAR2(5) INDEX BY
     BINARY_INTEGER;
  -- create an index-by table
  symbol_tab    symbol_tab_typ;
BEGIN
```

Nested Tables

Nested tables and index-by tables are very similar, and the syntax to create them is also similar. Use the TYPE statement, just as you would for an index-by table, but leave out the index by binary_integer clause:

```
TYPE type_name IS TABLE OF element_type [NOT NULL]
```

The NOT NULL option for nested tables works the same for all collections: All elements must have values. The *element_type* can be a record, but this record must contain only scalar fields and can use only database datatypes (no PLS_INTEGER, BOOLEAN, or SIGNTYPE).

Both nested tables and VARRAYs can be stored as columns in a database table, so the collection itself—not just individual elements—can be NULL. Oracle calls this whole-collection nullity "atomically NULL" to differentiate it from an individual element that is NULL. When a collection is atomically NULL, you cannot reference the elements in the collection without raising an exception. You can check for an atomically NULL collection with the IS NULL operator.

Nested tables stored in a database are not stored in the same data blocks as the rest of the table data; they are actually stored in a secondary table. Just as a SELECT without an ORDER BY is not guaranteed to return the data in any particular order, a nested table retrieved from the database does not guarantee that the order of the elements will be preserved between SELECTs. Because the collection data is stored out-of-line, nested tables are the better choice for large collections.

VARRAYs

VARRAYs, or variable arrays, have a maximum number of elements. They are thus bounded. A VARRAY is defined with the TYPE statement, like other collections, but the keyword VARRAY or VARYING ARRAY tells Oracle that this is a VARRAY collection:

```
TYPE type_name IS [VARRAY | VARYING ARRAY] (max_size) OF
    element_type [NOT NULL]
```

The *max_size* is an integer that defines the maximum number of elements allowed in the VARRAY. The VARRAY can have fewer elements than *max_size*, but it can never grow larger than *max_size* elements. The *element_type* is the datatype of the one-dimensional elements. If the *element_type* is a record, then that record can only have scalar fields composed of database datatypes (like nested tables). The NOT NULL clause instructs Oracle to require each element in the collection to have a value.

VARRAYs can be atomically NULL and can be tested for nullity with the IS NULL operator, just like nested tables. Unlike a nested table, when a VARRAY is stored in a database, it is stored in the same data blocks as the rest of the row. Just as the order of columns is preserved in a SELECT * on a table, so too will the order of elements be preserved in a VARRAY retrieved from the database. Also, because the collection is stored in-line, VARRAYs are better for small collections. Large VARRAY collections will result in data block chaining, and performance on the table may suffer. If you populate your VARRAY collection with an UPDATE, rather than when the row is inserted, you may want to increase the pctfree for your table to avoid this chaining problem.

Using Collections

Collections, like records, can be used at two levels:

- The whole collection can be manipulated.

- The individual elements in a collection can be accessed.

The whole collection is referenced with the collection name, and the individual elements are referenced with a subscript:

```
collection(subscript)
```

The subscript for an index-by table is a binary integer, which can be either positive or negative. The range of possible values is huge: from $-2^{31}+1$ to $2^{31}-1$ (-2147483647 to 2147483647). Because an index-by table can be sparse, you can use these subscripts in meaningful and creative ways. The subscript for a nested table or a VARRAY also represents the ordinal position of the element within the collection. You have less flexibility in how you can design meaningful subscripts, however, for these reasons:

- Nested tables start out dense (the opposite of sparse).

- VARRAYs stay dense.

- Both have subscripts beginning with 1.

Initializing, Populating, and Referencing Collections

Before a collection can be used, it must be initialized (instantiated). Instantiating a collection is automatic for index-by tables, but for nested tables and VARRAYs, you must use a special built-in function called a constructor. Nested tables and VARRAYs, if you recall, start out atomically NULL–that is, the whole collection is NULL, not just the elements. As in a record, values can be assigned to a collection *en masse* or piecemeal. Assigning values to elements in a collection requires use of *subscript notation* for the element. To assign one whole collection to another *en masse*, you simply use the assignment operator. Let's look at examples of initializing and populating collections.

Index-by tables are the simplest collection to initialize; you simply reference an element in the collection, and it's initialized:

```
DECLARE
  TYPE symbol_tab_typ IS TABLE OF VARCHAR2(5) INDEX BY
    BINARY_INTEGER;
  TYPE account_tab_typ IS TABLE OF accounts%ROWTYPE INDEX
    BY BINARY_INTEGER;
  symbol_tab    symbol_tab_typ;
  account_tab   account_tab_typ;
  new_acct_tab  account_tab_typ;
BEGIN
  -- initialize elements 147 and -3
  SELECT * INTO account_tab(147)
FROM accounts where account_nbr = 147;
  SELECT * INTO account_tab(-3)
FROM accounts where account_nbr = 3003;

  -- You can reference a field in an element
```

```
IF account_tab(147).balance < 500   THEN
  change_maintenance_fee(147);
END IF;
-- copy one collection to another
new_acct_tab := account_tab;

symbol_tab(1) := 'ORCL';
symbol_tab(2) := 'CSCO';
symbol_tab(3) := 'SUNW';
  -- pass the collection to a procedure
publish_portfolio(symbol_tab);
```

Nested tables and VARRAYs must be initialized with a built-in function called a *constructor*. The constructor has the same name as the collection and takes a variable number of arguments. Each argument will be populated into an element in the collection in the order that it appears in the argument list. If an argument is NULL, the element is initialized to NULL: The element is created but not populated. Elements that contain a NULL value can be referenced but do not contain data. Elements that have not been initialized cannot be referenced.

```
DECLARE
  TYPE stock_list IS TABLE OF stocks.symbol%TYPE;
  TYPE top10_list IS VARRAY (10) OF stocks.symbol%TYPE;
  biotech_stocks stock_list;   -- nested table
  tech_10        top10_list;   -- varray
BEGIN
  -- invalid, collection not initialized
biotech_stocks(1) := 'AMGN';

  -- we can test for nullity of the whole collection
  IF biotech_stocks IS NULL THEN
    -- initialize the collections with the constructors
    biotech_stocks := stock_list('AMGN' ,'BGEN' ,'IMCL'
      ,'GERN' ,'CRA');
  END IF;
  tech_10 := top10_list('ORCL' ,'CSCO' ,'MSFT' ,'INTC'
    ,'SUNW','IBM' ,NULL ,NULL);
  -- referencing the elements is now valid
  IF tech_10(7) IS NULL THEN
    tech_10(7) := 'CPQ';
  END IF;
  tech_10(8) := 'DELL';
```

In this example, you can see the nested table BIOTECH_STOCKS initialized with five elements. The VARRAY tech_10 is defined with a maximum of 10 elements, but only eight elements are created with the constructor. Of these eight, two contain NULL values and are populated in later statements.

To initialize a collection based on records, you must pass a series of records to the constructor. You cannot simply pass the fields for the record to the collection constructor. See the example that follows; we can pass the record single_quote to the constructor, but not the individual record elements. You may want to create a function that returns a record populated by the fields passed to it (a constructor function for your record type). The collection has a built-in constructor, but the record does not. To reference an individual field in an individual element, use a combination of subscript and dot notation:

```
declare
  TYPE stock_quote_rec IS RECORD
    (symbol    stocks.symbol%TYPE
    ,bid       NUMBER(10,4)
    ,ask       NUMBER(10,4)
    ,volume    NUMBER
    );
  TYPE stock_tab_typ IS TABLE OF stock_quote_rec;
  quote_list    stock_tab_typ;
  single_quote stock_quote_rec;
BEGIN
  single_quote.symbol := 'ORCL';
  single_quote.bid := 100;
  single_quote.ask := 101;
  single_quote.volume := 250000;
 --valid
quote_list := stock_tab_typ( single_quote );


  -- invalid
quote_list := stock_tab_typ('CSCO',75,76,321000);

  -- display the bid field in record one
  dbms_output.put_line(quote_list(1).bid);
```

Collection Methods

Collections come with a number of built-in functions in addition to the constructor. These built-in functions are called *methods* and are used to test, expand, shrink, and generally examine or manipulate the attributes of the collection. To use a method, you use dot notation, like this:

```
Collection.Method
```

Some methods take parameters and some do not. The methods are listed in Table 9.2 and explained in greater detail in the following paragraphs.

TABLE 9.2 Collection Methods

Method	Description	Usage Restrictions
COUNT	Returns integer number of elements in the collection. For VARRAYs, COUNT equals LAST.	
DELETE	Removes all elements in the collection.	
DELETE ($<x>$)	Removes element number x. If x is NULL, the collection is not changed.	Invalid for VARRAYs
DELETE ($<x>,<y>$)	Removes element x through y, inclusive. If y is greater than x, the collection is not changed.	Invalid for VARRAYs
EXISTS ($<x>$)	Returns Boolean TRUE if element x is initialized. Returns Boolean FALSE if element x is not initialized.	
EXTEND	Appends one additional element to the end of the collection.	Invalid for index-by tables
EXTEND ($<x>$)	Appends x additional elements to the end of the collection.	Invalid for index-by tables
EXTEND ($<x>,<n>$)	Adds x additional elements to the end of the collection, populating them with the contents of element n.	Invalid for index-by tables

TABLE 9.2 Collection Methods *(continued)*

Method	Description	Usage Restrictions
FIRST	Returns the smallest element number in the collection. For VARRAYs, FIRST always returns 1.	
LAST	Returns the largest element number in the collection. For VARRAYs, LAST always returns the same as COUNT.	
LIMIT	Returns the maximum number of elements in the VARRAY definition. For nested tables and index-by tables, returns NULL.	Not useful on nested tables or index-by tables
NEXT(<*x*>)	Returns the next higher element number above *x*. If *x* is the last (highest) element number, returns NULL.	
PRIOR (<*x*>)	Returns the next lower element number below *x*. If *x* is the first (lowest) element number, returns NULL.	
TRIM	Removes the last element from the collection.	Not valid for index-by tables
TRIM(<*x*>)	Removes the last *x* elements from the collection. If *x* is larger than COUNT, an exception is raised.	Not valid for index-by tables

COUNT   COUNT returns the number of elements in a collection. This is particularly useful for index-by tables because they can have widely spaced element subscripts. For VARRAYs, COUNT is always equal to LAST and less than or equal to LIMIT.

```
DECLARE
   TYPE stock_list IS TABLE OF stocks.symbol%TYPE;
   tech_10         stock_list;
BEGIN
   tech_10 := stock_list('ORCL','CSCO','MSFT','INTC'
```

```
    ,'SUNW','IBM' ,NULL ,NULL);  -- initialize 8 elements
    -- count returns 8
dbms_output.put_line(tech_10.count);
```

DELETE   DELETE is overloaded with three functions. The first, invoked with no parameters, truncates the collection, removing all elements. This overloading is the only one that will work on VARRAYs.

```
tech_10.delete;   -- remove all elements from tech_10
```

The second overloaded function, called with one parameter, removes the single element referenced by the parameter. This overloading is invalid for VARRAYs, since they cannot have elements removed from the middle of the collection.

```
tech_10.delete(4);   -- remove element 4 from tech_10
```

The third overloaded function, called with two parameters, removes all elements between the first parameter and the second parameter, inclusive. This overloading is invalid for VARRAYs, since they cannot have elements removed from the middle of the collection.

```
tech_10.delete(2,4);  -- remove elements 2,3 and 4
```

EXISTS   EXISTS is used to see whether there is an element with a particular subscript. It is frequently used to check for the existence of an element before the element is assigned a value. If the element does not exist and you try to assign a value to it in a nested table or VARRAY, you will raise an exception. EXISTS returns a Boolean TRUE if the element has been initialized and a FALSE if it has not been initialized.

```
IF tech_10.exists(7) THEN
    tech_10(7) := 'CPQ';
END IF;
```

EXTEND   EXTEND is overloaded with three functions. The first, invoked when no parameters are passed to it, adds a single element to the end of the collection. This new element contains all NULLs, so if you define the collection as NOT NULL, you should not use this overloading.

```
tech_10.extend;   -- add one element to tech_10
```

The second overloaded function, called with one parameter, adds the specified number of elements to the collection. If you try to extend a VARRAY past the limit, you will raise an exception. Also, the newly added elements are NULL, so if the collection has been defined NOT NULL, you should not use this overloading.

```
tech_10.extend(2);    -- add two elements to tech_10
```

The third overloaded function, called with two parameters, adds new elements and copies an existing element to the new elements. If you have a NOT NULL collection, this is the only overloading that you should use.

```
-- add 2 new elements and copy element 4 to them
tech_10.extend(2,4);
```

The EXTEND method is invalid for index-by tables, but you don't have to extend an index-by table; simply assign a value to the new element, and it is automatically initialized.

FIRST   FIRST returns the lowest element number in the collection. It is most useful for index-by tables because they can start with any number. FIRST on a VARRAY always returns 1. FIRST on a nested table will return 1 if the first element has not been deleted.

```
tech_10.first;
```

LAST   LAST returns the highest element number in the collection. It is equally useful on index-by tables, nested tables, and VARRAYs. For VARRAYs, LAST is always equal to COUNT and less than or equal to LIMIT.

```
-- return the highest initialized subscript for tech_10
tech_10.last;
```

```
-- loop through all elements in the varray tech_10
FOR loop_counter IN tech_10.first..tech_10.last
LOOP
```

LIMIT   LIMIT returns the maximum number of elements in a VARRAY definition. This function is useful when you are extending a VARRAY and don't want to extend it past the maximum value (which raises an exception). LIMIT returns NULL for nested tables and index-by tables.

```
IF tech_10.count < tech_10.limit
THEN
   tech_10.extend;
END IF;
```

NEXT   NEXT returns the next-higher element number in the collection. This is most useful for index-by tables, in which there are frequently large gaps in element numbers. It isn't of much use on VARRAYs, since the next(x) always equals $x + 1$. If the parameter is the last element in the collection, there is no NEXT and this method returns NULL.

```
IF blue_chips.next(4) <> 5
THEN
    -- Element 5 was deleted from nested table blue_chips
```

PRIOR   PRIOR returns the next-lower element number in the collection. This is most useful for index-by tables, in which there are frequently large gaps in element numbers. It isn't of much use on VARRAYs, since the next(x) always equals $x + 1$. If the parameter is the first element in the collection, there is no PRIOR and this method returns NULL.

```
IF blue_chips.prior(50) <> 49
THEN
    -- Element 49 was deleted from nested table
```

TRIM   TRIM is overloaded with two functions. The first, invoked with no parameters, removes the last element from the collection.

```
tech_10.trim;    -- removes last element from tech_10
```

The second overloaded function, called with one parameter, removes the last number of elements specified from the collection. If you try to trim more elements than are in the collection, an exception is raised.

```
tech_10.trim(3);    -- removes last 3 elements
```

The TRIM method is the only way to remove some, and not all, elements from a VARRAY.

Comparing Collections

As with records, you cannot directly compare two entire collections with a Boolean operator. Oracle does not know what would make one collection sort higher or lower than another, so it can't compare them. To compare collections, you can write a function that will return a scalar datatype and use this function for the comparison:

```
IF stock_list1 > stock_list2    -- NOT VALID
```

```
IF sort_collection(stock_list1) >
    sort_collection(stock_list2) -- VALID
```

You can also compare the individual elements within the collection, or you can use database objects with a MAP or ORDER function. Database objects are unlikely to appear on the SQL and PL/SQL exam and therefore are not covered in this book.

Summary

In this chapter, you read about both kinds of Oracle composite datatypes: records and collections. You saw how to create them, initialize them, and use them either with dot notation (for records) or with subscript notation (for collections). You also read about records defined implicitly with the %ROWTYPE attribute. Explicitly defined records and all collections require definition with the TYPE statement before they can be used. Nested table and VARRAY collections can be atomically NULL and therefore must be initialized before they can be referenced. Collections have a set of built-in functions, called methods, that you use to manipulate them. You also saw that you cannot compare either records or collections via Boolean operators.

The topics covered in this chapter that you are likely to find on the exam include

- The %ROWTYPE attribute and how to use it

- The inability to compare records or collections with Boolean operators

- The dangers of using SELECT INTO to populate a record

- Basic differences among the three collection types, such as sparsity, bounding, and database storage

Key Terms

Before you take the exam, make sure you're familiar with the following terms:

%ROWTYPE

%TYPE

Collection

Constructor

Dot notation

Field

Method

Record

Subscript notation

TYPE

Review Questions

1. Which line in the following PL/SQL block will raise an exception? Choose one.

```
1 declare
2   type company_rec is record
3     (id                number    not null
4     ,company_name    company.comp_name%type
5     ,sic_code         varchar2(5)
6     ,begin            date
7     ,contact_phone    varchar2(14)
8     );
9   comp_rec    company_rec;
```

A. Line 2

B. Line 4

C. Line 6

D. Line 9

2. Which line will define a record field *marital_status* with a default of 'S'? Choose one.

A. `,marital_status    varchar2(1) default 'S');`

B. `,marital_status    varchar2(1) := 'S');`

C. Either A or B

D. You can't set a default for a field.

3. Which field definition will define the field `account_nbr` with the same datatype and size as the column acct_no in the table vendors? Choose one.

A. `account_nbr    vendors.acct_no%rowtype`

B. `account_nbr    vendors.acct_no%columntype`

C. `account_nbr     ref vendors.acct_no`

D. `account_nbr    vendors.acct_no%type`

4. Which collection type can you *not* save into a database? Choose one.

   A. Nested table

   B. VARRAY

   C. Index-by table

   D. None of the above, you can save all three into a database.

5. Refer to the following PL/SQL block. Is the bouquet_typ record type valid?

```
DECLARE
   flower_typ is record
     (flower_name    varchar2(40)
     ,flower_color   varchar2(40)
     ,supplier_id    number
     );
   bouquet_typ is record
     (bouquet_name       VARCAHR2(64)
     ,price              NUMBER
     ,primary_flower     flower_typ
     ,secondary_flower   flower_typ
     ,tertiary_flower    flower_typ
     );
```

   A. Yes, a field in a record can be another record.

   B. No, fields must be composed of scalar datatypes.

   C. Yes, but records can only be nested two deep.

6. Refer to the following PL/SQL block. Which option is a scalar datatype?

```
DECLARE
  flower_typ is record
    (flower_name   varchar2(40)
    ,flower_color  varchar2(40)
    ,supplier_id   number
    );
  cursor flower_cur (supplier_in number) is
    select flower_name, flower_id
    from flowers
    where supplier_id = supplier_in;
```

A. flower_name

B. flower_typ

C. flower_cur

7. Can you define a field in a record to require a value?

A. No

B. Yes, with the NOT NULL clause

C. Yes, with the DEFAULT clause

D. Yes, with the CONSTANT clause

8. How can you compare two records for equality? Choose one.

A. Compare each field, using the comparison operator (=)

B. Use the comparison operator (=) on the two records

C. Both A and B

D. Neither A nor B

9. How can you copy the contents of one record to another? Choose two.

   A. Copy each field using the assignment operator

   B. Use the COPY method

   C. Use the DUPLICATE method

   D. Copy the whole record using the assignment operator

10. Which option can you *not* do with the following %ROWTYPE records? Choose one.

```
declare
    emp_rec1     emp%rowtype;
    emp_rec2     emp%rowtype;
```

   A. select * into emp_rec1 from emp where emp_no = 5;

   B. insert into emp values (emp_rec1);

   C. emp_rec1 := emp_rec2;

   D. if emp_rec1.salary > emp_rec2.salary then

11. How do you add elements to an index-by table? Choose one.

   A. Use the EXTEND method

   B. Just assign the value, and the element is added automatically

   C. Use the constructor to create the new element

   D. You can't add elements to an index-by table.

12. Using the following PL/SQL block, which collection is not valid?
Choose one.

```
declare
  type basic_rec_typ is record
  (name          varchar2(50)
  ,rank          varchar2(3)
  ,serial_nbr    varchar2(9)
  );
  type detail_rec_typ is record
  (basic_info    basic_rec_typ
  ,co_name       varchar2(50)
  ,unit_nbr      varchar2(12)
  );
  type platoon_list is table of detail_rec_typ;
  type buddy_list is table of basic_rec_typ;
  type spouse_list is table of varchar2(30);
  type discharge_dates is table of date;
```

A. platoon_list

B. buddy_list

C. spouse_list

D. discharge_dates

E. They are all valid.

13. Which of the following datatypes is not allowed in records? Choose one.

A. Boolean

B. Number

C. Date

D. VARRAY

14. Can you reference an uninitialized nested table? Choose one.

   A. Yes

   B. No

   C. Yes, but only to test for nullity

15. Which of the following can you *not* do with a VARRAY?

   A. Compare it to another VARRAY with the > operator

   B. Assign it to another VARRAY with the := operator

   C. Test it for nullity with the IS NULL operator

   D. Pass it to a procedure as a parameter

16. On which collection type can the EXISTS method be used? Choose one.

   A. Index-by tables

   B. Nested tables

   C. VARRAYs

   D. All of the collections

17. Which method would you use to find the bounding value in a VARRAY? Choose one.

   A. EXTEND

   B. LAST

   C. COUNT

   D. LIMIT

18. Which method can you use to skip over gaps in subscripts in a collection? Choose one.

    A. FIRST

    B. NEXT

    C. COUNT

    D. LIMIT

19. How could you append three elements to the nested table PRODUCTS, copying element 1 to all three? Choose one.

    A. Create each element with the constructor, then assign element 1 to each with the assignment operator

    B. Use the EXTEND method like this: `products.extend(3,1)`

    C. Use the EXTEND method like this: `products.extend(1,3)`

    D. Use the LAST method to position the collection pointer to the end, then use the EXTEND method like this: `products.extend(3,1)`

20. Which of the following will use a constructor to create two elements (thingamabob, dohicky) in the products nested table? Choose one.

```
declare
  type product_list is table of varchar2(30);
  products product_list;
begin
```

    A. `products.constructor('thingamabob,'dohicky');`

    B. `construct products using ('thingamabob,'dohicky');`

    C. `products := product.create('thingamabob,'dohicky');`

    D. `products := product_list ('thingamabob,'dohicky');`

Answers to Review Questions

1. C. `BEGIN` is a keyword and cannot be used for field or record names.

2. C. Both A and B are correct, but C is more correct.

3. D. The `%TYPE` attribute will define the datatype and size for a field at compile time based on the table and column referenced.

4. C. Index-by tables cannot be saved into a database.

5. A. Fields can be either scalar datatypes or records.

6. A. Scalar datatypes are atomic, like the predefined types `DATE`, `NUMBER`, and `VARCHAR2`. Records are composite datatypes. Cursors are not datatypes.

7. B. The `DEFAULT` clause will only assign an initial value if none is specified; the field can be explicitly set to `NULL`. There is no `CONSTANT` clause.

8. A. You can compare the individual fields in a record, but you cannot compare the whole record with the comparison operator.

9. A, D. Records don't have methods; only collections do.

10. B. You can assign one record to another, select * into a `%ROWTYPE` record, and compare the fields of a `%ROWTYPE` record, but you cannot use records in the `VALUES` clause of an `INSERT` statement.

11. B. The `EXTEND` method is used for nested tables and `VARRAY`s, but index-by tables do not need a method; you simply assign the value to a new element. A constructor is used to initialize nested tables and `VARRAY`s.

12. A. When a record is used in a collection, that record can only contain scalar datatypes. A record is not a scalar datatype, so `buddy_list` is OK, but `platoon_list` is not.

13. D. A collection cannot be used as a field in a record; all of the other listed datatypes can.

14. C. Uninitialized nested tables and VARRAYs can only be tested for nullity.

15. A. Collections cannot be compared with Boolean operators.

16. D. EXISTS is valid on all collection types.

17. D. EXTEND is used to append elements to the collection. For a VARRAY, LAST and COUNT are both used to report the number of elements in the collection. LIMIT is only useful on VARRAYs and reports the bounding value.

18. B. The NEXT and PRIOR methods are used to get the subscript numbers of the adjacent elements in a collection.

19. B. The constructor is only used once to initialize the collection; it is not used to append elements to it. The LAST method returns the subscript for the last element; there is no collection pointer.

20. D. A constructor is a built-in function having the same name as the collection type. It is used with an assignment operator to initialize a collection.

Exception Handling

ORACLE8i SQL AND PL/SQL EXAM OBJECTIVES OFFERED IN THIS CHAPTER:

✓ Describe PL/SQL exceptions

✓ Recognize unhandled exceptions

✓ List and use named PL/SQL exceptions

✓ Trap unexpected errors

✓ Describe exception propagation in nested blocks

✓ Customize PL/SQL exception messages

Exam objectives are subject to change at any time without prior notice and at Oracle's sole discretion. Please visit Oracle's Training and Certification Web site (http://education .oracle.com/certification/index.html) for the most current exam objectives listing.

In Chapter 7, *PL/SQL Basics*, you learned about the block structure of PL/SQL. Until this point, we have covered the header, declaration, and executable sections of this block structure. This chapter will focus on the last, optional section: the exception section.

Exceptions, Errors, and PL/SQL

Other languages have errors; PL/SQL has exceptions. This may seem like a simple semantic difference, but PL/SQL deals with exceptions differently from the way that most other languages manage errors. Some languages, like C, require error-checking for practically every function call. PL/SQL, on the other hand, is like Ada and has an all-inclusive method of dealing with errors. When any error occurs, program control branches unconditionally to the exception section of the current PL/SQL block. This makes the code much cleaner and separates error handling from normal processing. Oracle has made this error/exception handing extensible by allowing the programmer to *declare* other types of exception conditions, like Account_Overdrawn, that are violations of business rules, and not just violations of the PL/SQL language rules. This extensibility makes PL/SQL's exception handling robust.

In this chapter, our examples will use a model for order entry and fulfillment. This business model has interactive order entry modules that take customer orders and call procedures used for fulfillment.

Raising and Handling Exceptions

When a runtime error occurs, an exception is said to be *raised*. When an exception is trapped and not allowed to propagate outward, it is said to be *handled*. Errors in the compilation of a PL/SQL program are not exceptions that can be handled; only runtime exceptions can be handled. The raising and handling of exceptions are important tasks in PL/SQL programs, and understanding how these techniques are employed is an important topic to understand before you take the exam.

Raising Exceptions

There are three ways that an exception can be raised:

- By the PL/SQL runtime engine

- By a RAISE statement

- By a call to the RAISE_APPLICATION_ERROR procedure

When a database or PL/SQL language error occurs at runtime, an exception is raised automatically by the PL/SQL runtime engine. Exceptions can also be raised explicitly with the RAISE statement:

```
RAISE exception_name;
```

Explicitly raising an exception is how a programmer makes use of any custom exceptions he has declared. But the RAISE statement is not limited to just programmer-declared exceptions; you can raise any exception with the RAISE statement. For example, if you want to test your new exception-handler routines for a TIMEOUT_ON_RESOURCE error, you don't have to construct a test case that induces contention. You simply put a

```
RAISE TIMEOUT_ON_RESOURCE;
```

statement into your program for the test, and you will effectively simulate an ORA-00051 database error.

Custom-designed exceptions are where the RAISE statement really shines. For example, our order entry system takes orders. If the inventory for a particular item is too low to fill the order, we assign backordered status to the item and trigger inventory replenishment. We can put the exception-oriented code where it belongs—in the exception section—and keep our executable section focused on order fulfillment:

```
DECLARE
  inventory_too_low      EXCEPTION;
  -- other declarations here
BEGIN
  -- more code here
  IF order_rec.qty > inventory_rec.qty THEN
    RAISE inventory_too_low;
  END IF;
  -- more code here
EXCEPTION
  WHEN inventory_too_low THEN
    order_rec.status := 'Backordered';
    replenish_inventory(inventory_nbr=>
    inventory_rec.sku_nbr,min_amount=>order_rec.qty -
inventory_rec.qty);
END;
```

Handling Exceptions

The exception section of a PL/SQL block contains the code that lets your program handle an error condition. Trapping an exception occurs automatically when an exception is raised: Program control leaves the executable section and passes to the exception section. Once control is in the exception section, it cannot pass back to the executable section of the same block. Handling an exception involves executing the custom code that you put in your exception section for that particular exception condition. Frequently, this code will clean up after an error, such as closing open cursors or rolling back uncommitted data, but the code may also include other processing, like the inventory_too_low example from the previous section. Here is the general syntax for an exception section:

```
EXCEPTION
  WHEN exception_name THEN
    Code for handling exception_name
```

```
[WHEN another_exception THEN
  Code for handling another_exception]
[WHEN OTHERS THEN
  Code for handing any other exception.]
```

You place the exception-handling code for each exception into a separate WHEN clause. The WHEN OTHERS clause must be placed last and is a default handler, used to handle any exception that is not explicitly handled. You can think of the exception section as an IF, ELSIF, ELSE statement. Each WHEN *exception_name* corresponds to the IF or ELSIF, and the WHEN OTHERS corresponds to the ELSE. When an exception occurs and control passes to the exception section, Oracle will check to see if the exception has a specific handler; if it does, that handler gets executed. If the exception does not have a specific handler, the WHEN OTHERS handler, if present, is executed. There is no limit to the number of WHEN clauses in an exception section. Use as many as needed:

```
EXCEPTION
  WHEN inventory_too_low THEN
    order_rec.status := 'Backordered';
    replenish_inventory(inventory_nbr=>
    inventory_rec.sku_nbr,min_amount=>order_rec.qty
     inventory_rec.qty);
  WHEN discontinued_item THEM
    -- code for discontinued_item processing
  WHEN ZERO_DIVIDE THEN
    -- code for divide by zero errors
  WHEN OTHERS THEN
    -- code for any other exception.]
END;
```

When the exception is raised, control passes unconditionally to the exception section. This means control does not return to the code where the exception occurred. When the exception is handled and resolved, control passes to the next statement in the enclosing executable section. Here is an example:

```
BEGIN
  -- We nest PL/SQL blocks to simulate a procedure call
  DECLARE  -- start of inner block
```

```
      bad_credit  EXCEPTION;
   BEGIN
     RAISE bad_credit;
     -- control never reaches here; an exception occurred
   EXCEPTION
     WHEN bad_credit THEN
       dbms_output.put_line('bad_credit handled');
   END;  -- end of inner block
   -- control passes here after bad_credit is handled
 EXCEPTION
   WHEN OTHERS THEN
     -- control will not pass here from the bad_credit exception
     -- since bad_credit was handled
 END;
```

When an exception occurs and there is no local exception handler for that exception, control passes or propagates to the exception section of the enclosing block:

```
 BEGIN
   -- We nest PL/SQL blocks to simulate a procedure call
   DECLARE  -- start of inner block
     bad_credit  EXCEPTION;
   BEGIN
     RAISE bad_credit;
     -- control never reaches here; an exception occurred
   EXCEPTION
     WHEN ZERO_DIVIDE THEN  -- does not handle bad_credit
       dbms_output.put_line('divide by zero error');
   END;  -- end of inner block
   -- control does not pass to here, it goes to the
     -- exception section
 EXCEPTION
   WHEN OTHERS THEN
     -- control will pass to here since bad_credit was not
     -- resolved
 END;
```

Exception Propagation

Exceptions that are not handled propagate outward from the routine that detected the exception to the calling program. This outward propagation stops only when the exception is handled and resolved or when it reaches the outermost program. SQL*Plus, as an outermost program, usually handles exceptions by causing the current statement to fail, and then displays an error message. Figure 10.1 shows how an exception is propagated.

FIGURE 10.1 Exception propagation

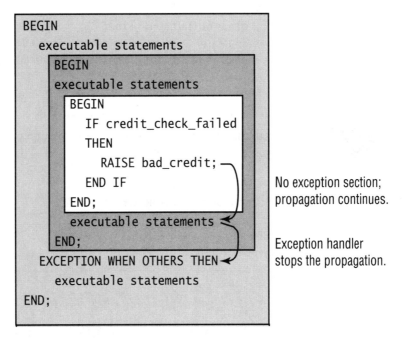

Exceptions raised in the declaration section of a PL/SQL block will pass control to the exception section of the enclosing block. For example, if you assign a text string to a date variable in the declaration section, an Oracle –1858 exception (Non-numeric character was found where a numeric was expected) will be raised and control will pass directly to the exception section of the enclosing block, as shown in Figure 10.2.

```
BEGIN
   DECLARE
```

```
        timestamp DATE := 'SYSDATE'; -- datatype mismatch
   BEGIN
     dbms_output.put_line('Inside inner block');
   EXCEPTION
     WHEN OTHERS THEN
        dbms_output.put_line(
   'exception handled in inner block');
   END;
 EXCEPTION
   WHEN OTHERS THEN
     dbms_output.put_line('
   exception handled in outer block');
     dbms_output.put_line(dbms_utility.format_error_stack);
 END;
```

Only exceptions raised in the executable section get passed to the exception section of the same block.

FIGURE 10.2   Exceptions raised in the declaration section

```
BEGIN
   executable statements

     DECLARE
       today DATE := 'SYSDATE'; -- can't assign text to a date
     BEGIN
       dbms_output.put_line('This line will not execute'):
     EXCEPTION
       WHEN OTHERS THEN
          --exception will not get handled here
     END;

   EXCEPTION WHEN OTHERS THEN
        exception handled here
END;
```

Exceptions raised in the executable section pass control to the exception section of the same block. If this exception section does not have a handler for the exception raised, then the exception will continue to propagate to the enclosing block's exception section. Figure 10.3 illustrates the program flow for exceptions raised in the executable section. Remember, a WHEN OTHERS clause will handle any exception.

FIGURE 10.3 Exceptions raised in the executable section

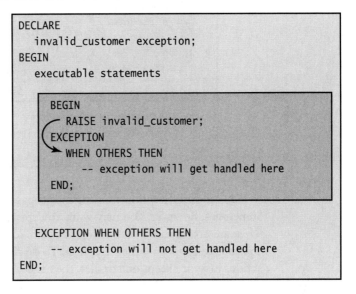

```
DECLARE
    invalid_customer exception;
BEGIN
    executable statements

        BEGIN
            RAISE invalid_customer;
        EXCEPTION
            WHEN OTHERS THEN
                -- exception will get handled here
        END;


    EXCEPTION WHEN OTHERS THEN
        -- exception will not get handled here
END;
```

Exceptions raised in the exception section of a PL/SQL block pass control to the exception section of the enclosing block, as illustrated in Figure 10.4. Exceptions raised anywhere other than the executable section always get passed out to the enclosing block.

FIGURE 10.4 Exceptions raised in the exception section

```
DECLARE
   invalid_customer exception;
BEGIN
   executable statements

      DECLARE
         today DATE;
      BEGIN
         RAISE invalid_customer;
      EXCEPTION
         WHEN OTHERS THEN
            today := 'SYSDATE'; -- data type mismatch
      END;

   EXCEPTION WHEN OTHERS THEN
      -- exception will get handled here
END;
```

Handling an exception will stop the propagation and resolve the exception. Sometimes, however, you may want your program to perform some actions when an error occurs (such as logging the exception via utl_file) and then continue to propagate the exception. To do this, you perform the desired actions in your exception handler, then execute the RAISE statement with no arguments. This RAISE statement will re-raise the current exception, allowing it to continue to propagate.

```
DECLARE
   order_too_old  EXCEPTION;
BEGIN
   raise order_too_old;
EXCEPTION
   WHEN order_too_old THEN
      DECLARE
         file_handle      UTL_FILE.FILE_TYPE;
      BEGIN
         -- open the file
         file_handle := UTL_FILE.FOPEN
```

```
         (location => '/ora01/app/oracle/admin/test/utldir'
         ,filename =>'error.log'
         ,open_mode => 'W' );
      -- write the error stack
      UTL_FILE.PUT_LINE(file_handle,
DBMS_UTILITY.FORMAT_ERROR_STACK);
      -- write the call stack
      UTL_FILE.PUT_LINE(file_handle,
DBMS_UTILITY.FORMAT_CALL_STACK);
      -- close the error log
      UTL_FILE.FCLOSE(file_handle);
      RAISE;    -- re-raise the exception
   END;
END;
```

Exception sections that use DBMS_OUTPUT or UTL_FILE to reveal an error stack or call stack may themselves raise exceptions if the output from FORMAT_xxx_ STACK returns a large value. Both stack routines can return up to 2,000 bytes, but utl_file.put_line is limited to 1,000 bytes, and dbms_output.put_line is limited to 512 bytes. If you use the previous code and don't allow for this possibility, you may raise an unhandled exception in your exception handler.

GOTO statements cannot be used to pass control from the executable section to or from the exception section:

```
BEGIN
  IF error_detected THEN
    GOTO error_label;  -- illegal, use a RAISE instead
  END IF;
  <<exec_label>>
  -- cannot get here from exception section
EXCEPTION
  WHEN OTHERS THEN
    <<error_label>>
    GOTO exec_label;  -- illegal
END;
```

Named Exceptions

Only named exceptions can be handled in their own WHEN clause in the exception section of a PL/SQL block. Oracle includes a number of named exceptions, declared in the package STANDARD. These built-in exceptions include the ones shown in Table 10.1.

T A B L E   1 0 . 1   Built-in Exceptions

Exception Name	Database Error	Description
DUP_VAL_ON_INDEX	ORA-00001	An INSERT or UPDATE would violate uniqueness on a unique index.
TIMEOUT_ON_RESOURCE	ORA-00051	A timeout occurred waiting for a resource, such as an exclusive table lock for DDL.
INVALID_CURSOR	ORA-01001	An attempt was made to perform an illegal cursor operation, such as fetching a cursor that has not yet been opened.
NOT_LOGGED_ON	ORA-01012	A call was made to the database without first establishing a connection.
LOGIN_DENIED	ORA-01017	An invalid username or password was supplied in the connect string.
NO_DATA_FOUND	ORA-01403	A SELECT INTO returned no rows.

TABLE 10.1 Built-in Exceptions *(continued)*

Exception Name	Database Error	Description
SYS_INVALID_ROWID	ORA-01410	An implicit CharToRowid conversion has invalid characters or format.
TOO_MANY_ROWS	ORA-01422	A SELECT INTO returned more than one row.
ZERO_DIVIDE	ORA-01476	An attempt was made to divide by 0.
INVALID_NUMBER	ORA-01722	An invalid character appears in a character-to-number conversion.
STORAGE_ERROR	ORA-06500	PL/SQL has corrupted or run out of memory.
PROGRAM_ERROR	ORA-06501	Internal PL/SQL error. Time to call support.
VALUE_ERROR	ORA-06502	A catchall kind of error indicating that a data value is invalid, due to size or type. Raised in conversion, truncation, or arithmetic operations.
ROWTYPE_MISMATCH	ORA-06504	Datatype mismatch between cursor variable and result set.
CURSOR_ALREADY_OPEN	ORA-06511	An attempt was made to open a cursor that is already open.

TABLE 10.1 Built-in Exceptions *(continued)*

Exception Name	Database Error	Description
ACCESS_INTO_NULL	ORA-06530	A database object, LOB, or other non-collection composite is referenced without first being initialized.
COLLECTION_IS_NULL	ORA-06531	An element in a nested table or VARRAY collection is referenced without first being initialized, or a method on an uninitialized collection is invoked.
SUBSCRIPT_OUTSIDE_LIMIT	ORA-06532	An element subscript higher than the bounding value of a VARRAY is used.
SUBSCRIPT_BEYOND_COUNT	ORA-06533	An element subscript higher than the initialized elements in a nested table or VARRAY is used.

Customizing Exception Handling

In addition to the standard named exceptions, you can declare your own named exceptions, such as those for violating business rules, or you can associate a name with a database error number. You can even assign an error number to a programmer-defined exception. These capabilities give you, the programmer, useful tools for managing exceptions and exception processing.

Declaring Your Own Exceptions

If you declare your own exceptions, you can include a WHEN clause in your exception handler for that PL/SQL block. The scope of the declared exception is the same as for a variable. Exceptions declared in outer blocks are accessible from that block and any sub-blocks, but exceptions declared in a sub-block cannot be handled by name in the enclosing block:

```
BEGIN
  DECLARE   -- sub block (or procedure call)
    insufficient_credit   EXCEPTION;
  BEGIN
    RAISE insufficient_credit;
  EXCEPTION
    WHEN insufficient_credit THEN
      --we can handle it here
      extend_credit(cust_id);
  END;  -- end of nested block
EXCEPTION
  WHEN insufficient_credit THEN
    -- NOT VALID, exception is out of scope
END;
```

If you declare an exception with the same name as a built-in exception, your references to that exception will resolve to your exception and not to the built-in exception. This is a bad practice as well, because the code becomes non-intuitive and more difficult to maintain.

Giving Names to Database Errors

If you want to handle an exception with its own WHEN clause, that exception must have a name. There are thousands of database errors but fewer than 25 with built-in named exceptions. When one of these unnamed exceptions needs to be handled, you can *associate* a name with the error number using the PRAGMA EXCEPTION_INIT statement:

```
PRAGMA_EXCEPTION_INIT(exception_name, error_number);
```

When you do this, you must first declare the exception name that you will use, then associate that name with an error number:

```
DECLARE
  invalid_table_name  EXCEPTION;
  PRAGMA EXCEPTION_INIT(invalid_table_name, -942);
BEGIN

EXCEPTION
  WHEN invalid_table_name THEN
    UTL_FILE.PUT_LINE(file_handle,
    'User '||UID||' hit a bad table');
END;
```

Another way to handle unnamed database errors (without declaring and associating a name with an error number) is to use the built-in functions SQLCODE and SQLERRM, which are declared in the package standard. *SQLCODE* will return the current database error number. These error numbers are all negative, except NO_DATA_FOUND, which returns +100. *SQLERRM* returns the textual error message. Your programmer-declared exceptions have a SQLCODE of +1 and a SQLERRM of User-Defined Exception. To have a programmer-defined exception return a different SQLCODE and SQLERRM, you need to number your exception with the RAISE_APPLICATION_ERROR procedure.

Numbering Programmer-Defined Errors

The RAISE_APPLICATION_ERROR built-in procedure is used to raise an exception and assign an error number and custom message to the programmer-defined error. The default error number for a programmer-defined exception is +1, and the default message is User-Defined Exception. This generic message from an unhandled exception will not help to identify the cause of the error. The RAISE_APPLICATION_ERROR procedure can be called from either the executable section or the exception section of a PL/SQL block and will explicitly raise the named exception with the specified error number:

```
RAISE_APPLICATION_ERROR(error_number, error_message
  [,{TRUE | FALSE}]);
```

The error number must be in the range of –20,999 to –20,000. The error message is a text string up to 2,048 bytes long. The TRUE and FALSE define whether this error message is added to the error stack (TRUE) or overwrites the error stack (FALSE). The default behavior is to overwrite the error stack, possibly destroying the information needed to troubleshoot or correct the problem.

```
IF product_not_found THEN
   RAISE_APPLICATION_ERROR(-20123, 'Invalid product code',
   TRUE);
END IF;
```

Summary

In this chapter, you read about how exceptions differ from errors and how PL/SQL manages error conditions. You saw how to raise and handle exceptions. We reviewed the named exceptions that come built into the PL/SQL language, as well as how to name other exceptions. We covered how exceptions propagate and where exceptions are handled when raised within sub-blocks. You also learned how to customize not only exception names, but also exception messages and error codes.

The topics covered in this chapter that are likely to be on the exam are

- Declaring vs. associating vs. raising vs. handling exceptions

- Exception propagation: when an exception is raised, where will it be handled

- How to use a programmer-defined error message with RAISE_APPLICATION_ERROR

Key Terms

Before you take the exam, make sure you're familiar with the following terms:

Associate an exception

Declare an exception

Exception

Exception section

Raise an exception

SQLCODE

SQLERRM

Review Questions

1. What is the PRAGMA exception_init used for?

   A. To declare an exception

   B. To associate an exception name with an exception number

   C. To handle an exception

   D. To associate a function with an exception number

2. What command do you use to induce an error condition?

   A. raiserror

   B. raise_exception

   C. raise

   D. exception

3. Can the RAISE_APPLICATION_ERROR procedure append the message to the existing error stack?

   A. Yes, this is the default behavior.

   B. Yes, but this is not the default behavior.

   C. No, the RAISE_APPLICATION_ERROR procedure always replaces the error stack.

4. What causes a TOO_MANY_ROWS exception?

   A. Your FETCH buffer is too small.

   B. A SELECT INTO returned more than one row.

   C. You performed a Cartesian product.

   D. Your array insert buffer is too small.

5. What does the following code do?

```
DECLARE
   invalid_action exception;
BEGIN
```

   A. Associates the `invalid_action` exception

   B. Raises an `invalid_action` exception

   C. Handles an `invalid_action` exception

   D. Declares an exception called `invalid_action`

6. In what ways can an exception be raised? Choose three.

   A. By the PL/SQL runtime engine

   B. By a RAISE statement

   C. By a call to the RAISE_APPLICATION_ERROR function

   D. By a call to the RAISE_APPLICATION_ERROR procedure

   E. By a registered alert process

   F. By a RAISERROR statement

7. What must be included in the exception code to propagate the current exception to the enclosing block?

   A. Nothing—once an exception is handled, the enclosing block cannot be notified of the error.

   B. The propagation can continue only by explicitly raising the exception by name in the exception section.

   C. The RAISE statement with no exception specified will re-raise the current exception.

   D. The RERAISE statement will re-raise the current exception into the enclosing block.

8. In the following PL/SQL code, what will the output and error stack include?

```
BEGIN
  BEGIN
    RAISE no_data_found;
  EXCEPTION
    WHEN OTHERS THEN
        dbms_output.put_line('ERROR in inner block');
        raise;
  END;
EXCEPTION
  WHEN NO_DATA_FOUND THEN
        dbms_output.put_line('No data found error');
  WHEN OTHERS THEN
        dbms_output.put_line('ERROR in outer block');
END;
```

A. ERROR in inner block

B. No data found error

C. ERROR in outer block

D. A and B

9. Your requirements say that all exceptions in your anonymous PL/SQL block must be logged. Will the following exception section meet these requirements?

```
EXCEPTION
   WHEN OTHERS THEN
      INSERT INTO error_log (timestamp ,err_code
                              ,err_msg, err_stack)
         VALUES (SYSDATE
                 ,SQLCODE
                 ,SQLERRM
                 ,DBMS_UTILITY.FORMAT_ERROR_STACK);
      RAISE;
END;
```

A. All requirements are satisfied.

B. The requirements are not satisfied.

C. The requirements are sometimes satisfied.

10. An exception that is raised in an exception section passes control to where?

A. The operating system

B. The executable section in the enclosing block

C. The exception section in the enclosing block

D. The WHEN OTHERS clause in the current exception section

11. In the following PL/SQL code, what will the output and error stack include?

```
BEGIN
  BEGIN
    RAISE no_data_found;
  EXCEPTION
    WHEN NO_DATA_FOUND THEN
        dbms_output.put_line(
  'NO data found in inner block');
    WHEN OTHERS THEN
        dbms_output.put_line('ERROR in inner block');
        RAISE;
  END;
EXCEPTION
  WHEN OTHERS THEN
      dbms_output.put_line('ERROR in outer block');
      RAISE;
END;
```

A. ERROR in inner block

B. NO data found in inner block

C. ERROR in outer block

D. All of the above

12. In the following PL/SQL code, what will the output and error stack include?

```
BEGIN
  DECLARE
  -- You can't assign text to a date
  today DATE := 'SYSDATE';
  BEGIN
    RAISE no_data_found;
  EXCEPTION
    WHEN OTHERS THEN
        dbms_output.put_line('ERROR in inner block');
        RAISE;
    END;
EXCEPTION
    WHEN OTHERS THEN
        dbms_output.put_line('ERROR in outer block');
        RAISE;
END;
```

A. ERROR in inner block

B. No data found error

C. ERROR in outer block

D. All of the above

13. Which of the following types of exceptions cannot be handled in an exception section?

A. Syntax errors

B. Database errors

C. Datatype mismatch errors

D. Divide by zero errors

14. In the following PL/SQL code, what will the output and error stack include?

```
BEGIN
  BEGIN
    RAISE no_data_found;
  EXCEPTION
    WHEN OTHERS THEN
      dbms_output.put_line('ERROR in inner block');
      RAISE;
  END;
EXCEPTION
  WHEN OTHERS THEN
    dbms_output.put_line('ERROR in outer block');
    RAISE;
END;
```

A. ERROR in inner block

B. No data found error

C. ERROR in outer block

D. All of the above

15. What function can you use to retrieve the error number for the current exception?

A. ERRNUM

B. SQLCODE

C. SQLNUM

D. You can only get the exception name, not the numeric code, for an exception.

16. What function can you use to retrieve the text associated with the current exception?

A. SQLERRM

B. SQLERRMESG

C. ERRORTEXT

D. ERRMSG

17. What clause do you need to include in your exception section to handle any exception not previously specified?

A. ELSE

B. WHEN ANYTHING ELSE

C. WHEN ANY OTHER

D. WHEN OTHERS

18. In the following block of PL/SQL code, what will dbms_output display?

```
declare
  invalid_code    exception;
begin
  declare
    invalid_code  exception;
  begin
    raise invalid_code;
  exception
    when zero_divide then
      dbms_output.put_line('Exception handled');
  end;
  dbms_output.put_line('No errors here');
exception
  when invalid_code then
    dbms_output.put_line('There is an invalid code');
  when others then
    dbms_output.put_line('Another exception occurred');
end;
```

A. Exception handled

B. No errors here

C. There is an invalid code

D. Another exception occurred

19. Which line will cause a compile error (a syntax error)?

```
1 exception
2   when sqlcode = -942
3     dbms_output.put_line('Invalid table name');
4   when others
5     dbms_output.put_line('Unhandled exception');
6 end;
```

A. Line 2

B. Line 4

C. Line 6

D. There will be no compile error.

20. Which line will cause a compile error (a syntax error)?

```
1 declare
2   54_resource_busy exception;
3 begin
4   raise zero_divide;
5 exception
6   when others then
```

A. Line 2

B. Line 4

C. Line 6

D. There will be no compile error.

Answers to Review Questions

1. B. `Exception_init` is used to associate (give a name) to an error number.

2. C. The `RAISE` command is used to raise an exception.

3. B. The default behavior is to replace the existing error stack.

4. B. A `SELECT INTO` can only return a single row. When it returns more than one row, the `TOO_MANY_ROWS` exception is raised.

5. D. This is an exception declaration.

6. A, B, D. `RAISE_APPLICATION_ERROR` does not return a value and so is a procedure. There is no alert process or `RAISERROR` statement.

7. C. While you can explicitly re-raise an exception by specifying the exception name in the `RAISE` statement, it is not the only way to re-raise the error. You can simply issue a `RAISE` statement without additional arguments to re-raise an exception, without ever having to know what the exception was.

8. D. The `WHEN OTHERS` clause in the inner block handles the exception and re-raises the exception to the exception section in the outer block. The outer block handles it in the `WHEN NO_DATA_FOUND` clause.

9. C. This one's kind of tricky. While all the information put into the ERROR_LOG table is great for logging the error, if the enclosing block or program encounters this exception and performs a ROLLBACK, the ERROR_LOG table changes will get rolled back, along with the other uncommitted changes. It would be better to use UTL_ FILE, which operates outside transactional boundaries. You could also construct an autonomous transaction procedure to insert (and commit) the ERROR_LOG entries. To learn more about autonomous transactions (which are not likely to be on the exam), see the Oracle Server Concepts reference.

10. C. Exceptions raised in the exception section get passed to the exception section of the enclosing block.

11. B. The exception is handled in the `WHEN NO_DATA_FOUND` clause of the inner block and does not propagate further.

12. C. Exceptions in the declaration section of a PL/SQL block cannot be handled in that block. They are immediately propagated to the calling program/block. The RAISE no_data_found line never executes.

13. A. Syntax errors are handled by the PL/SQL compiler and not the runtime engine; they cannot be handled in the exception section.

14. D. The exception is caught in the inner block. The message is displayed, the error is re-raised, handled again in the outer block, and re-raised. The unhandled no data found error propagates out to the calling program.

15. B. The built-in function SQLCODE can be used to retrieve the error number associated with the current exception.

16. A. The built-in function SQLERRM can be used to retrieve the text associated with the current exception.

17. D. The WHEN OTHERS clause will handle any exception that has not yet been handled.

18. D. The scope of an exception includes the block in which the exception is declared and any sub-blocks. The exception raised in the example code is not handled in the exception section of the block that the exception was raised in. As the exception propagates to the exception section of the enclosing block, it goes out of scope and becomes an unhandled programmer-defined exception. The exception that was raised is not the same as the invalid_code exception in the enclosing block, even though they have the same names. This explanation may seem confusing (as do some exam questions): Reread the code and keep an eye out for the scope of the exceptions declared and raised.

19. A. The WHEN clause can be used only with exception names. The SQLCODE function can be used in Boolean comparisons but not in a WHEN clause.

20. A. Exceptions must follow the same naming restrictions as any other identifier, such as variables. Identifiers cannot begin with a number.

Appendix A

Practice Exam

1. How do you implement relationships between entities of an ER diagram in the Oracle database?

   A. Create a primary key constraint

   B. Create a unique key constraint

   C. Create a foreign key constraint

   D. Create an index

2. Which stage comes after the Analysis stage in the application development cycle?

   A. Implementation

   B. Testing

   C. Design

   D. Development

3. Which datatype declaration in a column would compare `'MARK'` and `'MARK '` as the same.

   A. VARCHAR (10)

   B. CHAR (10)

   C. VARCHAR2 (10)

   D. LONG

4. What will happen when you enter the following command at the SQL*Plus prompt?
   DEFINE SALARY

   A. A user variable named SALARY is created and assigned a value of 0.

   B. The value of the user-defined variable SALARY is displayed; if the variable is not defined, a message is displayed stating the variable is not defined.

   C. A user variable named SALARY is created, and no value is assigned.

   D. The value of user-defined variable SALARY is removed.

5. You query the database with the following:

```
SELECT PRODUCT_ID FROM PRODUCTS
WHERE PRODUCT_ID LIKE '%S\_J\_C' ESCAPE '\';
```

Choose two PRODUCT_ID strings from the options that will satisfy the query.

A. BTS_J_C

B. SJC

C. SKJKC

D. S_J_C

6. The EMPLOYEE table is defined as follows:

```
EMP_NAME    VARCHAR2(40)
HIRE_DATE   DATE
SALARY      NUMBER (14,2)
```

Which query is most appropriate to use if you need to find the employees who were hired before 01-Jan-1998 and have a salary above 5000 or below 1000?

A. SELECT emp_name FROM employee
WHERE hire_date > TO_DATE('01011998','MMDDYYYY')
AND SALARY < 1000 OR > 5000;

B. SELECT emp_name FROM employee
WHERE hire_date < TO_DATE('01011998','MMDDYYYY')
AND SALARY < 1000 OR SALARY > 5000;

C. SELECT emp_name FROM employee
WHERE hire_date < TO_DATE('01011998','MMDDYYYY')
AND (SALARY < 1000 OR SALARY > 5000);

D. SELECT emp_name FROM employee
WHERE hire_date < TO_DATE('01011998','MMDDYYYY')
AND SALARY BETWEEN 1000 AND 5000;

7. What's the error in the following code?

```
SELECT state.st_name, st_code
FROM    state s
WHERE   st_code = 'TX';
```

A. When tables are not joined, a table alias name cannot be used in the query.

B. When a table alias name is defined, it must be used to qualify all the column names.

C. If a table alias name is defined, you cannot use the table name to qualify a column.

D. In the SELECT clause, you cannot have one column qualified and another column not qualified. It should be either all columns qualified or no columns qualified.

8. The table MOVIES is defined as follows:

```
MOVIE_ID              NUMBER(5)  PRIMARY KEY
NAME                  VARCHAR2(20)
LEAD_ACTOR            VARCHAR2(15)
VIDEO_STOCK           NUMBER(3)
DVD_STOCK             NUMBER(3)
GENRE                 VARCHAR2(8)
```

Choose the best query that shows the name and lead actor of the movie that has the highest number in DVD_STOCK.

A. SELECT NAME, LEAD_ACTOR FROM MOVIES
   WHERE   DVD_STOCK EQUALS (SELECT MAX(DVD_STOCK)
       FROM MOVIES);

B. SELECT NAME, LEAD_ACTOR FROM MOVIES M1
   WHERE   MOVIE_ID = (SELECT MOVIE_ID FROM MOVIES M2
     WHERE M1.DVD_STOCK = MAX(M2.DVD_STOCK));

C. SELECT NAME, LEAD_ACTOR FROM MOVIES
   WHERE   DVD_STOCK = MAX(DVD_STOCK);

D. SELECT NAME, LEAD_ACTOR FROM MOVIES
   WHERE   DVD_STOCK = (SELECT MAX(DVD_STOCK)
       FROM MOVIES);

9. What is the maximum number of rows the following query can return when successfully executed?

```
SELECT EMPNO, ENAME
FROM   EMP
WHERE  SALARY = (SELECT MAX(SALARY) FROM EMP);
```

A. 1

B. Unlimited

C. 0 or 1

D. 256

10. The table MOVIES has the following data:

MOVIE_ID	NAME	LEAD_ACTOR	VIDEO_STOCK	DVD_STOCK	GENRE
1245	OCTOBER SKY	JAKE GYLLENHALL	5	3	DRAMA
1356	ARMAGEDDON	BRUCE WILLIS	15	10	ACTION
2376	THE MATRIX	KEANU REEVES	8	5	ACTION
6745	BOWFINGER	EDDIE MURPHY	6		COMEDY
6644	CLUELESS	ALICIA SILVERSTONE		9	COMEDY

Consider the following query, then choose the most appropriate statement.

```
SELECT name, genre
FROM   movies
WHERE  genre = (SELECT genre
               FROM   movies
               WHERE  name = 'THE MATRIX')
ORDER BY 2, 1;
```

A. The query will result in two rows.

B. You cannot use the same table name in the query and in the subquery without using a group function.

C. The subquery will return more than one row; since this is a single-row subquery, the query will fail.

D. The ORDER BY clause cannot be used in the query.

11. Consider the following query that is used to select the name, salary, and difference in salary from the average. Choose the most appropriate option.

```
SELECT ename, sal, (sal-avgsal) diff
FROM   emp, (SELECT AVG(sal) avgsal FROM emp);
```

   A. The query will fail because there is no alias name provided for the subquery in the FROM clause.

   B. The query will not produce the intended result because a WHERE clause is missing.

   C. The query will fail because the column names are not qualified.

   D. There is no error in the query, and the query will deliver the intended result.

12. The table ADDRESSES is created using the following syntax. How many indexes will be created automatically when this table is created?

```
CREATE TABLE ADDRESSES (
NAME    VARCHAR2 (40) PRIMARY KEY,
STREET  VARCHAR2 (40),
CITY    VARCHAR2 (40),
STATE   CHAR      (2) REFERENCES STATE (ST_CODE),
ZIP     NUMBER    (5) NOT NULL,
PHONE   VARCHAR2 (12) UNIQUE);
```

   A. 0

   B. 1

   C. 2

   D. 3

13. Which clause in the CREATE VIEW command prevents updates to the base table through the view?

   A. WITH CHECK OPTION

   B. WITH READ ONLY

   C. WITH NO UPDATE

   D. There is no such option; if a user has privilege on the base table, the user can update the view.

14. Consider the following code, then choose the most appropriate option.

```
CREATE TABLE CUSTOMER (
CUSTOMER_ID    NUMBER (5),
CUSTOMER_NAME  VARCHAR2 (40),
ZIP            NUMBER (5)) AS
SELECT CUST_ID, NAME, ZIP_CODE
FROM CUSTOMERS
```

A. The code will create a table named CUSTOMER.

B. Column datatypes should not be specified when creating a table from another table.

C. ZIP is a reserved word and cannot be used as a column name.

D. When creating a new table from an existing table, you cannot specify a different column name.

15. The table CUSTOMERS has the following data:

```
ID    NAME               ZIP UPD_DATE
----  ---------------  ---------- ---------
L921  LEEZA              75252 01-JAN-00
B023  WILLIAMS           15215
K783  KATHY              75252 15-FEB-00
B445  BENJAMIN           76021 15-FEB-00
D334  DENNIS             12443
```

You issue the following command to alter the table. Which line of code will cause an error?

```
1  ALTER TABLE CUSTOMERS
2  MODIFY
3  (UPD_DATE DEFAULT SYSDATE NOT NULL,
4    ZIP NOT NULL);
```

A. Line 2

B. Line 3

C. Line 4

D. There will be no error.

16. Which line of code has an error?

```
1  CREATE VIEW ACTION_MOVIES
2  (NAME NOT NULL, ACTOR)
3  AS
4  SELECT NAME, LEAD_ACTOR
5  FROM MOVIES
6  WHERE GENRE = 'ACTION'
7  ORDER BY NAME;
```

A. Line 2

B. Line 3

C. Line 7

D. There is no error.

17. For which task would it be appropriate to use a FOR loop?

A. To assign value 50 to variable 1, if variable 2 is 100.

B. To insert 10 consecutive numbers into a table starting with 20.

C. To insert a record into a table until the value of variable 1 is equal to 20.

D. A FOR loop is not a valid structure in PL/SQL.

18. Which line of code has an error?

```
1 DECLARE
2   V_NAME    VARCHAR2 (40) := 'DAVID CLARK';
3   V_ID      NUMBER   (4)  := 1001;
4   V_STATUS BOOLEAN        := FALSE;
5 BEGIN
6   INSERT INTO EMP (ID, NAME, STATUS)
7 VALUES (V_ID, V_NAME, V_STATUS);
8 END;
```

A. Line 2

B. Line 3

C. Line 4

D. Line 7

19. How do you declare a variable in the PL/SQL block, if its underlying database column datatype is not known? (The table is DBTABLE and the column name is COLUMNX.)

A. V_X NUMBER;

B. V_X VARCHAR2;

C. V_X DBTABLE.COLUMNX%TYPE;

D. V_X COLUMNX.DBTABLE%TYPE;

20. Evaluate the following statement. What value of V_PRICE would assign the value of 'C' to V_GRADE?

```
IF V_PRICE > 1000 THEN
    V_GRADE := 'A';
ELSE
    IF V_PRICE > 900 THEN
        V_GRADE := 'B';
    ELSE
        IF V_PRICE > 800 THEN
            V_GRADE := 'C';
        ELSE
            IF V_PRICE > 600 THEN
                V_GRADE := 'D';
            ELSE
                V_GRADE := 'E';
            END IF;
        END IF;
    END IF;
END IF;
```

A. V_PRICE greater than 1000

B. V_PRICE greater than 800

C. V_PRICE between 801 and 900

D. V_PRICE between 601 and 800

21. What causes a WHILE loop to terminate?

    A. When the condition is evaluated to NULL

    B. When the condition is evaluated to FALSE

    C. When the condition is evaluated to TRUE

    D. The EXIT statement must always be used to terminate.

22. How many ELSE clauses can an IF...THEN...ELSIF statement have?

    A. 0

    B. 1

    C. Unlimited

    D. 64

23. Consider the following PL/SQL block. How many rows will be added to the table NUMBERS when this block is executed?

```
BEGIN
  FOR IX IN 5..10 LOOP
    IF IX = 6 THEN
        INSERT INTO NUMBERS VALUES (IX);
    ELSIF IX = 7 THEN
        DELETE FROM NUMBERS;
    END IF;
    IF IX = 7 THEN
        ROLLBACK;
    ELSE
        COMMIT;
    END IF;
  END LOOP;
  COMMIT;
END;
```

    A. 6

    B. 1

    C. 5

    D. 0

24. If C1 is a cursor defined in a PL/SQL block, what will be the value of C1%NOTFOUND after the cursor is opened but before the first fetch?

   A. TRUE

   B. FALSE

   C. NULL

   D. None of the above

25. When the following PL/SQL block is executed, what will be the value of V1?

```
DECLARE
  V0 PLS_INTEGER;
  V1 BOOLEAN;
BEGIN
  BEGIN
    SELECT COUNT(*) INTO V0 FROM EMP;
  END;
  BEGIN
    V1 := SQL%FOUND;
  END;
END;
```

   A. NULL

   B. TRUE

   C. FALSE

   D. The code will not work.

26. Which line of code has an error?

```
1 DECLARE
2    CURSOR c_emp IS SELECT empno, salary FROM emp;
3    R_emp  c_emp%ROWTYPE;
4 BEGIN
5    OPEN c_emp;
6    LOOP
7      FETCH c_emp INTO r_emp;
8      EXIT WHEN c_emp%NOTFOUND;
9      UPDATE EMP SET SALARY = SALARY + 500
10     WHERE  EMPNO =  c_emp.empno;
11   END LOOP;
12   CLOSE c_emp;
13 END;
```

A. Line 2

B. Line 3

C. Line 7

D. Line 8

E. Line 10

27. Using the following INVENTORY table instance chart, choose the SQL statement that will increase the base price of all items by 3% of the combined base_price and surcharge.

Column Name	sku	name	base_price	surcharge
Key Type	pk			
NULLs/Unique	NN/U	NN	NN	
FK Table				
Datatype	varchar2	varchar2	number	number
Length	16	50	11,2	11,2

    A. update inventory set base_price = (base_price + surcharge) * 1.03;

    B. update inventory set base_price = base_price * 1.03 + surcharge * 1.03;

    C. update inventory set base_price = (base_price * 1.03) + NVL(surcharge,0)* 1.03;

    D. None of these statements will achieve the desired results.

28. Which of the following is not a group function?

    A. SUM

    B. AVG

    C. GREATEST

    D. VARIANCE

29. If the current date is 1-Mar-2000, what will be returned from the following SQL statement?

```
SELECT LAST_DAY(ADD_MONTHS(SYSDATE,-2)) FROM dual;
```

    A. 30-Mar-2000

    B. 31-Jan-2000

    C. 31-May-2000

    D. 29-Feb-2000

30. What will the following SQL statement return?

```
SELECT MOD(25,5), MOD(8,2.5) FROM dual;
```

   A. 0 and .5

   B. 5 and 4.5

   C. 0 and 2

   D. This will raise an exception, since MOD can only operate on integer values.

31. You need to display the date column start_date in the format:
23Rd of September, 2000
Which of the following expressions will satisfy these requirements?

   A. to_char(start_date,'Dsp of Month, YYYY')

   B. to_char(start_date,'DDTh of Month, YYYY')

   C. to_char(start_date,'DTh "of" Month, YYYY')

   D. to_char(start_date,'DDTh "of" Month, YYYY')

32. What will be displayed from the following PL/SQL block?

```
DECLARE
  X  VARCHAR2(10) := 'TITLE';
  Y  VARCHAR2(10) := 'TITLE   ';
BEGIN
  IF X >= Y THEN
    dbms_output.put_line('X is greater');
  END IF;
  IF Y >= X THEN
    dbms_output.put_line('Y is greater');
  END IF;
END;
```

   A. X is greater

   B. Y is greater

   C. Both X is greater and Y is greater

   D. Neither X is greater nor Y is greater

33. Which statement will implicitly begin a transaction?

    A. GRANT

    B. SELECT FOR UPDATE

    C. ALTER

    D. TRUNCATE

34. Which data dictionary table can tell you who granted the DBA role to user BATMAN?

    A. DBA_ROLE_PRIVS

    B. DBA_SYS_PRIVS

    C. DBA_TAB_PRIVS

    D. None, you can't tell who granted the role.

35. What is the value of BALANCE in the CHECKING table for ACCOUNT_ID 'A' after the following PL/SQL block?

```
BEGIN
   UPDATE checking
     SET balance = 5000
     WHERE account_id = 'A';
   SAVEPOINT save_A;

   UPDATE checking
     SET  balance = 7500
     WHERE account_id = 'A';
   SAVEPOINT save_A2;

   UPDATE checking
     SET  balance = 3000
     WHERE account_id = 'A';
   SAVEPOINT save_A3;

   ROLLBACK TO SAVEPOINT save_A;

   UPDATE brokerage
     SET cash_bal = 25000
     WHERE account_id = 'A';
   SAVEPOINT save_X;

   ROLLBACK to save_X;
   ROLLBACK to save_A;
END;
COMMIT;
```

A. 5000

B. 7500

C. 3000

D. 25000

36. What does the following SQL statement do?

`ALTER USER sherry IDENTIFIED BY ann;`

   A. Creates user ann with the password of sherry

   B. Creates user sherry with the password of ann

   C. Changes the password to ann for user sherry

   D. Changes the password to sherry for user ann

37. What does the following SQL statement do?

`ALTER USER tommy QUOTA 2500 ON tools;`

   A. Sets user tommy's quota in tablespace tools to 2500 bytes

   B. Sets user tommy's quota in tablespace tools to 2500 kilobytes

   C. Sets user tommy's quota in tablespace tools to 2500 megabytes

   D. Changes user tommy's privileges on the table tools

38. If `emp_seq` is a sequence, what does the following SQL statement do?

`GRANT ALL ON emp_seq TO public;`

   A. Gives user public permission to select from the sequence `emp_seq`

   B. Gives user public permission to select or alter the sequence `emp_seq`

   C. Gives any user permission to select from the sequence `emp_seq`

   D. Gives any user permission to select or alter the sequence `emp_seq`

39. Which statement will remove the primary key PK_IMAGES from the table IMAGES?

   A. `ALTER TABLE IMAGES DROP PRIMARY KEY;`

   B. `DROP PRIMARY KEY PK_IMAGES;`

   C. `DROP TABLE IMAGES PRIMARY KEY;`

   D. `ALTER CONSTRAINT PK_IMAGES DROP;`

40. Which of the following check constraints is invalid?

A. CONSTRAINT CHECK (gender in ('M','F'))

B. CONSTRAINT CHECK (due_date > SYSDATE);

C. CONSTRAINT CHECK (bonus < salary)

D. CONSTRAINT CHECK (approval_code LIKE 'A%')

41. Which statement will disable the unique constraint SSN_uniq on the EMP table?

A. ALTER TABLE EMP DISABLE SSN_uniq;

B. ALTER CONSTRAINT SSN_uniq ON TABLE EMP DISABLE;

C. DISABLE CONSTRAINT SSN_uniq;

D. ALTER TABLE EMP DISABLE CONSTRAINT SSN_uniq;

42. Which option best describes when constraints are checked and the deferrability of constraint checking?

A. By default, constraints are nondeferrable and checked initially immediate. They can be set to deferrable and checked initially deferred.

B. By default, constraints are deferrable and checked initially immediate. They can be set to nondeferrable and checked initially deferred.

C. By default, constraints are deferrable and checked initially deferred. They can be set to nondeferrable and checked initially immediate.

D. By default, constraints are nondeferrable and checked initially deferred. They can be set to deferrable and checked initially immediate.

43. Which statement calls dbms_utility.analyze_schema with correct named notation syntax?

A. dbms_utility.analyze_schema(
schema->'SCOTT'
,method->'ESTIMATE');

B. dbms_utility.analyze_schema(schema=|'SCOTT'
,method=|'ESTIMATE');

C. dbms_utility.analyze_schema(
schema-|'SCOTT'
,method-|'ESTIMATE');

D. dbms_utility.analyze_schema(
schema=>'SCOTT'
,method=>'ESTIMATE');

44. Which of the following is an invalid trigger event?

A. after delete

B. before startup

C. after logon

D. after drop

45. Which of the following cannot be a field in a record?

A. A VARCHAR2 variable

B. A nested table

C. A %ROWTYPE record

D. A BOOLEAN variable

46. Which line in the following PL/SQL block will raise an exception?

```
1   TYPE emp_typ is RECORD (
        emp_no     VARCHAR2(20),
        name       scott.emp.name%TYPE);
2   emp_rec   emp%ROWTYPE;
3 BEGIN
4   SELECT * INTO emp_rec FROM emp
        WHERE emp_no=12;
5   emp_rec.emp_no := emp_seq.nextval;
6   INSERT INTO emp VALUES (emp_rec);
7 END;
```

A. Line 1

B. Line 2

C. Line 4

D. Line 6

47. Which line in the following PL/SQL block will raise an exception?

```
1 DECLARE
2   CURSOR stock_cur (symbol_in VARCHAR2) IS
        SELECT symbol, exchange, begin_date
        FROM stocks
        WHERE symbol = UPPER(symbol_in);

3   stock_info   stock_cur%ROWTYPE;
4 BEGIN
5   OPEN stock_cur('ORCL');
6   FETCH stock_cur INTO stock_info;
7 END;
```

A. Line 2

B. Line 3

C. Line 6

D. No exception will be raised.

48. Which collection type must be explicitly initialized with a constructor?

   A. Index-by table

   B. Nested table

   C. VARRAY

   D. Nested table and VARRAY

49. Which collection type can be sparse?

   A. Index-by table

   B. Nested table and VARRAY

   C. Nested table and index-by table

   D. VARRAY

50. What type of data structure is on either side of the assignment operator in the following PL/SQL statement?

```
symbols(x) := akadian.symbol;
```

   A. The field symbol in the record akadian is assigned to the element x in the collection symbols.

   B. The field akadian in the record symbol is assigned to the element x in the collection symbols.

   C. The element symbol in the collection akadian is assigned to the field x in the record symbols.

   D. The element symbol in the record akadian is assigned to the field x in the collection symbols.

51. An exception is raised in line 3 of the PL/SQL block below. Where is it handled?.

```
1 BEGIN
2    DECLARE
3       timestamp   DATE := 'SYSDATE';
4    BEGIN
5       call_some_proc
6    EXCEPTION
7      WHEN VALUE_ERROR THEN
8          dbms_output.put_line('value error');
9      WHEN OTHERS THEN
10         dbms_output.put_line('some other error');
11   END;
12 EXCEPTION
13   WHEN OTHERS THEN
14       dbms_output.put_line('unknown error');
15 END;
```

A. Line 7

B. Line 9

C. Line 13

D. Lines 9 and 13

52. In which PL/SQL section is a server error associated with a named exception?

A. Header

B. Declaration

C. Executable

D. Exception

53. What type of exception requires a RAISE statement?

   A. A named server exception

   B. A programmer-defined exception

   C. An unnamed server exception

   D. The RAISE statement is never required for an exception.

54. What is done in the following PL/SQL code?

```
INVALID_DATE    EXCEPTION;
```

   A. An exception is declared.

   B. An exception is raised.

   C. An exception is associated.

   D. An exception is handled.

55. What is done in the following PL/SQL code?

```
PRAGMA EXCEPTION_INIT(invalid_table_name, -942);
```

   A. An exception is declared.

   B. An exception is raised.

   C. An exception is associated.

   D. An exception is handled.

56. What does the following PL/SQL block do?

```
RAISE_APPLICATION_ERROR(-20123
, 'invalid_product_code', TRUE)
```

  A. Raises the previously defined exception invalid_product_code, with a SQL code of –20123, appending this error to the existing error stack

  B. Raises a programmer-defined exception, that does not have to be previously defined, assigns –20123 to the SQL code for this exception, and appends the error to the existing error stack

  C. Raises a programmer-defined exception, that does not have to be previously defined, assigns –20123 to the SQL code for this exception, and overwrites the existing error stack with this error

  D. Handles either the server error –20123 or the programmer-defined exception invalid_product_code

Answers to Practice Exam

1. C. A relationship between two tables is implemented in Oracle using foreign key (referential integrity) constraints. Foreign keys make sure that the value entered in one table is valid against its parent table.

2. C. Design is the next stage after Analysis. The stages of application development, in order, are Analysis, Design, Development, Testing, and Implementation.

3. B. The CHAR datatype fills the width of the column with spaces if the length of the column data is less than its length. Using CHAR, 'MARK' and 'MARK ' are the same. VARCHAR and VARCHAR2 store only the data and do not add spaces. You cannot compare a LONG column.

4. B. DEFINE is used to declare a CHAR datatype variable or to display its value if no value is provided. For example, DEFINE SALARY = 300.10 would create a variable named SALARY and assign a CHAR value of 300.10 to it. Using DEFINE SALARY would display its value. You can use these variables in queries. The variable name should be preceded by an ampersand (&SALARY):

    ```
    SQL> DEFINE SALARY = 300.10
    SQL> DEFINE SALARY
    DEFINE SALARY      = "300.10" (CHAR)
    SQL>
    ```

5. A, D. The substitution character % may be substituted for zero or for many characters. The substitution character _ does not have any effect in this query because an escape character precedes it, so it is treated as a literal.

6. C. You have two main conditions in the question: one on the hire date and the other on the salary. So, you should use an AND operator. In the second part, you have two options: The salary can be either more than 5000 or less than 1000. So, the second part should be enclosed in parentheses and use an OR operator. Option B is similar to option C except for the parentheses, but the difference changes the meaning completely. Option B would select the employees who were hired before 01-Jan-1998 or have a salary above 5000 or have a salary below 1000.

7. C. An alias name S is defined for the table STATE. Therefore, to qualify a column, only S can be used. You should not use the table name to qualify the column. Note that in this query, because data is selected from only one table, there is no need to qualify the column names at all.

8. D. A subquery must be used here, because you want to know the highest value in the DVD_STOCK column, and then use this value to get the name and lead actor of the movie. Option C conveys the same meaning, but you cannot use a GROUP function in the WHERE clause.

9. B. The query can return an unlimited number of rows. Since the equality operator is used for the subquery, the subquery can return only one row.

10. A. There is no error in the statement, and the query will return two rows. The subquery returns only one row with a value of 'ACTION', and the main query returns the name and genre of the two ACTION movies.

11. D. There is no error. It is not necessary to have an alias name provided for the subquery in the FROM clause. An alias name would improve the readability of the query. Column names must be qualified only if there is an ambiguity.

12. C. Oracle creates unique indexes for each unique key and primary key defined in the table. The table ADDRESSES has one unique key and a primary key. Indexes will not be created for NOT NULL or foreign key constraints.

13. B. The WITH READ ONLY option in the CREATE VIEW command is used to prevent any INSERT, UPDATE, or DELETE statements applied to the base table through the view. WITH CHECK OPTION is used to restrict the updates or inserts to the view.

14. B. When creating a table using a subquery, column datatypes should not be specified. The datatypes are derived by Oracle from the data selected or based on the base table. You may specify a column name and constraints for the new table.

15. B. When you're altering an existing column to add a NOT NULL constraint, no rows in the table should have NULL values. In the example, there are two rows with NULL values.

16. A. When defining views, you cannot specify constraints or datatype definitions. A view is a representation of data from underlying tables or views.

17. B. A FOR loop is used to repeat a task a fixed number of times. Option A would use an IF...THEN statement; option C would use a WHILE loop. Here is the code:

```
FOR X IN 20 .. 29 LOOP
    INSERT INTO TABLE_A (COLUMN1) VALUES (X);
END LOOP;
```

18. D. The INSERT statement will fail because a table cannot be created with the BOOLEAN datatype, so a BOOLEAN value cannot be directly inserted into a table. The BOOLEAN value may be converted to a SQL datatype using the DECODE function before inserting.

19. C. By declaring a variable with %TYPE, the datatype and width are assigned at runtime. The database definition may change and need not require a code change in the PL/SQL block.

20. C. V_PRICE greater than 800 and less than or equal to 900 would assign 'C' to V_GRADE. The IF statement is evaluated from the top down.

21. B. When the condition or Boolean variable in the WHILE loop evaluates to FALSE, the loop is terminated.

22. B. An IF...THEN...ELSIF clause can have only one ELSE clause; it can have many ELSIF clauses.

23. B. One row will be added. Although the loop executes six times, the value is inserted to the table only when the value of IX is 6. When IX is 7, all rows from the table are deleted, but the operation is rolled back.

24. C. %NOTFOUND and %FOUND would be NULL before the first fetch. They will be either TRUE or FALSE after the first fetch, depending on the fetch result.

25. B. SQL%FOUND and SQL%NOTFOUND will have Boolean values based on the previous SQL statement executed inside the PL/SQL block. SELECT COUNT(*) will always return a value.

26. E. When you're referencing record variables inside an explicit cursor, you should reference the variables with the record name, not the cursor name. Line 10 should read `WHERE EMPNO = r_emp.empno;`.

27. C. Options A and B do not take into account the possibility of `NULL` values in the surcharge column.

28. C. `GREATEST` is a single-row function that takes an arbitrary number of arguments.

29. B. This expression will resolve as follows:
```
LAST_DAY(ADD_MONTHS(SYSDATE,-2)) =
LAST_DAY(ADD_MONTHS(1-Mar-2000,-2)) =
LAST_DAY(1-Jan-2000) =
31-Jan-2000
```

30. A. `MOD` will return the remainder after dividing the first argument by the second argument.

31. D. The format codes needed are `DD`, day of month; `Th`, ordinal modifier; `"of"` a text string; `Month`, the month name spelled out; and `YYYY`, the four-digit year.

32. B. With the `VARCHAR2` datatype, trailing spaces are included in the evaluation, so Y would sort greater than X. If the X and Y were the `CHAR` datatype, they would be equal and option C would be correct, but X and Y are `VARCHAR2`, so option B is correct.

33. B. `SELECT FOR UPDATE` is a DML statement. The others are all DDL, which will implicitly end a transaction, but not begin one.

34. D. `DBA_ROLE_PRIVS` and `DBA_SYS_PRIVS` will report the GRANTEE but not the GRANTOR.

35. A. The savepoint `save_A` is set after the balance is set to 5000, and the transaction is rolled back to this savepoint twice.

36. C. The `ALTER USER` statement is used to change one or more attributes of an existing user account. The `IDENTIFIED BY` clause specifies a password to authenticate the user.

37. A. By default, when a number refers to a disk storage amount, it is measured in bytes.

38. D. The privilege ALL includes all the privileges that can be granted on that type of object; for a sequence, this includes select and alter. The grantee public is a special user that represents any user connected to the database.

39. A. To remove a primary key, use the ALTER TABLE statement with the DROP PRIMARY KEY clause.

40. B. SYSDATE cannot be used in a check constraint.

41. D. The ALTER TABLE statement with the DISABLE CONSTRAINT clause is used to disable constraints.

42. B. Deferrable constraints are a relatively new feature in Oracle, and the default behavior for when constraints are checked is backward compatible. Thus, constraints are checked immediately (not deferred). On the other hand, constraints are, by default, deferrable.

43. D. The correct symbol for use in named notation parameter passing is =>.

44. B. The following events are invalid: before startup, before logon, before servererror, after shutdown, and after logoff.

45. B. Collections cannot be fields within a record.

46. D. Records can only be used in the VALUES clause of an INSERT statement if each field is listed individually.

47. D. These are all valid statements. The exam may have tricky questions like this, so beware.

48. D. Index-by tables are the only collection that is initialized automatically; the other two must be initialized with a constructor.

49. C. Index-by tables can always be sparse, and nested tables can become sparse after deletions.

50. A. Records are composed of fields and are referenced with dot notation. Collections are composed of elements and are referenced with subscript notation.

51. C. Exceptions raised in the declaration section are handled by the enclosing block.

52. B. The `pragma exception_init` statement associates an error number with an exception name in the declaration section of a PL/SQL block.

53. B. Since the runtime engine has no knowledge of business rules or when to raise a programmer-defined exception, the programmer is responsible for identifying the error condition and raising the exception.

54. A. To create a programmer-defined exception, you declare it in the declaration section of the PL/SQL block.

55. C. You associate an exception name with a server error number with the `PRAGMA EXCEPTION_INIT` statement.

56. B. The `RAISE_APPLICATION_ERROR` procedure raises a programmer-defined exception. This exception does not have to be given a name previously. The number is assigned to the `SQL CODE`, and a `TRUE` in the third argument will cause the exception to be appended to the error stack rather than to overlay it.

Glossary

Symbols

%ROWTYPE   Attribute used in PL/SQL to declare a record variable. The variable is declared based on a table, a cursor, or another record variable.

%TYPE   Attribute used in PL/SQL to declare a variable based on a column or another variable. The variable is declared with the datatype and length of the referencing column or variable.

@   Used to execute a script file –@<filename>. Optionally, you may provide the positional substitution variable values.

@@   Used to execute a script file inside another script file. The called script file location is assumed to be the same as the calling script.

A

Aggregate Functions   Also known as group functions, functions that operate on groups of rows. These functions don't know how many arguments they will operate on until the data is fetched and grouped.

Anonymous Block   A PL/SQL block that is not named. Anonymous blocks may be present in the client tools or inside named blocks, or they can be run as programs from the server.

Associate an Exception   To give a name to a database error. Use PRAGMA EXCEPTION_INIT to associate a name with a database error number.

C

Cardinality   The number of distinct values. If a table has a cardinality of 1,000, it has 1,000 rows. If a column has a cardinality of 30, it has 30 distinct values (there may be 1,000 rows, but only 30 distinct values).

Cartesian Join   The result of not specifying enough join conditions when selecting data from multiple tables. If there are n tables, there should be at least $n–1$ joins to avoid a Cartesian product.

Child Table   The referencing table in a foreign key constraint; that is, the table with the foreign key constraint.

Cluster   An optional method of storing data. Tables that are accessed together or joined frequently (parent/child tables) can be stored together.

Collection   An ordered list of elements, similar to a one-dimensional array.

COMMIT   Makes permanent the changes made to the data. Changes are made using the INSERT, UPDATE, or DELETE statements.

Concatenation   The joining of two character string values. The symbol || is used in Oracle as the concatenation operator.

Concurrency   The condition when many users/sessions can access and modify data at the same time.

Consistency   A state maintained by the database. A statement/transaction sees a time-consistent image of the data plus any uncommitted data from the statement/transaction.

Constant   A memory location to store a value that cannot be changed in the program.

Constructor   A built-in function of nested tables and VARRAYs. A constructor is used to initialize the collection.

Control Structures   Lines of code to control the flow of the PL/SQL program. There are conditional and iterative control structures.

Correlated Subquery   A subquery that references the column names of the parent query in the subquery.

Currval   The sequence pseudo-column that will return the last number generated from the sequence number generator.

Cursor Attribute   An attribute that gives the status of the cursor. There are four cursor attributes: %ISOPEN, %FOUND, %NOTFOUND, and %ROWCOUNT.

Cursor FOR Loop   A powerful loop structure that can be used in PL/SQL to open, fetch, and close the cursor.

D

Datatype   A property of the data element. The datatype defines the rules; for example, the NUMBER datatype can be used for arithmetic.

Declaration Section The section in the PL/SQL block where you declare all the variables, constants, cursors, exceptions, and type declarations.

Declare an Exception To create a programmer-defined error.

Default Column Values Values specified in the column definition that are used to insert values to rows if the column value is NULL.

Deferrable A constraint that can have constraint checking delayed until the end of the transaction.

Delimiter A special character used to separate different statements in the PL/SQL program. A semicolon is the delimiter in PL/SQL.

Design Phase The most important phase in the application development cycle. In order, the phases of the application development cycle are Analysis, Design, Development, Testing, and Implementation.

Dot Notation The notation used in references to fields within records or in the invocation of collection methods.

DUAL A dummy table in Oracle, mainly used to execute SQL statements when there is no base table needed for the query to execute successfully. For example, DUAL is used to retrieve pseudo-column values such as SYSDATE or user.

E

Entity-Relationship (ER) Model A visual diagram used in the analysis and design stage of the system development cycle. The ER diagram shows the relationship between entities and their attributes and characteristics.

Environment Variables SQL*Plus variables that allow the programmer to customize its environment. These variables can be customized using the SET command.

Exception An error in an Oracle system.

Exception Section The section in the PL/SQL block where the error-handling routines are written.

Executable Section A mandatory section in the PL/SQL block. The executable statements are written here.

F

FETCH Retrieves a row from an open cursor. The FETCH command is used to retrieve one row at a time.

Field A component within a record.

FOR UPDATE Clause Part of the SELECT statement. When used in a cursor, the FOR UPDATE clause locks the rows returned by the cursor.

Foreign Key Constraint A constraint on one or more columns that requires one or more NULL values in the protected columns or requires the data values in all the protected columns to exist in a primary key or unique constraint.

Function A named, stored program in the Oracle server. A function must return a value and may have parameters to pass values to the function. Functions can be used in SQL statements. Functions are called in expressions.

I

Index A structure associated with tables and clusters, which is used to speed up queries. An index is an access path used to reach the desired row more quickly.

Index-Organized Table A table and an index stored together.

Initially Deferred A constraint that is set to delay constraint checking until the end of the transaction.

Initially Immediate A constraint that is set to perform constraint checking at the end of each statement.

Iterative Control A control structure that evaluates a set of statements repeatedly. A FOR...LOOP, WHILE...LOOP, or basic loop is used to code iterative control.

J

Julian Numbers The values Oracle uses to calulate dates. A Julian date refers to the number of days since January 1, 4712 BC.

K

Key   A distinct value in an index.

L

Labels   Identifiers used to label a block or a loop structure, or to branch control to a different part of the program using a GOTO statement. Labels are always enclosed in double angle brackets (<< >>).

LOB   Large Object in Oracle. A LOB is used to store large, unstructured data.

Lock   A resource collision avoidance mechanism.

M

Method   A built-in function of collections. Methods are used to manipulate the collection.

N

Named Block   A PL/SQL block that has a name. A named block can appear inside an anonymous block or may be stored in the database. There are two types of named blocks: functions and procedures.

Named Notation   The parameter-passing method, used for procedures and functions. It explicitly assigns values to parameters based on the parameter name.

Nested Block   A block within another block. You may have as many levels of nesting as needed.

Nextval   The sequence pseudo-column that will cause the generation of the next number from the sequence number generator.

NLS   National Language Support. NLS parameters and arguments allow you to internationalize your Oracle database system. NLS internationalizations include date representations, character sets and alphabets, and alphabetical ordering.

Nondeferrable   A constraint that must have constraint checking at the end of each statement and cannot delay constraint checking until the end of the transaction.

NOT NULL Constraint   A column constraint that requires a data value in the protected column.

NULL   An unknown value or statement. If used in the PL/SQL block, NULL says, "Do nothing." A NULL can be used as a filler when an executable statement is mandatory and you have nothing to do. Most functions return NULL when called with a NULL argument.

O

On Delete Cascade   A foreign key option that causes deletes on the parent table to automatically cause corresponding deletes to the child table.

On Delete Set NULL   A foreign key option that causes deletes on the parent table to automatically cause corresponding columns in the child table to be set to NULL.

Oracle Data Dictionary   A set of tables and views that store the metadata of the Oracle database.

Outer Join   A join used to select data from a table even if there is no matching row in the joined table. These are the rows that are not returned by using a simple join. A plus symbol surrounded by parentheses ((+)) is the outer-join operator.

Owner   The schema that owns an object. Owner, schema, and user represent a logical grouping of database objects in the database.

P

Package   A stored program that is a collection of program units like functions, procedures, variables, and so on. Packages are created with a specification and a body.

Parent Table   The referenced table in a foreign key constraint; that is, the table with the primary or unique constraint.

PL/SQL Engine   The technology that compiles and executes PL/SQL programs inside an Oracle server. The PL/SQL engine is integrated into the Oracle server and certain other Oracle tools that process PL/SQL programs. The engine processes procedural statements.

Positional Notation   The parameter-passing method, used for procedures and functions, that relies on the order of the parameters to determine which parameter receives which value.

Primary Key Constraint   A constraint on one or more columns that combines NOT NULL constraints on each protected column and a unique constraint on all protected columns. The primary key uniquely identifies any row in a table.

Private Synonym   A restricted alias to another object.

Procedure   A stored PL/SQL program that gets called as a statement. A procedure does not return any value directly, but you may pass values to and from the procedure using parameters. Procedures cannot be used in SQL statements.

Public Synonym   A global alias to another object.

Q

Qualify   To further specify a table or column name to avoid ambiguity. The table name is qualified with its owner or schema name; a column name is qualified with its table name or alias name.

Query   A SELECT statement used to retrieve already-saved data from the database.

R

Raise an Exception   To cause an error to occur.

RDBMS   Relational Database Management System. The most widely used database concept in the information technology world.

Record   A composite datatype.

ROLLBACK   An action that undoes the changes made to the database since the transaction began.

ROWID   The pseudo-column and physical address of a row in a table.

S

SAVEPOINT   A marker set in between DML statements in a single transaction to go back to a specific point.

Schema   A logical grouping of Oracle database objects.

SCN   System Change Number. A number that represents a committed, consistent image of the database. SCNs only increase with time.

Script File   A file that contains a set of commands that are run sequentially.

Self-Join   A join that occurs when the table is joined to itself in a query.

Sequence   An Oracle object that provides unique sequential numbers.

Single-Row Functions   Functions that operate on a single row at a time. These functions know how many arguments they will operate on at compile time, before any data is fetched.

SQL Buffer   The area in SQL*Plus where the last command executed is saved.

SQL*Plus   Oracle's native tool to interact with the database.

SQLCODE   A built-in function that returns the current database error number.

SQLERRM   A built-in function that returns the text of the current database error.

Statement   A single SQL command that can include subqueries.

Structured Query Language   SQL, the database-access language to query and manipulate data in the database.

Sub-Block   The block that appears inside a block in a nested block structure.

Subquery   A query inside a query.

Subscript Notation   The parenthetical notation used in references to elements in a collection.

Synonym   An alias name for an object. Synonyms can mask the owner or even the database of the object.

SYS   The schema that owns the Oracle data dictionary.

T

Table   The basic unit of data storage in Oracle. The data is stored in rows and columns.

Transaction   A logical group of DML statements considered a single unit. Together, the statements constitute an atomic view of data or an atomic change to data.

Trigger A stored program unit created in the Oracle server, which is attached to an event and executes when the event occurs. Prior to Oracle8i, a trigger was always attached to a table and the events were INSERT, UPDATE, and DELETE. In Oracle8i, triggers can be created for database-level or user-level events.

Truncate To remove all rows of data from the table.

TYPE The statement used to define a record or collection.

U

Unique Constraint A constraint on one or more columns in a table that ensures no two rows contain duplicate data in the protected columns.

User Another term used for schema. Schema, user, and owner represent a logical grouping of database objects in the database.

V

Variable A memory location to store a value, which may be used any number of times in the PL/SQL program. The value of the variable can be changed inside the program.

View A logical representation of data from tables. Views are stored queries.

W

WHERE CURRENT OF A clause used in UPDATE and DELETE statements inside an explicit cursor to point to the most recent row fetched.

Index

Note to the Reader: Page numbers in **bold** indicate the principal discussion of a topic or the definition of a term. Page numbers in *italic* indicate illustrations.

D

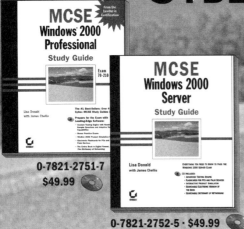

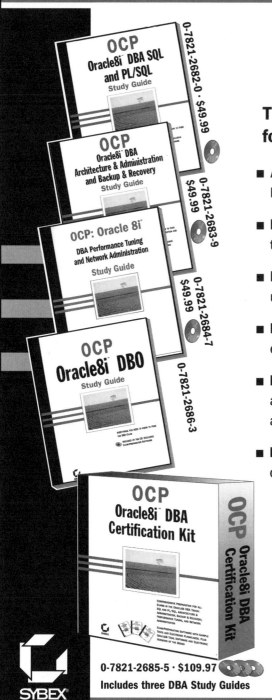

Oracle Software License Agreement